Start Your Own Computer Repair Business

Start Your Own Computer Repair Business

Linda Rohrbough
Michael F. Hordeski

McGraw-Hill, Inc.

New York San Francisco Washington, D.C. Auckland Bogotá
Caracas Lisbon London Madrid Mexico City Milan
Montreal New Delhi San Juan Singapore
Sydney Tokyo Toronto

pbk   1 2 3 4 5 6 7 8 9   DOC/DOC 9 9 8 7 6 5

Library of Congress Cataloging-in-Publication Data
Rohrbough, Linda.
    Start your own computer repair business / by Linda Rohrbough &
Michael F. Hordeski.
       p.   cm.
    Includes index.
    ISBN 0-07-911901-8 (pbk.)
    1. Computer service industry—Management.   2. Computers-
-Maintenance and repair—Management.   3. New business enterprises-
-Management.   I. Hordeski, Michael F.   II. Title.
HD9696.C62R643   1995
004.16'028'8—dc20   95-2013
                                                                CIP

Acquisitions editor: Brad Schepp
Editorial team: Robert E. Ostrander, Executive Editor
               Sally Anne Glover, Book Editor
               Jodi L. Tyler, Indexer
Production team: Katherine G. Brown, Director
                Wanda S. Ditch, Desktop Operator
                Linda L. King, Proofreading
Design team: Jaclyn J. Boone, Designer   EPC1
             Katherine Stefanski, Associate Designer   9119018

To Jessica Ann and Margaret Aileen.

Acknowledgments   We've had a lot of help and encouragement in the process of completing this book, despite some tough circumstances. Many thanks go to Brad Schepp, Senior Acquisitions Editor at McGraw-Hill, and his excellent staff for sticking with us.

In addition, we'd like to thank (alphabetically rather than in order of importance) Data Depot's Robert Hurt, Diversified Technigraphics' Don Thompson, Micro 2000's Stephanie Shore, and the sales team at Tech Assist.

Contents

Introduction

White-coated men talking in mathematical terms were the first to handle the giant magic boxes. That's not true anymore. Not only are the boxes many times smaller, but it is no longer necessary to have an education equivalent to that of a rocket scientist to be involved in the world of computers.

The magic is fast disappearing. Practical, increasingly portable, and attractive computers are expected to become as numerous as automobiles by the year 2000, delivering communication, expanded business opportunities, and increased productivity. Computers have become a necessity for anyone doing business in the Western world. And like any machine, computers have moving parts; they face failure and need repair. As the number of computers increases, so will the number of repair technicians. Somebody is going to have to fix all those computers!

Local, dependable, computer repair businesses are the ones with the advantage here. These types of businesses can move fast, with lower overhead, and provide customers with individualized care and service. The know-how to start one of these successful computer repair businesses, from the people who have done it, is in this book.

With case studies, interviews with the experts, and a look at the direction the market is heading, you'll discover the secrets to starting a thriving computer repair, maintenance, and teaching business of your own. The information offered can also be profitable for those considering computer repair on a part-time basis, as well as for individuals responsible for seeing to it that computers are cared for in corporate environments.

Chapter 1 details the opportunity in terms of projected growth of the computer marketplace, what services are and will be in demand, why a smaller repair business can offer more than the "big outfits," how long it takes to get established, and how other businesses have started from scratch to make as much as six figures.

Getting that start is the focus of chapter 2. You'll find ways to give your business that first crucial push, financial tips such as what income individuals can expect operating a PC repair business, how to set pricing, how to check the competition, and how to offer extra services that will help establish the business. Also included are tips on how to make contacts that will help get those first customers, how to get referrals, where to look for business, advertising on a tight budget, unusual ways to spark business, and how to make your customers think you're a genius (when you're not).

Chapter 3 explains the basic concepts of computer hardware and helps decode the terminology. Also, service issues, integration and its effect on repair, and trends in the repair business will be covered.

Software is one place where the individual computer repair business can carve out a niche, and chapter 4 explains how. Understanding the operating system, an integral part of the computer, and how it relates to the hardware and the application software can be the crucial edge in business success.

Examples of the most common hardware repairs are found in chapter 5. In a step-by-step approach, this chapter offers what to look for and what to watch out for as well.

Once the hardware is ruled out as the problem, many repair and service organizations step out of the picture, leaving the user holding the bag. Chapter 6 covers how individual computer repair technicians, with a "wholistic" approach to repair, can solve these sticky problems and earn loyal customers. It also offers information on the up-and-coming field of remote diagnostics, which can be performed without the repair technician leaving the comfort of the home or office.

Network specialization to boost income is the focus of chapter 7. Networking terms and concepts are decoded in this chapter. The most common trouble spots are also covered, as well as the tools to find and fix the problem. The second half of the chapter focuses on network certification, what it is and isn't, and what's required to get certified.

Chapter 8 looks at other money-making areas of specialization in the PC repair business. Income-boosting general certifications are covered, as are the most lucrative areas of repair specialties, such as laser printer and monitor repair. The focus is on areas with a future, coupled with training that's readily available.

Like any other business, computer repair has its own set of liabilities, trouble spots, quirks, and special requirements. Chapter 9 is focused on the common pitfalls of this business and how to avoid them. It includes tips on business licensing, insurance, avoiding liability, and even how to get paid.

Finally, chapter 10 covers additional services you can offer to boost your income. Most of these services give you the opportunity to double your hourly rate and offer the added benefit of bringing in repair customers. Plus, they're all related to PC work, so they don't require a lot of extra training to perform.

One more point: it's tempting, in a book like this, to begin listing the necessary skills you must have in order to succeed at computer repair. But rather than be like Albert Einstein's elementary school math teacher, who told him he'd never be any good at math, we will avoid making assertions as to what skills are necessary. The most basic need is to have an interest in the subject. If you've picked up *Start Your Own Computer Repair Business*, you've demonstrated enough interest to be qualified.

Whether that interest is motivated by a desire for the security of having your own business or whether you're just looking for a way to support your computer "habit," computer repair is certainly a fascinating and exciting opportunity. Now is a particularly opportune time with the move toward an "information superhighway," where people will be able to shop, go to school, play interactive games, communicate, and be entertained no matter where they live.

Your entry into the world of computer repair at this junction in history makes your services a "pit stop" on the information superhighway. You can be of benefit to both yourself and those you serve. Congratulations!

1 The opportunity

"The world does not owe men a living, but business, if it is to fulfill its ideal, owes men an opportunity to earn a living."

— Owen D. Young, 1847–1962, a lawyer/economist who served as chairman of the board at General Electric as well as an adviser to Presidents Harding and Truman.

Boston resident Eden Stone doesn't have a car, but that doesn't matter as long as she has her computer, according to *American Demographics*. In "What is a Luxury? It Depends," the Bostonian asserted that the computer was more important than a stereo, television, couch, washer, and dryer, all of which would be sacrificed first, if need be. In the same article, Vincent Fernandez of Tacoma, Washington declared he'd rather give up his car than his computer.

This growing trend, in addition to the overall expansion of the personal computer market, means opportunity for the person considering a business in computer repair. We'll look at the forces shaping this opportunity, as well as the advantages the individual computer repair business can have over established repair outfits.

The Roper Organization, who conducts a regular poll of consumers to determine which products consumers consider luxuries and which products are considered necessities, said millions of Americans are turning to the belief that computers are no longer a luxury. Only 4 percent of Americans considered their computers a necessity when computers were added to the Roper list of products in 1983, but that number climbed to 11 percent in the early 1990s and is expected to continue to grow.

The computer— from luxury to necessity

Among the more affluent, the numbers are higher. One in five adults with household incomes of more than $50,000 considered their home computer a necessity, and one out of four college students made the same assertion. The closet analogy to the current situation in the computer industry is when the automobile began to pepper the American landscape. Automobiles went from loud annoyances to luxury items to necessities. So it is with computers.

Nearly four million personal computers shipped in the United States in the first quarter of 1994, according to figures released by the market research firm Dataquest. That number is nearly 20 percent higher than the number in the same quarter in 1993. About 65 percent of the units shipped were from the top ten PC manufacturers, also known as original equipment manufacturers (OEMs), which were, in order: Compaq, Apple, IBM, Packard Bell, Gateway 2000, Dell, AST Research, Zenith Data Systems (ZDS-Group Bull), Hewlett-Packard (HP), and Toshiba.

Rapid computer industry growth spurred by SOHO

Continued increase in the personal computer industry is evidenced by the rapid growth up the "food chain" as component suppliers for personal computers report fantastic gains. The Semiconductor Industry Association reported explosive growth in the worldwide semiconductor market in the early 1990s. The group is forecasting that the worldwide market for semiconductors will grow about 20 percent a year to reach about $133 billion by 1997, fueled mostly by the demand in the small office/home office (SOHO) personal computer market.

Intel, with the lion's share of the component market for the majority of personal computers, has been reporting skyrocketing growth in both revenue and net income. The company announced earnings for its seventh record quarter in April of 1994, with income of $2.66 billion, a significant increase from the $2.02 billion it reported the quarter before. The company itself says it is the growth in the personal computer market that has boosted Intel to its current position as the world's largest semiconductor manufacturer.

Microcomputer manufacturers are targeting the growing home office and home markets to make up for lost corporate business, according to the Silicon Valley newspaper, the *San Jose Mercury News*. Lawrence Magid, in a column entitled, "Computer Firms are Living Off the Home Market" claims large companies are cutting microcomputer purchases because of corporate downsizing, so the OEMs have to go to the SOHO buyers.

From 1980 to 1992, an estimated 100 million personal computers have been sold. A total of 14.5 million units went out in 1992 alone. But according to predictions released by the market research firm Channel Marketing, PC sales are expected to continue to climb to a high of 100 million unit sales in 1999 (Fig. 1-1).

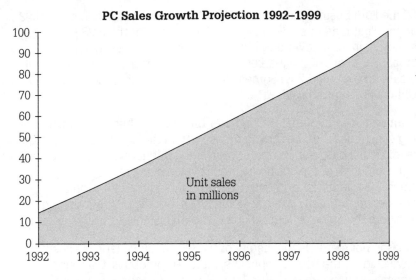

PC Sales Growth Projection 1992–1999

Unit sales in millions

1-1

The personal computer market overall is growing. Annual PC sales are projected to climb from 14.5 million units sold in 1992 to more than 100 million by 1999.

Home PC use continues to surge, as 34 percent of U.S. households already have a personal computer. A total of 36 million computers are in 33 million households. Personal computers sold for home use amounted to 9 million units in 1993, and that number is expected to reach 19 million by 1996, the marketing group said. But the number of computers in the home is predicted to surpass even the small business market, climbing to 42 percent by the end of 1996 (Fig. 1-2).

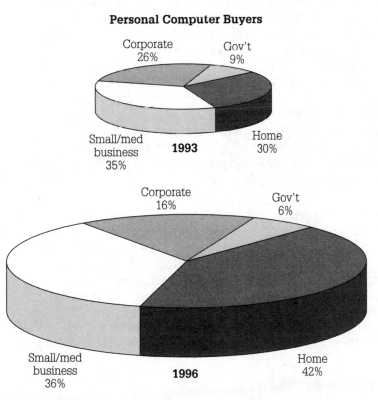

Personal Computer Buyers

Corporate 26%
Gov't 9%
Small/med business 35%
1993
Home 30%

Corporate 16%
Gov't 6%
Small/med business 36%
1996
Home 42%

1-2

Not only is the home market growing, but the entire industry is mushrooming as well. Nearly 6 million computers were sold for home use in 1993, but that number is expected to reach 19 million by the end of 1996, according to the market research firm Channel Marketing. An analyst said the home market will be "the biggest growth area we'll see in our lifetime, in any industry."

Small and medium businesses accounted for the largest market share in 1993 at 35 percent. That market share is expected to grow slightly to 36 percent by 1996. The corporate and government market segments are expected to decline from 35 percent of the market to 22 percent, but the numbers overall will be greater in every market segment. This is because the "pie" is getting bigger, Channel Marketing said.

Research analyst Joeann Stahel of Computer Intelligence/Infocorp agreed it is not the big companies that are driving the growth in the computer market, but the home and small business computer user. Her contention is home users are not buying computers to replace home game systems or even for "edutainment" (a combination of entertainment and education). Home computer users are primarily work-at-home types, who are either bringing work home from the office or starting home-based businesses, Stahel asserted.

Another reason not stated is the history of the love affair Americans seem to always have held for the new. Telephones, radio, automobiles, television, cellular phones—you name it and Americans have gone for it in a big way, even changing their culture, if need be, to make room for the new gizmo. Personal computers definitely fall into that category. No self-respecting businessperson today would be caught without a telephone or an automobile, or it seems, a computer.

Entrepreneurial fever spurs home market

The *American Forecaster Almanac* called the move toward self-employment "Entrepreneurial Fever." The publication sited lower computer and software costs as a factor in the move toward self-employment, in addition to applications such as computer-aided design (CAD) that give the small guy the same tools the big companies have. A number of other factors are at work converting more and more Americans into freelance entrepreneurs. Those factors are: the respect the U.S. business culture has for self-employment (the "self-made man" scenario); a sluggish economy in the 1990s that's forced layoffs of trained technical experts from traditionally secure corporate or military jobs; and aging baby-boomers with greater resources and access to credit who are looking for more satisfying work. One final factor listed was conformity. It's "in" to be self-employed, and the trend of people working for themselves tends to breed others who follow.

Smaller companies more recession-proof

Perhaps a more hidden motivation is the fact that small businesses have been a lot more resilient—more "recession-proof." Ruth Runyan, a statistician and economist at the U.S. Census Bureau, said smaller companies are doing better than larger companies in tough economic times. In the County Business Patterns report from the U.S. Census Bureau, small businesses with fewer than 10 employees grew 0.6 percent in 1991, while businesses with 10 to 100 employees declined 0.2 percent, and those with more than 100 dropped 1.7 percent. In the three years prior, from 1987 to 1990, large businesses grew three times faster than smaller firms. Runyan was quoted in

American Demographics as saying, "smaller establishments were less vulnerable to whatever was going on in the economy."

Yet, while the number of personal computers continues to increase, profit margins for computer manufacturers are falling. Years ago, you had to go to a specialized store to buy a computer. Now you can't go into any large retail store without seeing rows of the "magic boxes," each running its automated message to entice the consumer.

For OEMs, competition has become fierce, with large volumes and razor-slim profit margins. Many of the major computer manufacturers are complaining of falling profit margins, and all have taken steps to reduce overhead and cut costs. Even Intel, despite its sharp revenue increases, said it is seeing a trend toward a lower gross margin percentage.

While competition favors the consumer, it also makes it more difficult for computer manufacturers to offer after-the-sale support. Packard Bell, one of the first computer manufacturers to begin selling computers through consumer retail outlets, discontinued its toll-free support line in 1993. Company officials said several hours of toll-free customer support on a system ate up the slim profit margin the company made by selling the system in the first place.

Even with toll-free lines, the most common complaint is lack of support. A typical support story, Steve Houser, a resident of Denver, Colorado said he'd been enticed to buy a particular brand of computer due in part to the offer of toll-free support. That support never materialized because the toll-free lines were always busy, forcing him to dial the regular company phone numbers to get help. He never got the toll-free support he'd been offered.

Software vendors are struggling with support as well. Despite an outcry on the part of the hard-core computing community, the software market leader, Microsoft, started 900 number phone support to help finance the ever-increasing load of new computer users entering the market who need telephone help.

Competition has forced computer manufacturers to offer a one-year warranty, and many come with on-site service after that first year. But consumers are increasingly unhappy with the service provided. The typical scenario is the customer finds a problem with the computer, then calls technical support, but either the lines are busy or the caller gets connected to a seemingly endless line of voice-mail menus. When a real person finally does get on the line, there are often complaints of the call being routed to the wrong people, further compounding the frustration.

Ed Foster, editor of a leading computer industry weekly, *InfoWorld*, wrote 24 articles in an 18-month period dealing with complaints about customer

The support crisis

support concerning both hardware and software. The ZiffNet computer magazine database on the online service CompuServe had over 280 articles from various computer publications, such as *PC Magazine*, *PC Week*, *MacWEEK*, *Windows Sources*, *Digital News & Review*, *PC Sources*, *Government Computer News*, and even from the *New York Times*. Most of the articles were addressing serious support problems with computer hardware and software companies.

Foster said in an *InfoWorld* editorial, aimed at the publication's corporate and institutional business audience, that reader feedback indicated product support in the computer industry is a seriously neglected issue. He reasoned that part of the cause was harsh financial times coupled with price wars, in which product support always suffers. But another portion of the problem stems from the fact that computers are becoming easier to use and a commodity market. These factors in Foster's view, lead vendors to believe they don't need to do much for consumers.

While old-timers in the computer industry are used to calling vendors and getting the answers to tough problems, that's starting to change as well. The vendors simply don't have all the answers anymore. Foster reported that readers are complaining about technical support representatives who have advised them to go to an online service such as CompuServe, post their question, and hope another user can figure it out.

Keep in mind here that Foster is addressing mainly large business and corporate computer users, many of whom use their machines all day and teach others as well. This brings up the obvious question: If people who make their living at this struggle to get answers, where do people go who are new to computers?

Support issues become mainstream

As the number of computer users grows, the support problem is moving as an issue from the computer industry into mainstream publications. The *New York Times* addressed the support issue from another angle in the article, "Reining in the Rising Hidden Costs of PC Ownership; With Machines More Complex, Support is Vital, But Expensive." From a corporate standpoint, each PC costs an average of $40,000 over five years, and these costs are rising due to the growing complexity of computer systems and networks, the *Times* said. The costs associated with technical support, employee work habits, and administration can be more than the cost of the hardware and software. The *Times'* advice for cutting costs is to provide quality technical support so employees do not have to teach themselves and others, which reduces their productivity in other areas.

A *Wall Street Journal* article presented the problems of support in "Befuddled PC Users Flood Help Lines: No Question Seems to Be Too Basic." Two years ago, computer manufacturers said most of their calls were from "techies" looking for answers to complex problems, but now as much as 70 percent of the calls are from computer neophytes. The article describes an experience a Dell Computer support person had with a woman who was trying to get the computer's foot pedal to work. The "foot pedal" turned out to be the mouse, which she had on the floor. She obviously was used to working with sewing machines, which have similar-looking foot-pedal speed controls.

AST Research's Manager of Service Marketing Craig McQuilkin was quoted as saying that given a choice between using the manual that came with the computer and using the phone, people choose the phone. "It's a phenomenon of people wanting to talk to people," McQuilkin said. Indeed it is. Compaq, another of the "top ten," is reporting 8,000 calls a day on its support lines. Considering the continuing explosion in personal computer sales predicted by analysts, this is simply the tip of the iceberg.

The large repair companies, such as TRW (now owned by ComputerLand), show little interest in supporting the average PC user. The biggest complaints consumers have is that large repair companies often charge by the hour from the moment the technician's vehicle leaves the parking lot, until the moment of return. These companies are geared toward corporations, who have large numbers of computers and the money to sign up for large support contracts. In addition, most only deal with the hardware, avoiding problems having to do with software, which can be just as real and just as crippling as hardware problems. Other players, seeing the opportunity, are entering the service field, but these are also focused on the hardware and still leave much to be desired.

Established repair companies leave much to be desired

Tandy Corporation, which owns thousands of Radio Shack retail outlets nationwide, did a survey in which it found that individuals and companies are dissatisfied with their previous computer repair experiences. The survey results showed users are looking for local computer repair facilities they can count on. The company has decided to turn its 6,600 retail outlets into repair drop-off points, who send the repair items to one of its 116 repair centers.

The problem is, Radio Shack forecasts a 15-day average turnaround time that could stretch into a longer period. Users can get an estimate on repairs, but it could take $20 and two weeks to get it. Two weeks of "down-time" to a small business owner or telecommuter could mean nearly a month of lost business opportunities. In addition, users have to schlepp their computers to the local Radio Shack store, which for some will be like taking their sink apart and hauling it down to the plumber's shop to fix a leaky faucet. This type of service is hardly aimed at users who feel that their computer is a necessity.

In the strictest sense, computer repair is correcting problems with the physical components of the computer. But that still leaves a variety of avenues. While every shop did repair, many build new computers as well, which is a natural extension of the repair business. Some build computers equipped with add-on boards aimed at specific purpose, such as use by

Variety of ways to proceed

scientists collecting data for experiments. Others build computers to get business contacts for repair or at the request of clients. Still others offer consulting services, which range from advice for a particular problem to one-on-one tutoring.

Depot repair is another branch that deals specifically with repair of individual components that make up a larger portion of the computer, such as circuit boards, monitors, or hard disk drives. A depot repair shop often picks one or two specialty items and focuses just on those repairs alone. Often, computer repair technicians working at a retail level will turn to the more specialized depot repair shops for specific needs in special situations.

Consulting also falls under computer repair as many technicians find themselves doing one-on-one tutoring, training the client in the use of a specific software product or in the use of the operating system. In addition, consulting can include helping a client find the right hardware and software components to solve a specific problem.

The biggest strength small computer repair services have over larger outfits is the ability to offer a "wholistic" approach, so the clients can get that memory upgrade or the hard drive repair or find out why the new software upgrade won't work on their current computer. It is rare to find a one- or two-person computer repair business that doesn't offer a variety of the above-listed services to its clients, depending on the personality and interests of the business owner as well as the needs of the community.

Meeting the need

The growing parallels between the burgeoning computer industry and the automotive industry are becoming increasingly obvious. In 1991, there were 123.8 million passenger cars on the road, as recorded in the *Statistical Abstract of the United States*. Some estimates say there are as many as 100 million working personal computers in this country, and estimates are that over 40 million new computers were sold in 1994. Assuming some computers are placed on the scrap heap this year, that is still about one computer for every passenger car. In the article "How a Home Computer Can Change Your Life," *Fortune* magazine claims that there is now a computer in one of three U.S. households. Software giant Microsoft, a developer of software aimed at the business market, is now turning to the home software market. The $4.6 billion company is predicting its income from the home sales will jump from the current level of 10 percent to over 50 percent by the end of the decade.

The *Fortune* article quotes Stanford, Connecticut-based brokerage analyst John Maxwell, who said home computing will be the "biggest growth area we'll see in our life-time, in any industry." Put simply, there are going to be too many computers for computer users to go back to the manufacturer every time they have a problem or need the answer to a question. The closest analogy would be asking the owner of a Chrysler to drive the car to where it was manufactured for repairs. Of course, that's ridiculous. Already at overload now with support calls, computer manufacturers are simply not keeping pace with the increasing demand. Even if they could meet the demand, a phone call to a distant technical support technician is not going to be as satisfying to the consumer as a personal conference with a local individual.

It seems clear, then, that it is in the interest of the computer marketplace to have computer repair businesses be local and readily available. But what are the benefits to the person starting a computer repair business? The biggest benefit is the income, which is significantly above average. In addition, the repair business requires a minimal investment to get started, can be run from a home out of a garage or spare room, and offers flexibility both in the work and the hours. Further, the computer repair individual is judged by the ability to perform the work. Credentials, including college or vocational degrees, while helpful, are not yet required. Let's take each of these points individually.

Computer repair business benefits

Computer repair, maintenance, and teaching can either be a good part-time addition to another occupation or a good-paying business with above-average income potential. While some computer repair technicians interviewed for this book were making $18,000 to $25,000 a year part-time, others were pulling in as much as $60,000 to $75,000 a year full-time, working alone. But the income potential doesn't stop there. We talked to computer repair outfits who are doing well into the six-figure range. They've done this by finding a niche and specializing, although none of those businesses were one-person operations any longer.

How much can I make?

Because many repair businesses do the work on-site, it is not unusual at all to see thriving home-based computer repair businesses. While computer work offers good income, the "boxes" themselves require little in the way of storage space. They are sensitive to extremes of heat and cold and so need a relatively clean, temperature-controlled environment. An empty portion of a room, a spare bedroom, and an enclosed garage are all fine places to begin a computer repair operation.

Home-based repair does work

While there is no end to the tools you can get to make your job easier and more efficient, you don't need a lot of money to get started in the computer repair business. Most of the items you'll need, you probably already have. Starting from scratch and assuming you have to purchase everything, it could take as little as $3,000 and as much as $10,000 to get started. One of the most encouraging things about this business is you don't have to purchase everything at once; you can start with a minimal amount of tools and build as you go along.

Small initial investment

The good news is your hours are flexible. If you're working with business owners, you might find yourself working in the evenings more, as they need to be available during the day to their clients. If you aim at the more

Flexible hours

corporate market, you'll be working when the corporate world is available—usually from late morning to early afternoon. If you're doing depot repair, your hours will be even more flexible. Most repair businesses set their hours based on what suits both themselves and their customers.

Credentials not required

Since the computer repair field is still so new, there are no state or federal requirements for official credentials, as there are for plumbers, electricians, doctors, or lawyers. This means you can still enter the field of computer repair without any formal training as long as you can demonstrate to your clients that you can perform the necessary tasks.

Software and hardware vendors have started their own programs to test the expertise of individuals and offer certification to those who can pass the tests. This is to help protect the vendor's reputation and to provide support for the vendor's customer base. Some of the programs are quite challenging, such as the certified Novell engineer (CNE) certification offered by local area network (LAN) vendor Novell.

While these certifications can help a technician get business, they are not a requirement for entering computer repair nor are they a substitute for experience. Most technicians obtain the certifications they feel they need after establishing their business.

Some states require you have a license from the state department of consumer affairs in order to work on computers, laser printers, or photo copiers that belong to consumers. If you're working for corporate or business customers, the licensing doesn't apply. California is one such state that requires an Electronic Service Dealer license. This is issued by the Bureau of Electronic and Appliance Repair, which is part of the state's Department of Consumer Repairs. No credentials are required to obtain the license, but you must fill out the necessary paperwork and pay an annual fee to the state, which is under $150 per license. In California there is an electrical and an appliance license issued by the same bureau, but to work on computers you would only need the electrical license.

The idea behind the licensing is to protect both the business and the consumer. The licensing requires you issue an estimate for repairs before these repairs are done, and the consumer must be informed before repairs over the estimated cost are performed.

The license also protects you, as you're to clearly state on the form that you cannot be held responsible for lost, stolen, or damaged equipment while it is in your care. In case of a dispute, the state's consumer affairs department mitigates between you and the client. California requires you have a form for estimates that displays your business name, license number, and has check boxes for items brought in with the equipment such as cartridges, paper trays, and power cords. You'll need to check with your state's offices to see if such a license is required for you to work on home computers and peripherals in your state.

Every business has its downside, and computer repair is no exception. The most challenging portion of the business is keeping up on the technology, meaning you need to be willing to learn and keep on learning. Changes in the computer industry occur at an incredible rate. A few years ago, if you had told someone they would be able to see movie clips and television on a personal computer using compact disc (CD) technology, they might have thought you were crazy. But now, it's commonplace. That's the reason most computer repair technicians look through three or more computer industry publications each month. They also look for other reliable resources where answers to sticky problems can be found, and we'll talk about those resources later in the book.

The downside

We've explored the rapidly expanding market for the personal computer and the opportunities available for computer repair. We've also looked at the advantages and the downside of the business.

Let's Delve In

Jeffry A. Timmons, a professor at the Harvard Business School and author of *The Entrepreneurial Mind* said concerning the entrepreneurial dream: ". . . it is no wonder that so many have the dream, once you discover how the self-employed feel about themselves, what their work lives are like, and the economic rewards they earn. Uniformly, the self-employed report the highest levels of personal satisfaction, challenge, pride, and remuneration. They love their work because it is invigorating, energizing, and meaningful."

This description, while aimed at the world of self-employment in general, seems as though it were written specifically about the computer repair business. It's precisely what those interviewed for this book said about their work. So why wait any longer to find out about this stimulating business? Let's delve in!

References

Carlton, Jim. March 1, 1994. "Befuddled PC Users Flood Help Lines, And No Question Seems To Be Too Basic." *The Wall Street Journal* CCXXIII (41): B1, B6.

Dunn, William. January, 1994. "Small Business Takes a Licking And Keeps on Growing." *American Demographics* 16 (1): 14–15.

Fisher, Lawrence M. March 27, 1994. "Reining in the Rising Hidden Costs of PC Ownership; With Machines More Complex, Support is Vital, But Expensive." *New York Times* CXLIII (49,648): F10.

Foster, Ed. March 1, 1993. "Gripers Swear Product Support Needs a Hippocratic Oath." *InfoWorld* 15 (9): 39.

Kirkpatrick, David. February 21, 1994. "How a Home Computer Can Change Your Life." *Fortune* 129 (4): 100–104.

Long, Kim. 1993. *1994 American Forecaster Almanac.* Ithaca, New York: American Demographics Books.

Magid, Lawrence. April 10, 1994. "Computer Firms are Living Off the Home Market." *San Jose Mercury News* p1F(1).

Timmons, Jeffry A. 1989. *The Entrepreneurial Mind*. Andover, Massachusetts: Brick House Publishing Company.

United States Department of Commerce. 1993. *Statistical Abstract of the United States*. Washington, DC: U.S. Government Printing Office.

Waldrop, Judith. July, 1993. "What is Luxury? It Depends." *American Demographics* 15 (7): 13–14.

2 Launching your repair business

"The reward for work well done is the opportunity to do more."
— Jonas Salk, M.D., inventor of the vaccine to prevent polio.

You've already seen the outstanding opportunities in computer repair, but can you break into this rewarding field? You'll want the answer to this question before we move on into the nuts and bolts of the work itself. That's the purpose of this chapter. We'll explain what you need to have, where to get experience if you need it, how you can get the business to sustain you financially, and how to build your business.

We'll also introduce you to people who are currently operating repair shops both from their homes and from store fronts. Many of them started with little or no training, several faced career upheavals in today's uncertain economy, and some sold other businesses to enter the field of computer repair. These case studies will give you an idea of the rewards and challenges of the business, as well as insight into how you can build a successful business as well.

When a service is as much in demand as computer repair, it's not difficult to get customers; they're looking for you. But they can't find you if they don't know about your services. Also, like any other service business, computer repair will only be successful with repeat customers, and that means building trust is a crucial element. Once you've made contact, then you need to know what materials cost as well as what to charge for your time. Before we get into the nitty-gritty of the actual terms and work involved, we'll talk about starting from scratch, things you need to get started, unusual ways to advertise on a limited budget, building trust to get repeat customers, what to charge, and tips on how to get referrals.

Starting from ground zero

It is going to cost you some money to get started. You don't have to lay out all of the cash now, but you'll have to make an investment in what you're doing. If you're starting from ground zero, you might need to have at least a part-time job in order to stay afloat until the business takes off.

Of the 10 essential business rules offered by the Harvard Business School, the first is "Don't run out of cash," and the tenth is "Don't run out of cash." Keeping your cash flow up is crucial to your business survival.

Harvard Professor Jeffry Timmons says in *The Entrepreneurial Mind* that the successful start-ups keep their fixed expenses down. They combine hard work with avoiding purchases of equipment, office space, or vehicles, preferring to rent or lease instead. Buying used equipment isn't an option Timmons mentions, but it is certainly another viable option for saving money on needed equipment. So if you don't have an abundance of money or resources, don't be discouraged. Your probability of business survival is actually better.

To start, you'll need business cards, envelopes, and stationary. Nothing particularly fancy is necessary. After all, you'll probably want to see how things go before throwing a lot of money at your "look." But you will need something to hand out to people interested in your services and something on which to print invoices.

You'll also need some basic computer hardware, just as anyone with a new business. However, the computer and peripherals can serve two purposes: they can be used to lend a professional look to your venture at a lower cost than hiring artists and printers, and they can offer a training ground for you.

Get a computer

This is an obvious point. Practicing on the computers at your current job or at the school you attend is beneficial, but you need to have your own. You can pick up a computer at a swap meet or at a garage sale. The computer you get will be based a good deal on the type of repair you want to do. You might not need to own the state-of-the-art model in the Apple Macintosh computer line if you plan to work on Macintosh computers, but you should have a Macintosh even if it's an older one.

The biggest market is the Intel-based market, also known as the IBM-compatible personal computer (PC) market. This is the easiest and least expensive market to get into. In the PC market, you'll need to hedge your bets by obtaining a computer that will operate the graphical user interface Microsoft Windows as well as the more popular DOS operating system. This way, you can be versed in both.

Your own computer will also allow you to keep track of your client base, print business letters, and you can practice on it. Most repair folks I talked with started by tinkering with inexpensive, used machines they bought for that purpose.

Pay as little as you can for such equipment by keeping track of current prices for new or used computers and related peripherals. One way to do that is to go out and get a copy of *Computer Shopper* magazine. This publication has been a pricing mainstay for computer professionals for years and is literally packed with ads for everything from used computer systems to unusual components. While *Computer Shopper* contains articles, few computer repair shops said they read the editorial content, even though the magazine has begun to feature well-known computer industry writers. As for buying from the advertisers in the publication, some repair shops make purchases; others simply use the magazine as a plumb line and attempt to work with local sources. The thick, glossy publication is easy to find in computer stores or on newsstands that carry a wide variety of computer publications.

On a smaller scale, there is the *Processor*, available on a monthly, biweekly, or weekly basis, and *Computer Hotline*. Both are national publications that contain no editorial content—just advertising. Both feature ads for computer equipment and services and are especially useful for finding older, hard-to-find equipment and parts. Special services, such as rebuilding hard drives or print heads, are also listed. The main difference between the two is the *Processor* is aimed more at new equipment, while *Computer Hotline* focuses more on used supplies and equipment.

Once a year, *Service News* produces a special, glossy *Hardware Maintenance* issue dedicated to depot repair and spare parts. *Service News* is aimed more at the corporate market and reports monthly on issues such as user support programs from leading computer software makers to computer industry mergers and acquisitions. The *Hardware Maintenance* issue lists specific information on depots and spare parts providers with a cross-reference in the back that lists depots and part suppliers by the type of services or parts. This is where you can find less-expensive parts for proprietary PC or Macintosh systems and sources for workstation, minicomputer, and mainframe computer supplies and materials. Many of the companies listed offer catalogs you can request. You'll find the contact and subscription information in appendix A for all the magazines mentioned.

Another good source for pricing information is computer magazines, produced locally, that are given away in retail stores. These advertiser-supported publications are harder to find but are geared almost exclusively to area businesses, services, and events. The vendor advertising and the individual ads in the back will give you an idea of what the market value is for computer-related items in your location.

Computer swaps are also an excellent source for used equipment, parts, and pricing information. Just visiting one can be quite an education, as you'll see trends in the market and get tips on potential problems and answers by socializing there. If you love tinkering, you'll find the swaps especially addictive. You'll need to beware, though, as the used equipment is often sold "as is" and could have hidden problems. This is especially risky at an outdoor swap where there is no electricity, so you're buying computers you can't test first. On the other hand, you're in computer repair, aren't you? Here's a good chance to get a problem you can fix; just be sure you don't pay more than you're willing to lose.

You'll find computer swaps in your area by contacting a local computer user group or a local computer store and asking. The swaps might also be listed in the free, local computer magazines which you can also pick up by visiting a local computer store.

A laser printer can produce your promotional material

Get a laser printer, if you can afford it. You don't need to run out and purchase the top-of-the-line model, but a 300-dot-per-inch laser will allow you to print up your own business cards, letterhead, and envelopes as well as make your own brochures in small quantities, as you need them. MySoftware has an inexpensive package called "MyBrochures and Mailers" that works under Microsoft Windows and offers samples of preprinted papers with designs that you can whip out on your laser printer in a hurry. Sample designs are included in the software so you can insert the preprinted paper and simply fill in the blanks to get your business cards or letterhead. You can call the printing companies listed in the package toll-free to get catalogs of preprinted, matching cards, stationary, and envelopes, which you can order in small quantities such as 100 pieces.

You might be able to find laser printers used, but they're popular because they produce such professional results. You can expect to pay at least $500 for a new laser printer. The company that leads in laser printers, Hewlett-Packard, makes the HP Laser 4L model, which prints at 300 dots-per-inch, shuts itself off when not in use, and is less expensive to operate than other laser printer models. HP makes other printers that offer better print quality, and if you can afford a better printer you should get it. Your business image depends on it, and you won't be sorry. Also, I would stay with HP because many of the other printers in the market are basically HP printers. You can bet that HP will work with just about any software package you have, and if you decide to offer laser printer repair, you can experiment with your own printer.

Professionally printing your promotional material

If you decide to have your promotional materials produced by a professional printer, get the smallest quantity possible and come back for more when you need them. This is because even good-quality paper lasts less than a year before it begins to age and yellow. In addition, your ideas will probably change as you get into working in the field, and you might find that your interests and opportunities change. If, for example, you find yourself wanting to focus on monitor repair, it'll be tough to abandon all the money you spent on that huge pile of yellowing stationary that says, "I fix anything."

You might already have plenty of experience with computers and are ready to branch out on your own. But if not, you could volunteer in a nonprofit organization doing computer repair. If you have the computer knowledge, but not the retail experience, you could pick up the retail and pricing information by working in a software or hardware store part-time.

Gain experience without paying for it

Computer literacy organizations are springing up all over the United States, as well as worldwide. The focus is to get used computers to people willing to learn but unable to afford the equipment. If you're brand new to computer repair, volunteering for such a program has two advantages.

Volunteer to gain experience

The first is you'll be able to get hands-on experience repairing the hundreds of donated computers that come into these programs. I've seen volunteers working in an entire room full of old IBM-compatible computers, Macintoshes, printers, modems, and other peripherals. There's a good chance you'll see lots of oddball problems as well as plenty of unusual configurations while testing the machines and building working models.

The second advantage is getting to know others in the field. People running these programs tend to be leaders in the local computer industry. In Dallas, the Computer Literacy program is headed by Brian Nichols, an airplane pilot for American Airlines who is using his substantial free time to co-found CyberProductions. CyberProductions designs multimedia advertising materials and is attempting to set up an interactive, multimedia trade show for computer industry vendors on the Internet. In addition, the computers donated are stored in the INFOMART, a building in Dallas where the leaders of the high-tech industry congregate and where computer and high-tech trade shows are held.

Once the donated computers are repaired, they are used in teaching courses offered by volunteers in the program itself. These working computers are also given to organizations that are attempting to help people gain employment, such as missions on skid row and community social service programs.

Several students from local high-tech schools volunteer their Saturdays to the Dallas Literacy Program in order to sharpen their skills for future employment and just because they enjoy the work. Isaias Alverez, a student at DeVry Institute of Technology and President of the Society of Hispanic Professional Engineers is an example. If you would like to meet industry professionals and get real experience, this is certainly an inexpensive and fruitful way to start.

Mike Hordeski's company, Jablon Computer, received a donation of five old IBM XT system units with keyboards. These were repaired and donated to Creative Alternative for Learning and Living (CALL), a local nonprofit group that provides homes and training to disabled adults in California. They are used by the home supervisors as word processors. A CALL employee purchased one of the systems, and CALL used the profit from the sale to purchase monitors, printers, and other needed parts.

Other organizations that need help are those who receive donated computers. Overworked and underpaid, the people staffing volunteer organizations have little time to devote to computer repairs or teaching and are looking for volunteers. You can certainly visit these programs and offer your services in repair or teaching. Not only will this look good on a resume, but it will also give you the experience you need. To find out who needs help, call your county social services department or a local church and explain to them what you'd like to do. (This type of volunteer work also opens doors for gaining free publicity for your business, as we'll see further on.)

Work in the computer retail industry

Another way to get the experience you need is to work in a computer software or hardware store, especially if you need experience in the retail end concerning how much to mark up materials. Many department stores have computers for sale and have a high turnover in part-time employees. Retail computer stores offer openings as well, and you might even be able to get a position at a computer repair shop.

This is a commonly used strategy that has already been proven in the computer industry several times. Intel, the microprocessor manufacturer, was started by a group of former employees from another semiconductor manufacturer, Fairchild Semiconductor. David Mahoney left computer manufacturer, Data General, to be one of the co-founders of Banyan Systems in Westboro, Massachusetts. Banyan has become one of the major companies in the PC networking area, with 700 employees.

Profile

Fred Chapman
Weatherford Electronics & Computer Services, Weatherford, Texas

"You can end up working 24 hours a day, 7 days a week," explained Fred Chapman, owner of Weatherford Electronics & Computer Services. This statement might seem quite a surprise when you consider Fred's business is in a community of 15,400 just west of Fort Worth, Texas.

Fred was a diesel truck mechanic for Ryder Truck rental, but an injury to his back left him permanently disabled. He was suddenly thrust into the position of finding a new occupation. The counselors at the Texas rehabilitation commission offered him training for a new job, so Fred took tests to see what kind of job he might be suited for.

He ended up at Weatherford College in the Industrial Electronic Technology program. It took him three years to complete a two-year

Associate of Applied Science degree, but it was while he was earning that degree that he became interested in computers. Fred also had disability income to help him financially during this difficult time.

A computer-aided design (CAD) course had Fred in a fix because it was just about impossible to spend the kind of time necessary to get the assignments done in an on-campus computer lab where everyone was competing for computer time. Fred's instructor suggested the budget-conscious move of building a computer for CAD homework, since Fred didn't feel he could just go buy one. With the instructor's help, Fred built the computer. It was during this process that he and the instructor realized Fred had a knack for this type of work.

After that, Fred and a friend started fixing older computers in their spare time. During his time at Weatherford College, Fred made contact with the county purchasing agent and ended up doing some repair on the school's computers. The school did have another computer consultant, but the other consultant had a bad reputation, so they hired Fred instead.

Fred said he heard nothing but bad comments about the other consultant. The demand for an honest consultant was high, and Fred remembers people commenting about the other consultant, "He sells you a computer and then you can't find him."

During his studies, Fred divorced. He was left with the full responsibility for his one-and-a-half-year old son. "I needed to make a decision to quit or start a real business." He made the decision so fast, he was clear down at the county offices to get a business license before he realized he didn't have a business name. Because he was going to electronics school he decided to call it Weatherford Electronics & Computer Services. Now it's only computer services, but Fred already has the stationary and the name is known, so he hasn't changed it.

He set up an office and shop in one room of his three-bedroom mobile home and said his business volume tripled almost immediately. It was tough at first, though, because his first big customers were nearly an hour's drive in Dallas, and he had to pay cash for all the parts he needed to do repairs. Fortunately, he made friends with a banker in Weatherford who agreed to a 30-day note on Fred's signature alone. He was also able to get 30-day net terms with his suppliers, some of whom have manufacturing facilities in Taiwan.

The right suppliers gave Fred the ability to get parts, such as Intel Overdrive upgrade microprocessor chips, which Dallas suppliers were unable to get in quantity. He put an ad in one of the county papers advertising a lower price than the Dallas distributors and was pleased with the response.

"It's also important to get the right distributor who will take care of me so I can take care of my customers," Fred explained. When parts under warranty fail, Fred needs to get the replacement part back in the computer as quickly as possible. "A long-term RMA (returned merchandise authorization) on a part hurts my business. My supplier will cross-ship. I can't afford a two-week turnaround on an RMA."

In a year the business was too large for the trailer, so he rented office space. He also turned down some work to keep from growing too fast and avoided oddball machines from new customers or work that would interfere with work he'd already taken.

He has a second technician, hired full-time about a year ago, in addition to a full-time secretary. The friend that helped him with repairing used computers when he started out is also on his payroll, but only part-time because he has a full-time job elsewhere.

While he has a yellow-page ad, Fred admitted he gets the vast majority of his customers through referrals. He makes a point of taking time to explain what he's doing, why, and what it will cost. He also concentrates on recommending a plan of action that will help the customer the most instead of always looking at his "bottom line." Word gets around in a small town fast when someone is unhappy, Fred claims. He also offers a one-year parts and labor warranty on his work.

Fred's a strong believer in following up on customers. "People in my business are getting the reputation of used-car salesmen, and I'm out to try to change that." His schedule is to call within a week of the service, then call again in 60 to 90 days, then at 6 months. "But most customers call back before the 6-month call with some more work for me," Fred added.

One of the ways he's freed up some of his time, besides hiring employees to handle some of the workload, is to have parts delivered instead of picking them up. The other step he's taken is to ask customers to bring the computers to him, instead of traveling on-site whenever possible.

When he has to go on-site, he charges a flat rate for the call based on whether its in the city or in the county. Other repair services start charging per hour on service calls from the time they leave the office until they pull back into the parking lot. Using a flat fee has helped his popularity with customers.

Fred claims another competitor came into the community, opened a store, made money at first, but only lasted a year and a half before he went bankrupt. The reason his competitor didn't last was he wouldn't back up his service and he used cheaper components, according to Fred. "This business is so easy to get into, and it's easy to make money fast, but when it comes to support and the long haul, they (other consultants) don't make the grade."

A particular warning sign is when a new computer store offers a longer warranty than anyone else. "If Conner, NEC, and other suppliers only offer a one-year warranty on their parts, where do these stores get longer warranties than their suppliers?" However, a warranty isn't valid if the store isn't in business. "These stores come in, sell fast, get out. Sometimes they just move on the other side of town with a new name, and then they don't have to take care of the warranties."

"People underestimate the consumer. Sooner or later the person will realize you've taken advantage of him." In his effort to never underestimate the customer, Fred "specs" the repair or upgrade job in detail, including listing brand names, model numbers, and hard disk buffer size of the components he recommends. Then, for comparison shopping, he provides the customer a list of questions to ask. This could be seen as offering too much detail, but Fred says people come back. He's also been known to take people back in the shop and show them the motherboard he uses, explaining why he buys a more expensive motherboard instead of the one advertised in the *Fort Worth Star Telegram* for $100 less. "I don't sell. I educate."

There have been tough times when he considered giving up the business, saying to himself, "I'm going to walk out of here and go to work for someone else." And there are still days when his back injury keeps him out of commission, but he realizes there are too many benefits in working for himself to stop now.

The business does tend to have a cycle, Fred noted. "There will be two or three weeks where it's really busy, then other times that the phone doesn't ring." He's learned, however, that the quiet times are the times to do cleaning, inventory, bookkeeping work, and other items that were neglected during the busy period, before the next rush comes. He says these cycles give him time to catch his breath. He's also noticed cycles in the repair work. He might have a ten-day period of nothing but repair on laser printers, or a cycle where he does nothing but fix computers "blown out" by a local storm.

He also contracts out some repair work to depots such as deep laser printer work, chip-level diagnostics, and monitors. He said depot businesses, also known as "bench tech guys" don't really talk to people, but they have lots of work if they're good. He finds the depot businesses at local computer events, such as computer swaps. "You can learn a lot from people at the swap."

Reciprocal relationships in which he gives and gets referrals is another way Fred gains business. For example, he made friends with a Radio Shack manager and is careful to take good care of the customers she sends him. He said it's a win-win relationship because it makes her look good and it makes him look good. He also contracts with programmers for custom applications clients need and offers service contracts.

As for his plans for the future, Fred said he doesn't want to be "IBM or CompUSA. I'd like to have five technicians doing repair and oversee the operation."

His advice to start-up computer repair businesses is, don't let somebody else take care of too much while you're growing, don't grow too fast, and keep your fixed expenses low. "You don't need a lot of advertising really. What you need is to put out good-quality work."

Business is looking for you

Once you have some experience, your own equipment, and a small stock of promotional material, it's time to go round up business. *American Demographics* says the demand for health and business services will grow faster in the 1990s than in the 1980s. Computer and data processing services, among the business services expected to grow, will account for 800,000 new jobs at a growth rate of 5.3 percent a year, according to the Bureau of Labor Statistics.

These statistics mean you can go out armed with the knowledge that computer repair and services are in demand, and that trend is predicted to increase between now and the year 2005. What you have to do is help customers find you by either placing yourself where they are or by getting them to come to you.

Give customers a taste of your excellence

While computer swaps and user groups are the place to get used equipment, information, and experience, they're not the place to find customers. Folks in these places are not looking to pay for repairs or information. You need to position yourself as an authority in the places where the people willing to pay are going. These people are in business either for themselves or for a company and don't have time to troop around the countryside to find out what they need to know. They're also looking for credible people with knowledge they feel they can count on.

Jay Conrad Levinson, in his revised-for-the-'90s book *Guerrilla Marketing*, said the trend in customers is toward people who are ". . . more demanding, less forgiving, in a hurry, and appreciative of warmth and attention to detail." These people need to see your work. More directly, Levinson advised service businesses to allow potential customers "a taste of your excellence."

So where do people who are demanding and in a hurry go for computer information and where can you give them a "taste?" Why, at courses or seminars, especially those offered by credible schools that take one day to a few weeks.

Teach a computer course or seminar

Teach at nonprofit schools   What those who attend courses at nonprofit schools don't know is that most instructors, especially those teaching single-day or evening courses, are offered very low pay for their teaching work, and there is a high turnover rate in these positions. The school draws those with "life experience" to teach by offering public exposure and credibility to the potential instructor. This is a way many computer repair businesses and consultants in other fields gain customers.

Many times the courses are offered based on enrollment, so if a certain number of students don't sign up, the course doesn't run, and the instructor doesn't get paid. However, the schools are careful to deluge the area with flyers or catalogs promoting both the courses and the instructors. Learning Tree University, an accredited, nonprofit institute in the Los Angeles area, sends out over one million catalogs every two months to the residents of the San Fernando Valley. Not every school is able to promote itself as thoroughly, but you can bet they are attempting to reach the local community because that's where they find students.

The self-employed are drawn to this kind of work because they are the only ones who will accept the uncertainty and low pay. Most of the teachers teach one or two classes, and most leave altogether once their businesses are established.

Not every person in a course will be a candidate for consulting. Some will actually use what you have to say and solve their own problems. Others will spend the entire session confused (the "overload" syndrome) and dismiss the course entirely. But there is that percentage that will see that you know what you're doing, decide the job is too hard for them, and hire you.

To get into the position to teach, expect to wait several months. It takes time to produce catalogs and even more time to set up courses and instructors. To get in as an instructor, look for courses you think you could teach, even if you might have to do some work to get ready. These schools are often open to suggestions, so watch what they're doing now and feel free to suggest something along the same lines.

Send your resume, business card, and brochure, if you have one, to the person in charge of curriculum planning for the computer courses. One of the best ways to find potential openings is to scan the course times for a particular offering and look for "staff" as the instructor. That means they didn't have anyone to teach the course when the catalog was printed and are actively looking for someone. They might have found someone in the meantime, but this is an opportunity for you to contact the school and ask if they need an instructor for the course.

You might find that these schools are poor and don't have enough computers. If you can come up with a computer course that doesn't require students to have "hands-on" time with a computer, you'll have an easier time selling it to the school. Those institutes with computer labs often have them tied up every minute because hands-on classes are preferred by students, and the school can charge more for such a class. You might be more successful with a subject that doesn't require an actual computer, or maybe only one computer (such as a computer virus course), and then work your way into teaching the more popular "hands-on" courses.

Once you begin teaching, pushing your consulting services is not what you want to do. You want to build relationships with the students as people. Levinson emphasizes the human bond before the business bond. He claims an effective marketer "first makes the human bond" by treating the person in all interactions like a person "with a family, a business, hobbies, interests, opinions—and then like a customer." His assertion is those business relationships that put the human bond first are long-lasting, repeat customers, while business-first relationships are fragile.

Do make sure, however, that all your students leave your course with your business promotional materials or at least your business card. You don't know when they'll need you or refer you to a friend. Also, don't forget that many people who have computers purchased the machines so they could work at home. Those employees are often more credible to their employers and are listened to when they make suggestions. Many a computer repair technician has gotten ongoing work in private businesses, corporations, or government facilities through the referral of a student.

Teach adult education classes   Similar teaching opportunities are available in adult education and vocational programs sponsored by your local school district. These are much better paying positions, often with medical and insurance benefits. Most of the courses are several weeks in length at night and on weekends, at a high school or vocational campus. School district facilities are more likely to have computer labs where you can teach with one or two students to a computer.

In these programs, the schools are looking for teachers with life experience, such as five years or more of computer experience, but do not require a teaching certificate. If you have the experience, you can often get into teaching quickly if you promise to take college courses over a period of time to pick up the teaching credential. You'll need to contact the main office of your school district for more information.

The drawback here is these courses are often heavily funded, meaning students pay little and might have waited on a long list to get into the course. This means many of your students will be people with a lot of time on their hands and not an overabundance of money to throw at problems. But you can still pick up clients in these courses, and you'll get the added benefits of exposure in the school's promotional materials, free daytime hours, and steady, reliable income.

Once you have a teaching credential, you can also begin exploring options such as teaching at state-operated extension courses at a junior college or university. There are two advantages here: the pay can be much better for the time you spend, and the income of the individuals taking the courses is likely to be higher.

Winn Rosch, author of one of the leading computer repair books, the *Winn L. Rosch Hardware Bible*, said upstart computer repair businesses should consider offering a free diagnostic check. Rosch suggested taking a Saturday and inviting local residents to bring their computers for optimization and a free check—no pressure, no sales.

Offer free computer clinics

The only catch in doing this is you'll need to do a virus check on each machine first before you do anything else. If you do not scan for those destructive, rogue programs, and you use the same disk on each computer you check over, you could be liable should one of the people attending your clinic come up with a virus.

Another twist on the computer clinic idea is to do the clinic as a fund-raiser in conjunction with a community nonprofit group with a small charge for the computer checkup that goes to the charity. The added benefit here is the event might be publicized by local newspapers, as well as television and radio stations, provided that the details were sent to these media sources on the letterhead of the nonprofit organization. This opens up the activity further so your clinic could be held at any one of a number of places, like the high-school gym or the local library, which is helpful if you happen to be working from a home office. Even if you've decided to rent office space, you might want to consider doing a fund-raiser for a credible nonprofit group so you can reap the potential publicity and gain the association.

You can make up stickers and place one on each computer you check so these potential customers then take home their computer with your business sticker on it. If they have a problem and they've gotten to know you, they're likely to give you a call. You could offer to repair problems, suggest upgrades, and demonstrate your excellence. Marketing books, available at your library, are full of promotional ideas like this one that you can adapt for your business.

How to become a local expert

You can give speeches on computers for local groups and work on becoming a well-known local computer expert. Gloria Michels, a professional publicist, in her book *How to Make Yourself (or Anyone Else) Famous* said there are two reliable ways to generate "newsmaking action." Both methods have to do with giving because ". . . giving is so unselfish and rare that it commands attention whenever it happens." The two ways are: giving a speech or giving something away.

Clubs and organizations in your community are looking for speakers for their programs for the coming year. Michels reasons that almost anyone can become a speaker at one of these events if they can come up with something that suits the group's interests. Such groups include the Chamber of Commerce, the Rotary, the Friends of the Library, professional real estate groups, the Historical Society, and others. The way to find these groups is to watch your newspaper for listings of meetings or speeches.

In her book, Michels has come up with simple forms for readers to fill out so they can mesh what's interesting about themselves personally with whatever they are trying to promote. For example, an insurance company president was also interested in antique maps as a hobby, so Michels suggested he offer to give a speech to the Historical Society entitled, "What antique maps tell us about Lake County real estate today." A young man who had been in street gangs and in trouble with the police combined his interest in kids and his experience with gangs to give a speech to the local PTA titled, "How to protect your children from street gangs."

You'll need to come up with an interesting topic based on your experience and the interests of groups in your area. Then write a letter to the program chairman of the group in which you say you'd like to speak, outlining the benefits of the your speech and when you could be available. You should also include a photo, a resume, and a business card. Then wait a week or two, and if you don't hear from the program chairman, call and ask if the materials were received. At that point, you'll find out if your speech is of interest to the group, and you can ask about the publicity plans, offering your services to help. Michels' book offers information and tips concerning how to deal with newspapers, magazines, and radio stations to get publicity, as do a number of other books on public relations. You should get some of these types of books, available at your local library, and study them.

Michels said it was by making speeches that the insurance company president became an authority for the press. By looking through their archives of past stories and people, reporters found references to the company president's speeches and began calling him for quotes on related topics as they came up. The same thing happened to the young man who was a former gang member. There is no reason you can't take the same route as well.

It happens. You get a customer. Now you need to know what to charge. Prices per hour vary based mostly on how experienced and established the repair individual is, as well as how difficult the work is. Computer repair technicians work hourly for about the same rates as plumbers and electricians for standard repair work, about $40 to $65 per hour. You'll find that hourly rates in an area such as New York City will be considerably higher than in most rural farming areas.

How to set your pricing

It also doesn't seem to matter much in hourly rates whether the technician travels to the site or has a storefront. In our interviews, some shops charge for travel time; others don't. It seems to be the more established repair businesses that charge for travel time as well as the actual time on site.

When you are starting out, you can absorb the travel time for short trips, say 15 or 20 minutes one way. If the travel time is much more than this, quote an amount to the customer first. You can combine some activities for longer trips so that you can justify the extra travel time. For example, if a job takes you to a nearby town or business area you normally do not go to, you can take along some of your flyers and do some prospecting.

Repair businesses that charge per job are charging hourly and adding the cost of materials. This isn't particularly difficult to calculate if you know the cost of materials and how long it takes to perform a task. Most shops will diagnose a problem and offer an estimate for the repair without charge, if the customer wants to bring in the computer. Small businesses and individuals are more comfortable with the by-the-job charge, since they can plan their expenses better, but if you misjudged the extent of the repair, you might end up losing on the deal.

None of the technicians interviewed ever worked for less than $20 an hour, and some make several hundred dollars an hour. The ones who charged $20 an hour said they did so when they were first starting. The highest hourly wages are gained for difficult, detailed work like recovery of crucial data off trashed hard disk drives or repair of specialized systems that do specific tasks, such as computers that collect data from other machines.

How to charge more

The most obvious way to find out what you can charge is to find out what others are charging and then set your prices accordingly. Customers are not always driven by the lowest price, so if you can offer something your competitors don't, like more personalized or faster service, you can get business even if your price is higher. Those with vendor certifications, like the Novell's Certified Network Engineer (CNE), can also command higher rates, even if they're not dealing with a network, simply because they have the certification. Information about where to call for specifics concerning the main vendor certifications is in appendix B.

In addition, if you can become an authorized service center for a computer manufacturer, you can also charge more. Vendors are looking for a track record and are likely to require a minimum sales or repair volume, which varies depending on the size and sales philosophy of the vendor. The larger vendors are more likely to demand higher sales or repair volumes. They will also expect you to have a storefront, and you must take classes on products offered by the vendor.

But once you make the vendor's list, customers who call the manufacturer for help are referred to your shop for repairs. You are also given a special telephone contact number for support, so when you get a problem that you can't figure out, you can get right into the technical support department and get the answer. Neil Wyenn of Granada Hills, California-based CPR Computer Repair has several such arrangements with vendors such as Epson. If you look through the phone book, you'll also see other computer repair shops advertising as authorized repair centers for popular manufacturers.

The manufacturers try to limit the number of authorized service centers in an area. They also might require your shop to meet their criteria, such as a certain amount of floor space or a sales volume level. Vendor requirements vary, so it's best to call around. The phone numbers of the most popular vendors are listed in appendix B.

You can also talk to the vendors directly at large trade shows, such as Fall COMDEX, the industry's largest U.S. trade show, focused on the computer industry and held each November in Las Vegas, Nevada. If you buy frequently from a hardware or software vendor, you might receive free tickets to the show in the mail. This is a good place to locate vendors you are interested in, ask questions, and get on the mailing list for material about becoming an authorized service center. There are other trade shows as well, ranked by attendance in Fig. 2-1, but Fall COMDEX is the best known. More information about this show and other top trade shows in the computer industry can be found in appendix A.

Another avenue is to obtain a service contract from a third-party service organization such as Bell Atlantic Services. Bell offers repair services to original equipment manufacturers (OEMs) of computer and telecommunications equipment. The company has a network of independent repair facilities that subcontract computer repair work throughout the United States. Using the services of local facilities as subcontractors allows the

MediaMap: Top Computer Trade Shows

Trade Show	Location	Attendees*	Exhibitors*
COMDEX/FALL ('93)	Las Vegas	172,848	2,169
PC EXPO	New York	120,283	835
COMDEX/Spring	Atlanta	100,000	1,104
WINDOWS WORLD	Atlanta	100,000	1,104
FOSE	Washington DC	75,000	500
NAB	Las Vegas	72,000	900
MACWORLD Exposition and Conference	San Francisco	69,500	540
NetWorld+Interop	Las Vegas	60,000	600
Personal Computer & Electronics Expo ('93)	Long Island	53,000	200
SEMICON	San Francisco	50,054	1,178
GRAPH EXPO/EAST ('93)	Chicago	45,000	526
AIIM Show & Conference	New York	42,000	337
Networks Expo ('93)	Dallas	41,243	450
Strictly Business Computer Expo	Minneapolis	36,000	900
PC EXPO ('93)	Chicago	35,867	230
ComNet	Washington DC	38,000	438
Networks Expo	Boston	33,712	365
Seybold ('93)	San Francisco	32,000	250
UNIX EXPO ('93)	New York	31,503	355
National Design Engineering Show	Chicago	31,495	1,003
Wescon ('93)	San Francisco	30,000	1,300
DB/EXPO	San Francisco	30,000	200
Showbiz Expo	Los Angeles	29,834	500
VISCOMM ('93)	New York	26,739	495
International Business Expo	Las Vegas	23,887	534
ACM SIGGRAPH	Orlando	25,000	275
Tech Net/Imaging	Washington DC	23,332	540
SUPERCOMM/ICC	New Orleans	21,632	494
A/E/C SYSTEMS	Washington DC	21,350	500
Graphic Communications 3	Philadelphia	20,000	300

*The attendee and exhibitor numbers are for 1994, except as noted.

2-1

Here's a list of the top U.S. trade shows, put together by MediaMap. As you can see, Fall COMDEX is the largest, but there are several other significant shows around the country.

company to offer a wider service area to its customers. Several types of contracts are used, including hourly, flat rate, and time and materials. The fees paid are generally competitive with computer repair rates in the area. Calls for service are relayed from the manufacturer to a central office of the third-party service organization to the local repair facility. The needed parts are usually sent by the manufacturer to the local repair shop, and defective parts are returned to the manufacturer. Contact information for Bell Atlantic Services is in appendix B.

Get Repeat Business

You have customers, but you need them to come back. Repeat business is what staying in business is all about. In the 1990s, it is attention to customers as people that strengthens business relationships.

Customer Care

Harvey MacKay, successful businessman and author of several books, including *Beware the Naked Man Who Offers You His Shirt*, insists that you need to write down details you uncover about people when you meet them, like how many kids they have, their interest in baseball cards, or the fact that they're struggling with an aging parent. Then, before you talk with them the next time, you read over your notes looking for those details. MacKay stresses that how much you know about someone doesn't bother the person—if they think you care.

If you're worried about the time you'll spend conversing instead of working, you can relax. Jay Conrad Levinson maintains you do not need to spend a lot of time socializing with your customers to transfer this sense of caring. However, Levinson emphasizes that each time you do interact, the human element should come first.

This extends to your work on your customer's computers. A contact manager software package will help you keep records of each customer's history. One of the ways to tell people you care is to keep detailed records on their computer system. It will take discipline, but you'll need specifics on the make, model, and system configuration of the computer, why Mr. Jones saw you last, and what you did. This will be incredibly valuable information the next time they contact you for help.

Business profile

Computer Specialist, Public Service Company of Colorado
Denver, Colorado

Steve Houser's story is one of a young man who didn't know what he wanted to do or even what he could do. Steve simply tried every opportunity that came along until he found his niche, and the respect he was looking for, in computer repair.

He started as a cook at a restaurant out of high school, but he needed more money so he took a better-paying janitorial position with Colorado's electric utility, Public Service Company of Colorado (PSCo). He attended college part-time as an architecture student and got married, but found that starting a family forced him to quit school. He started doing odd jobs on the side to earn extra income, but found it draining and difficult.

Looking for an alternative, he noticed that job transfers were an option at PSCo. Steve set about looking for an internal job opening where he could get marketable, on-the-job training. "I decided that instead of four years of college, I'd spend four years learning a skill," he said.

He tried being a lineman but hated the work. Desperate, Steve took drawings he'd done in architecture school and tried to get a job in the company's Drafting Department. He ended up drawing the locations of gas lines by hand. When PSCo brought in a computerized system for drafting that used workstation computers and the program AutoCAD, Steve jumped at the chance for more training. This was despite the fact that his new job location was in a downtown facility, which meant more driving and parking costs, but no further compensation. With low seniority in the department, Steve decided he had nothing to lose.

He soon found he had a talent for the computerized drafting work and was asked to train other people in the department. Later, the Computer Maintenance Department asked for a person in the Drafting Department who could be used as a link. In this way, the Computer Maintenance Department could train someone to handle routine tasks by being instructed over the phone instead of sending a computer maintenance technician downtown for everything that came up.

The company originally intended to rotate the extra responsibility between people, since no additional pay came with the added responsibility. They tried several people, but discovered not everyone was deft at handling this task. Since Steve could perform his work and handle the repair and support as well, the management made the decision to stop rotating the job and let Steve handle it.

After two and a half years, a job in the Computer Maintenance Department opened up. The job posting said applicants should have a technical degree in electronics, but Steve said he knew the people in the department so well by then that they encouraged him to apply. He did and got the job!

As part of a team of six employees in Computer Maintenance that handles work on 23,000 pieces of equipment, Steve's had the opportunity to work on just about everything. In addition, Steve has been able to take vendor training classes on hardware troubleshooting and repair at company expense. He has 11 certificates from these classes, including credentials from Toshiba on laptop computers and hard-to-obtain certifications from Apple Computer.

Now the opportunity is opening up for Steve to start his own computer repair business. PSCo has announced layoffs are coming and says it plans to get its computer repair services from a third-party source. Steve has already been offered a job by aerospace contractor Martin-Marrietta and believes he'll be offered a job by the firm taking over the PSCo computer repair work as well. But when the layoffs actually do come, Steve plans to use the substantial severance pay coming to him to start his own computer repair company in the southern suburbs of Denver where new housing is springing up.

One of the things Steve loves most about the computer repair business, besides the work, is the respect he receives. "When I was a janitor, even though I made good money, people would kind of pull their hand back from shaking mine when they found out what I did. That doesn't happen now."

Recommend upgrades

But why wait for them to contact you? If you have specific information on your clients, you can look for opportunities to serve their computing needs with upgrades to the system they already have. That architect who's so cramped on disk space should know that hard disk drive prices have dropped again, and he can get more space for a lot less than the price you quoted him six months ago. Or how about the families with kids who have computers? A multimedia upgrade might make sense, as much of the new educational software is multimedia. And there's that accountant who lost his hard disk drive. Could he use a tape backup drive?

In *Beyond Computing*, an IBM magazine for business and information technology users, John Murphy of Metro Computing in Gibbsboro, New Jersey says that many corporate managers are turning to upgrades to prolong the life of their PCs. These upgrades include new monitors, graphics cards, additional memory, larger hard disk drives, math coprocessors, and central processing unit (CPU) upgrades.

Many users have discovered they have to upgrade their computer shortly after the purchase, according to a Channel Marketing survey of 1,000 PC buyers. The Dallas, Texas-based market research firm said the top five "I wish I'd gotten . . ." complaints among PC buyers were more internal expansion slots and external drive bays, a better monitor, more memory, a bigger hard disk drive, and the need for a 5.25-inch drive in addition to the 3.5-inch drive that came with the computer. This means there is an upgrade market with the burgeoning new computer user market as well as with those who have owned their computers for some time.

In addition, your best resource for new business is old customers. Marketing experts say you can increase your sales volume by 20 percent simply by offering new services to existing customers. They already know you, so they'll be more open to listen to what you have to offer. A postcard in the mail is an excellent approach. You might even want to do a regular mailing to all your customers advising them of new items and reduced prices to keep yourself and your business visible.

Revive the lost art of the thank-you note, with a twist

Think back. When was the last time you bought some big-ticket item and received a thank-you note from the salesperson who sold it to you? Fred Chapman, owner of Weatherford Electronics and Computer Repair, says part of the reason his business is predominant in his city is because he follows up after the sale. He calls within a week or so of a purchase or repair to ask how things are going and to make sure customers are happy with the service from his shop and the performance of their computer.

These stories are not unusual. This follow-up-after-the-sale advice is standard fare in most how-to sales books. With thank-you cards, birthday cards, holiday cards, postcards, and so on, effective salespeople start working on the next sale while the first sale is still warm .

But you're in the computer business and there are many ways to say "thank-you" using a computer. You could record a "thank-you, is there anything else we can do for you?" message that the computer delivers by phone using a voice mail/modem add-on card. How about printing up the notes using software and hardware you sell? You could also send a note via electronic mail to the customer's electronic address if they have one. If not, you could use electronic services, such as MCI Mail, to mail the note for you. This is more than just a way to say thanks; it can be a way to get more business. Computer owners have a tendency to love new technology and might go for the answering machine board and software that called their phone or a modem and software for electronic mail access. If you're not feeling creative, a phone call or a short, handwritten note is better than doing nothing.

Levinson had particular advice for service businesses. He said, "Find out what your prospects want, how they'd describe an ideal business such as yours, what benefits they most want. Then offer what they want and need and become the business that they want, stressing the benefits you offer."

Find out what customers want, then give it to them

Can it be that simple? Just ask people what they want and then try to give it to them? You'd be surprised how many computer repair shops and other service businesses want to make those decisions for the customer. If you think about it a moment, it probably won't take you long to remember the last time you wanted to purchase something and the salesperson "patted you on the head" and told you, "We don't think that's right for you."

Co-author Linda Rohrbough has a client, a mom-and-pop-shop plumbing business, that wanted a state-of-the-art multimedia computer system with all the bells and whistles. They knew what computer they wanted, and she was to add a fast modem, a spectacular monitor, and software for remote access. When she was purchasing components, several suppliers asked her what the equipment was for. When she told them, the suppliers laughed and said a business like that didn't "need" all this high-end stuff. They were right, of course. A mom-and-pop plumbing operation could run its business on one of the first PCs ever made, but they didn't want a low-end computer. Had Linda "pooh-poohed" her customers, she would have lost the sale.

It is easy to forget that "wants" and "needs" are relative and totally subjective. If you present the pros and cons of giving your customer what they want, they're willing to pay for it, and it doesn't violate the law, then there shouldn't be a problem.

Asking customers what they want is the beginning step in advertising. This is why companies pay big money to get those people to stand out in the shopping mall and ask you questions about what brand of mouthwash you prefer and why. Effective advertising begins with market research, which is precisely what you do when you begin asking customers what they want. Levinson suggested simply cold-calling businesses, starting the conversation by saying, "Can I have two minutes of your time?" Tell them you do computer repair and ask them what they think the perfect computer repair business would be like.

When you have your answers, begin gearing toward delivering those items to the customer, and advertise that you deliver those added items or services. You might have to come up with some questions to ask to prime the conversation. Here are a few samples:

Does the business prefer that the repair person come on site, or do they mind bringing the computer to you? Would it be helpful to them if you did a tape backup of their computers and gave them the tape? (If they don't have tape backup drives and you have a portable, parallel tape backup unit, they are likely to call you to get the information restored when they need it. Be sure to slip a business card or sticker about your services inside the tape cartridge case.)

It is also important to keep up with what your customers want by asking them what they require, what they expect, and what they consider good service. According to Joan Koob Cannie, in her American Management Association book *Keeping Customers For Life*, customer satisfaction is a moving target. It changes on a regular basis. Cannie's advice is to ask customers every few months what they need, then make adjustments to your business services and advertising accordingly.

A whopping 96 percent of unhappy customers will not complain to you directly, but they will complain to ten other people. But more importantly, Cannie points to an MIT study that claims about 80 percent of technical innovation comes from customers.

Sometimes you'll need to study the ideas to interpret them into a business opportunity. For example, the widespread complaining about a lack of an affordable and quick package delivery was not interpreted into an overnight delivery service until Federal Express came along. (By the way, Federal Express goes to extremes to keep its "absolutely, positively overnight" promise, including chartering a jet at a loss to the company so deliveries are on time.)

Few customers will have refined the opportunity for you. Most will express their comments in terms of a complaint or an inconvenience. Don't let negative comments stop you from seeing other money-making products and services that your clients want!

You have the advantage

We believe one of the reasons small business in general is performing so well in the current economic environment is because it can move and adapt faster than large companies or corporations. The main advice to corporations is a concept called "empowerment," meaning the person who has the responsibility for the task or the customer should have the authority to make decisions necessary to get things done right. However, empowerment can be difficult for large companies to incorporate. After spending years training people to adhere to a bureaucratic environment where risks are avoided, it might be difficult to turn around and get those same employees to step out on a limb and make decisions by themselves.

For example, Jan Carlzon, head of SAS Scandinavian Airlines, was able to change the company's balance sheet from an $8 million loss to a $71 million profit in two years. In his book, *Moments of Truth*, he said the turnaround was due to implementing empowerment. In one instance, a plane load of customers were delayed by an equipment failure. The gate attendant announced there would be free coffee and donuts during the delay, a move to help ease the situation. However, the airline's kitchen wouldn't cooperate with the "unauthorized" move, so the attendant went to a competitor and purchased the coffee and donuts out of her own pocket. The gate attendant was opposed by her own company, but Carlzon was able to prove he was serious by giving the attendant a commendation and seeing to it she was reimbursed.

In contrast to empowerment, consider your own city's motor vehicle bureau. Like most bureaucracies, your time and needs are on the bottom of the priority list. Further, the people working there are hardly motivated to see that you're satisfied. The employees are not rewarded for taking risks, and they are heavily penalized for mistakes. So those serving you play it safe, adhering strictly to a predefined set of rules without wavering. You only go there because your desire to continue to drive your car is greater than your aversion to long lines and rude clerks.

Then consider the small business, where the customer is very likely to be served by the same person each time. This is an environment where the customer can be personally known and where mistakes, if made, can be quickly corrected. There's also room here to bend the "rule" in a special case, should the need arise.

The bottom line is people are interested in dealing with businesses that care about their needs, their convenience, and their priorities. They want to be in the driver's seat. They expect the businesses they deal with to have figured out their problem and the answer because that's the only reason they've agreed to let go of their money. They want to deal with bright, motivated people who can make decisions and get the job done without a lot of red tape or hassle. They don't like dealing with problems or mistakes, but they understand if it can't be helped, especially if they feel the service provider is doing everything possible to remedy the situation. In short, they're like you.

These facts and the skyrocketing demand for computer repair services give you the advantage. You can deliver. Now let's look at how.

References

Cannie, Joan Koob. 1991. *Keeping Customers For Life*. New York, New York: AMACOM division of the American Management Association.

Levinson, Jay Conrad. 1993. *Guerrilla Marketing, Secrets for Making Big Profits from Your Small Business*. Boston, Massachusetts: Houghton Mifflin Company.

MacKay, Harvey. 1990. *Beware the Naked Man Who Offers You His Shirt*. New York, New York: W. Morrow.

Michels, Gloria. 1988. *How to Make Yourself (or Anyone Else) Famous*. New York, New York: Cross Gates Publishing Company.

Murphy, John A. November/December 1993. "Upgrading PCs—Pumping Up the Power." *Beyond Computing* 2 (6): 56–58.

Timmons, Jeffry A. 1989. *The Entrepreneurial Mind*. Andover, Massachusetts: Brick House Publishing Company.

Waldrop, Judith. March, 1994. "Career Opportunities to 2005." *American Demographics* 16 (3): 18–21.

3 The basics

"One machine can do the work of fifty ordinary men. No machine can do the work of one extraordinary man."

— **Elbert Hubbard, founder of the Roycroft shop in New York for artistically printed and bound books. Hubbard died when a German submarine torpedoed the British ocean liner Lusitania during World War I.**

While a cynical programmer or design engineer might say otherwise, computers are amazingly reliable, just like automobiles. And, like automobiles, obsolete PCs that were state-of-the-art in the 1970s, such as the Osborne and the Apple II, are still being lovingly used by die-hard fans all over the world. Many computers are tossed aside because they have fallen behind in the break-neck race for performance—not because they've quit working. The top-of-the-line PC sold today will be obsolete in a few short years if the advances in computing continue at the rate they've kept for the last 20 years.

From a repair and upgrade standpoint, our interest is more in what's wrong with computers than what's right about them. To talk about what's wrong, you will need to recognize the basic components of the computer and understand how those components work together. Even if you already understand the components, it is important for us to define the terminology so later references to common repairs and specialized "tricks" make sense to you.

Our point of view evolves from the personal computer arena, since that's where the majority of the repair business opportunities lie. Once our terms are defined, we'll talk about standards, integration, obsolescence, and breakdowns, and we'll consider how those issues are affecting computer repair.

The subassemblies

In one sense, a computer is a computer is a computer. Computers these days, regardless of the manufacturer, work in very much the same way. They all have at least one central processing unit (CPU) and a storage place called *memory* for data entering and exiting the processing unit. Other major portions that make up a computer include: the motherboard, mass storage, power sources, keyboard, monitor, peripherals, and ports. These parts of the whole computer, usually manufactured as separate subassemblies, are often replaced as one of the basic steps of computer repair.

The processor

The first computers used racks of big vacuum tubes that gave off light and heat, attracting insects. When an insect would fly into an early computer, it would cause a failure, which is where the phrase, "a bug in the system" came from. Vacuum tubes have been replaced with modern transistors that are too small to be viewed without a microscope. Intel's latest processor, called the "Pentium," contains 3.1 million transistors in a flat, square-shaped piece of silicon about 3 inches in diameter. Semiconductor manufacturers are spending billions to make processors that are used in just about everything from automobiles to household appliances.

Know your processor   In computers, it is imperative you know what processor is in the machine you're working on. The characteristics of this central chip, also known as the microprocessor or central processing unit (CPU), determines the capability of the computer itself, including what kind of software and the other components you can add. It might also be the clue as to why something the user wants to do doesn't work. Snooper, one of the shareware programs included with this book, will tell you what processor is inside the PC you're looking at and how fast that processor is.

Processor speed   The processor will have a capacity for processing data, measured in bits, and a clock speed measured in megahertz (MHz). A *bit* is the smallest amount of data the computer is capable of storing, and the clock speed can be thought of as how often the processor cycles through an operation on the data.

The easiest way to explain this is by using the wheelbarrow analogy. Let's say the processor's capacity is like the amount of dirt a wheelbarrow can hold, the clock speed is like the number of trips that can be made with the wheelbarrow, and the data processed is the dirt we're moving. The amount of dirt that can be moved in a given amount of time with a wheelbarrow depends on the amount of dirt that the wheelbarrow can hold as well as the number of trips that can be made in the time period.

Processors are designed to operate chunks of bits measured by the bit width. The first processors used in personal computers had bit widths of 8 bits and were called 8-bit chips. Newer processors like the Pentium are able to handle 64 bits at once and are called 64-bit chips.

In general, a larger wheelbarrow is going to move more dirt. But it is possible that a smaller wheelbarrow could move more dirt than a larger one, if the smaller wheelbarrow made more trips. So a 16-bit processor running at 33 MHz could be faster than a 32-bit processor running at only 16 MHz.

Processor naming conventions   Processors in general have long been "named" using numbers, such as Intel's product line, the 8088, 80286, 80386, and 80486. These chips were then commonly nicknamed by dropping the "80." This was until Intel discovered in a court battle with its competitors Advanced Micro Devices and Cyrix that it couldn't defend numbers as trademarkable names. In its latest release, Intel broke tradition and renamed its newest processor, which would have been the 80586, the Pentium.

There are several types of memory. We'll describe each type and its function in the computer.

Memory

Read-only memory basic input/output system (ROM BIOS)   The built-in memory that performs the computer's startup functions is known as the read-only memory basic input/ouput system (ROM BIOS). The ROM BIOS or BIOS is often programmed into a single chip that plugs into the main board of the computer. The BIOS chip activates the peripherals and provides a standard set of functions for the processor. Other devices that contain a processor, such as a printer, will have their own BIOS as well.

The power on self-test (POST) in ROM   The ROM BIOS also contains a set of self-test routines called the power-on self test (POST). These test routines are run through each time the computer is started. If there is an error, the computer will halt. An experienced computer repair technician can watch where a computer halts in the POST and get a pretty good idea of where the trouble has to be occurring. In addition, the BIOS issues POST codes, numerical values that can be read by special equipment or are displayed on the monitor if the computer gets far enough in the start-up that the video display is working. If the POST doesn't get far enough for the video display to work, a system of beeps through the PC speaker will be issued by the BIOS to indicate the status of the test. A healthy computer system will issue a single, short beep if the POST was successfully completed. We'll talk more about the POST and POST codes in chapter 5 when we discuss common problems and the tools needed to fix those problems.

When we talked with repair technicians, we asked them what were the most common repair problems they ran into. Here are the top three answers.

The three most common repairs

- Hard disk drive
- Power supply
- Video card

Note: there didn't seem to be one component that came up more often than the others, so this order is not a ranking, but is listed alphabetically.

Random access memory (RAM)   The storage area for data to be operated on by the processor is commonly known as random access memory (RAM) or dynamic RAM (DRAM). When a reference is made to the computer's memory, RAM is usually what is meant.

The RAM is used as a scratch pad for data to be manipulated by the processor then placed back into the memory area once the processor is finished. The processor and the two types of memory (ROM and RAM) are crucial to the operation of the computer. A failure in these components is usually fatal.

Single in-line memory modules (SIMMs)   Recent developments in RAM have the several chips that make up a portion of RAM together on small boards that then plug into sockets on the main board. These small, finger-length boards are known as SIMMs (single in-line memory modules). Most of the older computers use RAM chips lined up in rows with individual sockets, while newer computers use SIMMs. You might also run into SIPPs (single in-line pin package), but SIPPs have faded from use. SIPPs are very much like SIMMs, but instead of standard circuit board connections, they have comblike connectors in the form of individual pins that stick out from the bottom of the small boards. These connectors are fragile and can be easily damaged when SIPPs are installed or removed. All three types of memory, RAM Chips, SIMMs, SIPPs, are shown in Fig. 3-1.

3-1

A random access memory (RAM) chip, a single in-line memory module, and a single in-line pin package. SIMMs and SIPPs integrate the smaller RAM chips into a single circuit board. SIMMs are the most popular. Micro House

RAM Chip

SIMM

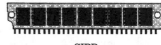
SIPP

Cache   It's tough to talk about computers very long without running into the term "cache." A *cache* (pronounced "cash") is a small block of RAM that holds frequently used instructions and data. If the processor is using an instruction or set of data frequently to complete an operation, the data or instruction is sent to the faster cache instead of the regular RAM. This speeds up the overall speed of the computer, and over a large number of operations it becomes significant. Peripherals, hard disk drives, and other subassemblies are likely to have their own cache to speed up computer performance.

The motherboard

The CPU and the RAM chips usually plug into a main circuit board, often referred to as the "motherboard," system board, or main board. This board also contains connectors or "slots" for the insertion of other, smaller circuit boards that enable the computer to communicate with a host of other devices. The ROM BIOS is usually in the form of a chip that plugs into the main board, and the RAM chips might also have their own sockets or SIMMs. The CPU chip might have its own socket, or it might be on a small processor board that then plugs into a connector on the main board. The Dell

3-2
The Dell System 4xxDE motherboard depicted is equipped with a slot for a CPU board. (See Fig. 3-3.) In this particular case, the ports, video, and drive controllers are all integrated onto the motherboard.

motherboard in Fig. 3-2 has a slot for a CPU board. Figure 3-3 shows all the components of this Dell motherboard.

The motherboard is a piece of reinforced plastic with circuits that enables communication between all the components and devices of the computer. These days, circuit boards are made in thin layers on which the circuits are printed in a silk-screening process. The components sit on the surface of the boards, soldered to pads that are part of the circuit. The layers are needed for interconnections in all but the most simple boards. Holes are drilled through the boards, and these holes are plated for the connections between the layers of circuit tracks or "traces."

The process of placing the components on top of a board is called *surface mount technology*. The biggest dangers to motherboards, or any circuit board for that matter, are static electricity, physical bending of the board, dust, and heat.

Heat concerns   Large chips like the processor can produce local heating effects that are detrimental to the motherboard. This is a significant problem in the most recent, high-transistor-count microprocessors. An ideal electrical circuit should never dissipate heat, but the fact that there is always some resistance in the conducting material causes some of the electrical energy to escape in the form of heat. While some advances have been made in

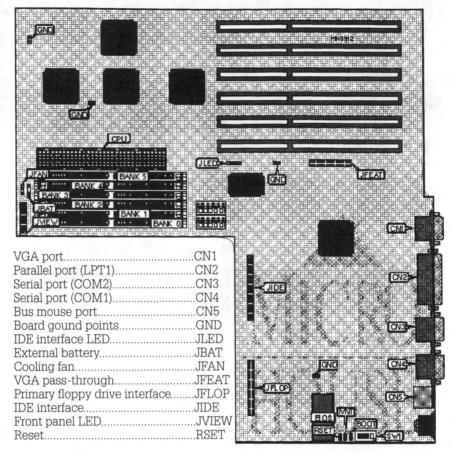

The diagram shows the components of the Dell System 4xxDE motherboard depicted in Fig. 3-2. Note the six expansion slots in the upper right and the banks of SIMM slots on the left-hand corner. Micro House

VGA port..CN1
Parallel port (LPT1)..........................CN2
Serial port (COM2)...........................CN3
Serial port (COM1)...........................CN4
Bus mouse port................................CN5
Board gound points..........................GND
IDE interface LED.............................JLED
External battery................................JBAT
Cooling fan.......................................JFAN
VGA pass-through............................JFEAT
Primary floppy drive interface........JFLOP
IDE interface....................................JIDE
Front panel LED...............................JVIEW
Reset..RSET

superconductive computer research to come up with materials that won't resist the electrical current, heat is still a problem. A processor with 3.1 million transistors can warm up the board it is placed on so much that the board bends physically, breaking some of the connections, or "traces," between circuits. This is especially true in hot weather.

In addition, the small tracks and the danger of heat makes the traditional practice of soldering in new chips or components to the motherboard especially tedious and risky. The buildup of dust also intensifies the heat problem. A thick dust layer can act as a blanket, coating the motherboard and its components as well as blocking the flow of air to the interior of the computer.

Mass storage

Mass storage used to be a matter of convenience, but now is a necessity. This storage can be anything from tape, much like the tape used in sound recording, to large-capacity hard disk drives designed for storage of computer data. The instructions that tell the computer what to do, known as software, and the data software manipulates have both grown too large to be loaded into the computer's memory without some means of mass storage.

Forms of mass storage   Mass storage has come in many forms. Both strips of paper and cards with punched holes have been used. The cards looked a lot like long index cards with square holes punched by an operator at a machine with a keyboard. In each case, the holes corresponded to the keys typed into the "keypunch" machine.

Punched cards go all the way back to the end of the American Revolution when they were used to control looms. They were used to count heads in the 1890 census and this type of coded card became one of the inventions IBM used to make its name when it first started.

In the case of cards, one instruction to the computer was typed on each card. The cards were then read one at a time by the computer so quickly that the sound was reminiscent of quickly shuffled cards at a poker game.

Tape, the same stuff used for audio recordings, is also used for mass storage in tape cartridge backup units and is still used as the main storage facility by many mainframe computers. Tape has the disadvantage of being sequential, meaning the computer has to read past a lot of material to get to the material you want it to use.

Random access storage has become the most widely used storage, starting at floppy disk drives and going up to hard disk drives and compact disc read-only memory (CD-ROM). Random access is faster because you don't have to wait as long for your data. The device can go directly to the location in which the data is stored and read it. These mass storage devices and the circuit boards that connect them to the computer will make up a significant portion of your repair business.

Formatting   All mass storage devices must go through a process called *formatting*. Formatting prepares the storage medium for recording data by dividing it logically into smaller parts that are clearly labeled by location. This allows the computer to write data to the medium and then record in a central location the address of where that information starts. On PCs running DOS, the central location where all beginning data addresses are stored is called the file allocation table (FAT), while on Macintosh computers it is the hierarchical file system (HFS). Without formatting it would not be possible to define an address for data written to the mass storage medium so the data could be retrieved again.

Floppy disk storage   Floppy disk drives involve a rust-coated, round piece of flexible (or "floppy") plastic with a hole in the middle, housed in a plastic sheath. Through an opening in the sheath, a coil called the read or write head uses an electrical charge to polarize the coated magnetic particles or read the polarization already there. Polarizing the rust on the plastic is called "writing" to the disk, and determining what polarization is already there is "reading" the disk. A spindle holds the disk while spinning it so the polarized information moves past the read head. The magnetic polarization is interpreted into digital signals, which are fed into the computer.

Each of the particles on the disk acts like a small magnet, which can be given a positive or negative polarity (north or south pole). Small areas on the disk are given a polarity depending on the number of digital ones and zeros. The changes in polarity as the head moves past these areas actually indicates a one or zero. Different schemes are used, but in the simplest form a polarity change, called a flux reversal, can represent a one, while the absence of any change represents a zero. Some schemes insert a flux reversal after consecutive zeros. This and similar tricks are used to provide synchronization pulses and improve the reliability of reading and writing data.

By writing the zeros and ones in combinations of a standard digital code, decimal numbers as well as other characters, such as the letters of the alphabet and punctuation symbols, are represented. A table in appendix D shows the decimal values of the characters you see on the screen on a PC.

Hard disk storage   Hard disk drives are similar to the floppy disk drives in that they also have a coat of particles that can be magnetized and data written to the drives is written in predefined areas called *tracks* and *sectors*. If you can imagine putting the tip of your finger on a spinning disk, the circular path your finger would trace is a track. Each track is divided into equal-length sections, and those sections are called sectors.

While data storage is much the same, hard disk drives require an additional format procedure that floppy disk drives don't require. The drives require a time-consuming low-level format, then a high-level format much the same as the formatting done on floppy disk drives. Low-level formatting identifies portions of the drive that don't meet the rigid standards necessary to hold data, though there is usually a map from the manufacturer that describes in detail what portions of the drive should not be used for data storage. This is true of every drive made, and these portions are marked using software. To make up for the deficit, the capacity of any given hard disk drive is always larger than what is advertised.

Low-level formatting writes the tracks and sectors to the drive. It is usually done on any hard disk drive just once, unless some severe damage has occurred, although more recent hard disk drives come with the low-level formatting already done. These popular drives, known as integrated drive electronics (IDE), are not supposed to be low-level formatted a second time, and the manufacturers say the drive should never be low-level formatted by the user. However, clever diagnostic software makers have come up with products that will low-level format IDE drives, though they recommend the practice be avoided if possible.

The spinning disks inside hard disk drives are aluminum or ceramic platters hermetically sealed inside a case to keep dust and other contaminates out.

Since the disk is rigid, the heads can be much closer to the surface and the disk can spin much faster. A single human hair is 100 times thicker than the space between the surface of the drive and the read head. Even a particle of smoke could cause damage to the data stored on the disk.

These factors allow the disk to hold a good deal more data, but the performance and construction of the drive are much more involved. The "clean rooms" where these drives are assembled require many times the cleanliness of a hospital operating room, down to recycling the air for impurities.

The read heads on a hard disk drive float on the air generated by the spinning platters, never touching the surface of the platters unless the drive is not operational. If the head touches the surface of the drive, that is called a *head-crash* because the action permanently destroys that area of the coating, and prevents it from ever holding any data. Most drives built now are designed to move the read-head over a portion of the drive that is never written to, called the *landing zone*, where the head is "parked" when the drive stops spinning. Old hard disk drives do not have this capacity and require a program to "park" the heads before the computer is powered down.

Hard disk platters traditionally spin at 3,600 revolutions per minute (RPM). However, in refining the production and capacity of these drives, the manufacturers have discovered that speeding up the RPM rate allows for more data storage. Many of the new drives spin at 4,500 RPM. Newer drives also contain more data in a smaller size or "form factor." Two-and-one-half inch drives, a half-inch wide, have been announced by drive makers in capacities of well over 600 megabytes (MB). Prices per MB of storage space are also dropping, making it less economical to repair hard disk drives.

Access speed and capacity are the two most important items to know about a hard disk drive. Obviously, the larger the storage capacity of the drive, the more data it can hold. The average access time, measured in milliseconds (ms), is an overall measure of how fast the drive can find stored data. There are other measures as well, such as the data transfer rate, which has to do with how fast the drive can read or write the data once it's been found. A fast hard disk drive can considerably improve the performance of a PC.

The interface between the drives and the PC   Hard and floppy disk drives as well as other devices such as tape backup drives, communicate with the central processing unit (CPU) via a circuit board that plugs into a "slot" on the motherboard. This board is commonly known as the drive controller board, and it must be compatible with the recording scheme used in the drive. Some newer motherboards have built-in drive controllers (usually for the floppy drives), and IDE drives have the controller built into the drive itself. IDE drives still do require a board that plugs into an expansion slot on the PC, but the intelligence is built into the drive itself, not the circuit board.

Hard disk installation concerns   Hard disk drives have a further wrinkle when it comes to installation. The computer's BIOS has built-in a table of specifications for hard disk drives. The table will have the unformatted capacity of the hard disk drive, the number of read-write heads, the number of cylinders, the number of sectors per track, the start reduced write current cylinder (RWC) or start write precompensation cylinder (WPC), and the address of the landing zone. We know that the heads read and write data to the disk (called the platter), but hard disk drives have a head on both the top and the bottom of each platter and can also have multiple platters. A cylinder is the sum total of the areas each of the heads can read on their respective platter without moving, as Fig. 3-4 illustrates.

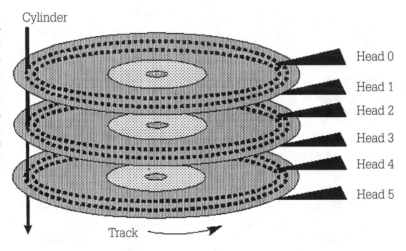

Cylinder

Head 0
Head 1
Head 2
Head 3
Head 4
Head 5

Track

When a new hard disk drive is installed in a computer, the specifications of the drive needs to be found in the BIOS in order for the drive to work with the computer in question. Two drives might have the same storage capacity, but one might not be supported by the BIOS. For example, the *Pocket PCRef* by Thomas Glover (Sequoia Publishing, 1993) lists a 212MB drive made by Conner Peripherals, the CP3200F, as having 8 heads, 1366 cylinders, 38 sectors, not applicable settings (NA/NA) for the RWC/WPC, and an automatic (auto) landing zone setting. The same book lists another 212MB drive made by Maxtor Corporation, the 7213A, with 4 heads, 1690 cylinders, NA for the tracks/sectors, NA/NA for the RWC/PWC, and an (auto) landing zone. The BIOS of an Everex 286 machine we have will not support either hard disk drive, but it is possible a BIOS could support one drive and not the other, even though they are both 212MB drives. It is not the manufacturer of a drive that matters, but making a match between the BIOS specifications and those of the hard disk.

Since this has proven to be a problem, BIOS makers have added a setting that is user-definable, usually the last entry in the BIOS listing, so you can put the settings of your hard disk drive in and make it work. This is especially attractive with IDE drives, where the intelligence to make the drive work is in the drive and not dependent on the BIOS. The biggest problem from a repair standpoint is attempting to determine the specifications for a drive that you're unfamiliar with. These specifications are also being added to computer books, such as the third edition of The *Winn L. Rosch Hardware Bible* (Brady, 1994). Pocket-sized reference books, such as the before-mentioned *Pocket Ref*, are also hitting the shelves containing these specification tables and adding DOS commands, printer error codes, lists of manufacturer's phone numbers, and other tidbits.

The complementary metal oxide semiconductor (CMOS), a part of the BIOS, is a special type of chip designed to help the PC maintain needed information when the power is off. The complementary part of the name means that all of the transistor switching is balanced so the needed power to operate the chip is miniscule. The small amount of power needed to maintain the CMOS is supplied by a backup battery. These chips are too expensive to use for all of the computer's memory, but they are used in other battery-powered devices like watches.

The CMOS

The CMOS is little more than a small area of storage, but it serves the function of maintaining the time and date information as well as the information about what is connected to the computer, such as the specifications of the hard disk drive. Without it, the computer cannot remember from one session to the next whether it even has a hard disk drive.

Many older computers came with a disk specifically for the purpose of changing the CMOS settings, including the time, date, floppy disk drives, and the specifications of the hard disk drive. You'll be fortunate to run into a situation where the user still has that disk. That information is part of the BIOS on most computers made these days and can be brought up on the computer's screen by either pressing the Delete (Del) key on the keyboard while starting up the computer, or by pressing a combination of keys at the same time. These keys could include: Ctrl, Alt, Esc; Ctrl, Alt, S; Ctrl, Alt, Insert; or others, depending on the manufacturer. In addition, the CMOS battery, which used to be soldered onto the motherboard has been improved in one of several ways, such as clipping it to the motherboard so it can be easily replaced. Some manufacturers have gone as far as to partially sidestep this problem with the addition of a rechargeable battery. The battery recharges while the computer is running. However, these batteries still wear out. They can only be recharged a certain number of times and eventually have to be changed. This will probably occur after a period of five years or more.

The newest CMOS storage is known as *flash memory*, a relatively new development where CMOS information can be stored and changed as needed as well as retained without battery or power supply energy. This flash technology is also being implemented for the BIOS as well. This means a

BIOS can be upgraded in the field by the user via a floppy disk containing the new BIOS information.

The power supply

The conversion of electrical power from the wall outlet to power the different components of the computer is done in the power supply. The power supply is a crucial component in personal computers since all devices that require electrical power depend on it. The 110 volt alternating current (ac) power from the wall outlet is converted to 5 volts and 12 volts direct current (dc). The 5 volts dc is used for most of the computer circuitry, while most of the 12-volt power goes to mechanical devices such as the motors that spin the floppy and hard disk drives. Both positive and negative polarities are provided for the 5- and 12-volt sources, with most of the current going to positive loads. A premium power supply will condition and control the voltage coming from the electrical outlet so there are no extreme highs or lows in the voltage fed to the computer's subassemblies.

Within the power supply is a fan that is often mistakenly interpreted to be only cooling the interior of the computer case. It is not. This fan is mainly designed to cool the components inside the power supply to prevent overheating and since this air also moves past the circuit boards, some cooling also takes place there. Some units have another fan that directly moves air over the circuit boards including the motherboard. The newer heat-generating processors, like the Pentium, might also have their own small fan to prevent heat problems.

Like heat, dust is an enemy of the power supply, just as it is the enemy of the other internal components of the computer. It can accumulate on the fan blades and get into the bearings of the fan motor, causing noise and friction problems. It can also coat the internal components of the unit, acting like a blanket.

The keyboard & monitor

The most recent additions in computing history have been components that allow individuals to enter information and view what they've entered immediately. These are the keyboard and monitor.

The keyboard connects to the motherboard and allows the user to type in data and give the computer instructions. Keyboards vary and are often a cause of problems because they simply wear out or are abused with coffee spills and the like. But many of these problems are easy to fix.

Monitors are also for the user, not the computer. A recent development in the history of computers, a monitor provides feedback to the user concerning what is happening with the computer and the data. Built much like a television, monitors connect to the computer using a circuit board.

However, very recently, computer monitors have begun to be used for television viewing via television reception cards that fit to the motherboard and convert the analog television signal to a digital form that can be displayed on the monitor. This way users can switch between computing and television or do both simultaneously. It is also possible, with enough mass storage, to capture the digitized television signal and manipulate it with software. The stored video sequence can also be captured and sent back out to a videocassette recorder (VCR) with the use of video capture circuit boards that connect to the motherboard. Sending video out to a VCR to the computer is called "printing to video tape" and is the basis for a new type of publishing—video publishing. Like desktop publishing, video publishing is expected to become a multimillion dollar consumer market.

The bus

The data highway that connects the processor, the memory and all the devices is called the *bus*. A typical bus is made of two sections, an address bus and a data bus. Each device connected to the computer has an address in memory where it can be reached. Data traveling in the computer is also assigned an address that gives the data a location to be stored and fetched for processing at a later time.

In a typical bus operation, the address bus broadcasts the address assigned to the data to all the devices in memory. The device with the correct address then responds (called an acknowledge), and the outgoing data is sent over the data bus to that location. The advantage to this scheme is it doesn't matter where a device is located on the bus. The device will get the data it is meant to get. This scheme allows you to connect several devices to your computer and move them around as long as you tell your computer about it, so it can make the necessary device address changes.

Bus types   Various bus types include: Industry Standard Architecture (ISA) and the Extended ISA (EISA) for the PC, Apple Computer's NuBus for the Macintosh, IBM's Micro Channel, Digital Equipment Corporation's TURBOchannel, Motorola's VMEbus, Intel's MULTIBUS, and the small-sized STD bus.

To handle video, a type of data that takes up a lot of room and must be moved through the computer's bus quickly in order to be displayed on the computer's monitor, Intel has developed the Peripheral Component Interconnect (PCI) bus standard which is being adopted by both the Macintosh and PC computing markets. Another video bus standard competing with PCI is the VESA VL-Bus, also known as the "local bus" standard.

These bus standards mean different expansion slots and different cards designed to fit those expansion slots. Figure 3-5 shows an add-on card with a Small Computer Systems Interface (SCSI, pronounced "scuzzy") for controlling compact disk read-only memory (CD-ROM) drives. This card is made for a standard ISA bus PC. Figure 3-6 is of another SCSI card to perform the same function, but made for a PCI bus. Note the variations in the connectors at the bottom of each card.

3-5
The connectors on this Small Computer Systems Interface (SCSI) card are designed for use in an Industry Standard Architecture (ISA) PC bus.

3-6
The Small Computer Systems Interface (SCSI) card depicted here is designed to perform the same functions as the ISA SCSI card in Fig.3-5, but it is designed with connectors for the Intel Peripheral Component Interconnect (PCI) bus standard. PCI offers faster performance, especially for graphics and video applications.

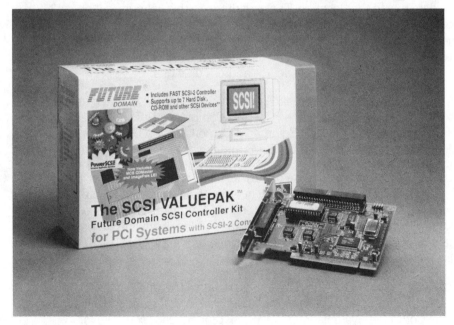

Multiple-bus PCs   Some PC manufacturers have included more than one bus technology in their machines. For example, Fig. 3-7 is of a MicroFLEX-PCI/VL/100 from clone manufacturer Micro Express of Santa Ana, California. In this unit the Micro Express has included both PCI and the local bus to accommodate add-on cards for the VL-bus and the specially made expansion slots for PCI cards.

3-7
Micro Express has included both the PCI and the local bus on the motherboard of this computer to accommodate both standards.

Chip sets are available from various manufacturers to facilitate the work of the bus, connecting the processor to memory and peripherals to the processor. Some chip sets offer special features like power management to save battery-life by varying the clock speed, or *write-back cache*. A write-back cache holds data from the CPU to be written to mass storage or to memory during periods when the CPU isn't processing. The effect is to speed up read and writing performance.

Interrupts

Interrupts are signals that interrupt the central processing unit (CPU) from normal operation to act upon a special demand situation. Your doorbell and telephone could be considered interrupt devices. In the computer, interrupts are assigned priority levels that determine how quickly they are recognized and acted upon. Once the interrupt has the attention of the processor, all other tasks are suspended while the processor handles the task required by the interrupt. These signals are typically assigned specific RAM memory addresses and are usually used by devices connected to the computer, such as a modem, for input/output operations. Personal computers usually have several interrupts for use by add-on type devices.

Direct memory address channels

Direct memory address (DMA) channels bring data directly into the computer's memory and bypass the processor altogether. The DMA channel allows large blocks of data to be transferred on personal computers without bogging down the processor, and the advantage is the speed at which data can be moved. Peripherals such as network cards and optical scanners often require a free DMA channel in order to bring data into the computer for use.

The number of input/output (I/O) addresses are limited in personal computers. Most peripheral devices require an available address on the bus as well as an interrupt or DMA channel in order to work. The more devices added to the computer, such as a network card, a scanner, or a modem, the smaller the chance that a memory address, an interrupt, and a DMA channel will be available when they are needed.

Peripherals

The items added to a computer system are termed peripherals, though the definition of whether or not a device is a peripheral depends in part on how widely adapted it has become. Printers, mice, optical scanners, modems, CD-ROM drives, barcode readers, and a host of other devices that can be added to a computer to increase its functionality are termed peripherals. Other specialized devices such as motor controls for factory automation are also peripherals.

The installation and repair of these devices is an important part of the computer business. The business with some peripherals is in installation, as items like mice, barcode readers, and modems are usually replaced rather than repaired. As already stated, a peripheral is likely to require a free location in memory in addition to an interrupt or DMA channel in order to operate. It might also need a "port," which is the physical connection to the computer.

Ports

Ports are hardware locations where peripherals plug in. The majority of peripherals available for a computer will be designed to plug into an existing serial or parallel port already available on the computer. The ports are for input and output (I/O) and often are connected to a circuit board or card that takes up an expansion slot within the computer. Each port also requires an interrupt.

Serial ports, also known as a "serial interface" on PCs, also called RS-232 connections, come in either 25-pin or 9-pin types. They are most widely used for modems, though printers can also use the port if they're specially designed to do so. Parallel ports, or "parallel interfaces" are either 25-pin or use a special Centronics interface and are most widely used for printers. Typical ports, integrated into a motherboard.

Another special kind of port, the SCSI, allows devices designed for its use to be "daisy-chained" with one connected to the computer and the rest connected one to another via cable. This is a convenience, as several different devices can be connected to the computer without the problem of an additional memory address and interrupt for each one. Macintosh computers come with a built in SCSI port and workstations, minicomputers, and even mainframe computers often are equipped with SCSI ports. PCs usually require that a card be added to the computer to allow SCSI functionality.

The case

All the subassemblies or components that we've referred to are all neatly fitted into a case, except the monitor and keyboard. The case helps shield the user from electromagnetic radiation and is also supposed to help prevent the computer from generating radio interference. Cases are varied, but they usually come in a variation of two forms, a standard flat case and a tower case, as shown in Fig. 3-8. The components are placed in a chassis, motherboard first, then the other components are added. The chassis often has openings in the back for the exhaust from the power supply fan and slots so the ends of circuit boards placed in the PC can be accessed from the outside. The way in which cases close does vary, but usually the lid slides on from the back of the unit, then is fastened at the back with screws.

3-8
While cases for PCs are varied, most all stem from these two basic designs.

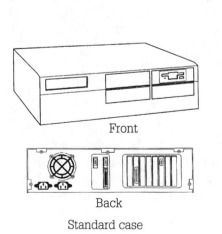

Front

Back

Standard case

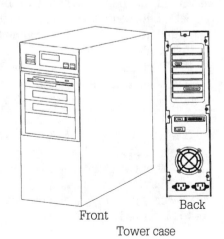

Front

Back

Tower case

Profile

Steve Sacco
AMCOM Consulting Services, Agoura Hills, California

AMCOM Consulting Services is Steve Sacco's second computer repair company. His first was in a partnership of four, which he said had a severe drawback and one fatal problem. The drawback was everything had to be done by a committee meeting. The fatal problem was the other partners had a tendency to miss customer appointments. Steve said he stayed with it for a while, but finally decided he'd rather be "the master of his own destiny."

Previously, Steve had worked for several companies in Southern California doing customer phone support, acting as a field service engineer, and starting training classes. He was first attracted to working in his own business because the companies he worked for either went out of business or moved out of the state, and he kept finding himself looking for another job. He also disliked the rigidity of the schedule imposed on him by the corporate environment. "I hated working 8 to 5, hated having to worry if I was 5 minutes late coming back from my lunch." Steve started AMCOM in 1986, working from a spare room in his home.

In the beginning he knew he needed more experience on the retail side of the business, so he talked an independent software company in the area into allowing him to work in the store for free in exchange for information about how the business and pricing was done. He also worked out a deal so that any hardware repair work the customers needed would be referred to him in exchange for allowing the store to keep a percentage of the profit Steve made on the repair.

A friend introduced Steve to the Los Angeles Unified District adult school program. At first, Steve made up a resume showing all the teaching and classroom experience he had with the companies he'd worked for, but the officials at the school district said that wasn't what they wanted. He was instructed to go through and change the resume to reflect the five years of his technical experience. Steve redid the resume, agreed to go to college to get the hours necessary to get a teaching credential, and was immediately hired to begin teaching computer courses at the high school in the evenings.

As for advertising, AMCOM has taken out a total of one ad in the Southern California issue of the free computer paper, *MicroTimes*, from which AMCOM got two calls. Steve says he hasn't advertised since, getting all his business by word-of-mouth. "I didn't want to build a big company. But I make sure I treat my customers like friends by treating them as I would like to be treated myself."

After his experience with partners, Steve said he decided to train one of the students from the high school electronics class when he needs extra help, and pay the student as he would an independent contractor.

AMCOM now offers repair of both Macintosh and IBM-compatible PCs, as well as instruction in the operating systems DOS and Windows. Steve also offers instruction for popular software packages such as WordPerfect and dBASE, and he is a WordPerfect certified software engineer (CES). His clients include the University of California at Los Angeles (UCLA), the Veteran's administration, and the Las Virgenes school district.

Most of his work is computer repair and upgrading. There is a lot of interest in upgrading, and Steve encourages the upgrades because they're a good buy for the customer. "If something fails, I'll replace it with something faster—such as replacing a 286 motherboard with a 486 SLC motherboard. I can do that unless the machine is a propriety model, like an Epson, Compaq, or IBM." The "brand-name" computers are difficult to upgrade without parts from the manufacturer, and the manufacturers' parts tend to be expensive, often several times more than parts for a clone. "I encourage my customers to buy clones, and that way they won't get into a proprietary system that uses custom-made parts that only come from that manufacturer," Steve added.

Upgrading sometimes is complicated, as he replaced a computer with a 286 motherboard with a 486 SLC motherboard only to find that the computer wouldn't boot consistently. It turned out that the reset signal was coming up too fast for the computer to work, so he had to solder a capacitor on to the reset line in order to get the computer to work. There was a substantial amount of work involved, but Steve didn't charge them for all his time, since the work was for his largest customer. "I try to treat people fairly, the way I'd like to be treated myself."

As for stock, Steve said he used to keep more parts around, but when prices fell several years back, he lost several hundred dollars. Now all he keeps in his truck is a motherboard, a couple of 1 megabyte (MB) single in-line memory modules, both a 3.5-inch and a 5.25-inch floppy disk drive, a video card, an input/output card that also has an integrated drive electronics (IDE) interface to control floppy drives and hard disk drives, a power supply, and a keyboard.

Besides upgrade business, Steve says he sees a lot of hard drive failures, power supply failures, and monitor problems. While he can repair monitor problems, he prefers to subcontract the work. He sends monitor work to a depot repair shop in Texas who works for a flat rate of $75 per monitor. He subcontracts all but minor printer repairs to a printer depot. This saves him having to buy specialized tools and keep schematics for monitors or printers.

He also sends out laptop computers to a depot for repair. "When you get inside one of those things, there's just a spider web of wires. The biggest problem is getting it back together once you've taken it apart."

To find the depot repair shops, he depends on referrals and the phone book. He looks for fast, honest, and capable people he can depend on, who charge a flat rate. However, it is more difficult to find flat-rate depot repair in printer work, he admitted.

When he makes an appointment with a customer, he uses First ACT from Symantec to print a template file for a 3-copy NCR form he calls a field service report. The report form includes places to record the customer information, the date of the appointment, and an explanation of the service needed. Steve transfers the customer information to his customer database on his hand-held Sharp OZ 7000. Once on site, he chooses the customer from a list in the Sharp, and presses a button to start the unit tracking his time. When he's finished, he records the actual repair and time to the field service report, has the customer sign the report, gives them a copy, and then uses the information in the Sharp to prepare his billing each month. He also has a written copy of the field service report to send in with his bill and one for his own records. He also uses QuickBooks, from Intuit, to help him track his billing and overdue accounts.

Besides the fact that he likes to use the Sharp hand-held computer, Steve says it helps business. "Customers are impressed, the more high-tech you are." He also encourages the use of Windows. "If Windows is set up properly, it's a lot easier for people to use."

Steve's pet peeve is customers who try to get him to lower his prices by quoting prices from other sources, such as newspaper classified ads. His response varies, but he said he usually ends up reminding people that he has plenty of work and if they feel more comfortable with the price in the ad, then they should pursue that source.

The best part of the business, besides allowing him to afford and play with the computers, is taking long, late summer breaks to camp and hike in the mountains around Southern California when his business slows down.

Standards

While the subject of standards could be considered terminally boring, it is really quite crucial to the business of computers in general and repair in particular. In order for components of various computers to be interchangeable, the manufacturers must build them to common specifications, which include how the computer talks to the component and how the component will respond. These specifications are known as standards.

A standard example

For example, a standard in the telecommunications industry is the Hayes command set. The modem commands designed by Hayes, an Atlanta, Georgia-based modem manufacturer, have been adopted industrywide as the standard for modems. Any software that supports the Hayes command standard should work with any modem that also supports the Hayes standard. This can be thought of as both hardware and software speaking the same "language."

Standards exist in just about every part of the computer industry, but there is no rule that says a product must conform to the established standards. For example, it is possible to purchase a modem that is not Hayes compatible, meaning it does not understand the Hayes command set. Such a modem is likely to be a problem because it will not work with the vast majority of telecommunications software. If you were the one to recommend this modem to a customer, that customer is probably going to be angry with you because the modem won't do what the customer expects it to, and that is simply work with the available software.

The bottom line is products that conform to existing standards are easier to work with, while products that don't might or might not work. While you don't have to know every nuance of each standard, it is part of your job to be aware of the existing standards and to look for products for your customers that conform to these standards.

Standard versus proprietary

Standards are good for the consumer and consumers know that, so hardware manufacturers like to talk about standards and interoperability (also known as "open systems"). Meanwhile, you might find these same companies are scrambling around making their systems proprietary.

The usual reason given for proprietary designs are that they're "better" for the consumer, as the design offers some added benefit not available elsewhere. For example, several manufacturers, such as Compaq, are going to proprietary disk drive designs with 26-pin cabling rather than the standard 40-pin cables. The upshot to the consumer is proprietary systems cost more in replacement parts and service, whether the repair comes from a third party or from the manufacturer.

There are two sides to the coin in the manufacturer's view. One side is if a good design is being widely adopted for something in demand, like a smaller-size floppy drive, but someone else owns the design, then as a manufacturer you have to either come up with another design to perform the task or face paying the designer for the original design. This happened with the hard-plastic-enclosed 3.5-inch floppy disk drive. When that drive was developed, other computers, such as models from the European manufacturer Amstrad, were being marketed that had a 3-inch drive. The Amstrad 3-inch floppy never became widespread although you might find it still used in the dedicated word processor machines sold in mass market retail stores and office supply centers.

Obviously, paying for a design is not what manufacturers care to do unless they have to, so they either come up with something totally different or walk the legal line of adopting as much as they can without being accused of stealing the original design. With two designs so close and nothing particularly advantageous about either one, it is usually the design that has the widest acceptance that ends up being the one adopted.

This has been going on in business for probably as long as business has been conducted. Vice-President Al Gore, in addressing the Information Superhighway Summit held in Southern California at UCLA in 1993, referred to the early days of the establishment of railroads as an analogy to the computer industry. It seems that each railroad company made its track a different size than any other railroad company so that only its trains could run on track it laid. The scramble was to lay track quickly in order to control as much of the market as possible.

Formed in 1918 in the United States, the American National Standards Institute (ANSI) handles voluntary standards for public and private sectors, including the computer industry. ANSI represents the United States to both the International Standards Organization (ISO) and the International Electrotechnical Commission (IEC), both headquartered in Geneva, Switzerland. The ISO handles all standards except electronics and electrical, which are the concern of the IEC. The ISO offers a certification program for vendor products that is very highly regarded in the European community.

ANSI sets standards for programming languages, telecommunications, electronic communication of transactions between companies or electronic data interchange (EDI), and mass storage devices such as magnetic tape, diskettes, and cartridges. While ANSI participation is voluntary, those products that don't conform to ANSI standards have a much tougher time gaining acceptance.

The biggest problem with ANSI standards is it takes literally years for the organization's committee to produce a standard. It took nearly six years for an ANSI committee to set standards for the popular, low-level computer programming language "C." This means the battle for standardization in the realm of new technology might have already been fought in the marketplace before it ever became officially "standardized." In many cases a standard in the works becomes obsolete before it is officially approved.

Waiting for the market to standardize is the argument for "trailing edge computing" and the reason the "leading edge" of technology is often referred to as the "bleeding edge." Attempting to make fresh, often nonstandard hardware and software work is a painful and grueling job. But with components that have been out for long enough to become standard—meaning widely supported by the hardware and software companies if not officially adopted by ANSI—the job is a much simpler one.

Your customers will be looking to you to help them make decisions about technology purchases. They'll expect you to know if the technology they're buying from you is compatible or not. If they decide to walk the high-tech tightrope of leading-edge technology, they'll also expect you to know the risks they're taking. This isn't as difficult as it might sound, if you're keeping up on the industry the way you should be. You can count on us in this book to point out standards in various areas of the industry wherever we can.

Compatibility

Compatibility is related to standards, but is not the same thing. From the standpoint of repair, standards are a much more complex issue, but compatibility is more important. Two systems might be compatible, in that they can both use the same software and information can be swapped between the two, but that might be the extent of their compatibility. The open systems talk is going hand-in-hand with a proprietary approach to building systems. Compatible from a repair standpoint is the ability to move components or subassemblies from one system to another.

One of the biggest problems in repair is the inability to get parts that will fit computers from the "name brand" computer manufacturers. Clones often mean a less complex repair job because they are made from standard parts where the subassemblies are interchangeable with parts from other clone manufacturers. Here's an example. A business has an Epson 386SX and wants to upgrade. When the Epson was purchased it was one of the "name brand" manufacturers in the computer market and the business paid a premium price for it. When discussing the upgrade, the business is told they can simply replace the motherboard with a 486 SLC motherboard for around $200. This includes moving the monitor, video card, hard disk drive, floppy disk drives, tape backup, and modem, to the new motherboard in the old case.

Before the business gets a chance to make the upgrade, the system begins to act quirky, displaying error messages that aren't repeatable and noise begins coming from the power supply. Just as our business begins the process of backing up the quarterly financial records, the computer quits.

Sounds like a good time for an upgrade, right? But it turns out the inexpensive clone motherboard on which the upgrade price was based will not fit in the Epson chassis. In addition, the power supply is made by Epson so it can only be turned off and on by a proprietary switch attached to the front chassis of the computer. These two facts alone mean a new 386SX motherboard is going to cost about $400, and a replacement for the Epson power supply is going to cost another $200. The Epson dealer where the system was purchased has gone out of business, but a call to Epson discloses an authorized repair facility nearby. The problem that made the system fail altogether was a short in the mouse that was blowing a fuse on the motherboard. It took three trips to the repair facility and the mistaken order of a new keyboard from Epson to find out the mouse was the culprit. The repair bill was $150.

After a week of downtime, the business is unable to pay its employees because the computer was not up to generate the checks and has the added problem of time lost in record keeping necessary to keep things going. Having lost all faith in the Epson, the business asked that the hard disk drive be backed up onto tape at the repair facility. The owners then purchased a new state-of-the-art clone computer with a larger hard disk drive, an upgraded monitor, and a higher capacity tape backup from a different repair facility and had their data from the tape restored to the new machine.

This illustrates the main problem with the "simply replace the subassembly" theory. If the machine is made by one of the top ten computer manufacturers, it is unlikely that clone replacement parts will fit. While the clone manufacturer is often using the same components as the top ten manufacturers, the subassemblies for repairs are designed size- and fit-wise so they must be ordered from the manufacturer at a premium price. Figure 3-9 illustrates this point with the layouts of two motherboards, an Epson Equity 386SX/16 PLUS and a 486 SLC board from Austin Computer Systems. Note that the Epson board has four expansion slots, and the I/O ports are integrated into the motherboard. This means the Epson chassis will only have four slots on the back for the addition of add-on boards, not the normal eight slots that clone cases offer. The Epson board is also larger and rectangular at 304.8mm by 272.8mm compared to the square 220.0mm by 220.0mm 486 SLC board.

There are ways to find out how proprietary the components used in a particular PC are. *Computer Sources* magazine has an excellent section every month called "Rip Off the Lid" where they go inside and examine the parts and makeup of PCs from a variety of manufacturers and including photos. In a "Rip Off the Lid" article, writer Doug Wilson took an in-depth look at the components that make up the Ambra Pentium DP60PCI computer and found the machine used the same motherboard as the Gateway PCI Pentium the magazine reviewed the previous month. Ambra is a clone maker, but also a "virtual corporation" of IBM. The manufacturers of each of the Ambra's subassemblies were identified and discussed, and benchmarks were taken.

A second article in the same issue went through the process of building an "Ambra look-alike" listing the subassembly sources and parts. In this article, "Sourcing an IBM Ambra DP60PCI Look-Alike," *Computer Sources* was able to beat the Ambra's $3,699 price tag by about $550 for a single computer.

Epson America
Equity 386SX/16 Plus

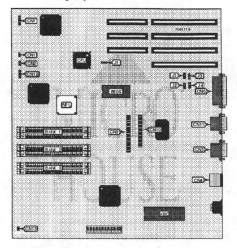

Austin Computer Systems
486/SLC 25

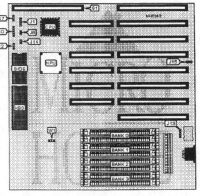

3-9
While the user wanted to replace the motherboard in the Epson 386, the proprietary design of the case prevented the introduction of the inexpensive Austin 486 SLC board into the chassis. The differences in the two boards are illustrated here. The lack of expansion slot openings in the Epson case and the rectangular design of the chassis were the two main factors preventing the upgrade.
Micro House

CN1 = Battery	CN11 = Serial port (COM 1)
CN2 = Speaker	CN12 = HDD access LED
CN3 = Keyboard/mouse	CN13 = Power LED
CN5 = VGA connector	J1 & J5 = Video switches
CN6 = Parallel port	J2 = Password enable
CN7 = CPU/Power LED	J3 = Monitor type
CN9 = IDE interface	J4 = Mouse enable
CN10 = Floppy drive interface	

J1 = Speaker
J7 = Turbo switch
J8 = Turbo LED
J12 = Monitor type select
J13 = External battery
J14 = Reset switch
J15 = Clear CMOS memory jumper
S1 = 16-Bit external cache memory card expansion port

Micro House is also an excellence source. The company publishes the Micro House Technical Library on CD-ROM, which includes technical specifications and illustrations of motherboards, hard drives and controllers, and network interface cards. Look-ups can be done by manufacturer, by the type of chip sets on the product if you don't know the manufacturer, and by other criteria as well. The library has over 2,000 motherboards alone that it can display on your computer screen in a moment, along with size and component information as well as switch and jumper settings. It includes definitions and troubleshooting tips and is updated quarterly. A single copy is under $400, and with the quarterly updates it is about $650.

The buying habits of consumers are not likely to change when it comes to buying proprietary systems, meaning there is still a market for component repair. This is especially true when the replacement subassembly costs more than the time and effort needed for component repair, as it often is in the cases involving "name brand" computers. You do have the option of using one of the many service firms that specialize in repairing boards for a single name-brand manufacturer like IBM. These firms will often provide a short turnaround time for boards sent to their facility or sell you a repaired board along with taking yours in exchange, much like many automobile parts service firms.

Integration

From the time that room-size computers started to do arithmetic, integration of the components has been a priority with engineers and designers. The process of combining the functionality of several different parts into one part offers a variety of benefits to the manufacturer and consumers. The benefit to the manufacturer is lower cost, especially if the functionality of the components can be preserved with fewer materials. In addition, storage, inventory, and handling costs tend to be less. For the consumer, lowered manufacturing costs mean lower price tags for goods. Usually this also implies that the item will take less physical space.

Integration is only possible in the computer industry when the component being integrated works in a manner that has become widely accepted enough to be considered a "standard." For example, the mouse connection has been integrated into most PC motherboards as has the video graphics array (VGA) controller for the computer's output to the monitor. Both of these components have reached a level of demand high enough that they're considered "standard," and so it makes sense for manufacturers to integrate them into the computer's main system board.

Analysts are predicting a trend toward integration that will mean computer repair personnel are going to find themselves replacing subassemblies rather than repairing failed components. If the subassemblies are cheaper than the repair, the logical course is to replace the subassembly.

For example, if a component on the motherboard fails, it could be cheaper to replace the motherboard than to spend the time necessary to determine which of the components failed, then desolder and replace the component from the multilayer circuit board. There is always the chance that the component or board could be damaged during the process. At normal hourly charges for repair, and assuming the case of the computer is not an odd shape or size, the customer is going to pay less if a new clone motherboard is installed because it takes less time.

Falling prices affect the picture as well. A perfect example is repairing hard disk drives. Many depot repair shops did a thriving business when drives were expensive and they could be repaired at a fraction of their cost. Now, with many hard disk drive prices so low, it just doesn't make sense to pay more for repairing these drives than it costs to buy a new one.

Another example of integration is the multifunction I/O boards available on the market now. It used to be that a separate drive controller board was necessary for the hard disk drive, the floppy disk drives, and any tape drives. Now, a single, multifunction drive controller board can be used for all three drives, as well as controlling the input/output (I/O) devices such as serial, game, and parallel ports. National Semiconductor just announced a multifunction I/O board that not only includes the IDE controller, the floppy controller, serial, parallel, and game port, but also includes an Ethernet connector for adding the PC to a local area network (LAN).

Integration doesn't necessarily mean there is no subassembly work available for integrated products. For example, if the motherboard has an integrated super video graphics adapter (SVGA) and the customer wants to go to a higher resolution video graphics card because of a special need, such as photo retouching on the PC, the integrated video can be disabled via switches on the motherboard and a new video card can be substituted in one of the expansion slots. This might not work for everyone because integrated motherboards tend to have fewer expansion slots. It's likely that a user who wants a high-resolution video card will also want a CD-ROM drive, an optical scanner, and an internal modem. Unfortunately, if there are only three expansion slots, there won't be room for four boards on that particular motherboard and some other option might have to be found, such as using an external modem that connects to an existing serial port.

Obviously, this is not good news for the third- and fourth-party repair shops out there who have been making a living doing component repair. But that market has not dried up yet. Integration requires standardization, and as long as the computer industry is moving as quickly as it has been from one fleeting standard to another, integration is frustrated. A manufacturer who wants to integrate must be assured there is a wide enough market for sale of the boards to justify the expensive process of changing the design and manufacturing process. Depot repair is still a lucrative field and because of overnight delivery services, depot repair sites can be located in a single portion of the United States and still serve customers nationwide.

In addition, integration is beginning to involve more than just computer components. As demonstrated by the new Sharp OZ-9520, integration of the keyboard, touch-screen, pen-based computer is already a reality (Fig. 3-10). With the additional fax/modem peripheral, users can now send and receive faxes and connect to online services such as CompuServe, GEnie, and others. With it's introductory price of $749.99 and the fax/modem an additional $179.99, these and other hand-held computers like them are definitely candidates for the depot repair market.

3-10
Integration of fax/modems and other peripherals in smaller and smaller designs are becoming more popular. The expense of these smaller computers make them worth repairing, but some specialization is needed. We see these emerging designs as opportunities for new depot repair facilities.

Profile   John White
Servonics Corporation, Wareham, Massachusetts

John White started the Wareham, Massachusetts-based repair depot Servonics in 1983. "Starting is easy. Staying in is hard," John said concerning his beginnings with Servonics.

Prior to starting Servonics, John had electronics training that he received during his enlistment in the U.S. Navy and on-the-job training later with RCA Research Labs in Needham, Massachusetts. He started the business because he found during his field work that customers were looking for a place to get their hardware repaired.

The money in depot repair isn't in the repair of leading edge hardware, but is in equipment that is one or two generations behind, John maintains. Talking about PCs based on Intel's newly released Pentium processor, John quipped, "I won't even be interested in those machines for another five years."

Servonics specializes in video repair, including monitors and terminals, but takes repair work on just about any PC repair and offers laser printer repair as well. The company once had offices in Philadelphia, Chicago, and Los Angeles but has found it can service its long-distance customers more effectively using United Postal Service (UPS). Locally, Servonics offers repair services at the rate of $70 an hour with a 2-hour minimum within a 70-mile radius of its location.

Competition from upstart computer repair businesses has forced Servonics to begin looking for another niche market. "People who used to be our customers are now in business for themselves," according to John. "I prefer to deal with large companies rather than individuals," John added, but he stays in the business of servicing individual customers.

John says he has "retired" twice, allowing his son and daughter-in-law to run the business. But when changes in the industry have required a change for Servonics to survive, John has come back in and worked to build the business again.

Some of his most lucrative work in the past came from big companies and he's seeking an opportunity for doing that type of work again. At one point he worked for Data General, a company that made its own memory boards. Servonics obtained a service contract with Data General and repaired its memory boards by the thousands. "The lucrative work is in taking a problem away for a big company," he said. "A small problem for a big company is big profit to a small company."

His plan is to find a big company with a small problem Servonics can solve. The way he'll do that is the way he always has; he'll just call and ask. "I start with the purchasing department of a large company and ask, 'What's the thing that gives you the most problems that you have to send out to a vendor?'" John said he doesn't need to have contacts at the company; he can just start cold-calling purchasing departments and find out what he's looking for fairly quickly. He starts with purchasing because they're the ones doing the buying.

For example, a large company might have invested entirely in 286- and 386-based PCs. They're not going to just throw that investment away.

Once a company has a volume of a certain machine, they get locked in. The benefit of going to a faster computer, companywide, might not outweigh the problems associated with the change. "Once you have 1,000 computers, who cares if a new computer is a little bit faster doing an invoice?" John remarked. Servicing those PCs is a lucrative business.

While the parts for 286- or 386-based PCs might be getting scarce, John makes it his business to go to auctions, swaps, and keep his eyes open for older machines he can use for parts. Machines that a company has been leasing that come off the lease are an inexpensive parts source as well, he added.

When asked what his regrets are, John said if he had it to do over he would have given his managers an equity interest in Servonics. Those managers, one after another, went off to start their own businesses. John feels that if they'd had a personal investment in the success of Servonics, he'd still have those people and that would have ensured continued growth.

Resources

Fortunately, there are a host of good books to help you understand the hardware. Most are aimed at allowing individuals to perform their own hardware upgrades and repairs, while others are aimed at the professional. If you feel like you need the basics, Aubrey Pilgrim's *Build Your Own 486/486SX and Save A Bundle* from the Windcrest division of McGraw-Hill goes into illustrated detail on items as basic as how to fasten the motherboard to the chassis, how to adjust the placement of floppy disk drives into the drive bays, and connecting cables.

Upgrading and Maintaining Your PC by Ulrich Schueller and Hans-George Veddeler (Abacus, 1993) offers a more in depth treatment with many accompanying photos. The Winn L. Rosch *Hardware Bible, Third Edition* is also an excellent in-depth treatment of PC hardware and repair.

If it's the Macintosh that your interested in, you'll learn a lot from Bob Brant's *Build Your Own Macintosh and Save A Bundle* (Windcrest/McGraw-Hill, 1991). Apple has several technical reference manuals available in book form as well. We offer some Macintosh basics, troubleshooting hints, and sources in appendix F.

Your search for reference material is best started at your local library. If you decide the book in question should be an addition to your personal library, you can order it. The books we've referenced here and others are listed in detail in appendix A.

Evolution from software to hardware

Software is a big part of the integration issue. When Bill Gates, co-founder of software giant Microsoft, started it was necessary to type in perfectly a series of commands to the forerunners of today's PC, in order to get the machine to boot or start. Now those instructions are built into the BIOS chip. As software instructions to the computer become standard, these instructions are built into the hardware. Computer instructions built into the hardware are always faster than those in software read from a disk drive. Apple is a prime example of this, as the basic commands that make its graphical operating system function are built into proprietary ROM chips. In this way, the Macintosh allows its users the luxury of a built-in user interface that doesn't demand hard disk space. The migration to this type of hardware integration is already beginning on the PC, as video cards are being introduced that offer parts of the code used in Microsoft Windows built into chips on the video card.

The basic computer components, processors and memory, are appearing in various subassemblies and peripherals in order to speed up operations or add functionality. A computer within a computer, processors and memory are commonly being used in video cards to speed up the display and enhance the resolution of images. Processors are also being called upon to handle compression of video. One minute of full-motion color video with stereo sound can take up between 40 and 60 megabytes of hard disk space. A built-in processor can condense the video, called compression, so it will fit in as little as one-tenth the storage space. The processor is used to compress and decompress the video on-the-fly for playback on the computer screen.

Processors are also used in most laser printers along with memory. Some laser printers even have an internal hard disk drive for storage of type styles known as fonts. This speeds up the printing process and allows the computer user to perform other tasks while printing is occurring.

Conclusions

The rules keep changing in computer repair, due to the changes in computer technology. The trend is towards more subassembly replacement as the cost of parts goes down. Depot repair, considered a dying art by some, appears to be facing changes, not demise. The annual *Hardware Maintenance* issue for 1993 published by *Service News*, said that while depot repair was so specialized in the past that most end-users didn't know depots existed, these shops are finding that their customer base is shifting. The self-maintainer and the original equipment manufacturer (OEM) are the customers of the 1990s for depots. In the effort to reduce expenses, large companies are becoming self-maintainers looking to farm out work, and they are more willing to work directly with repair depots. The trend is to have someone on staff in the company who can troubleshoot problems and coordinate repairs. Large companies have a stronger tendency to buy name-brand computers as well, so component repair is compelling compared to subassembly replacement.

But the explosive growth happening in the consumer PC market is also increasing the demand for generalized repair services focused on the individual or small business. These repair shops might find depot repair a handy tool in their toolkit of repair options, but subassembly repairs will probably be their strongest repair alternative.

The problem for the generalized computer repair business is correctly troubleshooting the problem to begin with. Once the problem is located, the alternatives to fix it are usually obvious. The integration of the hardware and the layers of program that make the hardware work makes repair a confusing and sometimes difficult issue for users. The hardware might be confirmed to be functioning, but a problem might still persist. Computer repair businesses have the opportunity, and perhaps will even be forced, to offer a more "wholistic" approach to computer repair—by getting involved in the software end as well. From operating systems to applications, that crucial software component is our focus in the next chapter.

References

Computer Sources. May, 1994. "Sourcing an IBM Ambra DP60PCI Look-Alike." Computer Sources 3 (12): 42–44.

Glover, Thomas J. 1993. *Pocket PCRef.* Littleton, Colorado: Sequoia Publishing.

Kessler, Nancy. October, 1993. "The Dawn of the New Depot." *Service News Hardware Maintenance* 13 (12): 4–8.

Wilson, Doug. May, 1994. "Inside the Ambra Pentium DP60PCI." *Computer Sources 3* (12): 36–40, 46.

4 Software

"All wish to possess knowledge, but few, comparatively speaking, are willing to pay the price."
— Decimus Junius Juvenalis, a satirical poet of ancient Rome.

Software is the crux, the essential element in computing that makes the entire industry fly ahead at its current windswept pace. Without software, nothing worth spending money on happens. Yet the majority of existing computer repair professionals will not deal with this aspect of computing. It is our contention that the marketplace is becoming increasingly intolerant of that approach. Serious opportunities await those who will take the time to learn both the hardware and the software.

But besides an increasing expectation on the part of the marketplace, there's another reason to know something about software. Software-related computer problems often masquerade as hardware difficulties. If you don't know the difference, you might replace a hardware subassembly and face the embarrassment of having the same problem crop up again because you didn't get to the cause. For example, if the environment files on the PC are set incorrectly, it might appear as though a portion of the hard disk drive is unreadable. If you understand both the functions of hardware and of software, you'll be able to recognize when a problem could be software related, saving yourself time and embarrassment. We'll explain what to look for in this chapter.

Software is divided into two categories: the operating system (OS) and applications programs. Just like everything else in the computer industry, the lines between application software and the operating system are blurring as more and more operating-system vendors are building applications into their products. This is an integration issue very much like what we discussed in the last chapter with hardware. But because a knowledge of the software is so crucial to successful hardware repair, we'll give you an overview of the role of the operating system software that controls the operation of the personal computer and the application software that actually produces the results people want.

The operating system

In the book *Gates*, the story of how Bill Gates and Paul Allen started the world's leading operating system software company Microsoft, there's a detailed description of how a user had to go about starting up one of the very first personal computers. The Altair, built by Albuquerque, New Mexico-based MITS in 1974 is described by the book as "a toy, a joke" by today's standards. "Every time you turned the machine off, it would go utterly blank. Merely to get it to do anything after you powered it up, you had to `bootstrap,' or `boot,' it with half a hundred sequences of instructions entered by flipping switches. If one of those instructions had been entered incorrectly—one flip among hundreds—the machine would refuse to do anything at all."

The Altair was so popular with electronics enthusiasts that MITS could barely keep up with the demand for build-it-yourself kits, much less ship the computers already assembled. This despite the fact that it took either eight or sixteen on/off flips of the toggle switches per instruction, just to enter a "dumb" little program that would make the Altair's lights blink on and off.

The operating system's role in the boot process

Still built on the same principles, operating system software comes standard with personal computers. It is no longer necessary to go through all that switch flipping. You simply turn the machine on and it does its own bootstrapping. (By the way, if you feel intimidated by the "old timers" in this business who seem to judge your knowledge by whether or not you know who invented the DOS forerunner CP/M, then read *Gates*. It will bring you up to speed in a hurry.)

Part of the boot process in PCs is built into the BIOS of the computer in the power on self-test (POST). When the power switch is turned on, the BIOS performs quick tests on the PC, and at some point it usually allows the user an opportunity to get into the BIOS to make changes (assuming the BIOS information is built into the PC and not stored on a floppy disk). The computer will usually display the type of BIOS and the current CMOS settings as well as the key sequence to press in order to get in and change the BIOS settings.

Once the computer completes the diagnostics, it reads the CMOS, and will then look for the operating system. It looks first on the floppy disk drive for a disk with the operating system and then to the hard disk drive. The most basic instructions the computer needs in order to boot are in the "kernel" of the operating system. The kernel is usually located on the hard disk or floppy disk on the very first track, or track 0, which was so labeled during the formatting process.

Operating systems abound. While you will usually hear about Microsoft's disk operating system (MS-DOS), the graphical operating system Microsoft Windows, IBM's Operating System/2 (OS/2), and PC-DOS, there are many others. Since Microsoft did a lot of the work on IBM's PC-DOS and OS/2, you'll find many similarities between those operating system products and its MS-DOS or Windows. Most people consider MS-DOS and PC-DOS interchangeable. This is partly because the operating systems from Microsoft and IBM will both support the same applications software.

The variety of operating systems

Owned by network vendor Novell, Unix is a popular choice, available in a number of different and incompatible versions known by the names of the companies who have modified the core of this operating system. There's the Santa Cruz Operation (SCO) Unix, Hewlett-Packard's HP/UX Unix, Sun's Solaris Unix, Apple's A/UX Unix, IBM's AIX Unix, the NeXT graphical Unix operating system, and so on. You'll find Unix in government and university computer centers used by scientists and engineers. Stock brokerage firms and many brokerage firms that deal directly with the stock market use Unix as well. Unix is also the basis of the popular electronic infrastructure known as the "Internet."

Unix will run on PCs as well as workstation computers, minicomputers, and mainframe systems. If you find yourself working on Unix-based PCs, you can pick up the operating system commands from one of many books that probably can be found at your public library. There is no shortage of Unix books, but we recommend as a starting point *Peter Norton's Guide to Unix*, a book by Peter Norton and Harley Hahn.

The operating system with the lion's share of the computer market worldwide is DOS. Microsoft Windows is number two, but since Windows is the only operating system that requires DOS in order to operate, it gives the DOS numbers a boost. In fact, many market analysts lump PC-DOS, MS-DOS, and Windows together, calling the entire market segment "the DOS market."

Microsoft's newest version of Windows, Windows 95, doesn't require DOS "underneath." An updated version of DOS, MS-DOS 7.0, is also in the works. However, users are slow to adopt major operating system changes, so expect to see the old versions for some time.

IBM's graphical OS/2 operating system is gaining market share and will run the same applications programs, PC-DOS, MS-DOS, and it will even run Windows and all the Windows applications. However, it requires more hardware, meaning it is more expensive to run. IBM is trying to change that, but it is fighting an uphill battle against the entrenched Microsoft. Windows and MS-DOS are licensed directly from Microsoft by the top ten PC manufacturers and come on the hard disk drives of the vast majority of the computers sold today. Since users get the operating system for "free" they'll be reluctant to pay for and trouble with installing anything else.

OEMs have been known to make changes to the operating system and put their own name on it. PC maker Compaq is one to do this. It is important to note that operating system upgrades or bug fixes from Microsoft might not work with an OEM version of DOS. Any updates or revisions have to come directly from the OEM, or a retail version of DOS can be purchased that will overwrite the vendor's version. The problem with installing the more standard DOS over the vendor's version is it might overwrite special features the vendor had written to perform additional functions with its hardware, such as the ability to switch to a power-saving mode with a couple of keystrokes.

The job of the operating system

The job of the operating system is to act as a traffic cop between the hardware (the BIOS) and software programs the user sees, such as word processing programs, spreadsheets, and so on. Operating systems, with the BIOS, control input/output operations such as drawing what you see on the computer screen and directing data to and from peripheral devices such as printers and modems. Each operating system has its own "language" and can be told to perform rudimentary functions using typed-in commands. These commands can be typed into the computer by the user to perform basic functions such as copying information from a hard disk drive to a floppy disk drive.

As operating systems have progressed, they've taken over functions that the person writing applications software used to have to handle, such as the management of data locations on the mass storage device. Programmers used to have to write into their programs the instructions for the computer to find an unused space on the floppy disk, then go to that location, such as track 2, sector 7, and write the data. The location of the data would have to be remembered in the application program so it could be retrieved later. Now all you need to know is the label or "file name" to be given to the data as a group, and the operating system handles where it is stored and keeps track of the storage location.

As we discussed, that "address book" or table has different names, depending on the operating system, but since we are coming from a PC orientation, we'll refer to it as the file allocation table (FAT). The FAT is located at track 0 of the floppy disk or hard disk drive where the data is stored. Most operating systems maintain two copies of the FAT, a working copy and a backup, and DOS is no exception. The FAT is especially important in PC repair because a user's information can still be out on the hard disk intact, but if the FAT is damaged or erased the data stored on the drive might appear to be gone.

DOS & how the PC works

DOS is the most widely used operating system, so we'll use it for our more specific examples of how things work from now on in this chapter. As we've said, the BIOS is set to look at the first floppy disk drive, designated as the letter A and a colon like this, A:. If the operating system is not found there, it will look on the hard disk drive, or the C: drive.

More recent BIOS releases allow you to go into the CMOS settings and change that sequence so the computer looks at the C: drive first for the operating system, rather than the A:. Some people set their machines this way to reduce the boot-up time and the wear and tear on the floppy disk drive. If the hard disk should fail, it is a simple matter to restart the computer, enter the CMOS menu, change the settings, and then start from a bootable floppy.

Once the machine boots DOS, it places a prompt on the screen, with a flashing cursor to indicate it is ready for the user to type in a command. It uses the letter of the drive it booted from for the prompt. So if it boots from the A: drive, the prompt will be A>, and if it was from the hard disk, the prompt will be C>.

The DOS kernel

Three files, called the "kernel," form the basis of what's needed to start the computer. The IBM version of DOS, PC-DOS, calls these files IBMBIO.COM, IBMDOS.COM, and COMMAND.COM. Microsoft's DOS, MS-DOS, uses the files MSDOS.SYS, IO.SYS, and COMMAND.COM. Both IBM and Microsoft decided two of the three files should be hidden from the user's view, so only COMMAND.COM is easily found by inexperienced users. The kernel is loaded into RAM, but the COMMAND.COM file is constantly referred to during a computing session, especially when one application program is ended and another is begun. Thus, it must be accessible by the computer.

Back when computers only had one or two floppy disk drives for mass storage, you would boot from the system disk (also known as the bootable floppy) with COMMAND.COM on it, take that disk out and put in a disk with your application program on it. When you finished working with the application program, you'd have to scramble around on your desk to find that system disk to put back in the drive. Without that disk with COMMAND.COM on it for reference, the computer would "hang," just sitting there running, but not responding.

You might still find yourself making those floppy disk swaps should you run into a computer with a hard drive problem you want to fix. However, hard disk drives have stopped all that disk swapping by serving both the operating system and the application software on a larger, internal disk drive that the computer can easily access.

COMMAND.COM tip

You'll find that inexperienced users like to erase COMMAND.COM. This usually happens by accident when users are attempting to remove unused files. The most common scenario is the use of the delete command with the DOS wildcard,

```
DEL *.*
```

which if used at the DOS command prompt can delete COMMAND.COM as well as all the files in the most basic directory of the hard disk, the root directory. The users might then be able to execute a program and work like normal, but when they exit the program, the system will display the error message "Bad or Missing Command Interpreter" and the computer will hang.

This can also occur if the users copy all the files from a bootable floppy into the root directory using the copy command with the DOS wildcard. If all the files are copied, the system files from a different version of DOS can be copied over the system files on the hard disk.

Since the problem didn't occur immediately after the users executed the copy or delete instructions, they might not see a cause-and-effect relationship between using the instructions and the problems they now face. Restarting the computer could produce a "nonsystem disk" error message, depending on the BIOS in the particular PC.

Check for the same DOS version While it is easy to restore the system files back to the hard disk, your problem will be to make sure the system files you restore are from the same version of DOS as the one deleted. Copying system files from a different DOS version than the one used to format and partition the hard disk drive can cause the problem to occur again, or at the worst, could cause the loss of all the data on the drive.

How to restore the DOS kernel To correct the problem, be sure you have the correct DOS version on a bootable floppy, boot from the A: drive and use the command:

```
SYS C:
```

to copy the system from the floppy back to the hard disk drive (the C: drive).

You can help prevent this scenario by write-protecting the system files using the DOS attribute command. The command and its use is described in appendix D. You'll find other tips on when to use the DOS commands in there as well.

The environment files

The final portion of the boot process is the execution of two files, the CONFIG.SYS and the AUTOEXEC.BAT. These files are optional and their purpose is to set the environment of the system. They're called "environment files."

The CONFIG.SYS File The CONFIG.SYS file is executed first and contains commands to load "device drivers" into the computer's RAM. These device drivers are software instructions for peripheral devices and usually come on a floppy disk included with the peripheral.

For example, CD-ROM drives usually have one if not more device drivers that need to be loaded into RAM to make the drive work. Most of the time, when adding these devices to a computer system, you simply put the included disk into the floppy disk drive, type "install," and follow the instructions in the manual accompanying the peripheral to copy the device driver to the hard disk drive and add the command to run the driver to your CONFIG.SYS file.

As an important side note, you might need a modem and access to an online bulletin board service, the most popular being CompuServe, to quickly get updated device drivers for special cases in which your clients are having problems. From these online sources, you can also obtain bug fixes and enhancements you need to solve problems.

In addition to device drivers, the CONFIG.SYS also sets up the use of RAM by the computer for reading and writing to the disk drive, the number of files that can be open at one time, and the dynamic use of portions of memory called data stacks. Two of the most important statements in the CONFIG.SYS are the FILES and BUFFERS settings.

CONFIG.SYS tip   One of the places to look if you get an error message that a file cannot be opened is in the FILES statement of the CONFIG.SYS. The FILES statement sets how many files the computer can have open at one time. We once had a user who called and said his telecommunications software, which had worked up until now, suddenly gave the error message "unable to open file" when he tried to log on to a favorite bulletin board. It had worked before.

We ran tests on the hard disk drive, used diagnostic software to look for corruption in the telecommunications software files, and racked our brains. It turned out that our user had changed the files statement in the CONFIG.SYS file so only five files could be opened by the computer at a time because he thought he'd save memory that way. Though the telecommunications software worked, the file with the information needed to log onto the bulletin board was the sixth file, and the computer was set so only five files could be open.

Our user knew just enough to be dangerous. The number the FILES statement (see Fig. 4-1) is set to in the CONFIG.SYS file does not take up additional memory. Common settings for the FILES statement are from 60 to 99, although you might use any value up to 255. It is the setting in the related BUFFERS statement that takes up additional memory. Buffers are memory reserved for each disk buffer to hold data during disk read and write operations. Each buffer requires 512 bytes of memory, so prudent buffer settings can save memory.

Most software programs these days require a buffer setting of at least 30, and in our example in Fig. 4-1, the setting is 32. If DOS is loaded into high memory, then the buffer space is taken from high memory as well. We'll discuss high memory and the importance of low and high memory in the memory management section later in this chapter.

Sample CONFIG.SYS File

```
STACKS=9,256
DEVICEHIGH=C:\DOS\SETVER.EXE
DEVICEHIGH=C:\DOS\HIMEM.SYS
DOS=HIGH
FILES=99
BUFFERS=32
DEVICEHIGH=C:\DOS\EMM386.EXE RAM
DOS=HIGH,UMB
DEVICEHIGH=C:\DOS\DBLSPACE.SYS /MOVE
```

Sample AUTOEXEC.BAT FILE

```
@ECHO OFF
LOADHIGH C:\DOS\SMARTDRV.EXE
SET MOUSE=C:\MOUSE1
C:\MOUSE1\MOUSE.EXE /Q
PATH C:\;C:\DOS;C:\WINDOWS;
SET TEMP=C:\DOS
PROMPT $P$G
WIN
```

The AUTOEXEC.BAT file   The AUTOEXEC.BAT is executed next. It automates routine tasks such as setting up where the computer looks for commands, expanding the DOS prompt to include more information for the user, loading files for devices into memory, and automatically starting programs, such as Windows.

You will always find these files in the root directory of the disk they're stored on. This is important because if you want to access an environment file, you need to know how to tell the computer where the file is. The root directory is the place the computer looks first for things it needs, and the root directory indicates the highest level of storage—the top of the pile, so to speak. It is designated by the drive and a single backslash, "A:\" or "C:\". The location of the file along with any subdirectories it is stored in, the file name, and the extension is called the "path." So, the path for the AUTOEXEC.BAT would be C:\AUTOEXEC.BAT, and the path to the CONFIG.SYS would be C:\CONFIG.SYS.

The AUTOEXEC.BAT   also contains the PATH statement, which informs the computer of all the places, including directories and subdirectories, it should automatically look for a command each time one is given. We'll talk more about directories and subdirectories later, but for now, each entry in the PATH statement is separated by a semicolon (see Fig. 4-1).

AUTOEXEC.BAT tip   You might want to note this troubleshooting tip. Check the path statement in the AUTOEXEC.BAT file if a user complains that a program that was working before has suddenly stopped working. You'll need to know the subdirectory in which the program is stored, but you might find that the PATH statement has changed and no longer contains the path where the program is found. Installation of another program, another user fiddling with the path statement, or other mishaps can cause this problem.

How to change the environment files   Unlike the other files up to this point, the CONFIG.SYS and the AUTOEXEC.BAT are simply text files that can be changed. NEVER MAKE CHANGES TO THESE FILES WITHOUT MAKING COPIES OF THEM FIRST. You always want to keep copies of these crucial files to roll back to so you can always set things back to the way they were when you started.

To make changes, you can use the program Edlin supplied with MS-DOS in early DOS 5.0, and Edit, supplied with later DOS versions. You can also use a word-processing program, if you can be sure and save the file as text-only.

To edit the AUTOEXEC.BAT file shown in Fig. 4-1, you can take a shortcut and type "EDLIN C:\AUTOEXEC.BAT" or "EDIT C:\AUTOEXEC.BAT" depending on which version of DOS you are using. You don't have to worry if the commands you type at the DOS prompt or in these editing programs are uppercase or lowercase because DOS translates all the letters you type into uppercase when the commands are executed.

Edlin, the text-only editing program delivered with the first version of DOS in 1981, remains cryptic and tough to use, requiring you to memorize its commands and displaying one line at a time. But it's fast, it is already on the PC in versions of DOS before 5.0, and it works if you know how to use it. Many repair technicians have learned it for those reasons. Edit is much easier to use, follows standard conventions for application programs, includes online help, and has replaced Edlin in the 5.0 or above versions of MS-DOS. This fact will probably make Edlin obsolete in just a few more years. Just in case you need it, information on using Edlin is in the DOS.TXT file on the included disk. You'll find information on Edit there as well.

You should either feel comfortable with any DOS editor you'll find or carry an editor you know as part of your repair tools. For your convenience, we've included QEdit, a quick text-only editor that easily fits on a single disk and can be used for viewing and editing PC environment files. The instructions for using QEdit are in appendix C.

Keep copies of the environment files   Many of the problems you'll encounter will be from customers who will tell you that the system used to work, nothing changed, and now the system doesn't work. The customer might believe they didn't change anything, but you need to be able to recreate the environment you had when the system was working. There are several reasons the user might believe nothing has changed. Perhaps the user installed software that made changes they're unaware of, or maybe someone else was involved. Perhaps nothing really has changed. You'll need to know that as well to start looking for failure elsewhere, such as in the hard disk drive.

The only way to know is to make copies. Once you've finished your editing and the system is working, you'll want to make a copy of the environment files and the device drivers to a bootable floppy. Another alternative is to create a subdirectory on the hard disk drive; name the drive with your initials and copy all the environment files and device drivers to it. Snooper, the configuration look-see program included with this book, can help you accomplish either of these two options. This way, if a new problem arises, you'll have something to compare with the current situation to help spot the cause of the problem.

The file allocation table (FAT)

One of the main jobs of the operating system is to keep track of files stored in mass storage. The operating system is responsible for working with the hardware to format a mass storage medium, such as a floppy disk, and then create the table where later file addresses will be stored. The user enters the command to prepare the disk for data by typing "format" at the DOS prompt. The operating system also keeps track of the mass storage by assigning the various drives attached to the system letters or numbers to designate one from another.

DOS uses letters and a colon, with the first floppy disk drive designated the A: drive. The designation B: is usually reserved for a second floppy disk drive, and the hard disk drive is usually the C: drive. Other drives can be added, such as a CD-ROM drive (which is usually designated drive D:), and each additional drive is designated by the next available letter of the alphabet after the letter "C."

Clusters   Once the disk is formatted, the file allocation table (FAT) is created. The FAT is a directory of the files on the hard disk drive. During the format operation, the disk's sectors are grouped into "clusters" whose addresses are then recorded in the FAT.

When data is written to the disk, DOS looks at the FAT to see where the next available cluster is, then has the drive go out and write the data to that cluster. Clusters can be between two and sixteen sectors in size, depending on the size of the hard disk drive.

If the cluster fills up, but there is still more data to be stored on the disk, DOS looks for the next available cluster, writes this next cluster address in the first cluster entry, and instructs the computer to continue writing the data to the second cluster address. If there is still more data, the third cluster number is written to the second cluster, and the process continues until all the data is written.

How DOS deletes files   When the user tells DOS a file is to be deleted, then DOS goes to the FAT and removes the first letter of the file name from the FAT, then marks all the clusters related to that file as available for new data. The next time data is to be written to the disk, the clusters now marked available are used.

Note that the deleted data is still physically in the cluster locations, at least until more data is written to the disk. This is why data can be recovered, if it is deleted, as long as nothing else has been written to the disk since the deletion. If something else has been written to the disk, chances of recovering the file intact get slimmer, though there might be the possibility of recovering part of the data.

This storage method, while an efficient use of the available space, can sometimes separate related data by a distance that slows disk access. This problem is called disk fragmentation. We'll discuss how to handle fragmentation in the "PC maintenance" section of chapter 8.

A note of caution A note of caution here is prudent. Microsoft has changed the basic structure of the way the FAT handles data every so often, which causes havoc with utility programs that go in and address the FAT directly. The last time was when DOS 5.0 came out and both Norton Utilities in versions before 6.0 and Central Point Tools before version 7.0 caused thousands of DOS 5.0 users to lose data. We had a client who used the Norton Utilities version 5.0 to attempt to recover some deleted files under DOS 5.0 and lost all the data on his hard disk drive. The moral of the story is, avoid use of a utility software product on a newly released version of an operating system.

Disk partitions

Partitioning might become a distant memory to all except those around before DOS 4.0, but it is still a concept you might have to deal with. Partitioning is dividing the drive into portions and creating a space where the operating system loads information it needs.

All drives must be partitioned, but in the early days users had to create several partitions for their larger hard disk drives because at that time DOS couldn't access a disk larger than about 32MB. To be able to use the additional disk space offered by drives larger than 32MB, the drives had to be partitioned. To DOS, each drive looked like another physical drive designated by a letter of the alphabet.

Partitions before DOS version 4.0 Users with one of the popular Seagate 40MB hard disk drives before the introduction of DOS 4.0 had two partitions. On those drives, it was customary to have a 32MB C: drive and just a sliver of storage, just over 8MB, on another logical drive designated as the D: drive. When the hard disk drive was installed, the drive was low-level formatted using either third-party software or the DOS DEBUG command. The DOS program FDISK was used to set up the partitions.

How to recognize prepartitioned drives These days, drives come from the manufacturer low-level formatted, and they might even be partitioned as well. The partition is where the operating system kernel is stored, so if the drive boots when it is installed without your doing anything, then you know the partition has already been created for you. You might still need to use FDISK to partition the drive and the FORMAT /S command, but some drives come with even those functions already accomplished.

You also need to know that FDISK also creates the master boot record (MBR) and the partition table, both stored in the partition. The partition table directs the computer to the partition with the operating system files needed for booting.

Why create more than one logical drive?   Partitioning a drive into more than one logical drive is still done, but only for two reasons. One is because the drive is larger than the 512MB single partition size limit that DOS 4.0 and higher imposes. The other reason is to run two different operating systems on the same machine.

If the drive is partitioned, an operating system such as OS/2 or Unix might reside on one logical drive, with DOS on the other. OS/2 will handle a partition up to 2GB in size, and it will still run DOS applications, which makes it attractive for large companies with very large customer or parts databases. The computer's environment files are then configured so the user can choose which operating system will boot when the computer starts.

Files & directory structure

Users often find the file naming and directory structure in DOS rather confusing. We'll cover both here.

Files   Files are a collection of data that for some reason or another goes together, such as it was created at the same time or it has related information, like the text of a letter. Under DOS, the file name can only have eight characters separated by a period from an optional three-character extension, such as REPAIRBK.DOC.

Filename conventions   There are naming conventions in the industry that apply to extensions to identify the type of file. For example, files with extensions of .EXE, .COM, and .BAT are recognized by DOS to be instructions the computer is to execute. Files with the extension .DOC and .TXT are usually documents or text files. The file name extensions are not hard-and-fast rules, but some programs, including the operating system, are designed to recognize and act on files with certain extensions.

Each file name has to be unique, even if only one character is different. Also, because of its digital system, each character has a unique numeric value (see the ASCII character table in appendix D). This means the computer sees zero as a different character from the uppercase letter "O". If a new file is added, and the new file has the exact same file name as an existing file, the computer will simply copy the new information over the old file.

The directory structure   As we've already said, the most basic directory, or the beginning directory, is called the root directory. The backslash character (\) separates one directory from another. Essentially, the directory structure is a way of giving files longer names, so one file can be distinguished from another. This way, you can have more than one file with the same name, as long as they're in different directories.

The place where a good explanation of directories would be helpful is in the case where you as the friendly PC repair person come into an office and someone has a computer where every file is out on the root directory of the hard disk drive. Now there's a formula for disaster. If these folks haven't called you complaining of missing data, they will soon.

So it is much easier to say to the person, "Look, computers are stupid. They only know the file name has to be different and you only have eight characters to make it different. So let me show you a way to store this stuff on the hard disk so that you don't lose anything."

Then proceed to explain that a directory is a way to add to the file name. So instead of eight characters, you get eight more to add and that way you can make each file different. Using this technique, you can create a directory called "CLIENT" and copy your file LETTER.DOC to the client directory. After you copy the file, the new file name is C:\CLIENT\LETTER.DOC.

While this approach could have the misguided effect of teaching customers to create a new directory for each letter they type to get a longer file name, it will at least allow them to better understand directories. Using this approach, you can then explain that every letter that begins with the file name C:\CLIENT can be handled as a group. This means they can be easily copied, backed up, or deleted without losing or affecting other data stored on the hard disk drive.

Directory names follow the same rules as file names. But the convention is to use just the eight-character file name and ignore the extension. One thing you don't see very often is directories with extensions, but that is an option.

Know your DOS commands

It is possible, and in PC repair it is often necessary, to give commands directly to the operating system. This means that you need to know the operating system commands.

Parameters   Operating system commands are usually one word to which you can pass "parameters," which are a shorthand way of giving the command additional instructions. The parameters are always separated from one another by a space, and the order in which they are given has meaning.

Taking the DOS COPY command as an example, to copy LETTER.DOC, from the root directory of the hard disk drive to a floppy disk, here's the command we'd type.

```
COPY C:\LETTER.DOC A:\LETTER.DOC
```

After you type in a command, you always press the Enter key to get the computer to act. In this case the parameters are the file name LETTER.DOC, and it is separated from the command by a space. The first file name is the file to be copied, and the second is the new name of the file name, which includes the drive that we want the file copied to.

Commands you need to know   The main commands you'll need handy for PC Repair use are: MD, CD, COPY, XCOPY, DIR, VER, PROMPT, CHKDSK, ATTRIB, and FORMAT. EDLIN or EDIT and DEBUG are useful if you want to set up hard disk drives on older PCs. MS-DOS 5.0 adds MEMMAKER, a utility for optimizing memory space, UNDELETE, and UNFORMAT. MS-DOS 6.0 includes DoubleSpace, a compression utility designed to get more space out of your hard disk drive. The most current version of MS-DOS, version 6.22, has changed the compression scheme and renamed the utility DiskSpace. Version 6.22 also adds the useful commands SCANDISK.EXE, DEFRAG.EXE, and MSD.EXE. We'll talk about where these commands are used as the opportunity arises. If you need to learn the commands, we've included instructions on using them in the DOS.TXT file on the included disk.

Get yourself a "cheat sheet"   Most of the common operating system commands you'll memorize fairly quickly once you use them a few times. However, remembering the parameters can get complex. Most technicians carry a small "cheat sheet" of DOS commands and parameters that they can quickly reference.

The Pocket PCRef from Sequoia Publishing is one such resource, containing a quick reference to the DOS commands and parameters as well as hard disk specification tables and the phone numbers of popular hardware and software manufacturers. A quick look in a computer bookstore or well-stocked general bookstore should turn up one, if not more, of these handy, portable reference books. You can also use the DOS.TXT file and Qedit, included with this book. You can carry both files with you on a single disk.

Where to go for more DOS help   If you need more help, there are a number of reference books to tutor you in learning DOS commands. Your library is likely to have a number of books on the subject. MS-DOS versions 5.0 and 6.0 or higher also offer online help in the form of an alphabetized list of the commands from which you can simply pick to get more information. To find out what version of DOS is on the machine, type "VER," press Enter, and the computer will tell you.

Tips for giving instructions over the phone

1. Have the user read back to you every character of the prompt so you know where they are. If need be, have the user type "Prompt PG" at the DOS prompt so you get a full reading of their current path position at each DOS prompt. Since users don't always understand the path, they're usually not where they say they are. If users are not where you think they are, your commands won't work.
2. Say "asterisk," not "star." Instruct the user to type Shift-8 to get the asterisk.

3. Tell the user when to press the Enter key or when to click the left mouse button. If using the mouse, be sure to specify how many clicks. One click on an icon highlights it, two clicks executes the underlying program. You might want one click to highlight the icon, then direct the user to read its properties to you as outlined later in this chapter.
4. Tell the user when to type spaces.
5. Use remote control, if possible (see chapter 6).

Batch files

DOS commands can be written together, or "batched," meaning saved together one per line in a file with an eight-character file name and the extension .BAT. You can write batch files to perform functions for your users, such as start a program for them. The user can then start the automated process by simply typing the name of the batch file.

If a program the client wants to use doesn't come with a batch file to start it, you can make one so all the user has to remember is a single word, instead of having to change directory, type the file name, then remember how to get back to the root directory. You can also add the directory of the program the client wishes to start to the PATH statement and do the same thing, but using a batch file allows the user to automatically start a file in the program on a regular basis.

You can also use batch files to make a simple menu/pick list so the user can simply type the number of a program to start the program, like Clark Waggoner of Oklahoma-based Clark Waggoner ComputerWorks did. Clark and his son created a simple program they set up for their customers who do not have Windows so programs can be started by simply picking the program from an on-screen menu. This is not only a convenience for the customer, but it serves as a constant reminder of Clark and his services.

Executable files supersede batch files   One thing you should know is if an .EXE and a .BAT file have the same eight character filename, the .EXE is the one the computer will execute. For example, if you have two files and one is START.EXE and the other is START.BAT, when you type START, the .EXE version will be the one chosen to execute by the computer. The START.BAT file will never be executed. In order to get the computer to execute the .BAT file, you'll have to change the filename, then type the new filename to get the .BAT file to work.

DOS shell

In DOS 5.0 and higher, a shell program has been supplied for starting programs and multitasking. Most new users find the shell difficult to use, but you might have users who prefer it to the DOS prompt and to Windows. You can use a mouse there, and it is possible to switch between running programs using the shell if you choose "Enable Task Swapping" from the "Options" menu.

You can also see a tree structure of the directories and subdirectories. To start the shell, type DOSSHELL at the DOS prompt. You can also add the command to start the shell to the end of the AUTOEXEC.BAT for users who want the shell to start automatically each time the computer starts.

Memory basics & limitations

The operating system has a lot to do with the use of memory in the PC. When the first PC was designed by IBM, the company decided that one megabyte of memory would be all the PC would ever need and designed its system accordingly. This was back when a 64-kilobyte program was big.

To backtrack, one bit is the smallest amount of information that can be stored. Eight bits equals one byte. A thousand bytes equals one kilobyte (K). A thousand kilobytes equals a megabyte (MB), and a thousand megabytes is equal to a gigabyte (GB). We could keep going, but you get the idea. (Actually the "1,000" is really 1,024, but it's an industry convention to say a thousand.)

Memory above 640K   The long and short of it is that IBM took the upper 384K of memory and broke that up into portions for all the different types of devices. Several portions are allocated for video adapters alone. Each type of monitor has a memory space reserved just in case a user might want to add that type of monitor. So monochrome monitors have a reserved spot in memory, as do Hercules monitors (which add graphics capability but not color). There's also memory space reserved for color graphics adapters (CGA), extended graphics array (EGA) adapters, and video graphics array (VGA) adapters. The rest of the memory is reserved for other utility functions.

Memory below 640K   The lower 640K was designated for software programs to use. For a long time, that 640K was plenty, but when you get into the realm of multitasking with color and a graphical user interface (GUI), the 640K is no longer adequate. The problem is compounded by recently developed peripherals that require software drivers be loaded into memory, such as CD-ROM drives or optical scanners. Each time one of those drivers is added it uses up some of that precious 640K of lower memory. Since everyone copied IBM's design, all compatible PCs have the same memory limitations. We could physically add more memory to the computer, but we couldn't use it.

The 640K barrier   So the problem became, "How can we get around this limitation?" One of the ways is to "trick" DOS into using the memory above 640K for programs. That is done by a software driver in the lower 640K pointing the program to a memory location above 640K. This works most of the time, but it has its limitations.

In addition, the software drivers loaded into the AUTOEXEC.BAT and CONFIG.SYS could be loaded into upper memory, and sometimes the upper memory included portions allocated but not used by video adapters. After all, most people only had one monitor, so the rest of that reserved memory could be used for something else. The problem is that the "pointer" software directing the software driver to upper memory might take up more of the 640K than the actual software driver itself. And because of the way memory space was divided, the order in which software drivers are loaded could make a difference in how much lower memory would be left. Sometimes a mere 1 or 2K of lower memory made the difference as to whether a program would run and just a few more K could significantly speed up performance. Additional memory above 1MB could be added and used as well.

Memory management software   Companies like Santa Monica, California-based Quarterdeck Office Systems made a name for themselves with QEMM, whose sole purpose was to squeeze out every drop of lower memory by shuffling device drivers and programs around. Quarterdeck also makes Desqview, a program that allows you to multitask or switch from one running program to another.

Quarterdeck made presentations around the country computer user groups and trade shows. The product had a real appeal to memory-hungry users as it could free as much as 700K of lower memory in certain cases. This was accomplished by shifting, shuffling, and tweaking drivers in the environment files, adding QEMM commands to the files, and changing the order in which drivers were loaded.

The problem was, this memory arrangement was not always a stable proposition. First of all, you had to reboot the machine several times, trying out the best memory arrangement. (Quarterdeck did later make things so you only had to reboot once.) In addition, if you added a new software application or peripheral, you had to start over, tweaking your memory and moving device drivers.

Windows heralded as memory barrier answer   Windows, Microsoft's graphical operating system, was to solve the memory problems. It did solve most of them, but only in programs written for the operating system. DOS software applications, though they would run under Windows, faced the same problem, only worse because now Windows took up an additional chunk of that lower memory! IBM's OS/2 tried to solve the memory problem by taking DOS out from underneath its graphical operating system. It ran DOS applications and Windows along with Windows applications, and broke the memory barrier, but it required so much hard disk space and memory that it discouraged many of its potential followers from giving it a try.

Memory management added to DOS   Once Microsoft introduced MS-DOS 5.0 with its memory management options and multitasking, the market began to move away from third-party memory management products. While MS-DOS 5.0 provided the user with the tools to configure memory, it was up to the user to edit the environment files to find the optimum configuration.

Like using QEMM, this practice could take hours and change significantly with the addition of a new device or software application. With the introduction of MS-DOS 6.0, there was MEMMAKER, a utility for optimizing memory. MEMMAKER automated the process, automatically moving device drivers into high memory, calculating the best configuration, and editing the environment files.

MEMMAKER   From a PC repair standpoint, the bottom line is that while you could spend a lot of time tweaking a customers environment files to get the optimum amount of lower memory, it takes less time to use MEMMAKER. Using MEMMAKER is no guarantee that everything the customer wants to run will work in memory MEMMAKER makes available. But it is a fast and reliable way to configure memory.

File compression

Compression is an old idea, but has become popular recently with the introduction of software products able to perform the compression and decompression invisibly to the computer user, allowing for more disk storage space at little extra cost. Several small software companies specialized in software programs for compressing files. One of the most popular is PKWARE of Brown Deer, Wisconsin with its PKZip product line. PKZip became well known because it is used on bulletin board service to compress files so they take less time for users to download using their telephone line and a modem. When users are being billed for phone line access and the time they're on the bulletin board, compression is a desirable option.

What is compression?   Compression itself is a way to take redundant portions of a file and represent them with symbols that take less space. In a simplistic example, if you could replace the character string "the" with one character, you could make this book smaller. So to compress the book, we take all the redundant characters and replace them with unique single characters. Then to uncompress it for someone to read, we reverse the process. Computers are good at this type of tedious task and perform it quickly.

There are two ways to perform compression. One is to analyze the document to be compressed and represent as many characters as possible with a single character, which takes more time. The faster way is to skip the analysis and just perform a standard compression. Analyzing the file produces a smaller compressed file while files compressed quickly are not usually as small. Files that are machine readable have pretty much been compressed as much as they're going to be and so compression on these types of files is usually not very fruitful. Machine readable files are programs that have been put through a process called compilation. Compilation changes the language the programmer used to create the program into code that the computer can execute directly and quickly.

Disk compression

Compression turned a corner when Carlsbad, California-based Stac Electronics and several other small companies introduced the idea of real-time, seamless file compression for PCs. As programs expanded in functionality with a corresponding expansion in the amount of disk space they took, the computer-user community found itself in pain.

There were all kinds of programs to be purchased, but disk space was at a premium. Just buy another disk drive? These folks had thought of that, but discovered that a transition from the old style MFM drives to IDE hard disk drives left them in the cold. Millions discovered they couldn't upgrade to a larger hard disk drive because their BIOS didn't support IDE drives.

In addition, prices were still high, and upgrading the BIOS was a painful and risky answer. At that opportune time, Stac Electronics, among others, came out with a software compression scheme, and the company claimed it doubled the capacity of your hard disk drive.

One big compressed file   In general, compression works by compressing all the files on your hard disk to a single file. The computer boots from a separate logical drive created by the program (usually drive H:), loads the compression software into memory, and then proceeds to compress every program on the drive into a single, large file. The file is called a "virtual" drive and looks just like the C: drive of the computer, often with its own FAT.

And for some users, the computer didn't even slow down. The reason is the time it takes to compress the data is often offset by the savings in writing nearly 50 percent less data to the disk. Even with a performance hit, users are still attracted to compression, which gives them the equivalent of a second hard disk drive with a purchase of software that is less than $100.

Compression and disk space estimates   Of course, the actual amount of compression you get on your hard disk depends on the type of files. If you have all programs and hardly any pure data, such as documents, databases, or spreadsheets, you're not going to get anywhere near double the disk space.

Another problem was the various compression programs would estimate the disk space, based on the past compression ratio, when the user asked for the remaining space by typing the DIR command from the DOS prompt. If you think you have 20MBs of disk space left, and you install a program that takes up 15MB, in reality you might not have enough disk space to install the program.

A San Francisco computer user sued Stac Electronics over its Stacker compression product. The suit accused Stac of false advertising because of the company's printed and verbal claims that users could "double their disk space." Evidently, this San Francisco user didn't double his disk, probably due to a high ratio of programs to user files on his hard disk drive. Stac settled the case out of court without revealing the details of the settlement other than to say it would add "actual compression results might vary" on its packaging.

DOS versions with and without compression   Microsoft has been in and out of the compression business since the advent of MS-DOS 6.0 because of legal fighting with Stac Electronics. The bottom line is MS-DOS 6.0 has DoubleSpace compression, MS-DOS 6.2 has an improved version of DoubleSpace, MS-DOS 6.21 doesn't have DoubleSpace at all, and MS-DOS 6.22 has compression technology Microsoft calls DiskSpace.

The 6.22 version also includes the updated ScanDisk utility for diagnosing and correcting disk errors and Doublegard, a utility Microsoft says adds an extra layer of protection for data. Since all four products were released in about a year's time, and Microsoft is the leader in operating systems, you're likely to find all four versions out there.

Disk compression complicates PC repair   Disk compression complicates PC repair by requiring you to have tools that can handle compressed drives, especially in data recovery situations. We talk more about the data recovery issues in chapter 8 when we deal with areas of specialization.

Compression also takes up valuable lower memory, so it is possible that applications your clients want to run might not work with disk compression in place. However, it is a way to stretch disk space when circumstances make upgrading a PC's hard disk impossible or impractical, and therefore it can be a tool to help your clients as well.

A short tale of MS-DOS 6.0

MS-DOS 6.0 was launched at the "World's Largest User Group Meeting" in June of 1993. Major computer user groups around the country watched a live satellite broadcast from San Francisco of Bill Gates and DOS Product Manager Brad Chase demonstrate DoubleSpace and the new automated memory management utility MEMMAKER.

DoubleSpace was the feature of interest. Microsoft had talked with several compression software companies, including extended talks with Stac Electronics, about licensing compression technology. However, Microsoft ended up licensing its DoubleSpace compression technology from Verisoft, a Stac competitor. Microsoft's adoption of compression technology was a strong endorsement to the computing community, but Stac didn't see it that way.

At one point, during the satellite broadcast introduction, Gates unexpectedly reached under the table and pulled the plug of the computer when DoubleSpace was in the middle of setting up a compressed drive. Gates did the same thing during the MEMMAKER demo. The demonstration was a success and users were lined up outside their respective meeting places afterward to buy the program from software dealers already set up to take orders. Sales of the MS-DOS 6.0 upgrade were off the charts, with more copies of the upgrade selling in the first 90 days after its release than the combined total retail sales of DOS 5.0 and Windows 3.1 combined.

But computer users being what they are, all over the country people were pulling the power plugs on their computers while compressing with DoubleSpace or using MEMMAKER. As it turns out, if you pulled the power plug when the Windows driver SmartDrive was flushing its disk memory (or cache), you could lose data from the hard disk drive.

In addition, MS-DOS 6.0 shipped with a small bug in the new Windows Undelete command that let you bring back deleted files with illegal characters in the file name, such as the "*" or "?" characters.

Microsoft released MS-DOS 6.2 in the spring of 1994, (skipping 6.1, IBM's newest release number for PC-DOS). The version changed the SMARTDRIVE.SYS cache utility, making it a more conservative read-only cache instead of read-write cache and fixing the Undelete illegal file name problem. Meanwhile, Stac Electronics filed a lawsuit against Microsoft, claiming the company had taken its compression technology and incorporated it into DoubleSpace.

The compression in DOS 6.0 was more transparent to users than Stac's, as it was called from a "hook" in the operating system itself. Microsoft accomplished this by loading the device driver that provides the computer access to the compressed drives, DBLSPACE.BIN, into memory before any environment files were executed. Another device driver, DBLSPACE.SYS, was then loaded into the CONFIG.SYS file to move DBLSPACE.BIN out of upper conventional memory so it wouldn't conflict with any other device drivers that needed the memory space. The hook also made DoubleSpace so transparent that the user no longer needed to worry about the environment files when loading a new software program or peripheral onto the system. This had been a problem with third-party compression programs.

Stac immediately took advantage of the new hook in DOS, introducing a version of its software compression product, Stacker, which not only took advantage of the feature, but also required MS-DOS 6.0 in order to run. Microsoft counter sued.

The legal battle went to a jury trial. Microsoft was ordered by the court to pull both MS-DOS 6.0 and the newly released MS-DOS 6.2 off of retail shelves. (Users with the operating system product were unaffected.) Microsoft countered by introducing MS-DOS 6.21, a version of the operating system without the DoubleSpace compression technology at all.

Microsoft also tried to get an injunction to pull the Stacker product that required MS-DOS 6.0 off retail shelves, but to no avail. Stac, meanwhile, was floundering financially, blaming the enormous expenses of the suit.

In the Summer of 1994, Microsoft again countered by shipping yet another version of DOS. This time it was MS-DOS 6.22 with a new compression technology named DiskSpace.

A federal district court directed Microsoft to pay Stac $120 million and Stac to pay Microsoft $13.4 million. But both companies decided to settle out of court before any money changed hands. The settlement ended with Microsoft's purchase of nearly 17 percent of Stac and a cross-licensing agreement giving each company the rights to the technology named in each suit.

Windows basics

Windows, from Microsoft, wasn't the first graphical user interface (GUI) to come long, but it has taken the PC market by storm. A graphical interface, which gives the user some clue as to what to do, is easier to use than a user interface with a C> and a blinking cursor in the upper-left-hand corner of the screen. Figure 4-2 shows a typical Windows 3.1 opening screen.

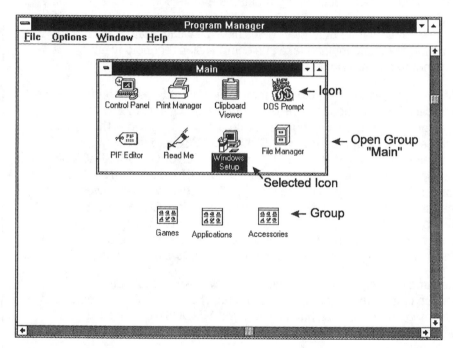

4-2
A typical Windows opening screen. There are four groups, but the "Main" group is open. The Windows Setup icon is highlighted or "selected" in the Main group.

The first version of Microsoft Windows was introduced in 1985, but it wasn't until the version 3.0 release in 1990 that the program really caught on. Introduced in the fall of 1991, Windows 3.1, also known as the "multimedia" version, included "Multimedia Extensions"—software support for data types new to the Intel-based PC, such as sound, animation, and video. The product also included the software drivers needed for adding popular PC sound cards.

The *Wall Street Journal* reported that Windows 3.1 sold over 3 million copies during its first six weeks of availability. Microsoft has since released Windows 3.11, with few changes, except a different box and hologram image to attempt to thwart counterfeiters.

The true measure of an operating system's success, as well as the successful adoption by the market of a computer platform, is the number of software applications available for it. Windows is clearly in the lead with more software applications than any other operating system, according to the Software Publisher's Association.

If you can manage to learn Windows, you'll have a leg up on many existing repair business owners. While Windows has been around a while now and is growing in popularity, many PC repair businesses haven't bothered to learn to use it. Steve Sacco of AMCOM Consulting Services was reluctant to move to Windows and frankly admitted he didn't like the operating system. Learning an entirely new approach to computing can be a challenge, especially when you have a thriving business to keep up with. But Steve was forced into it by the demands of his customers and his work. Now he's a Windows evangelist, saying that if it is set up properly, Windows can be much easier for new users. His knowledge of Windows helps him help his clients, cuts down on his phone support calls, and makes his life easier as well.

The bottom line is we feel Windows configuration problems will provide more repair business, if you can learn to troubleshoot and diagnose these problems. This section will give you the basics, and a Windows troubleshooting section in chapter 6 will give you the information you need to overcome more complex Windows problems.

Windows knowledge is an advantage

A little background

Windows introduced pictures and animation to PC users. Macintosh users had been enjoying those benefits since Apple Computer's introduction of the Mac, and while they had sounds to go along with the pictures, the Macintosh did everything in black and white. Windows was in color, a factor that swayed many a Macintosh user to switch to the Intel-based PC platform.

However, the true birth of the graphical operating system on PCs was at Xerox's famous Palo Alto Research Center (PARC), a think-tank where the best minds were known for coming up with innovative, high-tech ideas. Somehow, though, Xerox never pursued the graphical operating system or the Altos personal computer it had come up with to run the graphical operating system. By the time Xerox woke up and attempted to patent the concepts, it was past the legal time limit to do so. If you're interested in the story behind the Altos, get a copy of *Fumbling the Future: How Xerox Invented, Then Ignored, the First Personal Computer* (William Morrow, 1988).

Windows and integration   Windows is going the route of the entire computer industry in integrating popular functions and utility programs that once had to be purchased separately, right into the operating system itself. A sage programmer, who asked to remain unnamed, said: "Today's utility is tomorrow's menu option." Peter Norton, known for the Norton utilities and several excellent books on the PC, said the business of the utilities market consists of looking for holes in the operating system and filling them, mindful of the fact that the developers of the operating system will eventually fill those holes themselves. You can expect to see an increasing trend toward integration of applications into the operating systems from vendors, especially as the market standardizes on certain types of applications.

Windows' modes

Windows was originally designed to accommodate slower PCs with less than 1MB of memory. In version 3.0, to continue that compatibility, even though faster PCs with more memory capacity were entering the market, Windows had a "real mode" setting, so it would still run on slower computers.

Version 3.0 also had a standard mode and a 386 enhanced mode. Standard mode was popular for 286-based PC, required 2MB of memory, and was fast so it was often used for 386-based PCs as well. It provided access to extended memory and allowed users to run DOS applications in full-screen.

The 386 enhanced mode takes advantage of the hardware capabilities of the 386 processor to allow more than one DOS application to run at a time. It also allows for copying of text from one DOS program to another. Version 3.1 of Windows dropped real mode altogether.

Windows offers another structure on top of DOS. It can solve some of the directory problems users associate with DOS, but it has to be set up for the user by someone who knows both the DOS structure and the Windows structure. As we go on, you'll see why.

The mouse

Windows is mouse-dependent. While you can function in Windows without a mouse, it is uncomfortable to do so. Once just a whimsical accessory, the mouse on the PC has become so integrated that most motherboards now come with an integrated mouse port. Called a "bus" mouse, this port sends the mouse signals directly into the bus instead of through a serial port. Mice that work through the serial port are still available, but the bus mouse is becoming the most popular mouse type.

Also known as a pointing device, the computer translates the movement of the mouse on the desktop surface (or on a mouse-pad where it can get better traction) to the movement of an on-screen cursor, usually an arrow. Most mice have two buttons, though the left mouse button is rarely used. "Clicking" or pressing the left mouse button once selects the on-screen object to which the on-screen arrow is pointing. Two left button clicks close together causes the computer to act.

Mouse software settings   Software that comes with the mouse can be set to make the right mouse button the primary button for those who are left-handed. The software can also be set to control the sensitivity of the mouse, such as how close together the clicks need to be for the computer to take action and how fast the mouse moves.

Figure 4-3 displays the Mouse Manager menu that comes with the Microsoft BallPoint mouse for the portable computing market. The menu is accessible from within Control Panel in the Main group. An illustration of a track-ball mouse from a tutorial that comes with the software is shown in Fig. 4-4.

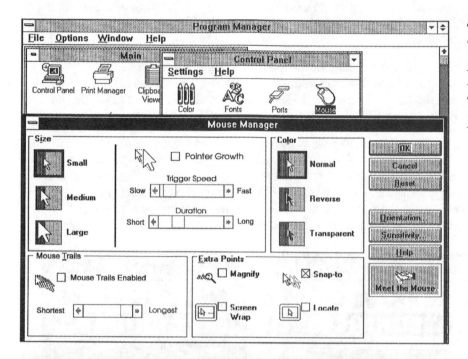

4-3
Software settings control the functions of the mouse in Windows. Shown is the Mouse Manager software settings screen that comes with the Microsoft BallPoint mouse.

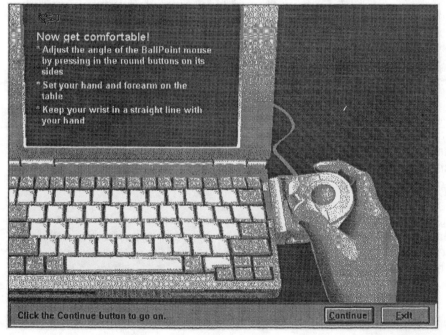

4-4
Mice vary in size and shape. Shown is a Microsoft track-ball mouse. This mouse is equipped so it can be used by either left- or right-handed users without modifying the software settings.

Windows still requires DOS knowledge   While users appear to get along with Windows without knowing much about DOS, repair people aren't that lucky. Because Windows is still based on DOS, it still uses the DOS file structure and requires knowledge of DOS file naming conventions in order to set up software products to work with its interface. In other words, behind the scenes the same DOS-like stuff is happening, but the user is unaware of those events.

Windows behind the scenes   The buttons in Windows are simply animations. The computer tracks the location of the mouse at all times and when the mouse is in a certain area, a click or double click starts a program, just like typing a file name and pressing Enter in DOS.

As you can see from Fig. 4-5 of the opening screen from the Micro House Technical Library, the button click animation requires two pictures that use shading and a fast screen draw to create a visual three-dimensional effect. In Fig. 4-5, "The Encyclopedia of Hard Drives" button on the left is in the normal position. On the right, the button has been redrawn due to a mouse click in the screen area where the button is shown. Note how the shading has changed.

4-5
As you can see from this example, the button clicks in Windows are animations. Once the mouse button is clicked when the mouse is within the area of the button, that portion of the screen is quickly redrawn to the shaded button on the right, then back again to the image on the left.

When the user lets up on the mouse button, the computer quickly redraws that area of the screen back to the way it was in the image on the left, then activates the program to start "The Encyclopedia of Hard Drives." Each button or menu option in a Windows program is linked to program code underneath that activates not only the on-screen animation, but also a series of commands that starts that portion of the program.

Program groups, items, & icons

The basic structure in Windows is the "Program Group" and the "Program Item." As shown in Fig. 4-2, each group has the same appearance. Groups are used for structure. They have no correlation to DOS directories and their names are arbitrary. Microsoft provides a few Groups of its own for users, such as the "Main," "Games," "Accessories," and "Startup" Groups.

Groups contain "Program Items" that can be assigned pictures or "icons," as shown by the open "Main" group. The icons represent Program Items that can be run by the user. Icons can be moved from group to group by the user and one icon can be copied so it might appear in several groups. Program Items placed in the special Startup group activate automatically when Windows is started.

How to make new groups   You can make new groups by going to the "File" menu in Program Manager and selecting "New." The "New Program Object" box will appear, as shown in Fig. 4-6. Windows will then ask if you wish to create a "Program Group" or "Program Item" in the New box. Select "Program Group" and you'll see something like Fig. 4-7.

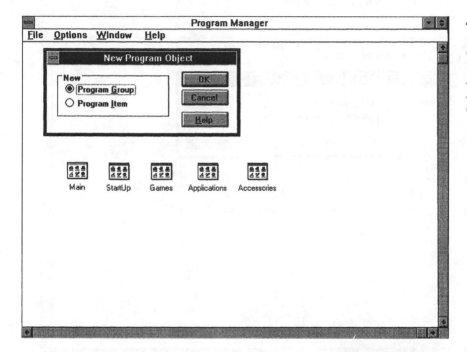

4-6
Once the "File" menu option "New" is selected, this box offers a choice between a new group or a new icon within an existing group.

4-7
In creating a new group, Windows prompts you for a description of the group.

You can type in a name for the new group in the "Description" box, as we did to make a PC Repair Tools directory, and Windows will fill in the "Group File" name for you after you click on "OK." The group file is assigned a name ending with the extension .GRP and is placed in the Windows directory, as shown in Fig. 4-8.

Sizing windows   Group windows, and Program Manager itself, can be sized. This is significant because if there are more icons in the group than can be viewed at one time due to the size of the window, a slider will appear along the side or the bottom of the window, or both, as shown in Fig. 4-8. The slider indicates that the view within the window can be moved to reveal objects not yet seen. This is so the other icons can be viewed and activated as well, and is known as a "virtual" screen.

4-8
Once you offer a group description, Windows will assign a name based on the description with the extension .GRP and place the new group file description in the Windows directory.

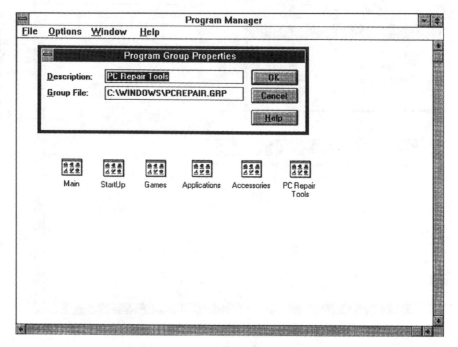

How to set up an icon for a non-Windows program   As we said, icons in windows indicate programs, and each icon is called a "Program Item." To show you, we're going to set up an icon for a DOS .BAT file to send a page eject character to a laser printer.

This .BAT file is helpful if you've pressed the Print Screen key on the keyboard, and the laser printer indicates it has something to print but hasn't "moved a muscle." It's waiting for a page eject command that it isn't going to get from the Print Screen function, so this .BAT file gives it that command. (We've placed this file, EJECT.BAT, on the disk included with this book.)

To run this batch file, you could go to Program Manager's menu, select "File," then "Run," and type "C:\UTILITY\EJECT.BAT" in the "Command Line" box that appears, then click on "OK." (We keep this .BAT file in a UTILITY directory on our own C: drive.) In fact, you can run any DOS or Windows program this way, provided you know the DOS command to start the program.

But we'd like to have this EJECT.BAT file available at the click of a button, so we want to create an icon for it in the new PC Repair Tools group. To do this you'll need to open the PC Repair Tools group, then select "File" from Program Manager's top menu, and "New" from the options there. When the New Program Object box appears, select "Program Item," click once on "OK," and the "Program Item Properties" box opens, as shown in Fig. 4-9.

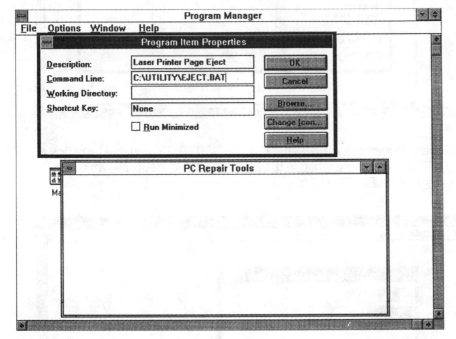

4-9
To place a new icon in a group, the group must be open. Once you select Program Item from the New Program Object box, this Program Item Properties box opens as illustrated.

In the "Description" box, you can type "Laser Printer Page Eject," mindful that what you type here, both uppercase and lowercase will appear exactly as we type it under the new icon. In the "Command Line" box type "C:\UTILITY\EJECT.BAT". You could also use the "Browse" option to fill in the Command Line box by clicking on "Browse," selecting the UTILITY directory, picking EJECT.BAT, and clicking "OK," as shown in Fig. 4-10.

The "Working Directory" box lets you designate what directory the program will use to store files it creates. It does not have to be the directory in which the program resides, but if you don't designate an already existing directory, Windows will use the one where the program is located. Since we know the

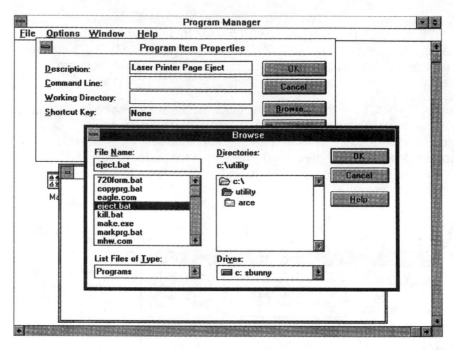

4-10

The Browse button allows you to pick the program you want to associate with your new icon from a list of programs available as shown.

"Working Directory" will automatically be C:\UTILITY, you can just click on "OK." Now you have an icon in the PC Repair Tools group, shown in Fig. 4-11, to execute the EJECT.BAT file.

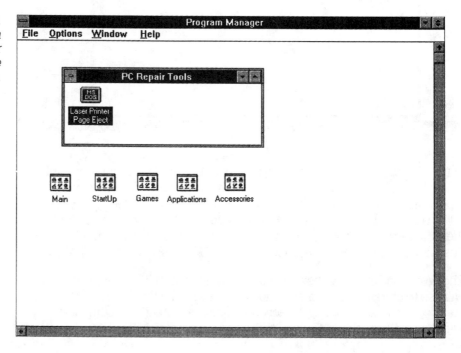

4-11

We've created a new icon that will execute our EJECT.BAT utility in the PC Repair Tools group.

How to change an icon   You can change the icon from the Windows default to one that's not so plain and better represents the function of this Program Item. To do so, highlight the icon in the open PC Repair Tools group, go to the Program Manager menu, choose "File," then "Properties." Note how Windows filled in the "Working Directory" box with C:\UTILITY, which is the directory location of the .BAT file.

Professionally developed programs designed to run under Windows supply their own icons with the program. However, since the .BAT file doesn't come with an icon, you'll have to select one from those available in Program Manager, as Fig. 4-12 illustrates. Click on "OK" and the "Change Icon" box brings the icons available in the Windows file "PROGMAN.EXE", (Fig. 4-13). Moving the slider displays 46 icons, including the one Windows always uses when there isn't an icon available. But there's no icon that looks like a printer.

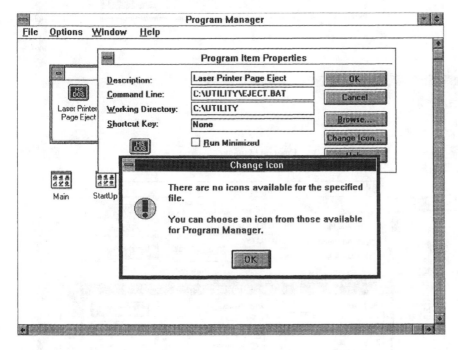

4-12
Windows knows there is no icon assigned to the EJECT.BAT file, but offers us the option of choosing an icon.

Fortunately, you can go to another group of over 100 icons supplied by Windows 3.1 and look there. Click on "Browse" and the Browse box appears, showing the location of the PROGMAN.EXE file in the Windows directory. As shown in Fig. 4-14, look for the file MORICONS.DLL in the list of files on the left. You can move the slider or type the file name in the box labeled "File Name" at the top left, then click on "OK." A new group of icons will appear in the "Change Icon" box. You can choose the lined paper icon, as we have in Fig. 4-15, then click on OK, and click on "OK" again in the Program Item Properties box.

4-13

More than 46 icons are available in the PROGMAN.EXE file. They can be cycled through using the slider.

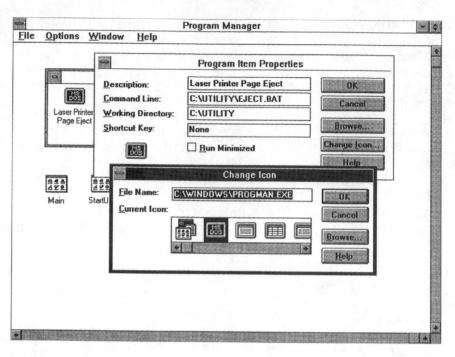

4-14

Windows 3.1 offers another group of icons in the file MORICONS.DLL.

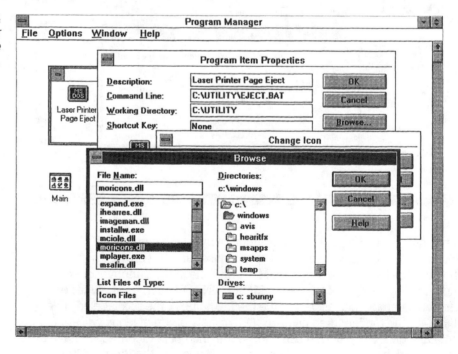

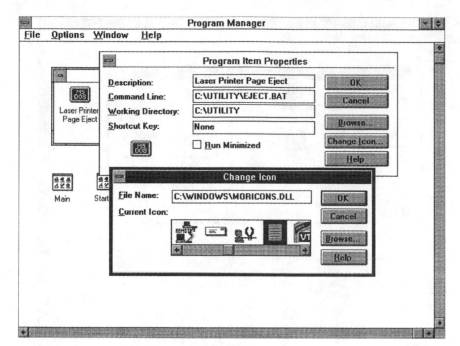

We've decided to choose the icon that looks like lined paper for our laser printer page eject utility.

If you use the Properties command from the Program Manager File menu on a group or an icon that already exists highlighted, you can see all the path and working directory information on an existing program. This can be useful if you need to know where a program's files are and where it is storing data files.

Getting to DOS from Windows

If you just want to go out to DOS from Windows, you can do so by clicking on the DOS icon in the Main group shown back in Fig. 4-2. Microsoft calls this DOS window a "virtual" PC. You can run some diagnostics, DOS commands, and programs from here. Die-hard DOS users will find it refreshing to get out into the environment they know best.

Windows displays a message when you enter this DOS "world" that reminds you to type "Exit" and Enter to go back to Windows, Alt+Tab to switch to Windows leaving the DOS screen active, and Alt+Enter to switch between a full-screen display and a partial display. You should experiment with these functions, as they can be quite useful.

Windows utility programs

Figure 4-16 shows how Windows has incorporated several utility functions. The Windows Accessories group offers several of these functions. If you know how to use these built-in functions, you can use them on any Windows-based PC.

The accessories include: a simple word processor (Write) that offers fonts; a drawing program (Paintbrush); a simpler word processor that offers the automated insertion of a time and date stamp (Notepad); a way to automate

4-16

The Accessories group offers several common functions. Two of the more useful are the word processor, Write, and the Calculator. However, the Media Player can be used to play back a couple of video clips offered with Windows 3.1, and the Sound Recorder can be used to record and edit custom sounds.

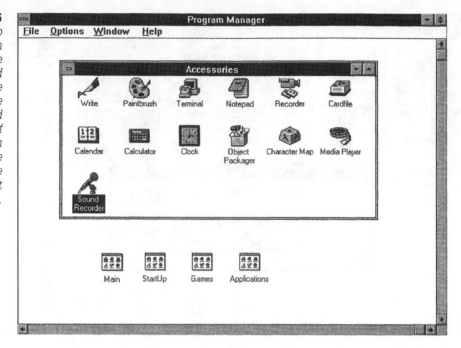

tasks (Recorder); a utility for inserting objects such as sound or video into standard applications (Object Packager); a way to easily pick unusual characters such as copyright symbols or registered trademark symbols, for use in another application (Character Map); a utility for playing back multimedia data such as video or sound files (Media Player); and a utility that allows you to record and edit your own sounds (Sound Recorder).

Video playback For those interested in seeing video playback on their PC, Microsoft has included two video files, FLYMTN8.AVI and RSHMRPH8.AVI, both located in the AVIS subdirectory of the WINDOWS directory. FLYMTN8.AVI is a fly-through between two mountains, and RSHMRPH8.AVI shows the transformation between the original Mt. Rushmore and the mountain after the presidents' likenesses were finished.

Sound recorder The sound recorder requires the installation of a sound card and use of a microphone that plugs into the sound card to record sounds. This means users can add their own sounds to events, such as the opening and closing of windows, or to their documents. Adding sound to documents is called voice annotation, and while it is much talked about, not many people are using it.

Sound and video files tend to be large and disk-space hungry. The only practical way to transmit a document with these extra files attached would be over a network. It's usually easier to simply call the other person and explain what it is you want them to know, rather than to attach a voice annotation.

However, Compaq is building sound chips onto the motherboards of its PCs and in some companies have even added telephones, attached to the side of the monitor, for receiving regular phone calls as well as adding voice annotations to documents. The phone also solves the problem of listening to voice annotations in a document without everyone else in the office having to hear the message.

Windows also provides a multitasking environment, meaning you can work with more than one program at a time. Shifting from one program to another is easy using the key combination Alt+Tab. When a program is running in the background it can be "minimized" or displayed only as the icon (the one used to start the program). When in full-screen mode, the program is said to be "maximized."

Configuration

Screen savers   Windows also provides screen savers that switch on automatically at a given time interval of no activity. Most monitors these days don't have problems with "burn in," where an image left on the screen for a long time becomes so permanent that it leaves a "ghost" image on the monitor that never goes away. But with Windows' password protection, a user can leave the computer, and when the screen saver comes on, it will hide whatever was on the screen.

User confusion in Windows tip   Here's a tip. Users often start up a program by double-clicking on an icon, then either switch to another program or leave the PC, allowing the screen saver to come on. In either case, Windows reduces the running program to an icon, which can even be hidden from view.

We had a case like this in which data in a DOS-based accounting program that ran under Windows would be updated in some portions of the program but not in others. For example, a check would show up entered in the register, but that data would be missing from the trial balance. What we discovered is the user would start the accounting program, leave the PC for a while, and the screen saver would come on. When the user came back, the accounting program full-screen display would be gone, with just the small icon in the corner showing the program was running.

The user, not realizing what was happening, would start another copy of the accounting program. Since the first running copy had files open and the second copy opened up data files from another portion of the program, some data would get updated in one part of the program but not in another.

There are two ways to handle this problem. One is to teach the user to hold down Alt and press Tab several times after coming back to the PC to scroll through what applications are already running. In the case of the accounting software, we wrote a batch file using Norton Batch Builder that we used to start the accounting program from the icon. The Batch Builder program checked to see if any other copies of the accounting program were running each time the icon was double-clicked. If another copy was running, that copy was maximized. If not, the accounting program was started. Of course, this required that the client have a copy of the Norton Desktop for Windows, but in this case he did.

Password protection   As a security measure, Windows can be set to require a password in order to allow anyone access to the screen once the screen saver has been activated. The password must also be entered when the computer comes up for the first time. This is not tight security, since anyone who knows what they're doing can bypass Windows at bootup and access the data on the PC, but it does provide some security. However, it is beneficial in a network setting.

The screen saver, the password options, and some options to customize the appearance of Windows are all found in the Control Panel, an option available in the Main group. Printer and mouse setup options are also available under Control Panel.

You should disable the password when you're working on a PC running Windows. If it is left on, you could get locked out. You can do so by clicking on the Desktop icon in the Control Panel group, then clicking on the Setup button under Screen Saver. Make sure the Password Protected box is unchecked.

Windows "tips" or "Easter eggs"for unforgettable business cards

Most users would like to be able to change the settings in Windows, but they don't know how. You could make your business card memorable by printing on the back of it the keystrokes for Windows "Tips" like this:

Windows Tips
Change Password -- Main, Control Panel, Desktop,
Alt-U, Alt-P, Alt-S.
Change Colors -- Main, Control Panel, Colors
Make Your Own Color Set -- Main, Control Panel,
Colors, Alt-P, Choose colors,
Alt-S to save with new name.

Another attention-getting business card would be one that has an explanation of how to activate the Microsoft Windows 3.1 Easter Egg on the back. Sought after by computer enthusiasts, Easter Eggs are undocumented animations that usually list those who worked on the program.

Windows Easter Egg
To activate hidden animation in Windows 3.1, hold down the Shift and Ctrl keys, open the Help menu in Program Manager, and select "About Program Manager." Double-click on the Windows icon in the window that opens. Nothing happens the first time you do this. The second time there's a message and a waving flag. The third time, a list scrolls by of people who worked on Windows heralded by a figure who looks like Bill Gates. You may find if you repeat this process, the appearance of the figure changes.

There are Easter Eggs in other application programs as well such as Microsoft Excel, Microsoft Word for Windows, CorelDRAW!, PC Tools for Windows. The Macintosh platform also has Easter Eggs. We doubt anyone would throw away a business card that had such an interesting tidbit on the back.

How to change Windows device drivers   If you change a printer, network driver, monitor, or upgrade the mouse, you might find you need to install a new software driver. To do this, you need the original Windows installation disks or the disk provided with the new peripheral. Windows will allow you to pick the item from the list, if it is available, and then ask for the installation disks in order to install the driver.

On computers where Windows is preinstalled, the manufacturer will either provide Windows installation disks or provide a special program that allows you to make a set of installation disks. The installation disks are necessary, so you should encourage your clients to make them and keep them available.

How to install a new device driver   For example, if you want to install a new printer in Windows, you can go to "Main," "Control Panel," then "Printers." From the Printers menu, you select "Add" and a list of printers will be presented. The printer will probably be on the list, and when you select the correct one, Windows will ask you for the first disk of the installation set of disks so it can copy the printer software driver to the hard disk drive.

If you have a printer that is not listed, you can pick the "Install Unlisted or Updated Printer" selection and click "Install." You will need a disk that hopefully came with the printer, so Windows can copy the correct printer driver to the hard disk drive. You can also do this if you have received an updated printer driver from the manufacturer of the printer.

You can install as many printer drivers as you think you'll need and then set the one you want to use by going into this menu, highlighting the printer you're interested in, and clicking "Set As Default Printer," then clicking on "OK."

File Manager

If you work in Windows, you'll find File Manager very helpful. Located in the main group, File Manager is Windows' answer to implementing the DOS commands. Under the "File" menu there are options for creating and removing directories, copying files, changing file attributes, and a number of other activities. One of the strongest features of File Manager is the ability to quickly delete an entire directory with all associated subdirectories. The "Disk" menu offers utilities to format floppy disks of varying capacities and make bootable disks, or system disks, as well. While File Manager is more graphical, you'll still need to know the basic DOS command syntax to use File Manager effectively.

Backup, antivirus, compression utilities   File Manager offers a number of additional options. In conjunction with later versions of DOS, such as MS-

DOS 6.0, it offers backup and antivirus utilities. If you own the Norton Desktop for Windows product, File Manager will display the Norton tools under a "Norton" menu option.

You can even get a graphical view of the DoubleSpace compression ratio, if compression is in use, from the "DoubleSpace Info" option under the "Tools" menu as shown in Fig. 4-17. Chapter 4 of the *Microsoft Windows 3.1 User's Guide* that comes with Windows offers a thorough explanation of the capabilities of File Manager. It's fast reading, especially if you already know the DOS command structure, and definitely worthwhile.

4-17
If the hard disk is compressed, you can get a graphical view of the compression and the space left using this "DoubleSpace Info" option located in the "Tools" menu under File Manager.

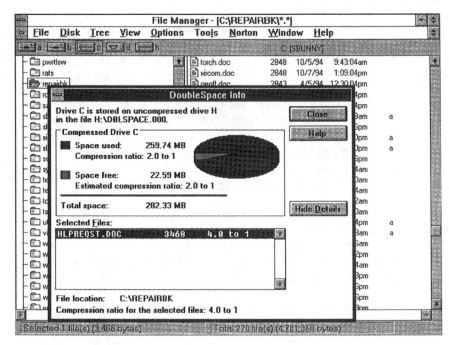

Windows Clipboard

Windows offers a way to exchange data between documents through the Windows Clipboard. A block of text or a drawing can be saved to the Clipboard using the "Copy" command found under the "Edit" menu of any Windows application, then pasted into another Windows application using the "Paste" command.

How to copy text from non-Windows applications   Text from non-Windows applications can also be copied to the Clipboard if Windows is running in 386 enhanced mode. You simply press Alt-Spacebar to open the Control menu, then type Alt-E for Edit and K for Mark. (You can use the mouse to open the Control menu and select these options as well.) Then you can either hold down the shift key while pressing the arrow keys or hold down the left mouse button while moving the mouse to highlight the text.

Once the text is highlighted, press the Enter key, and the text will be copied into the Clipboard. You can also place text into non-Windows applications from the Clipboard by putting the cursor where you want the text inserted in the application, pressing Alt+Spacebar, E for Edit, and P for Paste.

Knowledge of the Windows Clipboard is more helpful in using Windows than in repair work. However, it is something you can show clients that will help them, and that makes you more valuable.

When you configure Windows, the settings go into environment files for the program known as the .INI (pronounced "in-ee") files. There are two .INI files, WIN.INI and SYSTEM.INI. These are text-only files, much like the AUTOEXEC.BAT and CONFIG.SYS files, and are read by Windows when it starts.

INI files

WIN.INI contains information about the desktop, fonts, sounds, individual applications, and applications that should be started automatically when Windows starts. SYSTEM.INI is aimed at providing information about the hardware such as Windows mode settings and software drivers. A typical Windows .INI file might go on for two or three pages.

Application programs for Windows might have their own .INI files as well. You can see and edit all the environment files for Windows, including the .INI files, using the SYSEDIT.EXE command. From the Program Manager "File" menu, choose "Run" then type SYSEDIT and click on "OK." The System Configuration Editor box will open displaying all the environment files ready for editing.

When new Windows applications are installed, it is common for these applications to go into these .INI files and make changes. The changes might slow down the system, or the user might decide the program takes too much disk space for the amount of benefit it provides.

A good example was a particularly attractive set of application software called "Icon Do-It" from Phoenix, Arizona-headquartered Moon Valley Software. The program offered 200 designer icons, but the big attraction was its 15 animated icons. One icon was a California Raisin that danced on-screen like John Travolta in "Saturday Night Fever." Another was a butterfly that actually moved its wings up and down, looking like the real thing had decided to light on your monitor.

The problem was that the animated icons ate up so much of the computer's system resources, that processing slowed to a crawl for actual, productive work. So while Moon Valley made a big hit, after a while people wanted to uninstall the program. The trick then was getting the application all the way out of Windows.

Uninstalling Windows applications

Attempting to uninstall an application from Windows is like trying to get a big, pink, sticky wad of bubble gum off your shoe on a hot day. It's messy and difficult. Changes could be made by the program to the environment files, the Windows system files, and new files could have been added to both the Windows directory and the System subdirectory under Windows. The .INI files alone are text files that can be eight or more typewritten pages in length.

Another problem with uninstalling is the uninstall process might not be performed until after other changes are made to the system. One program might be replaced with a new one, or the user might find the program doesn't do what was expected after a period of time.

How often does the problem of uninstalling a Windows application come up? To give you an idea, the Software Etc. stores announced that the application Uninstaller for Windows from Microhelp of Marietta, Georgia was third of the top ten best-sellers in the chain's Productivity program category.

Uninstall programs don't always work at completely uninstalling an application. They're intelligent enough usually to fix the environment files and the Windows system files, but they often leave stray files that will never again be used. Some are memory resident, which can also be a problem. If the application installed its own video driver into the Windows system files, and the uninstaller doesn't put the correct video driver back, you could end up with a situation where Windows simply won't run.

Most uninstall programs also require that they be run before any installation is made. No software program can replace a backup, however, and we recommend you have one before installing any new software program to a system.

Manual uninstallation   One of the ways to uninstall a Windows application manually is to use the SYSEDIT command and look for changes the installed program made to the environment files. The program might have been considerate enough to back up the environment files before it changed them, so look for the same file names with the .BAK extension. This can be very much like handling a razor blade, however, so it should be done with extreme care. One thing to do before you edit anything is to make a copy of each file with the .BAK extension, or use your initials as the extension so you can backtrack if you need to.

Make backups before installation   The best insurance against these problems is to train your clients to make backups before they install any new software or software updates to their system. We recently had a case where an accounting software package sent our client an update. We've worked hard to emphasize backups, and our client made a complete backup before the update was installed. It was a good thing.

The first thing that happened was the client couldn't open some of his accounts in the accounting software. Then he noticed entries he'd never seen before showing up in his chart of accounts. Finally the accounting software began locking up, and he had to warm boot the computer to get out of it. It turned out that the update added a menuing program that produced memory conflicts with Windows. Things got so bad that at one point, double-clicking on the accounting software icon actually rebooted the computer.

Fortunately, our clients had that backup. We were able to restore the system back to where it was before the installation of the update. We attempted first to restore just the accounting program and data, but discovered the update made changes to Windows as well. We had to go out to DOS and use a DOS version of the backup software to restore the entire environment.

You can figure on running into "cousins" of Windows. Microsoft Windows for Workgroups 3.11 is peer-to-peer networking software that allows every PC on the network to share the resources of every other PC. Analysts at Computer Intelligence InfoCorp say Windows for Workgroups is gaining popularity in the peer-to-peer networking market.

Windows' "cousins"

There is another version of Microsoft Windows available—the New Technology version dubbed "Windows NT." Bill Gates himself has aligned Windows NT in the Unix camp, according to a *Computerworld* report. It appears Windows NT has many Unix-style commands and is aimed at the high-end networking environment.

The main differences from a repair standpoint is that Windows NT is designed to be a multiuser system, it doesn't have DOS underneath, and it has a database for configuration information called the Configuration Registry. This is where all the environment settings are so there are no .INI files, nor are there AUTOEXEC.BAT and CONFIG.SYS files.

Users installing NT have a choice between the DOS FAT or the New Technology File System (NTFS). The look and feel of the program is nearly identical to Windows, but it does allow for longer file names, something users have been clammering for. The next release of Windows is boasting similar features to NT, like long file names and no DOS underneath.

There's a possibility you might run across Windows NT in large government or corporate sites, but fortunately, it is very much like Windows 3.1, and with a little extra research, you should be able to navigate it. However, tuning and configuring NT might require further research on your part.

The entire purpose of the operating system is so computer users can work with software applications. Software applications range from the standard fare of word-processing, database, and spreadsheet applications to a practically unlimited range of programs designed to do almost anything you

Application software

can think of. And there are thousands of applications available generating billions of dollars each year in the software industry.

The Software Publisher's Association says the leading categories sales-wise are word processors, spreadsheets, and databases in that order. Home education software was the fastest-growing category, and entertainment software is also showing significant market gains.

Of the word-processing programs, the leaders are Microsoft Word for Windows, WordPerfect for Windows, and Lotus' Ami Pro for Windows. Leading spreadsheet applications for Windows include Lotus 1-2-3, Microsoft's Excel, and Borland's Quattro Pro. The database leaders are Microsoft's FoxPro for Windows and Access for Windows, Borland's dBASE for Windows and Paradox, and Lotus' Approach.

If you're advising customers on a purchase decision, you'll want to consider recommending an integrated software tool set, such as Microsoft Office or Lotus Smart Suite. These sets offer word processor, database, spreadsheet, and communications functionality all for one low price. The applications in these tool sets are widely supported as well, so your users won't be left with some oddball application that nothing else works with.

Software support

A Dataquest survey of the consumer software market said just over 5 percent of home users are currently paying for software support, but a surprising 30 percent indicated their willingness to pay for such support. Those numbers are expected to increase as free support from vendors declines. Here's another opportunity for you, if you can gain a working knowledge of at least one of the leading products in each major category.

Rare indeed is the computer user who knows if a problem with an application is hardware or software related. Users don't care how you fix a problem as long as it's fixed. PC repair technician Tim Zimmerman, owner of Southern California-based MicroServ, said customers have no tolerance for a repair person who can't diagnose a software problem. "You have to know both the hardware and the software," he added. Fortunately, learning the software on the market is easier than you think due to the Common User Access standard, which allows you to translate the basic knowledge you gain from one application to others.

Common User Access (CUA)

The Common User Access (CUA) guidelines were set forth by IBM sometime back and have been adopted by the leading players in the software development community. The idea is to make things easier for computer users by making the user interface as much the same as possible across all applications.

As you can see from our earlier Windows figures, the menu options at the top of CUA compliant applications are: File, Edit, Search, Options. Pressing the Alt key and the first letter of the top row of options usually opens a "pull-down" menu. Each option in the menu can be accessed by then pressing the first letter of the menu item, so the keystrokes "Alt-F" then "O" allow the user to open a file.

You can also use the keyboard arrow keys to move to an option by pressing Alt, which will put you on the top menu, then moving with the left or right arrow key to the item you want and pressing the Enter key to open the menu. You can then move down to the menu selection with the down arrow and press Enter when the option you want is highlighted. Moving the mouse highlight to the items and clicking will work as well.

While every software tool you'll use might not conform to the CUA guidelines, pressure from the user community is forcing developers who didn't want to make the move to do so anyway. You'll find that the new DOS applications and software upgrades are using the CUA guidelines as well.

This standard has also driven software prices down, according to software company leaders such as Philippe Kahn, president and chief executive officer of Borland International. Kahn stresses that the CUA standard implemented in GUI interfaces, such as Windows, makes software programs so similar in appearance and functionality that the three leading software categories have almost become commodities.

As software prices fall, more home and small business users can afford the name-brand software used in a corporate environment. This is one of the factors that levels the playing field for the home user competing with large companies for business.

Shareware is the general term used for both true shareware software and "freeware" or "public domain" software. Because of the difficulty that has grown up around penetrating the retail distribution channels, many upstart software authors have decided to distribute their programs through an elaborate, grass roots system known as the shareware distribution channels. Software distributed in this manner is available in abundance.

Shareware & public domain software

Professional distribution houses have sprung up offering catalogs of shareware titles available, which they sell for a distribution fee that is routinely less than $10 a disk and sometimes is as low as $2 to $3 a disk. This is a service charge to you for making the disk available. Several Shareware vendors offer CD-ROM disks of their latest software titles on a monthly basis. We've included several Shareware sources for your convenience in appendix C. You'll also find shareware distributed at computer user groups, computer swaps, and on computer bulletin boards.

True shareware is software distributed on a try-before-you-buy basis. Authors place a statement in their software informing users to register if they like or use the software. Most authors try to keep registration costs low and offer added incentives for people to register. One of the biggest incentives for registration is to receive support and to be informed directly of updates to the program.

SemWare, makers of the QEdit text editor included with this text, and Apogee Software, which makes popular games, have built impressive software development companies by distributing their products in this manner. Shareware author George Campbell, developer of the Burn-In software included in this book, said that on the average, about 10 percent of the users of Shareware register their software.

Other software, developed with public monies or by generous software developers, is given away or placed in the "public domain" and is therefore called public domain (PD) software or freeware. The Eject utility included with this book is PD software. No registration fee is expected or required, and no support is offered.

Often shareware titles, distributed electronically or by a vendor involved in distribution, are compressed. All the files are squeezed into a single file with an unusual extension, such as .ZIP. If the title is "zipped," the shareware compression utility PKZIP from PKWare includes the PKUNZIP routine needed to decompress the software title. Other compression schemes are used as well, such as ARC from System Enhancement Associates, which places the .ARC extension on compressed files. You can expect anyone using compression to distribute software will offer a copy of the program needed to uncompress the titles.

Configuring software applications

Because of the hassle involved in setting up new software programs, you might find yourself being called in to do just that. The main advantage of Windows is programs written for the operating system do not have to be configured in as much detail. When installing non-Windows programs, it is necessary to tell the program about the type of monitor you have, the type of printer, whether or not you have a mouse, a sound card, and so on.

With Windows, all you have to do is make these selections once at installation. Then the application software program developed to run under Windows gets all that information from Windows directly. Windows can also buffer printing so you can keep working while printing.

How to run DOS applications under Windows   However, many applications that users want and need to run are DOS applications. Most users want to run their DOS applications under Windows, if they can. Your job will often be the one of setting up these DOS applications to run under Windows, especially in home and small business situations. It also might surprise you to discover that your customers will want you to set up their DOS-based games as well. This isn't easy to do.

DOS software applications, and especially games, have a tendency to bypass the operating system and talk directly to the hardware. This speeds up screen draws, which increases the action in the game—something game developers insist is a necessity.

This type of program is labeled "ill-behaved," while software that works through the operating system is "well-behaved." Ill-behaved software can also cause havoc in memory use, and memory conflicts can shut the system down, a fact that makes use of ill-behaved software in a multitasking environment impractical.

Games are also memory hungry and often cannot use memory above the lower memory available for DOS applications. If the computer user has disk compression, a CD-ROM drive, and other peripherals that might take up lower-memory space, the chances of getting a game to run under Windows are slim. The user might be able to exit Windows and then run the game. However, fewer and fewer users are willing to learn the DOS commands necessary to make DOS software work outside of Windows, which compounds the problem.

Conclusions

Finding out why the machine doesn't work requires knowledge of both the software and hardware. As we've seen, if the problem can be isolated to a software problem, then leaving the user with the problem because the hardware is fine will make for a less-than-satisfying experience for the customer.

Knowing Windows will help. There are books on Windows out there and again, a trip to the library first might save you time and money.

Now that we understand the terms, how the hardware works, and how the software works, we can talk about troubleshooting. That's what the next chapter is about—how to find the problems and the tools to fix them. We'll also talk about computer viruses, which can masquerade as hardware problems.

References

Hays, Laurie. July 2, 1993. "IBM's OS/2/2.1 Debut is Modest Success, but Launch of Rival Windows NT Looms." *The Wall Street Journal* pB5(W) pB2(E) col 1.

Manes, Stephen. 1993. *Gates: How Microsoft's Mogul Reinvented an Industry and Made Himself the Richest Man in America*. New York, New York: Doubleday.

Lindquist, Christopher. July 5, 1993. "Gates Says Windows NT is a Form of Unix." *Computerworld 27* (27): 15.

5 Hardware troubleshooting & tools

"Ability will never catch up with the demand for it."
— Malcom S. Forbes, publisher of the renowned semimonthly journal of business and finance, *Forbes* magazine.

It's time for you to go out on a service call. What now? This chapter is designed to give you a basis from which to start troubleshooting the computer hardware.

Because it's tough to talk about troubleshooting without mentioning tools, and vice versa, we'll do both. You'll learn which problems repair technicians see most often, and which tools you'll need. We'll list the hardware and software tools for you again at the end of the chapter, and in appendix C we'll list the vendors offering these tools.

In the beginning, we'll talk about the repair call itself, including questions you can ask on the phone before you go out that will help you take the right parts and tools. Then, starting with a dead PC, we'll lead you through the various levels of possible problems and solutions. But first we need to go over a basic threat to sensitive electronic equipment, and that is static electricity.

Static electricity

The first thing you have to be aware of before working on any electrical equipment is static electricity, also known as electrostatic discharge or ESD. This discharge can be dangerous in a computing environment because the charge in a single static electric shock is many times more than computer components are designed to handle. Less static electricity than you can feel is able to destroy delicate integrated circuits. Your body can be holding static electricity from when you combed your hair, put on a sweater, or walked across the carpet, and that electricity is just waiting to discharge.

The static charge is always looking for earth, so you should be grounded, or connected to something that will eventually lead the charge to the earth. Wrist straps are available for you to wear while working on a computer. These can be attached to the outside of the power supply, which is grounded through the electrical outlet. Static mats for your workbench are also available.

There are also bags, boxes, and foam products available to protect components from static electricity during transport. You'll see these packing products at any electronics supplier or at your computer dealer. You can also buy antistatic wipes for cleaning surfaces that hold your computer equipment.

Antistatic packaging, sprays for electronic equipment

Antistatic sprays are available to keep static electricity down in the vicinity of the PC. A spray bottle with a mix of fabric softener and water can also be used for static spray. It will pick up more dirt from the environment, but it can be used on carpet and used to wipe down surfaces near computer equipment.

The problem with some facilities you might visit during repair trips is the outlets might all be three-prong, but that third prong might not be connected to an earth ground. This is something to check for in older buildings where it appears that the wiring has been upgraded. Figure 5-1 depicts a wrist

How to check for a ground

5-1
This wrist strap not only grounds you to protect computer equipment from stray static charges, but it also checks the outlet and determines if a true ground is present.

Jenson Tools

grounding system from the Jensen Tool catalog that also checks the outlet to be sure the receptacle is properly wired. It can be used with the wrist strap provided or with other wrist straps as well.

Investigation

It's diagnosing the problem, not the actual fix, that often takes the time and requires the most expertise when it comes to PC repair. Most subassembly repairs take less than half an hour for the experienced technician and some can be done in under fifteen minutes, such as replacing a power supply or a floppy disk drive. Even replacing an entire motherboard can take less than an hour. It's finding the problem that's the challenge.

Use your senses

Your best allies in finding a problem in a system are your own senses and your powers of deduction. When a suspect PC starts, you will gain experience listening for that light, crackling sound that indicates power is reaching the display tube in the monitor, even though the screen is still blank.

You'll want to listen for the fan motor, reach behind the PC to feel for a draft of air from the fan, look for the lights, listen for the whirring sound from both floppy disk drives, look for a flash of the lights on the keyboard, and listen for the beeps the computer makes as it starts. When there are problems, you'll be visually scanning the components while using your sense of touch to search for bent pins, loose connections, or a chip that's farther out of its socket than the others. As you gain experience, you'll know how things should look, sound, and feel, and your senses will be the first to tell you something isn't right.

Standard steps in a repair situation

Your deductive powers will come into play when you take the information you gain from doing your own analysis, the information you might glean from the customer, and your own knowledge of how the system functions to come up with a diagnosis. In the pursuit of a repair you might perform several or all of the following steps, usually in this order.

1. Ask questions (over the phone, if possible) about the problem.
2. Research any documentation that might apply.
3. Attempt to reproduce the problem.
4. Perform investigative tests.
5. Come up with a diagnosis.
6. Act on the diagnosis (fix the problem).
7. Attempt again to reproduce the problem (a check that the fix worked).
8. Identify ways to prevent future problems.

With a little experience, these steps will become second nature to you. Most of them are obvious. However, we'll give you some tips on a couple of them before we get into the actual hardware troubleshooting itself.

Questions to ask

If the PC won't boot, you have a different set of problems on your hands than if it will boot. The person who operates the computer in question is a primary source of information. You want to locate that person and ask a few key questions.

One of the assumptions you might make is that the computer or subassembly in question worked at one time. Don't make that assumption. The first line of inquiry is to find out if the computer worked before and if so, if it functioned properly then. If it hasn't worked before, that fact takes a good deal of pressure off you in your attempts to make it work now. It also means you're on your own in getting it to work.

If it has worked in the past, you're second question is, "When did it stop working?" If you discover that the computer stopped working after the big storm last night, or after some other significant event, then you've got a significant clue as to where to look for the problem.

Ask what the computer is or isn't doing. What you want is a detailed description of the symptoms. While some users might try to give you a diagnosis, you need to search for symptoms with a question such as, "Did you see any lights come on? Does it beep? Describe to me what happens when the problem occurs."

Another key question is, "What were you doing just before it stopped working?" What you're looking for is any software or hardware installed recently that could be causing the problem. If the machine was moved from one location to another, perhaps a cable wasn't reconnected or a card was jarred loose.

Find out if the current problem has occurred before. If so, you'll want to know if there's been any repair done previously on the system and if so, what steps were taken. Even if previous repairs were made, you are still in a position where you have to proceed as though no other repair had been attempted. You will want to proceed with greater caution, however, if you discover you're the third repair person who's been called on to fix this problem.

If manuals or documents that came with the computer, the peripherals, or the software in question are available, you'll want to have the user provide those to you. As you progress through the repair, you might want to refer to the documentation for hints, settings the user might have overlooked, support phone numbers, and other hints that might give you a clue to correcting the problem.

For example, you might find that the documentation clearly states that the software the user was trying to install needed a minimum amount of RAM, which wasn't available, and that was the problem. As you proceed with your investigation and the answer to the problem is not obvious, look for those, "Oh, by the way . . ." items in the documentation, as they might hold the answer. Of course, some users keep everything that came with the computer and meticulously file it away, while others don't. You can't expect users to have the documentation. That might be why they called you. You'll need to be prepared to brave forth on your own.

- How has it worked in the past?
- When did it stop working?
- Did you see any lights?
- Does it beep?
- Describe to me what happens when the problem occurs.
- What were you doing just before it stopped working?
- Has this problem occurred before?
- Was the computer repaired before?
- Where is the documentation?

Attempt to reproduce the problem

Once you've determined the symptoms and asked your questions, you want to attempt to reproduce the problem. If need be, have the client stay with you to instruct you on what actions are necessary to make the problem reoccur.

If you can reproduce the problem, then you've got something definite to work with. If you can't, then you might have an intermittent problem, which is the hardest kind to solve. The actions you take to try to diagnose the problem depend now on the symptoms the client gave you and your own knowledge and experience. We'll talk about symptoms and possible causes next.

Fatal errors

If the computer won't get through the POST and boot sequence, you have what's known as a "fatal error." Sometimes the problem is easy to pinpoint; sometimes it isn't. Your experience will be the biggest help to you, but here are some tips on what to look for.

Dead PC

If the computer shows no signs of life when the power is turned on, then it is obviously not getting any power. This is your classic "dead" PC syndrome. The probability is high that a switch is simply off or the machine is not plugged in.

Avoid embarrassment   While going through the step-by-step procedure described next might seem boring and obvious, you only have to be embarrassed once before you vow you'll never skip one of these steps again.

Check power cord   The most obvious is the system isn't plugged in, so you need to check that the power cord is plugged into the unit and into the wall outlet. If you have something else in the room that you can plug into the outlet to see if it works, such as a lamp, do that next. If the outlet is dead, there's your problem.

Check power strip   Power strips that sit under the monitor and control power to the computer are popular. You'll need to check that the PC's plugs are plugged into the power strip and that the power strip is plugged into the wall outlet. Check that the switches on the power strip are on and that the "master" switch is on.

The power strip often has a reset button on it, and an electrical surge can cause the unit to shut itself off from the incoming power. Pressing the reset button, usually located on the back, might get it working again. Switches on many power strips wear out after constantly being turned on and off, so you might try plugging the computer directly into the wall without the power strip and see if it works.

Check computer's power switch   It's common for the monitor and the printer, also plugged into the power strip, to work when the computer won't. That can be because someone turned the computer off directly at the switch located near the power supply or on the front of the computer, instead of using the power strip. You'll want to check that switch and make sure it's on.

The next thing to try is to try moving the plug of the item that is not working to another plug on the power strip. If that works, then you know the problem was the particular outlet socket on the power strip.

Check power supply   If it's just the PC that doesn't work and you can determine that a peripheral, such as the printer, is getting power, then it's time to look at the PC's internal power supply. Some monitors get their power from the computer's power supply, so if the computer is not getting power, the monitor might not work either.

You'll want to check the back of the case to see if the power supply fan is running, though you probably would have heard it. If the fan isn't running, it can be replaced, but a nonoperational power supply fan could mean the power supply has suffered from heat problems and needs replacement anyway. Internal components in the PC could also have suffered to excessive heat as well. If the fan is running, you'll need to check the voltage coming from the power supply by opening up the case.

Always be sure the computer is off before you open the case. You might want to physically pull the plug out of its connection to the power supply to be sure. On most PCs, you'll need a Philips screwdriver to get into the case by removing the screws that hold the top of the case, then sliding the case off from the front. Some of the tower models from IBM and Acer don't have screws, but open more like a book, with one side opening downward, revealing the interior.

You'll need a multitester, like the one depicted in Fig. 5-2, to test the output from the power supply. You can also use a digital multimeter, which offers numerical output. There are pocket-sized versions of both multitesters and digital multimeters available from sources such as the Jensen Tool catalog or retail electronics outlets such as Radio Shack.

5-2
A multitester is an essential piece of equipment for testing voltage, such as that from the power supply.

The power supply puts out voltages of 12 and 5 volts, routinely with both positive and negative polarities. To check the voltages, pull one of the power connectors from either a floppy or hard drive. This is a small 4-pin connector, usually made of a clear plastic material. If you look at the end of the connector going to the power supply, you will notice the corners are notched on one side, as in Fig. 5-3. If the connector is turned so the notches face

5-3
The connector from the power supply to components such as floppy disk drives is notched so it will only fit the connection one way. If you connect the probes from the multitester to the connections, you can measure to see that voltage within the proper range is being generated.

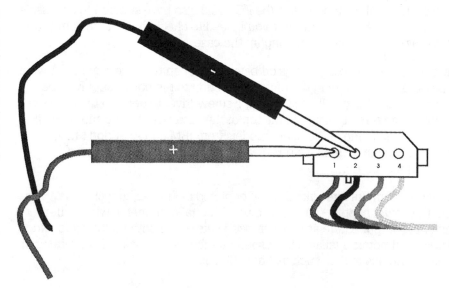

upward, the pins will be numbered 1, 2, 3, 4, and the following voltages should be present +12 volts direct current (Vdc), –12 volt return, +5 Vdc, and –5 volt return. You want to connect the probes of the multitester or multimeter to the power connectors from the power supply to see what voltage is being generated. Set the tester on direct current (dc), and be sure to correctly connect the probes.

Caution: Never plug in the power supply without it being connected to at least one other device; it could explode. To operate correctly, the power supply needs to be connected to something, such as a floppy disk drive, so it has a "load."

Acceptable power supply voltage levels   Each pair of wires, starting from pin 1 outside of the connector, carries either 5 volts or 12 volts. Anything from 4.5 to 5.5 volts and between 11.5 to 12.5 volts is acceptable. Voltages above and below those values indicate the power supply should be replaced.

Check for a short in a subassembly   A short in one of the items connected to the power supply could also be the culprit. To check, unplug the plastic power connections from each subassembly one at a time (the hard disk drive, each floppy disk drive, the motherboard), then plug in the power to the power supply.

If the power supply begins working after unplugging one of the subassemblies, confirm that this is the location of the short by plugging in the power connection again to that subassembly and then plugging in the power supply. You know you've found the subassembly with the short if, once again, the computer refuses to start. Once you've determined the subassembly with the short, you need to determine if it is cost effective to attempt to have it fixed or to simply replace the subassembly.

POST errors

If the computer has power and it appears something is happening, but it won't boot, the power on self-test (POST) is the place to look next. If you're getting beeps, but no boot and nothing on the monitor, you'll need to look at the codes for the particular BIOS in that computer.

Audible BIOS error codes   Unfortunately, all the audible BIOS codes are not the same. Some of the most popular audible codes are listed in Fig. 5-4. If you have the documentation that came with the computer, you can look up the POST codes.

Most of the PC repair technicians we interviewed have memorized the basic audible POST routines for the BIOSs they work with most often. They've said that by listening to the beeps and noting where the computer hangs up during the sequence, they feel they can isolate the area at fault.

Observe the POST sequence   Neil Wyenn of CPR Computer Repair of Granada Hills, California says he can usually tell where the problem is by

Common audible beep codes

1 short beep	POST test passed
No beep	Power supply or speaker
Beep doesn't stop	Power supply or motherboard
Short, repetitive beeps	Power supply or motherboard
1 long beep, 1 short beep	Power supply or motherboard
1 long beep, 2 short beeps	Motherboard
2 short beeps	Video
2 long beeps	Keyboard

observing the POST. Neil said if the keyboard lights flicker then stay on, and the computer doesn't make it the rest of the way through the POST, then he knows the problem has something to do with the keyboard. However, the keyboard error can also be caused by a short in the mouse or a fault in the keyboard controller circuits on the motherboard, and not necessarily be a problem with the keyboard itself.

POST cards   But there is another way. Various vendors offer POST cards—circuit boards that fit into a slot on the PC and offer a two-digit numerical code that lights up on the board to indicate the error. BIOS POST cards are set to the memory address that the BIOS issues its codes on, use the PC's power, and simply report the BIOS codes as they're generated. When a code "sticks" on the display, that's the code for the error. The vendors also offer a manual with popular BIOS codes and the accompanying meanings.

Some POST cards, such as the POST Probe from Micro 2000, and the QuickPostPC card from UltraX (Figs. 5-5 and 5-6) also offer lights to indicate the voltages from the power supply. Micro 2000 and the PocketPOST card from Data Depot also offer an adapter for use in PCs with the Microchannel architecture.

ROM POST cards   ROM POST cards are also available, and these cards have their own ROM BIOS. UltraX offers the Professional Hardware Diagnostics (P.H.D.) 16 with its own ROM, and Landmark has ROM POST, also with its own ROM. In order to use the independent ROM feature, you must exchange the ROM chip that comes with the software with the BIOS chip currently on the motherboard, although you can simply use the card as it is and read the BIOS codes. To do the exchange, you can use a chip-puller or a flat-head screwdriver to get under the chip on the motherboard and gently pry it up.

The big advantage in using a diagnostic card with its own ROM BIOS is if the ROM BIOS of the PC is bad, the system's components can still be tested. UltraX markets the Professional Plus as its premium diagnostic hardware product, offering the capabilities to perform a "burn-in," or extended test on component-level repairs. It can also be used to put in hours of testing to spot intermittent problems.

5-5
The POST Probe card from Micro 2000, shown with carrying case and Microchannel Architecture (MCA) adapter.

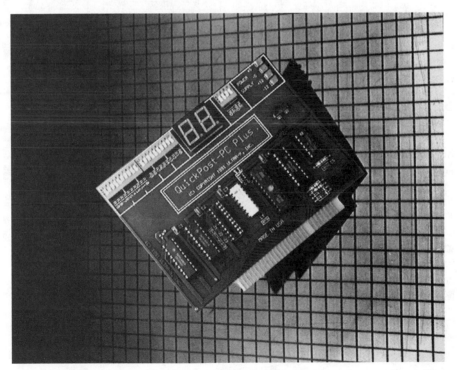

5-6
The QuickPostPC Plus POST card from UltraX.

American Megatrends, Incorporated (AMI) also offers a diagnostic card, the AMIDiag. This card comes with additional RAMLess Monitor chips, and so it works even if there is no RAM on the system. However, you do need a working CPU and a working serial port. The product requires you to connect a serial cable from the COM (serial) port of one system to the COM port of a working system and load the software VDEBUG that comes with the product. You also need to replace the ROM BIOS chips with the RAMLess ROMs provided by AMI. The serial link allows you to send commands to the system in question to determine the problem.

Either way, the cards put on an impressive light show for your client. Most experienced repair technicians have a POST card, but many said once they became familiar with the POST codes, they didn't feel a need to use the card. POST cards run anywhere from $100 plus to over $500. The ROM diagnostic cards are the most expensive.

POST keyboard error   If the problem is a keyboard error, make sure nothing is holding down any of the keys of the keyboard and check that the keyboard and mouse are plugged in securely. If you can, swap keyboards, either using one you have with you or swapping with another nearby PC, to be sure the keyboard is the source of the problem. If swapping doesn't make the problem go away, try swapping the mouse.

A sticking key on the keyboard could cause the error. If so, pry the key loose and clean underneath it. If it's the spacebar, forget it. The spacebar on most keyboards has springs underneath and if you get it off, your chances of getting it back on are just about nil. Some spacebars won't come off without breaking, which means a new keyboard.

Duplicate keystrokes using the ASCII character set   You can recreate a key if you need to, duplicating the key by pressing down the Alt key and entering the ASCII numeric code for the character on the numeric keypad. The numeric (decimal) values of the ASCII characters are available in appendix D. For example, Alt+65 will produce uppercase "A" and Alt+32 is a space. You might make a photocopy of the ASCII table and keep it with you for reference.

Washing a keyboard   You can wash a keyboard if you disconnect it from the computer, vacuum it out first, and then use plenty of distilled water. It is important to use distilled water because tap water has chemicals in it that will be left when the water evaporates, and those chemicals can create connections in the keyboard that weren't intended, causing a malfunction. Make sure the unit is completely dry before plugging it back in.

Obviously, washing a keyboard is a time-consuming procedure and one you probably wouldn't bother with if the keyboard is not an expensive one. Proprietary PCs often have specialized keyboards that are expensive, so it might be cheaper for you to spend some time cleaning the unit than to simply replace it. Since the cost of a new keyboard for most clone PCs is less than $20, there's not much repairing or cleaning you can do before you exceed the replacement cost.

POST video error If the POST indicates an error in the video, it's time to start checking connections. Check the connections in the back of the PC, especially if the unit has recently been moved, as a pin in the video connector might have gotten bent when it was reinserted into the video port.

Monitor on, but screen blank If the monitor comes on, but is blank, that's a problem with either the connection or the video card. You'll need to check both. Hopefully, you've inquired over the phone so you have an idea you might need a video card and have an extra one with you.

Reseat the video card Before you swap video cards, check the connection between the video card and the monitor and reseat the video card. Reseating the card means securing it down into the slot with even pressure across the top of the card.

You might also pull the card out, and using a number-two pencil with a new eraser, rub the eraser on the contacts at the bottom of the card in an effort to clean them. Be sure to "erase" or rub the contacts away from the computer so the erasings don't get down inside the case. Also, avoid rubbing away the metal on the contacts, and avoid touching the contacts of any card with your hands. You don't want oil and contaminants from your skin on those contacts.

Try a new video card Should you decide to try another video card, you might have to reset switches on the motherboard to accommodate a new video card or go into the setup and change the video, should it be different from the one already in the computer. The documentation for the computer should tell you. If you're not sure, try the setup first. If you have the Micro House Technical Library or a similar resource, it might help you to have printed out the information on the particular motherboard so you know the switch settings and the BIOS setup information before you go on site.

POST motherboard error If the error is a motherboard error, you can try reseating all the cards, checking for loose connections, and looking for physical cracks to the motherboard caused by heat. Chips sometimes "walk" meaning they move up out of their connections due to temperature changes that cause the motherboard to expand when warm and contract when cold. You should gently, with your thumb, push down on those chips on both ends in an attempt to get them to make contact again.

POST memory error If you get a memory error during the POST, also known as a parity error, you need to look at the memory chips. Remember that during the POST, the BIOS only checks the first bank of RAM, so if you get an error very early on that stops the POST, you can anticipate that the first bank of memory could be at fault.

You could get a parity error toward the end of the boot up process, when the computer is testing the rest of its memory. An error at that point makes memory past the first bank suspect. You'll want to note any address that might be given with a parity error, as that might prove to be a location in the bank of RAM that is at fault. Memory locations are given in hexadecimal (base 16) so you might want to get a calculator that can do hex-to-decimal conversions. Hex-to-decimal conversion tables are also available in those portable reference books with hard drive tables we've already mentioned, such as the *Pocket PCRef* from Sequoia Publishing.

Memory-chip testing equipment   The Jensen Tool catalog carries memory-chip testing equipment. These devices not only check the chips, but they also can be set to warm the chips before testing. Warming the chips allows you to recreate the environment the chip is running in and check for intermittent errors.

Memory test software diagnostics   Several commercial diagnostic software programs can also test the memory chips, should the boot process get far enough along that you can run them. These programs can even pinpoint the location of the problem. Tech Assist of Clearwater, Florida carries a variety of software tools aimed at specific troubleshooting tasks, including Ramalyzer. Ramalyzer is bootable in order to keep DOS out of the way while it checks RAM. The program can be configured to run multiple passes over all the RAM or just portions that are suspect in order to find the defective chips.

Other end-user tools, such as Winsleuth Gold Plus from Cypress, California-headquartered Dariana Software also test memory. Winsleuth and others can even display a graphical view of the motherboard, identifying the bad memory chip or chips. The problem with Winsleuth and end-user products like it is they require time to install and take up several megabytes of disk space. Winsleuth requires Windows 3.1, 4MB of hard disk space and 3MB of RAM. So while these products offer captivating animations, information to help users add components, and helpful utilities, they're not aimed at the serious PC technician, but at the end user. Generally, it is better to have one all-around diagnostic tool that can be run from a single floppy disk.

POST hard disk error   If the computer gets all the way through its other tests, but still won't boot, you could see a message like this, "Cannot Read Drive C: (A)bort, (R)etry, (F)ail?" or a hard disk failure message. The thing to do in this case is to insert a bootable floppy disk into the A: drive and try to boot again.

You'll want to use either bootable PC diagnostic software, such as PC-Technician from Windsor Technology, QuickTech from UltraX, Micro Scope from Micro 2000, or one of the other bootable PC diagnostics available. You can also use a bootable DOS floppy, but be sure you're using the same version of DOS as the version on the computer in question. Booting from a different

DOS version can damage the data on the hard disk. Always ask the clients if they have a bootable floppy disk or know what version of DOS they have.

If there are other PCs in the immediate area that have the same DOS version, you might want to create a bootable floppy using the DOS command "FORMAT A: /S" where the /S copies the system files to the floppy disk. Some technicians carry four or five bootable disks made with the most popular versions of MS-DOS (or PC-DOS if they work on IBM equipment). A set of such bootable disks would include DOS 3.3, DOS 4.1, DOS 5.0, DOS 6.0, MS-DOS 6.22, and PC-DOS 6.3. You'll also want to copy over from the DOS directory the appropriate DOS software commands.

Attempt to access the hard disk   Once you have a system disk or bootable floppy, boot from it and see if you can access the hard disk drive. If the system is set in the BIOS to access the C: drive first, you will need to enter the BIOS setup and change that so the computer accesses the A: drive first.

Once you've booted from the floppy, type C: and see if you can access the hard disk drive. If you can, the first step is to check for viruses. Most of the diagnostic software packages have virus-checking programs included, and there are shareware virus-checking programs as well.

Check for viruses   You'll want to do your virus check from a copy of the virus program and not the original disk. In fact, you'll want to do everything on a strange PC with copies of your original programs so that if a virus is found you can destroy the disks. We'll talk more about virus infection later in this chapter.

Check for the DOS kernel   If no viruses are found, you'll want to see if the DOS kernel is still there. Sometimes a prankster or an inexperienced user gives the command "DEL *.*" and deletes the DOS kernel. You can check for those files by running the directory command with the /A option, "DIR /A," which shows you all the files whether they are hidden or not.

You can also run the DOS command CHKDSK, and it will also tell you there are two hidden files, if those DOS kernel files are there. If the hidden files are not there, type "A:\SYS C:" to have the IO.SYS, MSDOS.SYS, and COMMAND.COM kernel copied from the floppy disk drive back to the C: drive.

Check hard disk controller   If the software cannot recognize that a drive is there, you'll need to check the hard disk controller card, both to make sure it is mounted securely in the slot and to see if the cables are properly connected. Look for the number 1 printed on the card near the connection to the floppy drive controller, then check to see if the colored stripe on the ribbon cable is on the side where the number 1 is on the connector. That colored stripe represents pin 1 on the cable. The stripe on the cable always goes to pin 1, so check this on the other cable connections as well.

The controller card could be bad as well, so you'll need to check. You'll want to get a copy of the CMOS settings before you remove the controller card from the slot. If you power up again with the controller card absent or the hard disk cables unattached, some PCs forget the CMOS settings for the hard disk drive. Check your diagnostic software for a copy CMOS command or simply print out the CMOS using the "Print Screen" key on the keyboard.

It is possible that the cable is just too near a heat source that also puts out electrical signals and that can cause intermittent data problems. We had a problem with a hard disk drive where, once the computer warmed up, we'd get a read/write error. We checked the drive, the cables, and the controller only to notice that one of the cables from the hard disk drive was laying across the top of the CPU. When we moved the cable away from the CPU, the errors stopped.

In addition, some of the hard disk controller cards are not compatible with CPU chips from manufacturers other than Intel. We know of another case where the hard disk drive on a motherboard based on a Cyrix 486 CPU wouldn't boot. Everything else worked fine, and the user, who was building the computer, was perplexed until he took the motherboard back to the supplier.

He discovered it was an incompatibility with the hard disk controller card, so he replaced the card and the system worked fine. Presumably, this problem wouldn't come up on a repair because the hard disk drive worked to begin with. But if you're called in on a repair and your controller card doesn't work on a clone-based system, you might have to check with the manufacturer of the card or the CPU to see if an incompatibility is involved.

Can't access drive, check for partition table   If you cannot access the drive, perhaps the partition table has been damaged or deleted. If you're using a software diagnostic tool, it might tell you a drive is there, but no partition table has been found, and it might ask if you'd like it to recreate the partition table. If you get this far, there's a good chance you'll be able to get the drive working again. The software will usually walk you through the rest of the steps at this point. You can also use the DOS command FDISK to check for the partition. We cover that in detail in chapter 6.

Let the drive warm up   When you open the case, power up the unit and see if you can hear the drive spin up. If not, you might have a drive with a bad motor or sticking heads. If the heads are sticking to the surface of the platters, sometimes it works to allow the drive to warm up, leaving the power on for a while, which might warm up the surface enough for the heads to loosen. This is more of a problem on older hard disk drives. If the user reports the drive works sometimes and other times it doesn't, this "sticktion" might be the problem. If the user reported a burning smell before the hard drive quit, you might have found a drive with a bad motor.

If the battery fails, the computer is going to forget everything because all of the CMOS settings will be lost. It won't boot from the hard disk drive and it won't know what time it is. It usually will boot from a floppy, however. In this case, you need to install a new battery. If the battery is soldered onto the motherboard, you're going to be faced with resoldering the battery.

Fortunately, more recent PCs offer batteries that are more easily replaced, but they vary from watch batteries to "AA" or 9-volt types. You might not know until you get there what type of battery you need. If you have a technical reference such as the Micro House Technical Library, you might be able to find the motherboard and the battery type there.

Once the battery is replaced, you'll need to reconfigure the CMOS to include the hard disk drive and the types and capacities of the floppy disk drives. This is where a hard disk reference guide comes in handy. If you are using a diagnostic program such as Micro 2000's MicroScope, then the software will attempt to talk to the hard disk drive directly to tell you the CMOS settings and even allow you to set the CMOS from within the program.

Stephen Bigelow is an electrical engineer, editor of two newsletters on troubleshooting PCs, and author of several books on computer repair. His experience with computer repair problems has lead him to opinions and insights into the repair business, especially in the area of component-level repair.

The trend in PC repair is away from "component" repair, or the replacement of individual parts. Instead, technicians are moving toward replacing an entire portion of the PC, which can include replacing circuit boards, and is termed "subassembly" repair. The main exceptions are in monitor repair and high-end electronics.

The cost of the component, the cost of the labor involved, the cost of the repair shop's overhead, and the needed profit margin to stay in business are the determining factors in whether or not a repair technician will choose to repair a damaged component or replace it. Technicians simply have to generate a certain volume of tested equipment per hour in order to make a living.

For example, Stephen estimated the cost to bring something in and have it fixed can be $50 or $60 an hour. When you consider it takes two hours to troubleshoot a part and it turns out the part is a $3 part, you can spend three hours, or $180 in labor, to replace a $3 part. That three hours includes finding the bad component, replacing it, and spending an hour testing.

On the other hand, if you're relatively certain the problem is on the motherboard, you can replace a motherboard in a half-hour, with an hour minimum labor charge. Even if the motherboard is a relatively new one, Stephen maintains that the cost of the average motherboard replacement

Dead battery—Lost CMOS settings

Why subassembly repair is replacing component-level repair

would be in the $200 range. So then there's no need to waste three hours of a technician's time.

Component-level repair has also become difficult, even if the problem component is easy to find, due to a lack of availability. One of the facts of life about PCs in general is they become obsolete very quickly. The net result of that is a small spare-parts market. Most of what is considered to be spare parts are coming from the original manufacturer.

In addition, once the faulty component is isolated, it falls on the technician to know what product to order. "It's not unusual to find a 15-digit part number that represents a simple 2K resistor. And there's no rhyme or reason to the part code," Bigelow said.

If you do know what to order, you might still face obstacles. Manufacturers often take a "quantum leap" from the individual components to a finished product. "If you don't know the manufacturer's bureaucracy, it can be tough to acquire a certain part," Stephen maintains.

Another problem in getting components is many of the parts are made overseas. For example, manufacturers of hard drive controllers might not have any individual parts available; that stock might be overseas.

Subassemblies tend to be more available than the individual products, and the chances are they'll be inexpensive. For example, it is not necessarily in the interest of a manufacturer of hard drive controller boards to provide the components to make another hard drive controller. That manufacturer would rather sell another hard drive controller than provide the parts to repair an old one.

Intellectual property issues can inhibit you from getting a needed part, even if you overcome other obstacles. This gets real "sticky" with custom integrated circuits (ICs) where they can be exclusive to a particular manufacturer. "If you know a highly integrated ASIC (application specific integrated circuit) has gone bad, you might not be able to get it because ASICs are proprietary," Stephen added.

In addition, subassembly repair takes less equipment. The problem can be isolated to a subassembly, and that means you don't need expensive equipment such as an oscilloscope, which is used to isolate specific problems in components. Stephen noted that many of the diagnostic software products available can do a very good job of narrowing down the problem, so the technician knows what subassembly to replace.

A repair shop should keep their parts, or subassembly inventory, to a minimum. The proliferation of parts these days makes it practical to only stock a few, standard components. "It's very impractical to stock parts because you don't know what parts to stock," Stephen advised. "You're better off to invest your effort developing contacts and your resources. If a SCSI (small computer system interface) adapter fails, what vendors offer the most for the lowest price? Let the manufacturer stock the parts. Your facility should be a technical facility."

Nonfatal errors

You'll find a number of errors or problems with computers that won't shut the machine down, but they will cause headaches for users. Some of these problems are intermittent, such as power supply fluctuations that can cause data loss. Others are more consistent, such as a floppy disk drive out of alignment. Again, finding the problem is the biggest challenge.

Run diagnostic software

One of the first things you'll want to do, assuming you can get the system to boot from a floppy disk, is run diagnostic software. This gives you a glimpse inside of the box and can help you make decisions about how to proceed next.

If you have MS-DOS 6.0, you can run Microsoft Diagnostics with the MSD command. Several professional, bootable tools are available that will also give you system information, such as: AMIDiag from American Megatrends, Incorporated (AMI); MicroScope from Micro 2000; PC-Technician from Windsor Technologies; QuickTech from UltraX; and others. These products are designed to be portable and fast. They contain a suite of tests and utilities to help you determine what is wrong with the system. These tools are listed in appendix C, as well as summarized at the end of this chapter.

We've also included in our shareware tools Snooper, a diagnostic tool from San Francisco, California-based Vias & Associates. Snooper is fast. It will give you a look inside the box, and it will create a log file of the configuration of the PC it is run on, which includes a complete listing of the environment files. The program lists the processor, memory, video cards, operating system version, and drives, both physical and logical. The complete manual for Snooper is in appendix C.

Intermittent errors could be from power supply

Power supplies are the culprit for many data loss and error problems that get blamed on software or on the hard disk drive. If the voltage the unit is putting out falls below the prescribed level, it can cause data to not be written to the disk or to be lost from memory. If the power level is too high, it can cause components to run at higher temperatures than normal and result in premature part failure.

Manufacturers will often use a power supply with the minimum amount of power in a PC, so if you add on peripherals that require additional power, the power supply might be overloaded. Most power supplies have a wattage label that you can check against the additional power needed by the installed boards. The rule of thumb is it's better to have a larger power supply than you need, rather than one that's just adequate or too small.

Veterans of the repair business have said over and over to check the power supply, especially when intermittent errors in the hard disk drive or other components show up. We've replaced power supplies on an educated hunch, even though the unit appeared to be putting out the correct amount of voltage when checked, and we have seen hard disk drive read/write errors go away. This can occur when the system demand for power is very near the wattage the power supply can provide. Power supplies can also be the culprit if the serial ports don't function correctly.

You can check the power supply over a period of time with PC PowerCheck, available for under $270 from Data Depot. This diagnostic card can either be placed into an empty slot on the PC or used alone to test a power supply without the PC. The card has a row of green lights that can be seen from the back of the computer. If all is well, the four lights will be on. But if there's too much voltage (overvoltage), too little voltage (undervoltage), too much noise (or ripple), or a power spike, then the green light on the line where the problem occurred will go out. Further, the card will indicate what occurred by lighting one of four yellow or red lights available for each voltage line.

Intermittent floppy disk drive problems

Floppy disk drives wear out. While they can be fixed, it depends on what a new floppy disk costs for the system in question as to whether or not the drive is worth repairing. As we said earlier, Compaq and IBM make its PCs with floppy disk drives that have proprietary connectors to the system and therefore will be significantly more expensive than standard disk drives. So it might make sense to repair, rather than replace, those drives. For example, IBM's PS/1 model PC uses a 3.5-inch floppy that was made especially for this unit. A replacement drive for the PS/1 is about four times the cost of a standard 3.5-inch drive.

One of the most frequent problems is the drives get out of alignment. There is controversy in the repair business as to whether or not software programs designed to align floppy disks can do so with enough accuracy to make it worthwhile. You can tell a drive is out of alignment because data written to a disk in that drive cannot be read by other computers, and vice versa. Special alignment disks and software are available to help you adjust the alignment on a drive using a screwdriver until the heads are back within the tolerances of the software. Data Depot offers such a product, Floppy Tune, for under $250.

However, the disk drive read/write mechanism is an analog system, while the alignment program is a digital system. While the software system might allow a technician to bring the drive into the manufacturer's tolerances, the argument is that it doesn't address other areas of alignment and won't perform as well as an analog floppy disk alignment tool.

The analog floppy disk alignment tools, at $350 to $1,500, are a significant expense. Some tools also require use of an oscilloscope and an analog alignment disk, while others only require an analog alignment disk. A digital software tool is in the $200 range. Either way, it takes an investment in order to align floppy disk drives at all. When new high-density 1.44MB drives are under $35, most PC repair shops have said it is difficult to justify the expense of an alignment tool unless you work on a significant number of floppy disk drives. If you are interested, the Jensen Tools catalog carries several different analog and digital repair tools. Data Depot also carries software and special disk for aligning drives.

Sometimes floppy disk drives simply have dirty read/write heads. The heads get dirty by picking up particles from the disks that can include particles from cigarette smoke or other airborne contaminates. You can buy floppy drive head cleaning kits at almost any computer retail outlet.

The standard procedure is to clean the heads once a year and not weekly as some of the cleaning kits advise. You want a kit that uses a fluid that you put on a disk that has a clothlike linen instead of plastic inside. Then you put the disk in the drive and try to access the drive, usually by entering A: from the DOS prompt, the drive spins the cloth against the read head.

UltraX provides head-cleaning disks and solution with its QuickTech Professional diagnostic software. Micro 2000's MicroScope diagnostic software has a special head-cleaning algorithm that moves the head up and down over the disk's tracks so the head is more thoroughly cleaned.

We've also included Cleaner, a shareware program from Rosenthal Engineering that will do a thorough job cleaning the heads of your floppy disk drive. But be forewarned. The cleaning is intense, and bargain cleaning kits might fail you by leaving bits of the cleaning disk all over the inside of the drive. Cloth-based cleaning disks and isopropyl alcohol are recommended. Rosenthal also offers cleaning disks for purchase.

If you happen to get a machine that was sitting in someone's garage for a while or someplace else where it picked up a lot of dust, you will probably need to clean the area around the heads as well. This is because the dust around the heads will work it's way onto the heads. You can purchase compressed air to blow out the dust or use a small brush in a cleaning fluid for this purpose. If you're using a brush, go over the area again using a brush without the cleaning fluid to get any excess. It is important to get as much dirt removed as possible before you clean the actual heads.

As we said earlier, hard disk drives can be affected by heat and cold, especially older units. If the drive will boot when it is allowed to warm up, that's an indication.

Intermittent hard disk drive problems

If you check the drive using diagnostic software and the number of bad sectors is on the increase, this could mean the drive is getting ready to fail. Hard disk drives come with bad sectors marked by the manufacturer and some bad sectors can develop after a period of time. However, bad sectors should not be showing up on a frequent basis.

If a piece of data is stored in a sector that is growing difficult for the computer to read, it could cause problems. The severity of the problem depends on whether or not the data is a portion of the drive necessary for the computer to boot, an application program, or data the user has stored.

Of course, bad sectors can also be caused by bumping the computer or dropping it a short distance. Power dips from line power fluctuations or intermittent power supply failure can cause the heads to drag on the platters or increase the frequency of read/write errors.

Diagnostic products for hard disk drives   Several utility products are designed to test and identify bad sectors and can even move the data in a faulty area to another location on the drive. Norton Disk Doctor (part of the Norton Utilities), PC Tools, SpinRite, Disk Technician Gold, PC-Technician, QuickTech, MicroScope, AMIDiag, Optune and other diagnostics aimed at both the end user and the professional are equipped for the task.

The Norton Disk Doctor and SpinRite are very popular with repair technicians, but unfortunately some of these tools are turning into end-user tools that must be installed on the hard disk drive. Norton Utilities, PC Tools, and Disk Technician Gold are all moving toward the end-user tool market.

Hard disk drive diagnostic tips   In addition, you might give the diagnostic software manufacturer a call if you come up with increasing numbers of bad sectors being reported, especially if the drive doesn't display other problems. There are bugs in these software products as well, and you might have found one. You don't want to be replacing a drive because of faulty software.

Clark Waggoner of Clark Waggoner ComputerWorks in Oklahoma told us he ran into a situation like that with a product on a drive. He suspected a problem, so he switched software products and the other software reported no problems. A call to tech support revealed the first product had a bug that caused it to report bad sectors in a certain kind of RLL drive.

The last thing you want to do as a technician is spend time installing software on a drive you think is unstable; you might need that time to get data the user needs off the drive. You can use DOS utilities such as Check Disk (CHKDSK), a utility for spotting problems with the FAT and giving you information as to how the disk space is allocated, how much memory is available, and logical problems with the FAT. MS-DOS 6.22 offers ScanDisk (SCANDISK), a utility aimed at a more thorough inspection of the physical surface of the drive.

Is a low-level format required?   If bad sectors or missing data are a problem on a recurring basis, sometimes a low-level format can solve the problem. But this should be a last resort because it permanently destroys all data recorded on the drive. Also, low-level formatting can take hours.

You'll hear a lot about low-level formatting from vendors who have developed the ability to low-level format IDE drives. IDE manufacturers told the public that the drives could not be low-level formatted by the end-user, as Modified Frequency Modulation (MFM) and Run Length Limited (RLL) drives can.

Because the IDE drives have a feedback mechanism to make reads and writes occur along consistent tracks as the drive turns, the problems with older drives where formatted tracks would "drift" is not a problem with IDE. Drifting tracks meant data stored there could no longer be read.

However, the utility software developers have figured out how to do a low-level format of an IDE drive and are offering products you can use for that purpose. CheckIt Pro Tests & Tools from TouchStone Software, MicroScope from Micro 2000, and QuickTech Professional from UltraX are some diagnostic programs that will low-level format IDE drives.

Checks to make before installing a new hard drive   If you end up installing hard disk drives, you'll need to be sure the BIOS of the PC can support the drive you plan to install. You might find yourself having to upgrade the BIOS in order to replace the hard disk drive on an older PC. Check with your hardware supplier first, making sure you have the model, the BIOS maker, version, and date to provide as background information. Older BIOS chips do not allow you to install the larger hard drives in use today. You might find yourself having to upgrade the BIOS in order to upgrade the hard disk drive on an older PC.

You might also need brackets to put a smaller drive in a bay that once contained a larger drive, especially if the old hard drive was a 5.25-inch drive and you're installing a 3.5-inch drive, so be sure to ask for those brackets. They should cost less than $5.

Hard disk installation software   As far as tools, there are some excellent software tools on the market to help. These tools are smart enough to guide you through the installation process, partitioning the disk, formatting, and setting up the CMOS. These tools are particularly helpful in setting up old drives, but on newer drives you probably won't need them and can simply use DOS.

One of the most popular third-party software tools is Disk Manager from OnTrack. PC-Technician, MicroScope, QuickTech, and other professional tools also provide similar functionality for installation of hard disk drives of any type. SpeedStor from Storage Dimensions is another highly rated installation tool. Most include documentation and help right there on the disk so you can go through and easily set up the drive. If you're installing IDE drives, these software tools can talk directly to the drive and can often get the information needed without any effort from you. These tools will save you many headaches and are highly recommended.

Intermittent memory errors

Intermittent errors in RAM can cause data loss, especially if the hard disk cache program, such as Windows' SmartDrive, is using that unreliable portion of RAM. Reading and writing to and from RAM that is unreliable can result in program and data files becoming corrupt and even damage to the FAT. These problems can make the hard disk drive look as though it was at fault. Other RAM-caused symptoms could be corrupted screen displays, problems with the operation of the mouse, or an inability to read from an installed CD-ROM drive. RAM is an area to check if the user is complaining about any of these symptoms.

Intermittent monitor problems

If the user is complaining about the appearance of the image on the monitor, it must be bad. Rarely do you hear users complain. If there are ripples or distortion in the on-screen image, it might be caused by something as simple as an electromagnetic source near the monitor. If monitors are too close together, even if they're on either side of a physical barrier such as a wall or a cubicle, each can affect the other. In addition, power sources near the monitor, such as a transformer for speakers attached to the computer, can cause this wavy, distorted effect. These magnetic fields, however small, are enough to affect the beam of electrons that is being projected onto the monitor.

The field produced by monitors is usually strongest from the sides or the back and decreases exponentially with distance. Two feet or more of separation between monitors is often enough to make the problem go away. The same distance from a transformer or other source of disturbance should solve the problem.

Other problems you might find include: missing characters, uneven or slow display, a jerky or skipping display, rolling, and other similar problems. If the characters on the screen are incorrect or missing, suspect the video adapter card. But if some of the pixels are the wrong color, then the monitor itself should be checked.

Intermittent errors in the ports

If the ports, serial or parallel, appear to be malfunctioning, the first step is to check the configuration of the software the user is attempting to use. Two devices set to the same port assignment will cause a conflict and neither will work. Windows allows you to configure the ports, both serial and parallel, for all Windows applications. Each DOS product must be individually configured to use a port.

On the serial port, you probably have a modem or pointing device hardware (such as a mouse) and telecommunications software or mouse drivers to deal with. On the parallel port, you're most likely dealing with a printer. If you are configuring telecommunication software, the software must be set to the correct serial or "COM" port, since there is often more than one.

Most of the diagnostic software packages will look at the serial ports, and will attempt to tell you what is using each port. A couple of the professional diagnostic software packages skip the last part because, technically, you can't really tell what's out there. The software that attempts to tell you what is using each port is making an educated guess based on widely adopted conventions for port memory addressing. Since it's an educated guess, the software might not always be right about what's out there.

There are devices that start at one COM port address but take up more than a single address, overlapping into the next COM port address. The overlap might be enough to cause a conflict and create problems, but the software might not be able to give you the overlap information. In our opinion, it is better to have an educated estimate of what's connected to the PC than none at all. Sometimes a visual inspection will tell you; it's fairly obvious when an external modem is attached to a PC.

For example, a user called recently saying the old bus mouse quit, so he bought a new serial mouse. The serial mouse worked fine in the DOS applications, but when he started Windows there was no mouse at all. This was easy to diagnose. The problem was in the way the mouse was configured in Windows, a conflict in the COM port settings.

Since the user had a bus port for the mouse and the bus mouse didn't cost anymore than the serial mouse, we advised that he trade the serial mouse for a bus mouse rather than change his Windows settings. We knew he had a modem and Windows telecommunications software, so going back to the bus mouse would avoid any further conflicts with the COM ports.

Parallel port errors   If the user is complaining about a printer problem, this falls to the category of parallel port difficulties. There could be several causes, including a malfunction with the port itself. It could be that the printer is not configured correctly for the software or not configured at all. Windows requires that you select a printer driver and a port, usually designated by LPT1 if there is only one parallel port.

A common mistake in setting up a printer that can use either a serial or a parallel port is to connect the printer from its serial port to the parallel port on the PC. This will produce garbled output. However, there are parallel cables sold that will work for this, since both ends offer 25-pin connectors—an arrangement that confuses new users. What the user often needs is a parallel to Centronics port interface, since most printers with both parallel and serial interfaces have a Centronics interface for the parallel port. Figure 5-7 depicts a standard Centronics connection on a parallel cable.

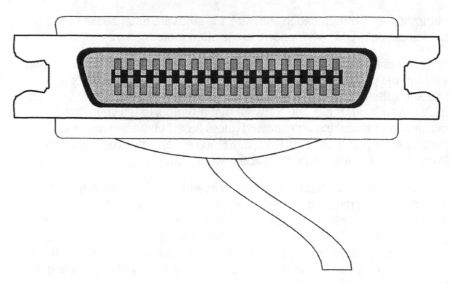

Another problem with laser and ink-jet printers is the printer can be accidentally configured in its internal software to only look for input from the serial port instead of the parallel port, or vice versa. It took us a trip down to Hewlett-Packard to discover this secret, and we have been careful to check to be sure the printer is properly configured ever since.

Troubleshooting mechanical port problems   A good piece of diagnostic software with loop-back plugs should help determine if there's a mechanical problem. Most of the professional software diagnostics, QuickTech, PC-Technician, MicroScope, include special loop-back plugs designed to fit the ports on the PC and work with the software to determine the problem.

With multi-I/O cards less than $20, it doesn't make sense to spend a lot of time fiddling with a bad port. The newest multi-I/O cards offer serial, parallel, game, IDE, and floppy drive interfaces all on the same card. You can use jumpers or dip switches, depending on the I/O card, to disable the functions you don't want.

If the ports are integrated into the motherboard, you should be able to set switches or move jumpers on the motherboard to disable the ports so you can use the expansion slots to install working ports. This is another instance where you'll need the documentation, either from the manufacturer, or from a third-party source such as Micro House.

Check the cabling   The cabling could be at fault if everything else is in order. You can use your multitester to test the cabling by disconnecting the cable, setting the meter to resistance, then touching one probe at a pin on one end and placing the other probe at the same pin on the other end. If you get a zero reading, the wire is OK. If the reading is infinity, then there is not a connection between the pins and you need a new cable. You might find it easier to carry extra cables that you know work for testing, along with "gender changer" plugs for the ends so you can change the ends of the cable to fit the situation as needed.

If you find yourself testing a lot of special or long cables, you might want to invest in a "breakout box" for cable testing. Serial ports are used to connect terminals to networks as well as to printers and modems. The breakout box actually lets you switch pin assignments so you can create different cabling setups and test existing ones. Breakout boxes provide a light show with as many as 100 light-emitting diodes (LEDs). A light glows for each pin that is receiving data. Most are portable for use on site, and gender changers are available. Many types are available, such as the Blue Box 100 RS-232 Breakout Box and Cable Tester from the Warwick, RI-based International Data Sciences (IDS) test equipment catalog.

The Small Computer Systems Interface (SCSI) is attractive because you can "daisy chain" as many as seven peripherals off a single SCSI interface and have them all work. This includes CD-ROM drives, hard disk drives, optical scanners, tape drives, and other devices. SCSI can also offer faster access to the peripheral in question. But problems with a SCSI device or port can be sticky since the interface is a "smart" interface that makes some decisions and must have some intelligence built-in, rather than a "dumb" interface like the serial or RS-232.

Small computer systems interface (SCSI)

For example, termination has been a big issue. Each SCSI device has a port on it to accommodate another SCSI device, which is how these devices can be chained together. If a special "cap" for the port, called a terminator, is not on the device at the end of the chain, or if it is removed and then the device is turned on, this can make the entire chain unoperational. Most of the time the terminator isn't removed unless the PC is moved or a device is either moved or removed from the chain. If the terminator problem arises, the computer case has to be opened and the SCSI card removed, reset, and reinserted to get the "chain" to work again.

Several products are available to help you troubleshoot, verify, and set up SCSI peripherals, including hard disk drives. Landmark Research International Corporation of Clearwater, Florida offers Landmark SCSI Certify with utilities for SCSI peripherals, especially hard disk drives. PC-Technician from Windsor will also help diagnose problems with SCSI hard disk drives and tape drives.

Neil Wyenn

CPR Computer Repair, Granada Hills, California

Neil Wyenn was a salesman for a computer disk drive manufacturer when he purchased CPR in 1987. While he bought CPR for a fifth of the asking price, he didn't know the company was dead and three of the remaining employees had given notice and were leaving within days of his actual ownership.

The only real assets were the four walls, a yellow pages ad, and the inventory. The two employees who remained were referring every phone call to other businesses, saying, "We don't do that."

That was the first problem he decided to tackle, Neil said. He asked the remaining technician if he could fix the items people were calling about, such as Apple and Commodore computers. The technician said he didn't know. Neil came to a compromise. "We decided to ask people if they'd be willing to bring the PCs in under the condition that if we could fix it, we'd charge the normal rates. If we couldn't fix it, we wouldn't charge them anything. So then [when a call came in] we could say 'yes,'" Neil said.

Neil then started going after authorizations. The business was already Epson and Leading Edge authorized, so he contacted AST, Citizen, Okidata, and NEC. "Once you have one authorization, it's easier to get others," Neil said. He's attended all the training classes required for authorization himself, then taught his technicians because he didn't want to lose the knowledge if he lost a technician. Authorization gives him the added advantage of having repair work referred to him by the vendors.

The printer authorizations were easier to get, Neil maintains. And once you know how to work on one, the others are all similar. This is especially true of laser printers, such as Canon, HP, Brother, Star, and Apple.

Neil says he's hired graduates of some of the technical schools but stopped because he found those students simply don't have the needed training. "Those schools would be better off just throwing a group of students in a room full of computers and parts. I've checked; those schools have old equipment that nobody has because they're too cheap to buy new or fairly new equipment," Neil added. He currently employs two technicians besides himself, two office people, and a bookkeeper.

As for location, Neil advises to open a small store in a place that has good parking in a nice industrial area near a major thoroughfare. "Make sure it's no more than two turns off the freeway," Neil said. Get a personable receptionist, make the front area look nice, and get a yellow pages ad, he added. Make sure there are no open computers where the customers can see them—don't let the customers see the repair side. "Let them walk into a business, not a fix-it shop," he said.

To keep up, Neil reads *Service News*, *Retail Week*, and vendor publications. He glances at as much as he can, but his time is at a premium. To make the most of his time, he telecommutes, doing his billing, payroll, and invoices at night from his laptop at home, connected by phone to his PC in the shop.

Neil said he feels that attempting to expand his current repair shop any further won't work. "I've filed almost the exact same tax return for three years now," Neil explained. To expand, he feels he'll have to open another store in a different location. And that's precisely what he plans to do.

Tools

You don't have to buy your tools in portable cases. You can probably carry all the tools you need to start with in a tough legal-size manilla envelope. But if you want to be taken seriously, you should begin investing in tools that are enclosed in portable carrying cases that make you look like you're serious about repair.

The tools you need include several sizes of Philips screwdrivers, several flat-head screwdrivers, long-nose pliers, one holding type of screwdriver that you can use to hold both slotted and Philips screws, a ¼-inch nut driver, and a small adjustable wrench. A small soldering iron is also needed if you run into changing some of the soldered-in batteries or need to reconnect a wire that breaks off. A small hand-held multitester or multimeter is also useful.

If you do extensive on-site work that involves changing motherboards or generally tearing the whole machine apart, you will find that often you do not have much table space or even floor space to work in. You can find yourself piling parts up on top of other parts. A top-opening bowling bag or doctor's type of bag works well since it takes up little floor space and can be loaded with lots of stuff like software and reference books.

You can get an assortment of screwdrivers and various other PC-aimed tools, like a chip puller, at almost any electronics store or from the Jensen catalog (Fig. 5-8). A more deluxe technician's toolkit, also offered by Jensen Tools, is depicted in Fig. 5-9. It includes a soldering iron as well as a wide variety of useful tools.

You will need to get disks to carry with you for your own use. You'll need disks in various capacities including: 3.5-inch 1.44MB, 3.5-inch 720K, 5.25-inch 1.2MB, and 5.25-inch 360K. You'll be able to format these disks in the various operating system versions you need and keep them with you. You might need

5-8
A simple technician's toolkit, this package offers the basics, including screwdrivers, nut drivers, and chip pullers.

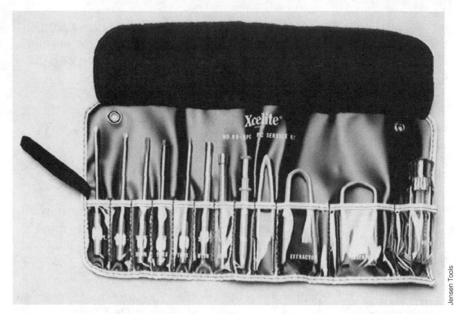

Jensen Tools

5-9
A more deluxe toolkit, this set has a case with extra storage and even includes a soldering iron.

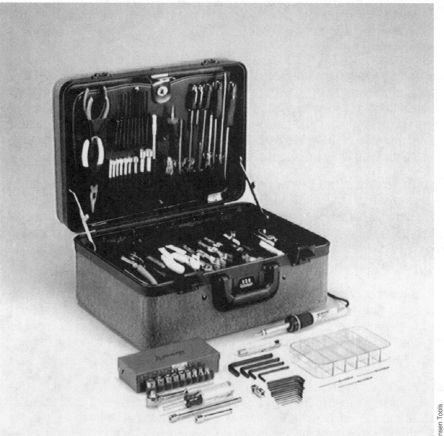

Jensen Tools

disks in the new 3.5-inch 2.88MB capacity if you're working in some facilities, though the 2.88MB capacity is not in widespread use.

You'll also need diagnostic software. You can use the DOS utility MSD, but you'll need something you can use in case MSD isn't available. We've included Snooper, a shareware diagnostic, on the disk included with the book to help you get started. However, Snooper is not bootable, and it can be helpful to have diagnostic software that is bootable. PC-Technician, QuickTest, and MicroScope are all bootable and aimed at the professional technician, while the CheckIt Pro and PC Certify products are aimed more at the mass market. Loop-back plugs should be included with diagnostic software, though some of the packages do the tests but require you to purchase the loop-back plugs independently. Other stand-by software tools in both Windows and DOS versions include Norton Utilities and PC Tools.

You should have a software tool for installing hard disk drives. That tool might be included with your diagnostic software, but most of the technicians we spoke with had a favorite hard disk installation tool, usually Disk Manager from OnTrack or SpeedStor from Storage Dimensions.

Other tools, such as cable testers, memory chip testers, and a portable parallel tape backup drive, are things you can pick up as you go along. You're most lucrative investment will probably be the parallel tape backup drive, as you can use that to offer additional services such as backup services as well as data recovery. It's especially helpful if you plan to specialize in network repair and services.

More specialized tools such as oscilloscopes require not only an understanding of how to connect them to the equipment, but also a knowledge of the type of wave pattern you're looking for on screen when you get an electrical signal. Tim Sullivan, owner of the computer repair service MicroServ of Colton, California said an oscilloscope is like a complex musical instrument; you have to practice everyday or you'll forget how to "play" it.

If you're interested in getting to know and use an oscilloscope, there is help available. A new introductory guide called the *Hands-on Guide to Oscilloscopes* by electronic design engineer Barry Ross offers step-by-step instructions on the devices and how to make accurate use of them. The book covers calibration, testing components, and circuits, as well as the methods for making accurate time, voltage, phase, and modulation functions. *Repairing PCs: Beyond the Basics* by Michael F. Hordeski shows how to use oscilloscope traces to check video cards, monitors, and faulty power lines.

As for software tools, we want to point out that a continuing features war is waged. This means that a new feature in one software product is usually duplicated in all the others after a short period of time. So rather than go through the products feature by feature, we've left that to the periodicals and are simply mentioning the products technicians are using the most.

For more information . . .

In appendix A, we've listed reference books that can be helpful in learning to do PC repair. However, often overlooked references are vendor manuals. The help files on disk and the manuals that come with software diagnostic tools are excellent sources of technical information. Repair technicians have said repeatedly in interviews for this book that they make a point of noting the manuals or help files that come with the products they purchase because the information is often helpful at a later date. You've already paid for this information; you might as well take advantage of it.

We've completed our general discussion of PC hardware troubleshooting. However, you'll find that additional income can come from software troubleshooting. That's what we'll talk about in the next chapter.

6 Software troubleshooting

"Consider the postage stamp: its usefulness consists in the ability to stick to one thing till it gets there."

— Henry Wheeler Shaw, writing under the pseudonym "Josh Billings" or "Uncle Esek." Shaw was well-known as a humorist in the mid to late 1800s.

From your customer's viewpoint, software problems are just like hardware problems; they interrupt the customer's work. And most customers can't tell the difference. They simply want the problem fixed. If you can fix these types of problems as well as hardware failures, you'll distinguish yourself from the crowd.

The first thing to know about software problems is they always occur because something in the configuration of the PC has changed. It's easier if you can get your client to tell you what changed, but that isn't always possible. It's your job to find out what's different, then make the necessary correction. The change is almost always one of the following four items: installation of new hardware, installation of new software, deletion of files, or a deliberate change made by someone.

Software can be the cause of a number of problems, including no boot, unexpected reboot, system hangs, inability to launch a program, unexpected characters or colors in the screen display, system "freezes" or lockups in the middle of a program, data corruption, and unexpected termination of a running program.

Chapter 5 covered what to do if the PC won't boot, a situation that can sometimes be a software problem. As we said in chapter 5, this could involve a missing or damaged partition table, or perhaps COMMAND.COM is not available. Computer viruses target the partition table and system files, attempting to erase or damage them. As we've already emphasized, your first check on any system should be for a virus.

Errors that interrupt the operation of the computer, such as system lockups and unexpected rebooting, are the telltale signs of a memory conflict. While these symptoms can be caused by a virus, another common cause is two software programs attempting to use the same memory location at the same time. If the system hangs while loading the environment files into memory, this can also indicate a memory conflict.

Unexpected program termination or a system freeze during the execution of a program can also be caused by memory conflicts or a lack of available memory for the program to use. Another related problem you'll see is a program your client wants to use simply won't run at all. This could be a new program the client wants to run or an existing program that worked before but mysteriously won't work now. You might also find that your clients want their DOS programs to run under Windows, and they will ask you to accomplish that task. Data corruption or data loss can be caused by several factors, including memory conflicts and unexpected rebooting. Software glitches or "bugs" can also be the culprits.

In this chapter, we'll talk about computer viruses, how to resolve software problems by scanning for viruses, looking for memory conflicts, examining and testing the environment files, Windows troubleshooting, getting DOS programs to work with Windows, and multiple-boot configurations. We'll also address remote diagnostics, how to recover lost data, and the crucial issue of backups. Finally, we'll cover some of the issues concerning glitches and compatibility in the software business, since you'll be acting as a liaison of sorts between the software companies and your clients.

Viruses

In November of 1983, Fred Cohen, a graduate student at the University of Southern California (USC) was credited with the introduction of one of a type of software that is dreaded in the computer world. He introduced it in a computer security class taught by Professor Leonard Adleman. Upon viewing the rogue program, Adleman was the first to dub it a "virus."

Viruses are programs, just like any other computer program. The majority of virus authors are between the ages of 15 and 21, according to the experts. What this means is you're more likely to find a computer virus in an environment where kids that age have access to computers, such as a university or a government installation affiliated with a university. Networked environments are another potential virus hot-spot.

While not all viruses are written to be destructive, most are. Viruses have been likened to graffiti. The same kid who wrote a bad word about the teacher on the chalkboard, using indelible marker, is probably the adolescent writing a computer virus now.

Virus symptoms vary, depending on the virus. Symptoms include hard disk crashes, computer lockup due to memory conflicts, missing or corrupted data files, unusual screen activity (such as characters appearing to fall off the screen or the entire screen turning upside down), and loss of all the data on the drive. Almost any problem that appears to be a hardware malfunction could be caused by a virus.

How viruses behave

In the strictest sense, a true virus was born to replicate and needs access to the computer's CPU in order to do so. That means viruses have to place themselves in the boot sector of a disk, attach themselves to a program that gets executed, or place themselves in the partition table. The Michelangelo virus is a primary example of a boot sector virus. The program spread because it placed itself in the boot sector of any disk, even one that wasn't bootable. Since most computers try to boot from the A: drive first, then go to the C: drive, the virus would infect computers because the infected disk was left in the A: drive. A user would access the disk, then forget and leave it in the A: drive. The next time the computer was started or rebooted, the computer would search the boot sector of the infected disk, and the virus got its chance.

Executable files or program files are another favorite place for viruses to attach themselves. These files have the extension .EXE, .COM, or .BAT. One of the popular ways to detect a virus that likes to infect these files is to measure the file, save the results, then do a comparison later. If there's a change in the executable files, that could mean a virus.

Data files, meaning standard files created by other programs such as documents, spreadsheets, and databases, are not places where virus programs can survive. Since these programs are never directly executed by the CPU, a virus attaching itself to a data file cannot replicate itself. However, these files can be corrupted or destroyed by a virus programmed to do so.

Virus infection tendencies

There have been predictions that a virus infection will occur on a large scale, brought on by the increasing popularity of networking. An increase in viruses distributed accidentally in packaged software and on the hard disk drives of computers has been part of the reason. But IBM says these predictions won't come true.

The company has made a dedicated study of virus infection in its High Integrity Computing Laboratory. IBM treats the lab very much like a hospital would treat an infectious disease clinic, meaning disks that go in do not ever go out. Jeffrey O. Kephart, a member of IBM's special virus lab, says research shows viruses are mostly spread by friends who exchange disks. His assertion is contamination will be found in pockets on machines used by people who have direct contact with each other. What this means from a repair point of view is if a virus is found, it makes sense to check the computers of people who have direct contact with the individual(s) who use the infected computer. This is also a way to get additional business.

Also, IBM said the oldest viruses are the ones you're most likely to find. In 1992 the company reported that the top ten computer viruses it found "in the wild" were all boot-sector viruses, and the top two accounted for one third of all the virus reports. Those two were the Stoned and the Form viruses.

Antivirus software

Some of the problems in finding a virus have to do with the way antivirus programs search for viral activity. These programs usually include "scanners" that look for a characteristic virus "signature" for known virus programs. The scanners look in the boot sector, the partition table, and executable files as well as memory. Virus writers have attempted to foil these attempts by creating "polymorphic" viruses that mutate so there is no one characteristic signature. This also means someone has to be hit by a new virus before the scanners can be coded to look for that virus's signature.

Another problem with signature scanning is combinations of programs can also create the same signature, causing the antivirus program to mistakenly report a virus when there is none. For example, Symantec's antivirus program reported the Cinderella virus in certain circumstances when the virus didn't exist, costing several business owners some big bucks in computer consulting fees. Should your antivirus software report a virus infection, you should try to confirm the report with the vendor of the antivirus software you're using. The vendor can tell you, based on the information you supply, if there's a virus or if you've found a bug in the scanner. You'll want to be sure there actually is a virus before attempting a cleanup.

Antivirus software programs abound, especially since shrink-wrapped software and even new computers have shipped with viruses. Even MS-DOS 6.0 includes Antivirus software, MSAV, and Windows 3.1 has a version, MWAV.EXE. Central Point Software contracted with Microsoft to include virus protection software with the operating system and is planning to provide updates as well.

McAfee and Associates have a popular shareware program for virus infections, VSCAN, which is distributed as shareware. A relatively new player, Stiller Research, is distributing its virus scanning software, Integrity Master, as shareware. Integrity Master has caught the attention of computer professionals because it checks for any data corruption and not just for computer viruses.

Unless the antivirus software found with the operating system of the user's hard disk drive has been activated each time the user inserts a new disk or starts the computer, it could be corrupted by a virus as well. You should keep your own antivirus software on a separate floppy disk and have a couple of copies available. If a verified virus is found, break the disk you used in half and throw it away. You can't afford to accidentally infect another computer, especially one of your client's PCs, with a virus.

Virus elimination

The only sure way to get rid of a virus is to boot from a clean floppy, use FDISK to rewrite the DOS partition, and then reformat the hard disk. This procedure will destroy all the data on the hard drive. You will want to install DOS and any application software from the original disks. If there is a backup available, you can restore only the data files from the backup. All floppy disks used on the computer are suspect and probably should be destroyed.

If you feel brave and know the virus is a boot sector one, you can try these steps to eliminate it without reformatting the disk. You can copy the system files from a clean, bootable floppy over the boot sector in an attempt to erase the virus. Use the command "SYS C: A:" where A: is the floppy drive and C: is the hard disk. There is also an undocumented MS-DOS switch in the FDISK command to recreate just the master boot record (MBR) without destroying access to all the data on the hard disk drive, as creating a new partition does. The command is "FDISK /MBR" and it works if the partition was created with MS-DOS. Use it with care. Some programs modify the MBR or master boot record in order to run, and these programs could crash if you use this command to rewrite the MBR.

Some antivirus programs claim to go through and eliminate the virus from the disk, even from executable files. The software does this by looking for the virus signature. If the antivirus software is not 100 percent accurate or the signature of the virus changes, then the virus might not be eliminated. Disk compression makes virus elimination a more complex process. If the drive is compressed, the computer uses the boot sector of the host drive. This means both the host drive and the compressed drive will need to be cleaned with antivirus software. Since virus cleanup is such a painful operation, the client might want you to go to the extra trouble of starting from scratch, just so there's no chance of further infection.

You can be sure your clients will be "loaded for bear," looking for whomever infected their computer with a virus. Nothing seems to make clients angrier than this senseless waste of their money and time. This is why we feel it is necessary to say again that you should take extreme care in checking for a virus on a computer you haven't worked on before, and you should destroy any floppy disks you use if you detect a virus. Your client will make it his business to find out where the virus came from, and if it was from you, you could very well be out of business.

PC repair sting operation

Here's an example of how a wholistic software and hardware approach can help you truly diagnose a PC as well as help you save your customer's data. This is based on the Southern California version of a report on a PC repair sting operation that was widely broadcast by various television news stations. The certification mentioned in the report is discussed in chapter 8.

Forty-percent of the computers sent out for repair might have nothing wrong with them, according to David Horowitz, the "Fight Back" consumer watch reporter for Southern California's Channel 2 Action News. In a sting operation set up by Horowitz and Don Doerr, owner of computer training firm National Advancement Corporation, a 386-based PC was infected with a harmless simulation of the Stoned virus in order to test the effectiveness of the average PC repair technician.

When the computer was started it displayed the following message on the monitor.

```
NO ROM BASIC
SYSTEM HALTED
```

Doerr and Horowitz went through the phone book and called three nationally known and reputable computer repair companies. As each technician examined the PC, he or she was being filmed by a hidden camera.

One technician, a woman, fixed the problem by replacing the hard disk drive. She said the data on the hard disk drive was unrecoverable and charged $250 for the repair. Another technician offered a $360 estimate to fix the computer. A third technician said he didn't know what was wrong and couldn't fix the PC, but charged $350 for the service call.

After the three technicians left, Doerr used a bootable floppy to boot the computer from the A: drive. He attempted to access the hard disk, and the computer responded with the message, "Invalid drive specification." Doerr then used Norton Disk Doctor, part of the Norton Utilities, to rebuild the partition table on the hard disk drive, restore the drive, and retrieve the data.

The worst part of the scenario, according to Doerr, wasn't that the technicians didn't know how to repair the PC, or their high repair rates. The worst part was they didn't have a clue how to get the data back. "If we had several months or several years worth of data with no backup, we would have been in serious trouble," Doerr said.

In a separate interview on the same subject, an unidentified computer user said a repair company was called out on a bad hard drive. The repair company said it would have to replace the hard disk drive and the data couldn't be retrieved. "As it turned out," the user said, "the hard disk drive was just sticking."

Horowitz's opinion was the repair technicians simply didn't know what they were doing. Certification is not required for computer repair technicians, he added, but there are groups who are attempting to change that. The thrust of the report was to promote a general and vendor-independent testing for technicians called Level 2 certification. The report concluded by advising consumers they should look for Level-2 certified technicians.

Software conflicts show up in memory when more than one piece of software attempts to use the same memory address. If you've asked your questions correctly, you'll know if some new piece of software has been added to the PC or a change has been made recently. This information might be the clue you need to solve the problem.

Memory conflicts

A big cause of software conflicts are terminate-but-stay-resident (TSR) programs, which sit in just a little bit of RAM, waiting for a user keystroke to bring them back to life again. A calendar program, scheduling software, software to animate on-screen icons, a telephone dialer—there are many packages designed to operate this way that have the possibility of stalling or stopping the normal operation of the PC. Users can install TSRs inadvertently during the installation of a new software program, not knowing the full implications of what they've added. Some programs are polite enough to ask if they can change the user's environment files so they can be loaded automatically each time the computer boots, but a user who doesn't know any better won't know that this might cause a problem.

TSR or memory resident software conflicts

TSRs are also more likely to be using a piece of memory that another application wants to use. They can also take up some of that precious lower memory available for DOS applications, which could be enough that some DOS applications won't work properly or at all.

Software upgrades can also be a potential source of conflict. An accounting package that worked just fine might slow to a crawl or refuse to work because the updated version requires more RAM. The confused user doesn't know what happened.

When you suspect a software conflict, here are the steps to take.

Steps to curing software conflicts

Interview the user The first thing to do is use the information the user gave you concerning the symptoms to see if you can recreate the problem yourself. If you can, you should get some insight as to what is happening.

Check the environment files The next step is to check the environment files. A common procedure is to make copies of the environment files and then boot with very simple AUTOEXEC.BAT and CONFIG.SYS files. See if the problem reoccurs. If not, add one line at a time (to one file at a time) to attempt to isolate the command or driver causing the problem.

If there are device drivers or special commands loaded by software applications, you'll need the documentation to determine what those commands do. You might find that parameters are passed to those commands to configure the device driver and it is important to know what those parameters, or switch settings, mean.

If you exit Windows to "tweak" the environment files, check the file attributes with the ATTRIB /A command first. Windows does write-protect the files and you'll find yourself frustrated if you go out to edit them, reboot, and find nothing has changed because the edits didn't take. You can use the SYSEDIT command in Windows to do your editing, but that means you'll need to wait for Windows to come up again each time to check the file settings. That might be fine if you're looking for a conflict between two Windows programs, but if you're looking at DOS applications, it's faster to take the WIN command that starts Windows out of the AUTOEXEC.BAT and work in DOS until you get the problem fixed.

Use multiple configurations   If the user needs memory for some crucial application to run, such as an accounting software upgrade for the current year, then look through the environment files for things you can eliminate. Each command costs memory, so each one you can eliminate will free up memory. For example, one client we know had network software drivers in his CONFIG.SYS file, but the computer wasn't connected to a network. The company that sold the computer had canned configuration files that it used to set up the PC, and since the company did a lot of work with other companies who had networks, it had the network commands, such as SHARE.EXE, loaded into the environment files. While the commands didn't cause any harm, they took up valuable memory. Once these commands were removed, the accounting software upgrade ran much faster because the removal added a few K of additional memory.

You might find that older versions of popular end-user utility products do not work well with operating system upgrades. Even utility software products can produce problems when used with new versions of the operating system. Both Norton Utilities and PC Tools in earlier versions had serious problems with DOS 5.0 and above that could cause data loss. When an operating system update is released, take care. Use your old utility software with it until the utility software developers release an update or enough time has gone by that reported problems will be common knowledge. Usually three to six months is long enough to reveal problems between utility software packages and the operating system update.

Windows troubleshooting

Windows 3.0, Windows 3.1, and Windows 3.11 are very similar and some of the same techniques can be used to troubleshoot all three. The minimum hardware recommendations for Windows in standard mode is an 80286 CPU, 6.5MB of hard disk space, and EGA monitor, and 1MB of RAM. The 1MB of RAM does not include the 340K set aside for system use. This means 640K lower or conventional memory and 384K additional memory is needed. Windows will run in this configuration, but this is a slow and painful way to proceed. A 386 or 486 with 4MB of RAM is much less painful. You can also anticipate Windows applications will need a minimum of 10 to 15MB of hard disk space each, so that is another consideration. If your customer is serious about getting some work done, this would be a good time to suggest an upgrade.

Problems that locked up the system in Windows 3.0 were called "unrecoverable application errors" (UAEs). Microsoft made changes in Windows 3.1 that made the operating system more stable and expanded the definition of errors under the heading "system integrity" errors. Sometimes system integrity errors are fatal, but most of the time Windows allows you to close down running applications and then exit. Sometimes, if the error is isolated to just a single application, that one application can be shut down and the rest of the system is unaffected.

To close an application that is no longer responding to you, you can press the CTRL+ALT+DEL key sequence, which usually restarts or warm boots the computer. However, Windows will ask whether the application should be continued or closed. If you say closed, Windows will close only that application and maintain the rest of the system. In this way, data loss either doesn't occur or is kept to a minimum. If you do have to exit Windows, you can usually continue by typing "WIN" at the DOS prompt to restart Windows.

Types of system integrity errors

System integrity errors under Windows 3.1 fall into four general categories: invalid opcode faults, general protection (GP) faults, page faults, and stack exceptions. All of these errors have to do with commands given the CPU that are illegal and/or cause memory conflicts. Invalid opcode is execution of an illegal instruction or "executing garbage." General protection faults are instructions that if executed would violate the protection features built into the CPU. The instructions attempted are not necessarily illegal themselves, but they are illegal in the context in which the attempt to execute them was made. Page faults and stack exceptions have to do with the use of system memory.

Understanding stacks

One of the things that will help you the most in troubleshooting Windows is understanding the concept of stacks. Stacks are like those spring-loaded piles of freshly washed plates in the buffet line at a restaurant. When you take one plate off, the other plates move up so you can easily take another plate from the top. In memory, stacks are the addresses of running programs. For example, if a program is running and you press the help button, that starts another program. The address of the first program is placed on the stack. When you finish the help program, the computer goes back to the stack to get the program that was running just before help was started. In this way the stack keeps track of the sequence of routines. The order the computer uses for the stack is called "last in, first out" or LIFO. Putting a program address on the stack is called a "PUSH" and taking one off is called a "POP." This is a simplistic example because larger programs are divided into much smaller programs or "modules" that perform single functions like redrawing the screen or saving a keystroke. Those modules are what are "PUSHED" and "POPPED" on and off the stack. But you get the idea.

If the computer can't find the next program to process, that's called an "internal stack failure." Usually you can just restart the computer, but sometimes you have to reinstall the operating system to get the computer running again. Stack overflows indicate you simply don't have enough memory.

To assist in finding what's causing these problems, Microsoft has additional documentation aimed at technicians and network administrators, the Windows Resource Kit. A separate resource kit is available for Windows for Workgroups that also includes the Windows 3.11 addendum. These documents include extra software drivers and are only available by special order at a nominal charge (under $40, including shipping and handling). Computer Discount Warehouse (CDW) carries the kits for all the versions of Windows, as well as other software and hardware, though you can order the kits through other retail software vendors as well. You can also download the kit and find tips and troubleshooting help by calling Microsoft's bulletin board service (BBS) at (206) 637-9009. (More information concerning the BBS settings and baud rates is in appendix C.) There are no charges or membership fees, but you have to pay for the call, and it can take a full hour to download all files needed to make up a single kit.

Windows diagnostics using Dr. Watson

When you consider the endless number of combinations available with all the different motherboards, CPUs, chipsets, display adapters, and device drivers coupled with the variety in operating systems and the nearly endless variety of software programs, troubleshooting problems by narrowing the field down to Windows still leaves an extremely large number of possible causes. Fortunately, if you're using hardware and software that is in wide-spread use, you have better odds of finding the problem simply because someone else has probably run into it before you and has found the answer.

One of the steps Microsoft has taken in helping to diagnose Windows problems is to develop a diagnostic TSR for Windows troubleshooting called Dr. Watson. Dr. Watson, (DRWATSON.EXE) wasn't included in Windows 3.0 but was shipped with the first versions of the Windows Resource Kit for Windows 3.0 and was available from Microsoft Product Support as an application note. The current version of DRWATSON.EXE is 0.80 and it shipped with Windows 3.1 and 3.11. You can find the Dr. Watson application in the Windows subdirectory. To run the program, select "File" then "Run" from the Program Manager menu, then type DRWATSON.EXE. If you click once on the Dr. Watson icon when it is active, the title bar will display the version number as shown in Fig. 6-1. If run with Windows 3.1 or 3.11, earlier

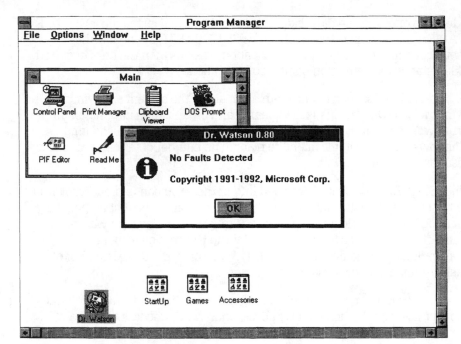

6-1

*To find out what version of
Dr. Watson, the Windows
diagnostic tool, is on your
system, start the program
running, then click on the
icon. The version number
is at the top in the
Title Bar.*

versions of the DRWATSON.EXE TSR can actually create GP faults or system
lockups. Microsoft cautions that only the 0.80 release be used for those
versions.

Dr. Watson's job is to look for system and application failures, such as GP
faults, and record it's findings to a file in the Windows directory called
DRWATSON.LOG. If you are looking to troubleshoot problems in a client's PC,
you might want to make a Dr. Watson icon and move it to the Startup group
so it starts each time Windows does. Later, you can view the log file the
program creates to get clues as to what might be the problem. This is
especially helpful if the problem is intermittent or if you happen to be doing
remote troubleshooting.

The DRWATSON.LOG file has three parts, each separated by a blank line. The
first part is the start and stop time and date of each time the program was
activated. If you see several starts and stops in a row, then you know those
were Windows sessions where no problems occurred. In the next two lines,
the first line explains the second. The first line will read like this:
"<APPLICATION NAME> had a <FAULT DESCRIPTION> fault at <MODULE
NAME> <CS:IP REGISTER>." The next line, starting with the "tag"
character string is the actual record of the error, with each description divided
from the next with a "$".

The <APPLICATION NAME> is the application you were in when the error,
<FAULT DESCRIPTION>, occurred. The <FAULT DESCRIPTION> is an

educated guess, or the most likely cause, of the error. Next is the <MODULE NAME> and its memory location. The <CS:IP REGISTER> field is the instruction in the stack that the application was on when the error occurred. CS:IP stands for instruction pointer code segment.

A "System Info" section offers information about the system and Windows. In Windows 3.1, Dr. Watson takes the name and organization information from what was given at the time of installation, but if you're troubleshooting Windows 3.0, those items might be blank. The number of tasks running is also given here.

The "Stack Dump" section is divided into frames. You can find out what was in the stack before the fault occurred in this section, in the first frame (0), by locating its memory location in the stack (the memory location was indicated in the third field of the tag line). Finally, the last section lists the applications running from the tasks list. Remember, the actual number of tasks running is in the System Info section.

Figure 6-2 shows an example of a problem description in a DRWATSON.LOG file. In this example, the Windows accessories word processing program "Write" had an error while the module "Display" was running. This would indicate a problem between the Write program and the currently installed video driver. The first step in troubleshooting this problem would be to change the video driver in the Windows Setup and then try using Write again.

6-2

Dr. Watson creates a log file, DRWATSON.LOG, that records the circumstances surrounding an error in Windows. This particular entry indicates a conflict between the Windows Write word processor and the current video device driver.

Dr. Watson 0.80 Failure Report- Wed Oct 5 14:59:44 1994
Write had a 'Code Segment (Read)' fault at Display 2:1d70
tagWRITE$Code Segment (Read) $Display 2:1d70$mov

You can also run the Microsoft diagnostic MSD by selecting "File," then "Run" under Program Manager. You'll want to know what display drivers and other hardware are out there before you change the video driver. If you end up calling Microsoft Product Support Services (PSS) (the numbers are in appendix C), you'll want to have both the DRWATSON.LOG file and the MSD results in front of you so you can offer a detailed description of the problem.

The Windows resource kit

Once you know what hardware you're dealing with, you might also find the specific conflict you're having documented in the Windows Resource Kit or in online forums maintained by Microsoft on CompuServe, GEnie, and Microsoft's own BBS. For example, the kit has a list of known problems between BIOSs from various vendors and Windows. Any BIOS dated prior to 1988 is suspect. Several popular BIOSs are listed as problematic with Windows. Phoenix specifically states that its BIOS dated 1988 or earlier should be upgraded. The Award BIOS prior to version 3.05 caused floppy drive read errors. The AST BIOS caused system lockups, GP faults, keyboard lockups, and network errors on AST Premium 286 machines. The DTK BIOS prior to revision 35 would not support IDE drives but would run Windows in enhanced mode, but the 35 revision could prevent 386 enhanced mode from running. Revision 36 of the DTK BIOS requires that the setup utilities be disabled in the CMOS. In each case, it is necessary to contact the manufacturer of the BIOS in order to get more information.

GP faults can be caused in Windows by cross-linked files. Cross-linked files are two files that have the same address in the FAT. Unexpectedly shutting down the PC, viruses, and other problems can cause cross-linked files. The place to start if you see a GP fault is to quit Windows and run CHKDSK (or SCANDISK under DOS 6.22) to find and correct cross-linked files. If you find cross-linked files with CHKDSK, you'll need to run the program again with the /F switch in order to fix the problem.

If the GP faults seem to occur with a specific application, there could be file corruption in the files of that application. The thing to do is reinstall the application and see if the GP faults go away. To make a clean install, you might want to delete the application first, usually by deleting the directory the application is in, so that the files are freshly installed on the PC.

Another troubleshooting tool for finding out what's causing GP faults is to start Windows using the command "WIN /D:XSV." The X, S, and V switches set parameters for memory use in Windows that can also be set in the SYSTEM.INI file. The X switch sets the expanded memory manager (EMM) to exclude the memory addresses from the hexadecimal value A000 to EFFF. The S switch turns off the ability for Windows to use the ROM address between F000:0000 and 1MB for a break point. The V switch works on Windows in 386 enhanced mode to bypass the ROM routine that handles interrupts from the hard disk controller, effectively stopping these interrupts. Performance is faster when the ROM routine handles the interrupts, but some hard drives won't support this.

If the GP faults go away when Windows is started with these parameters, then try exiting Windows and restarting Windows with the command "WIN /D:XS." If the GP faults return, you need to add the line "VirtualHDIrq=OFF" to [386Enh] section of the SYSTEM.INI file. Using SYSEDIT, you can search for the string "[386Enh]" then insert the line with the other commands, as shown in Fig. 6-3.

If the GP faults don't return when you start Windows with "WIN /D:XS," then try starting Windows with "WIN /D:X" and see if the GP faults start appearing again. If so, you'll need to insert the line "SystemROMBreakpoint=False" in the [386Enh] section of the SYSTEM.INI file using SYSEDIT. If the user is running third-party memory management software such as QEMM from Quarterdeck or 386MAX from Qualitas (headquartered in Bethesda, Maryland) this setting will need to be in the SYSTEM.INI file for Windows to run.

Troubleshooting general protection faults

6-3

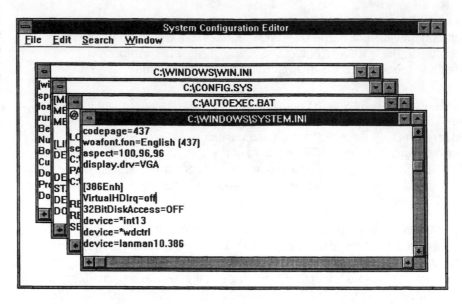

6-3
The SYSEDIT utility allows you to view and edit the environment files and the Windows system files WIN.INI and SYSTEM.INI.

Reinstalling Windows without losing settings

If you still can't get rid of the GP faults, you might have corruption in the Windows files themselves. At this point Microsoft recommends that you reinstall Windows, but do so by installing a new copy of Windows in another directory then copying over files you need so you don't lose your settings.

First, install Windows to a new directory name, then try to run the program from the new directory. We'll call the new Windows directory NEWWIN for our example. Try to run Windows from the NEWWIN directory. If it runs, then rename the files in the new Windows with the .GRP extension so they all have a .GRN extension. Exit Windows and from the DOS prompt type this:

```
RENAME C:\NEWWIN\*.GRP C:\NEWWIN\*.GRN
```

Rename all the .INI files to .INN by typing:

```
RENAME C:\NEWWIN\*.INI C:\NEWWIN\*.INN
```

at the DOS prompt. Then copy all the files and subdirectories from the NEWWIN directory to the original Windows directories by entering the following command:

```
XCOPY C:\NEWWIN\*.* C:\WINDOWS\*.* /S
```

See if Windows will run. If not, you need to delete the new and old versions of Windows and the applications and reinstall all of it from scratch. You could go through an extra step to see if one of the .INI files has incorrect settings, but it doesn't make any difference in the final outcome. If you want to do this, the steps are to rename the original .INI files to .INO by typing:

```
RENAME C:\WINDOWS\*.INI C:\WINDOWS\*.INO
```

then rename the .INN files to .INI with the command:

```
RENAME C:\WINDOWS\*.INN C:\WINDOWS\*.INI
```

and try to run Windows again. If the program runs now, the problem was caused by an incorrect setting in one of the .INI files.

If the file corruption problem continues and you've checked for viruses, the hard disk drive is the first suspect and the power supply is the second.

The availability of memory is another issue in Windows. If your customer complains of a sudden slowdown in the speed at which Windows operates, it could be fonts causing the problems. Especially if a new version of the graphics program CorelDRAW! or if new TrueType fonts have been installed, Windows performance can slow to a crawl due to the extra memory requirements of additional TrueType fonts.

Freeing up memory for Windows

To free up memory, it's best to delete the fonts that will not be used, as each installed font requires some memory. This can be accomplished by going to "Control Panel" in the Main group, then selecting "Fonts." You can disable the TrueType fonts by clicking on "TrueType" in the Fonts menu and then deselecting the "Enable TrueType Fonts" option. This can make things difficult, though, as every time you want to print something using the fonts, you have to go back in and enable the fonts again.

Some problems with Windows have to do with the multitasking environment and how applications release memory. If the user has been opening and closing several applications in a session and Windows begins to slow down, it could be because some applications just don't let go entirely of the memory they allocated for themselves, even if they're no longer running. So by opening and closing several applications, the amount of memory left after a while can decrease significantly. This problem can get to the point that it can crash the system. The only fix at this time is to close down Windows, then restart it again. You can counsel users to do this before a break or at lunch, when it won't be too disruptive.

Software tools are arriving on the market to troubleshoot Windows problems. Skylight from the RenaSonce Group is a Windows application that will give you graphical displays of memory usage, detailed descriptions of the hardware, IRQ and port usage, tasks running under Windows, and context-sensitive help. WinProbe from Landmark offers similar capabilities and provides printer tests. Norton Utilities and PC Tools both have Windows versions aimed at providing the same type of functionality and have even gone so far as to be integrated into portions of Windows. Again, the consideration is these products are aimed at the end-user, so they're going to take time to install, more time to use, and take up the client's hard disk space.

Microsoft's Object Linking and Embedding (OLE, pronounced "o-lay") is growing in popularity. OLE allows you to either link or embed "objects" into documents you're creating. This is helpful in repetitive documents that must be done regularly, on large projects, and in collaborative group projects over

Object Linking & Embedding (OLE) troubleshooting

networks. For example, you can take a spreadsheet document that a member of your team keeps current and link it to a report. If the spreadsheet is changed or updated, the spreadsheet shown in the report is automatically updated as well. If the spreadsheet is "embedded" into the report, you can double-click on it, and the application that created the spreadsheet will start, and you'll be allowed to edit the spreadsheet yourself. A document that has linked or embedded objects is called a *compound document*.

The registration information editor   In order to use OLE, applications must be OLE enabled, and they must be recorded in the Registration Information Editor. You can see what file types are registered by opening the Program Manager "File" menu, selecting "Run," entering "REGEDIT" in the Command Line box, and clicking on OK. If you enter "REGEDIT /V" you'll see a much more detailed view of the information stored in the registration editor. Windows applications that support OLE usually register themselves in this file upon installation. The files used to register are merged into the registration database and usually have a .REG extension.

Why compound documents might stop working   If compound documents no longer function the way they did, there could be several reasons. One is a change in the PATH command that keeps Windows from being able to find the directory for the application that created the embedded object. Another is a change in the registration editor. The file REG.DAT contains the needed registry information. If it is moved or destroyed, OLE won't work.

OLE enables a couple of other functions that aren't used by most users, but which could become disabled if OLE doesn't work. One is launching applications from File Manager by double-clicking on the filename that starts the application. The other is Drag and Drop printing, in which files can be moved from File Manager using the mouse and dropped onto the Print Manager icon for printing. Print Manager has to be running, but minimized for this to work.

Restoring REG.DAT   If the REG.DAT is missing or corrupted, you can have Windows restore the original registration database that comes with the program. First, quit Windows, then delete REG.DAT from the Windows directory. Restart Windows and run the Registration Info Editor, open the "File" menu, and choose "Merge Registration File." Highlight the SETUP.REG file (in the Windows SYSTEM directory) from the File Name list and click on the OK button. If you have other applications that use OLE, you'll have to add them to the restored database by using the Merge Registration File option, going into the directory where the application is stored, and looking for the .REG files. You might find some of the .REG files for applications developed by Microsoft in the Windows directory.

In order to run DOS applications under Windows, Windows creates a "virtual" PC, emulating a complete Intel 8086-based machine. This includes the memory, input/output devices, memory resident programs (TSRs), device drivers, and network software running when Windows is started. You can expect the overhead of this emulation to slow down your DOS application, but the slowdown is usually offset by the value of having the application so easily available and the ability to easily exchange text-based data with other DOS and Windows applications.

The first test as to whether or not a DOS application will run under Windows is to exit Windows and see if the application will run under DOS. If it won't run, it won't run under Windows either. Even though the DOS application runs on a "virtual" machine, the only memory available to it is the amount of memory left over after the environment files load all the environment settings and drivers. If that's less than the DOS application needs, then you can't run the program.

You can find out how much memory is available by running MEM at the DOS prompt if you're using DOS 5.0 or above. The CHKDSK command will also give you the available memory, and it is available in earlier versions of DOS as well as later versions. If the amount of memory listed as available is less than the DOS program says it needs on the outside of the box it comes in, then you don't need to hassle with an install to know there's not enough memory. You might also try to run MEMMAKER from the DOS prompt and see if you can free up some extra memory that way.

If the program will run from the DOS prompt, you can try it under Windows by using the "File," "Run" option from the Program Manager menu and type in the command to start the application. If this works, you can make an icon and run the non-Windows application under Windows. Windows uses a program information file (PIF) for each running non-Windows application to handle memory usage, priority, and the display options. If you don't create a .PIF file for an application, Windows uses _DEFAULT.PIF. You can modify and then rename the _DEFAULT.PIF in the Windows PIF Editor, found in the Main group, to handle a new DOS application you want to run under Windows (see Fig. 6-4).

At each box in the .PIF file setup, pressing F1 will bring you help for that item. You can give the DOS application a higher priority over other Windows and DOS applications if need be, by going to the Advanced Options section of PIF Editor. There you can check the Exclusive box to give the application more memory and more processor time than it would get under the default settings. This could be useful for a crucial application such as a telecommunications program, where it needs to have priority over other applications running at the same time.

The Detect Idle Time box, when checked, gives CPU time to other applications when the DOS application is not processing information. You

How to get DOS programs to run under Windows

Make adjustments with a PIF

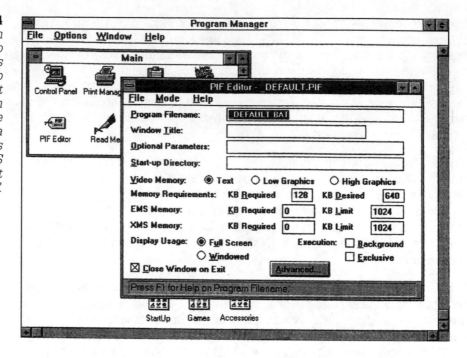

6-4

A file with the extension .PIF can be created to start non-Windows applications and to help configure the environment in which the application runs by using the _DEFAULT.PIF file as a starting point. Windows uses this file for any DOS application that doesn't have a .PIF.

might try unchecking this box if you're having trouble with an application that runs too slow or doesn't work right.

Some DOS applications come with their own .PIF files, and Windows provides .PIFs for a number of popular applications. You can have Windows set up applications with icons and PIFs for you, and the program will automatically set up an icon for all the programs it recognizes. In the Main group, double click on Windows Setup, click on "Options" then "Set Up Applications..." Windows will present you with the option of searching for applications it recognizes or allow you to specify an application. Applications that Windows recognizes are listed in the APPS.INF file in the SYSTEM subdirectory under the WINDOWS directory.

Allowing Windows to go out and search for everything it can possibly set up is a messy and inconvenient process. You can end up with icons all over the place, not knowing what most of them are for, and many will be for functions or programs you or the user don't want to see all the time. If you know the application you want to set up, it's best to just set it up yourself. Windows will ask you for the path of the program you want to set up and offer you a list of existing groups to pick from to place the new icon. The program will then give you the choices of programs it knows about that fit the path and filename you've provided. Pick one and Windows will set it up in the group you've selected.

If the DOS program won't run from the DOS prompt with Windows installed, all is not lost. There are options that will allow you to run the DOS application outside of Windows. Under MS-DOS 5.0 and higher, you can press F5 when you see the "Starting MS-DOS..." message to bypass loading the environment files and go straight to the DOS prompt. You can then check the amount of memory available and if it is enough, install the DOS program and forget running the program under Windows.

When you need to restart Windows, you can simply exit the DOS program and press the reset button or the CRTL+ALT+DEL key sequence to restart the PC. You can even create a .BAT file to start the DOS program from the root directory so the user can type a single word to start the program. Your client might not want to hassle with all of this, but it is an option.

However, a clean boot using the F5 option might still not work, as you might need the mouse driver or the CD-ROM driver in order to use the DOS program, especially if the program is distributed on CD-ROM. If you need to load special drivers, or a special configuration, you can set up a multiple-boot configuration using MS-DOS 5.0 and higher. A multiple-boot configuration is also an excellent option for a situation where several different people are using the same computer, but each needs to load different environment variables for programs or devices.

Figure 6-5 shows the CONFIG.SYS and AUTOEXEC.BAT files for a multiple-boot configuration. The MOUSE configuration starts the mouse driver but not Windows, while the WINDOWS configuration starts Windows, but not the

Booting without environment files

Multiple boot configuration

Multiple boot configuration example environment files

Note: MS-DOS 6.0 or higher only

Multiple boot CONFIG.SYS sample

```
[MENU]
MENUITEM=MOUSE
MENUITEM=WINDOWS

[MOUSE]
FILES=40
BUFFERS=20
STACKS=9,256
DOS=HIGH

[WINDOWS]
FILES=40
BUFFERS=20
DEVICE=C:\WINDOWS\HIMEM.SYS
STACKS=9,256
SHELL=C:\DOS\COMMAND.COM C:\DOS /P /E:256
```

Multiple boot AUTOEXEC.BAT sample

```
PATH=C:\;C:\DOS;C:\MOUSE;C:\WINDOWS;
GOTO %CONFIG%

:MOUSE
PROMPT MOUSE CONFIGURATION $_$P$G
C:\MOUSE\MOUSE.EXE
GOTO END

:WINDOWS
SET TEMP=C:\WINDOWS\TEMP
PROMPT WINDOWS CONFIGURATION  $_$P$G
WIN
GOTO END

:END
```

6-5
These are examples of CONFIG.SYS and AUTOEXEC.BAT files in a multiple-boot configuration. The MOUSE configuration loads the mouse driver, but not Windows. The WINDOWS configuration loads Windows, but not the mouse. To start the correct series of commands, the user simply chooses MOUSE or WINDOWS from a menu presented by DOS when the computer boots.

mouse. (The mouse will still work in Windows, but not in DOS applications with this setting.) You can just copy these files and modify them as needed for your own purposes. For each boot configuration, you'll need to specify a menu item with a unique name in the CONFIG.SYS. If you use these configuration files as a starting point for your own, please note that the file COMMAND.COM needs to be in the C:\DOS directory as well as in the root directory of the hard disk drive.

Since the CONFIG.SYS starts first, it passes the configuration name in a variable called %CONFIG% to the AUTOEXEC.BAT. The AUTOEXEC.BAT then executes the portion labeled with that value. You'll need an ":END" statement at the bottom of the AUTOEXEC.BAT and a "GOTO END" statement at the end of each set of commands to make this work.

When the CONFIG.SYS is set up with the [MENU] command at the top, then DOS puts up a menu after the "Starting MS-DOS..." message that lists each MENUITEM in the first section and asks the user to select by pressing the number of the choice. In our example, MOUSE would be choice number 1 and WINDOWS would be choice number 2. The system then puts the name represented by the number into the %CONFIG% variable and uses that value for the rest of the selections during the boot-up process.

In our example, the environment settings under the selection name are just as they would be in a separate environment file. We could have made some commands that are repeated common to both menu options by putting each command above the first menu option. Note that we've changed the PROMPT line in each one so the DOS prompt will indicate which boot configuration is active. You can do this for several configurations, if you'd like. Help for the multiple boot configuration process is available from the DOS prompt by typing "HELP MULTI-CONFIG."

Profile   Clark Waggoner
ComputerWorks, Sapulpa, Oklahoma

Clark Waggoner became interested in computers while he had another business of his own, an 18-year-old home-improvement company. He had to get a computer and accounting software to handle the accounting demands of his company and to take over a trust left to him by a family member.

He decided to sell his home-improvement business and go into computer repair after doing computer repair on the side for a couple of years. He rents an office but has his telephone set up to ring at both the office and at home so he's more available to his customers. He works on networks as well as individual PCs.

ComputerWorks keeps a small inventory of parts, such as a few hard disk drives, floppy disk drives, cases, video cards, and a motherboard or two. Clark tries to buy in lots of a half-dozen or so at a time from his supplier so he can get a better price. He's more conservative on his inventory of other parts than he is on floppy disk drives or monitors because pricing hasn't been as volatile in those areas. Clark said he's also careful to purchase his memory chips from a vendor that pretests every chip. It costs about 10 percent more to do it that way, but Clark says he's never had a bad memory chip.

When he started, Clark bought the phone number of another computer repair service that was going out of business. He got his first few customers from that number and from referrals. When the customers told the former owner of the repair business that Clark was treating them right, the owner gave Clark his entire mailing list.

When a new Yellow Pages came out that would combine the entire West Tulsa area, Clark was fortunate to be one of the first ones to sign up. He's pleased with his large ad in the phone book, but says the ad just breaks even with the business it generates. Since most of his business is from referrals, Clark feels as though the ad will pay off in the long run.

As for his services, ComputerWorks offers software troubleshooting and consulting as well as service and upgrades. "My basic goal is to be my customer's only computer support person," Clark added. Most of his customers are small- to medium-sized businesses, and he said he's worked with software of all kinds.

When he first started with computers, Clark and his son wrote a menuing program to get in and out of DOS programs without having to use DOS commands. For customers that don't use Windows, Clark adds the menuing program to their PC as an added bonus.

For customers who need upgrades, Clark gives a trade-in amount on used parts such as old system boards and hard disk drives. While the amount isn't large for trade-in parts, his customers appreciate getting something for their old parts.

He marks on the part he takes in trade what it came out of and why it was removed. Then once every two or three months he takes his used equipment down to a local computer swap and sells it. He says he's generated significant cash flow this way, and the practice allows him to give his customers a break on something they need.

Clark also tries to do most of his phone support without charge, unless it becomes excessive. "For every hour I charge out, I figure I have a five minute phone call coming down the line and I just figure that in. Telephone support helps build loyalty so they continue to buy from you when they don't necessarily have to," Clark stated. This is how Clark feels he is able to compete despite the proliferation of cash-and-carry retail stores that carry computers and accessories in his area. Problem solving skills are also important. "I can get the technical answer if I can get the problem narrowed down," he said.

For new people coming into the business, Clark says business skills are even more important than technical skills. "You might be the best technician in the world, but you need to be a business person first." What Clark means by business skills is the ability to see what customers need and what they want. "You want to satisfy the customer, then fix the PC," Clark maintains.

Remote diagnostics

End-user and remote diagnostics are both becoming increasingly popular. Some computer system manufacturers have always included diagnostics for the end-user to run on their systems to help technicians troubleshoot problems during the warranty period, and more are following this trend. Remote diagnostics are a combination of telecommunications software and diagnostics that allow the technician to operate the PC without having to be on-site. Remote diagnostics actually allow technicians to see the troubled PC's screen on their own computer screen and control the PC from their own keyboards.

Remote troubleshooting software

The first thing to note is these diagnostics only work if your user has a bootable PC. If the PC won't boot, even from a floppy disk, then the technician will have to see the machine. Computer manufacturers like IBM, Acer and Dell use the user-controlled option and include a disk with their PCs that have diagnostic software the user can run. When the user calls in for support with a problem, the vendor's help desk can ask the user to load the PC diagnostic disk and have the user report the results.

Micro 2000 has made that option available for the small repair shop with its MicroScope Client product. The repair shop buys a license for a certain number of copies of the Client software and one copy of the Technician's Manual. The shop can then sell the software to customers, or give it away, as part of its services. When a problem arises, the user is instructed how to run the Client software over the telephone. If an error occurs, an error number shows up on the screen. The user reports the number to the repair shop, who looks up the number in the Technician's Manual. The numbers are assigned by Micro 2000 and require the Technician's Manual to decipher.

Several vendors offer remote-control software. Some are for just diagnostics, and some are end-user products. AMI offers AMIDiag Remote, a remote diagnostic and monitoring system that a technician can use to start the software remotely, set the software to perform tests, then hang up the line because the software works without supervision. Before the technician hangs up, AMIDiag Remote sets the modem to answer mode, then logs its tests to a file. When the technician calls back, the remote PC's modem answers, and the technician can view the log file created by the software.

Data Depot's PC Clinic offers similar functionality, including the ability to shell out of the program to DOS to run DOS utilities. You can look at the interrupts and DMA channels, run CPU and math coprocessor tests, check the FAT, edit configuration files, edit the CMOS, scan for bad tracks, run performance tests, and even low-level format the hard disk drive. The product will also allow you to save and restore CMOS settings remotely. It comes with two disks, a control and a remote disk. A self-booting version of the remote control diagnostic is available as well.

Several end-user software packages can connect your PC to your clients, where you can run diagnostics remotely as well. Some of the most popular titles include: pcANYWHERE from Symantec; Carbon Copy from Norwood, Massachusetts-headquartered Microcom; CoSession from Iselin, New Jersey-based Triton Technologies; Close-Up from Santa Barbara, California-based Norton-Lambert; and ReachOut, offered by Vero Beach, Florida-based Ocean Isle Software.

These products and others work great in a DOS environment, which is where you'll be doing most of your hardware troubleshooting work. However, if you have clients who need you to be able to solve problems in the Windows environment, then the choices become more limited.

The most crucial part of connecting in Windows is getting the monitor device drivers to produce the correct screen display. If a relatively new, high-resolution monitor is involved, you might find yourself needing extra vendor support to get the program running. This could be time-consuming, as the vendor has to make adjustments to support a new display, and you'll end up calling customer support to see if an updated software driver is available. The vendors often have their own bulletin boards and offer updated software drivers on CompuServe for download, or both. You'll need to check with the vendor if you have problems with the display.

These Windows remote packages also make many changes to the Windows .INI files, so be sure to back up your .INI files before installing one, and make copies of your Windows and System directories. Then if you decide the software won't work for you, you can copy the original .INI files back, compare the Windows and System directories for files that need to be deleted, and be pretty much back where you were.

The biggest problem in actually running the remote software comes in if your client has a higher-resolution monitor than you do. If you end up troubleshooting some multimedia software package, you might find the communications slows to a crawl, even with fast modems, while your screen fills up with unintelligible goop. You might still be able to decipher some of the screen, or you might have to end the session and talk the client through the problem over the phone.

You can usually run DOS applications while connected in Windows, but some packages, like pcANYWHERE, require you to load a TSR in order to allow you to run DOS applications in full-screen mode. (You can still run DOS applications in a half-screen, however.) If the computer locks up, you'll find yourself having to reestablish the connection. Most of the remote software programs will allow you to set the modem in answer, and then you'll need to add the command to start the software to the AUTOEXEC.BAT. In Windows, you can simply move the software icon into the STARTUP group, and it will be automatically activated when Windows starts.

During a session, the host computer is the one everyone is viewing, meaning you want your client's PC to be the host so you see and operate his or her computer. However, you can still set things up so the client calls you, even though the client PC is the host PC. That way, the client pays for the call. For example, using pcANYWHERE, you can set up the software so Quick Connect dials you, but sets the session so the caller is also the host (see Fig. 6-6). In addition, you don't need two phone lines if you need to talk to the

6-6
PC Anywhere's Quick Connect option allows you to set the caller's PC as the host, so you can see the caller's computer, but the caller pays for the call.

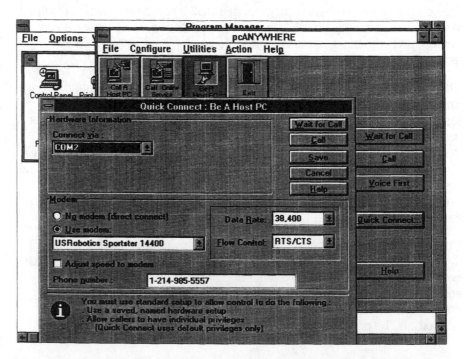

client. Knowing that most users probably have just one phone line, several of the remote control packages offer a "chat" mode, where windows open on-screen and you can type messages back and forth.

A fast modem will speed things up. You'll have fewer problems if you use a modem that is widely supported, such as the U.S. Robotics brand products. If you each have the same modem, that helps in troubleshooting the client's modem, if need be. Also, it should be obvious that the faster the modem, the more satisfying the experience. If the modem is a 14,400 baud or higher, the response time of each PC is acceptable, and the experience takes on a multiplayer game feel that clients like.

AT&T has a modem available that will transmit both voice and data over the same line, but it is still quite expensive for small business use. Look for prices to come down on those modems in the near future, which should make remote diagnostics even more popular and attractive to end users.

Bugs versus incompatibility

All software has glitches, known as bugs. The number of possibilities for conflicts in software is practically endless, and you need to be aware that eliminating all bugs is not practical and probably not even possible. However, when a bug is discovered, action on the part of the vendor is expected in the form of a bug fix that will stop the problem.

Conflicts arise among users and software companies in the definition of a bug. A software company might not consider a conflict between its product and a product from another vendor a bug. Users would consider such a problem a bug, especially if the conflict is between two pieces of software the users feel are both necessary to their business.

It's generally not expected that every software product developed should work with every other software product ever developed, especially when the other software is oddball stuff. What do we mean by oddball? We mean software custom-developed for a specific task, like a custom system to read milk output from dairy cows using analog input from milking machines, and software that is not in widespread use. It is expected, however, that a piece of software should work correctly with the world's most popular operating systems, especially if the software developer advertises that fact.

The reality is software conflicts exist. If the conflict is between a piece of accounting software and a popular networking program, the vendor probably will try to fix it. But if a game and a network program won't work together, the vendor probably won't try to fix it.

As the number of commercial software choices increases, so do the number of software conflicts. Software conflicts can lock up a PC, cause data loss, and make a user's life miserable. A software conflict can cause the PC's processor to go into an endless loop mode, and you might have to reset or even turn your

PC off altogether and wait 10 to 15 seconds for all the electrical circuits to stabilize before you can try again. Sometimes you can fix them, other times you have to ask your client to make a choice between the two software programs.

Software tools

The tools available for troubleshooting software problems tend to be limited. Many of the tools are already at your disposal in terms of operating system tools such as MSD.EXE, CHKDSK.EXE, SCANDISK.EXE, UNDELETE.EXE, UNFORMAT.EXE, and DRWATSON.EXE for Windows. The Norton Utilities, PC Tools, and other disk utilities also offer tools for finding problems in the FAT and partition table, undeleting disks, rebuilding the partition table, and other functions.

For remote diagnostics you can license the MicroScope Client for your customers. You can also set them up with a fast modem and a remote-control diagnostic package such as AMIDiag Remote or PC Clinic. Other programs you can consider for use in Windows and/or DOS for remote control include: pcANYWHERE, Carbon Copy, CoSession, Close-Up, and ReachOut.

Virus software is also a must. Shareware is a less-expensive alternative, though many of the professional software diagnostics we talked about in chapter 5 also include antivirus software. References to these packages are in appendix C.

One of the best investments you could make is to get yourself a copy of the Windows Resource Kit. If you think you might be working on Windows for Workgroups in a peer-to-peer networking environment, the Windows for Workgroups Resource Kit contains both the Windows information and the Windows for Workgroups information for only slightly more in the book form than the Windows Resource Kit. If you'd like to know more about networking before you decide, we cover that topic in the next chapter.

The last resort

No matter what kind of computer you happen to be working on, sometimes your experience will tell you the unresolved problem is a bug or defect in the software. Other times you won't have a clue. Either way, if you find a problem you can't resolve, you should call the vendor. Chances are you're not the first one who's called with this problem, and the vendors are getting wise enough to begin recording the problems and solutions. That means when you call, they've probably already handled it.

You can expect to go through tiers of customer support people before you get to someone who knows enough to give you an answer. Most customer support organizations are set up to save the most knowledgeable support personnel for the toughest problems. When you can begin to see that your attempts aren't working, you might want to get on the phone while you're still checking those last few things, so if you have to wait for the right person to talk with, you won't have to sit and twiddle your thumbs.

Some support organizations have a 900 number, and while that sounds cold and callous, it could be to your advantage. The staff on the 900 number are usually the highest tier of support because the company knows people are paying per minute for the call. That means the phones will be answered quickly, hold time will be kept to an absolute minimum or be nonexistent, and you can get your questions answered quickly. Several of the repair shops we've talked with carry a cellular phone and use 900 number support services because they can get their questions answered efficiently and quickly. When customers are paying between $50 and $70 (or more) an hour for your time, they don't mind paying $2.50 a minute for a few minutes so you can get an answer you need.

As you gain experience and expertise in doing repair, you might want to specialize. Specialization is one way you can boost your income, especially if you choose an area where the demand is high. Paul and Sarah Edwards, who make their living providing information on the work-at-home movement, say specialization is a must. While you need to know the more general aspects of PC repair we presented, you need to pick a niche in which you can be effective.

In the next chapter, we talk about specializing in network repair and the various training and vendor certifications that are available in this growing field. In chapter 8, we'll talk about industry-recognized certification both in general repair and in specific areas of the industry, how you can get certified, and where to get training and information to pass the certification tests. We also cover other lucrative areas of specialization that do not require certification, including data recovery, monitor repair, and printer repair.

7 Network specialization & certification

"Make yourself necessary to somebody."
—Ralph Waldo Emerson, Boston-born essayist and poet, 1803–1882.

If you want to be essential to someone, work on computer networks. Nothing strikes fear in the heart of a company's management more than discovering there is a problem with the network. This type of work does demand that you be more available, perhaps even on 24-hour call, but the financial rewards are better than general work on PCs.

If you decide you'd like to try network repair, you will need to understand how the network is designed and what to do when it is not working properly. You'll also need to consider the performance questions that can occur as technology changes. You should be able to offer suggestions to correct network bottlenecks and expand the network to speed up overall operations. And you might be called upon to suggest options concerning installation, upgrading, and maintenance.

Because there are many ways a network can fail, you will need to know how to detect those failures and make the appropriate repairs. By far the majority of network problems are in the cabling. The remainder of problems fall mostly into hardware or software configuration issues. You will also need to use techniques for diagnosing and treating both kinds of failure. The tools include cable testers, network monitors, and network analyzers.

Networks put the resources of several or hundreds of PCs together. This means sharing disk space, sharing use of peripherals (such as printers or faxes), and sharing messages as well. While networks are expensive, they are cost-effective compared to the hourly salaries of the firm's employees. Doing everything by hand is a very expensive proposition. So is duplicating equipment that sits idle much of the time. For example, why do three workers need three laser printers when one printer can be used for all three?

Thus networks are gaining popularity even in small offices where there are only a few PCs, as well as in large companies with hundreds of employees and hundreds of PCs. Those who can work on networks are also gaining popularity and can charge more for their expertise.

By far, the networking vendor you'll hear the most about and deal with the most is networking giant Novell. No matter what network you end up working with, you'll probably end up dealing with Novell or its products at one point or another. We'll discuss Novell as well as other networking software vendors in this chapter, so you'll be familiar with the popular products in each networking category.

In this chapter, we'll give you an overview of networks and the terminology involved, as well as some ideas as to the types of problems you might encounter and the tools to troubleshoot those problems. In the next chapter, we'll cover credentials for working on networks, or certification, and let you know what you need to do to obtain those certifications.

Networking terminology

Networking involves connecting PCs. If you log into an online service, such as CompuServe, you are connected to a network called a wide area network or WAN. Though you might end up working on WANs, we are going to limit our discussion to local area networks (LANs), where all the computers are in the same building or closely adjacent buildings.

Packet

The most fundamental term in networking is the packet or frame. Data moved in the network is divided into packets. Each packet has information added to the beginning that indicates the start of the frame, the sender, and the intended receiver. Each packet also has information added to the end of the data to indicate the end as well as other information. The beginning and ending information is determined by the unique set of predefined rules used on the network.

A simple way to think of this packet approach to data transfer on a network is to think of the data as a message scribbled onto a sheet of paper. The network, like a messenger service, takes the message and places it in an envelope addressed to the receiver, with the sender's return address added as well. If the data is transferred to another network, it is like the messenger service taking the envelope to Federal Express, which would then place that envelope in yet another envelope. Each network that receives the packet places it in yet another "envelope." When the packet arrives at its destination, the receiving workstation can be thought of as opening each envelope to take out the one inside until it gets down to the message, which it delivers to the user.

It is necessary to note that the term frame is more technically the part of the packet needed for the rules of the network. For our purposes here, it is enough to say the two terms are often used interchangeably.

Servers & workstations

Each network has a "server," which acts as a file repository, serving up the files to the rest of the PCs on the network as needed. It usually also handles sending output to the printer, or the print queue, and controls access to the files. It is equipped with a server adapter card. The number of PCs connected to the server depends on the capacity of the adapter and the server. The network operating system, located on the server, handles the transmission of data and security issues, among other things.

Hopefully, the server will be the fastest PC on the network. Each PC on the network is a "workstation" or a "client" that has network environment files that load the necessary drivers and configuration information into memory on top of whatever operating system is already running on the workstation.

Types of local area networks

LANs fall into three categories, based on the software: host-terminal, peer-to-peer, and client-server networks. Host-terminal networks mean the users have a monitor and a keyboard, but no CPU at their disposal. All the processing and storage is done on the host, which usually is a fast PC with a large hard disk and additional RAM. Some terminals are "smart" terminals with a certain amount of ability to store data or perform tasks, but for the most part everything is on the host and the data is moved back and forth to the workstations over the network.

Peer-to-peer networks are made up of workstations (or PCs) with CPUs, and each machine has the ability to store data and do its own processing. These machines are supposed to be "equal," but in reality one is usually used as a data repository just because it is convenient to do so. However, each workstation has access to the resources and peripherals of the others. Popular peer-to-peer networking products are NetWare Lite and Personal NetWare from Novell, LANtastic from Artisoft, and Windows for Workgroups from Microsoft. Both the Artisoft and Microsoft products work with Novell's NetWare.

Client-server networks are usually made up of workstations with CPUs as well, but one PC is the dedicated server. Each workstation can operate independently of the network, just as in peer-to-peer networks, but client-server networks are faster. This is because the server processes information requests for the workstations, then only delivers the requested information to the workstation, which cuts down on network traffic. Banyan's VINES and IBM's LAN Server products are both client-server network products.

The way in which the PCs are connected is the "topology" and is based on what tasks are to be performed. The bus, ring, and star topologies are the three most common. In the bus topology, all the workstations are wired along a single cable or "backbone." Ethernet and ARCNET frequently use the bus topology. The data traveling along the bus can be seen by all the workstations, but only the workstation to whom the data is addressed picks up the data.

The ring or Token Ring topology is like the bus, as the data can be heard by all the workstations and is addressed, but the bus or backbone is connected at both ends forming a ring. Physically, the ring looks more like a star with cable running to and from each workstation to the bus.

The star topology has only one cable running from each workstation to a hub, also known as a concentrator. The data passes through the hub, then to the individual workstation for which it is intended. ARCNET and unshielded twisted-pair Ethernet (or 10BASE-T) use the star topology.

Topology

The actual wiring between the PCs is the "media," and it determines the speed at which data can move. Unshielded twisted-pair (UTP) cabling, also used for modular phone lines, is a popular choice. There is a voice grade of this cabling and a data grade. Also known as 10BASE-T, the cabling is capable of transmitting data at the rate of 10 megabits per second (Mbps). While not particularly fast, this cabling is known for being less expensive and is therefore more commonly used. Faster 100-Mbps UTP cabling, known as 100BASE-T, is also available, but at a higher price tag.

Media

Coaxial cabling, much like that used for cable television service, is also an option. The choice for coaxial cable is sometimes made because the cabling is already in place within a building.

Fiberoptic cabling is an expensive alternative, although it offers the fastest data transfer speeds. It can also be difficult to install. It is sometimes used to link UTP Ethernet LANs across a distance, such as connecting network users in two separate buildings.

Two pieces of cabling can appear to be identical but have different transmission speeds. A common mistake is to splice together two differently rated cables, such as an RG-58 coaxial cable rated at 50 ohms and an RG-59 coaxial cable rated at 75 ohms. Usually, cable is labeled on the outside sheath as to its rating, so don't let this mistake happen to you.

A network adapter card, or network interface card (NIC), is placed in one of the expansion slots of the PC, and the wiring is attached to connections available on the card. Several companies make these network cards, including 3COM, National Semiconductor, and IBM. Adapters are also available that are portable and can be attached to the parallel ports of PCs for

Xircom

connection to the network. These "pocket adapters," such as the one depicted in Fig. 7-1, are mainly used for temporary connection of a PC and are mainly used for portable computers such as laptops.

If a server is involved, all the wiring goes to a special adapter card installed in the server. Software drivers then initialize the adapter cards when the server starts. An initialization routine is also performed for each workstation when it starts in order to connect it to the network.

Ethernet   Ethernet is the most common network. It was developed by Xerox in the mid 1970s and Xerox, DEC, and Intel made it a standard. About half of the installed base of network nodes use Ethernet. This includes PCs, engineering workstations, and minicomputers.

Ethernet is widely used for PC-based LANs, as well as minicomputer and mainframe computer environments. Ethernet is one of the major LANs used in the military and is used in DEC's DECnet LAN. Almost all Unix networks are also Ethernet based. Ethernet networks are available from a variety of manufacturers, including Novell, Gateway, Tiara, Interlan, Western Digital, Ungermann Bass, and Excelan.

Most Ethernet installations are the linear bus topology defined by the Institute of Electrical and Electronics Engineers (IEEE) 802.3 standard. Other IEEE standards are the twisted-pair Ethernet standard designated as 802.3 10BASE-T, and 802.5, which defines Token Ring.

There are three major cabling standards for Ethernet: thick Ethernet, Thin Net or thin Ethernet, and unshielded twisted pair (UTP). Thick Ethernet cable uses a coaxial cable that is about one-half inch in diameter. Attachment is made to the network bus cable using vampire taps, which clamp on to the cable and puncture it to make contact with the center core. These do away with splicing, which is typically done using N-type connectors. The original Ethernet systems used the heavy shielded coaxial cable, which has come to be known as thick Ethernet or thickwire.

Every network bus cable attachment needs a transceiver, which is attached to a network adapter card. A *transceiver* is a transmitting and receiving device, providing both input and output services to a device on the network. Some transceivers are built into the network adapter cards themselves, so no separate device is necessary. Others are separate, especially on networks using Thick Ethernet, in which transceivers come with transceiver cabling. The transceiver cabling connects to the adapter card via another cable called a drop cable.

Thin Net (or cheapernet) is another type of Ethernet cabling. The thinner coaxial cable is also known as Thin Net or thinwire. It is actually RG-58 coaxial cable and is similar to television cable, but slightly smaller in diameter. Devices designed to work with Thin Net usually connect directly to the cable with a T connector and bayonet-type network connectors (BNC) fittings. Most Thin Net interface cards have an on-board transceiver to eliminate the need for the drop cable and an external transceiver.

You cannot run Thin Net cabling as far as you can thick Ethernet cable. Each thick Ethernet segment can be as long as 1,500 feet, while thin Ethernet can only be reliably run for 600 feet. The total cable length of thick Ethernet can be nearly twice that of thin Ethernet, with 3,000 feet compared to thin Ethernet's 1,800-foot maximum. The biggest difference between the two is thick Ethernet can handle more than 10 times the number of stations at 1024, while thin Ethernet can only support 100 stations.

Lattisnet is another cabling method for Ethernet. It allows standard UTP telephone cable to handle the 10-megabyte-per-second (Mbps) Ethernet transmission rate standard. A device called a concentrator can be connected to each PC network adapter, which makes Ethernet function like a star-type of network. The IEEE 802.3 10BASE-T standard defines Ethernet specifications for 10-Mbps twisted-pair wiring.

There is also a distinction between voice grade 10BASE-T and data grade 10BASE-T cabling. If you have a choice, we suggest you opt for the data-grade cable because it is designed for network connectivity and will offer better performance. At greater cost, you can obtain 100BASE-T UTP cabling to speed up data throughput.

Token Ring   Another popular topology you'll run into is the Token Ring. Introduced by IBM in 1984, it was developed to provide connectivity for installations with a mix of computers. The IEEE 802.5 standard defines Token Ring as an international standard, and Token Ring has also been adopted as a standard by ANSI and the ISO.

The Token Ring passes a packet (also known as a frame or token) along the cabling ring. Each network adapter card accepts the incoming data and copies it for transmission, moving the data from one workstation to another. The workstation for whom the token is addressed is the station who acts on the data packet. The main disadvantage in this scheme is should one workstation on the network fail, the network can go down.

The hub of the ring uses a multistation access unit (MAU). Most MAU units have 10 ports. A stand-alone configuration can be formed with eight computers and can be connected to the MAU in an arrangement sometimes called a "canned" ring. The MAU senses which ports are used by workstations, using the remaining two ports to make connections to the ring. If a workstation should go down, the MAU bypasses the defective workstation, allowing the ring to continue running.

Token Ring network adapters or interface cards are available from IBM, NCR, Racore, Western Digital, Proteon, and others. Token Ring runs on a variety of cables, though the standard type is shielded twisted pair (STP), which looks more like lamp wire than telephone cord. The most popular type of STP is IBM Type 2, though you might find IBM Type 1, Type 3, and Type 6 also. The main ring can have a total length of 1,200 feet. The maximum distance from an MAU to a node, called the "lobe length," is 330 feet.

Network environment files

Computers on a network have environment files for automating the connection to the network, configuring the workstation to run on the network, and loading drivers to initialize the network adapter card. Taking Novell's NetWare as an example, the STARTNET.BAT, NET.CFG, and AUTOEXEC.NCF are the environment files used to load the various drivers and configuration information for the workstation. STARTNET.BAT is usually called as the last statement in the PCs AUTOEXEC.BAT and begins the preparation process for joining the workstation to the network. These network environment files are where you'll do most of your adjustments to get the workstation running on the network.

Protocol

The way the workstations communicate on the network is the network "protocol." These rules of network communication define the packet format of the data and error-checking to maintain the integrity of the data, as well as other things. Messages can even be transferred from one network to another via "routing" and "e-mail" (electronic mail) protocols.

A few popular protocols include the Transmission Control Protocol/Internet Protocol (TCP/IP), used by the government; AppleTalk, used by Macintosh computers; the Novell NetWare Core Protocols (NCP); NetWare Core Internetwork Packet Exchange (IPX); the Sequenced Packet Exchange (SPX); the Routing Information Protocol (RIP); and the Server Advertising Protocol (SAP). Sometimes you'll see the IPX and SPX used together and designated as IPX/SPX or IPXODI. Protocols are also referred to as "transport protocols." Usually, software drivers, whose names contain the acronyms listed above, are loaded during start-up of the workstation in order to facilitate communication with the network.

Gateway

A connection between two networks is called a "gateway." The gateway is usually a PC placed between a PC-based network and a mainframe computer to facilitate the transfer of information from one network to the other. The gateway PC is dedicated to handling the data from one network to the other and to performing protocol conversions for the data traveling back and forth. Gateways serve the added physical advantage of allowing the network users access to the mainframe computer without each having to be connected via separate wiring.

Gateways can also be used to access WANs, such as an electronic mail service for network users that is also connected via a gateway to a larger, public service such as MCI. In this manner, the network users companywide can electronically access each other and the world at large.

Bridge

A *bridge* is a dedicated PC used to connect two similar LANs. Bridges can improve the performance of the LAN by keeping the data traffic down. While the term bridge connotes the connection of similar networks, bridges can be used to connect networks with different topologies, such as Ethernet and Token Ring. Bridges can also be called a "data link relay" or a "level 2 relay."

Router

A *router* is also a dedicated PC on the network, but it is used to make sure messages are properly sent from one LAN to another LAN. Routers can balance network traffic loads, finding the best way to send a message even though several networks might be involved. Routers are also used to break up large LANs for security purposes.

Repeater

A *repeater* is placed in a length of cable to boost the signal coming down the cable. This is to address the problem of signal fading with both analog and digital signals traveling over a distance. In networks, the repeater is the simplest type of LAN interconnection device, and its function is to allow for longer stretches of cable between connected PCs.

Node A *node* is a device on the network. That device can be a client workstation, a file server, and a printer, or some other peripheral device. Each device or node has an identification number or string that identifies it on the network.

Network operating systems The network uses its own operating system, which is different from a single station PC operating system like MS-DOS. The network hardware, including the adapter cards and transmission over the media, is controlled by the network operating system (NOS).

The NOS can be one of the NetWare versions provided by Novell, or a NOS such as the 3Plus Open, which runs under OS/2 and uses 3COM's Ethernet network cards. IBM also markets networking software with its Token Ring cards. Networks can be multiplatform as well, such as the Banyan VINES NOS, which runs as a task under the Unix operating system.

Other NOSs include DECnet, TOPS, and NET/OS. DECnet was one of the first Ethernet-based networks. It was used for connecting Digital Equipment Corporation (DEC) minicomputers. Later versions also allowed DEC VAX minicomputers to act as file servers for PCs on a LAN.

The TOPS network from Sun connects PCs and Apple Macintosh computers together to share files on the same network. A peer-to-peer configuration provides low cost and low performance. It can be used for file sharing, but is limited in performance.

NET/OS is another network product that provides a simple, low-cost peer-to-peer network. NET/OS can emulate some of the NetWare low-level network routines like file locking. Proprietary network operating systems exist that only work with adapter cards from the operating system manufacturer. These include: ViaNet, Corvus Omninet, and 10 Net.

Another variation is "slotless LANs" or LANs that use the PC's parallel or serial port. They do not require a network adapter card, but work over standard RS-232 serial ports or parallel ports. An example is the PC-Interlink network product. Printer sharing, file exchange, and messaging is available for up to four PCs. The parallel port adapter plugs in, and a printer cable can then be plugged into the parallel adapter. You'll find PC-Interlink available in the Jensen Tool catalog. The product offers an inexpensive network interface, but the trade-off is in low-performance.

Novell Novell, with its billions in revenue, is the market leader in NOSs. Its main product, NetWare, is a proprietary network operating system designed to run on PC-based network file servers using an open architecture. The open architecture allows NetWare to be used with hardware from other vendors.

NetWare works with a variety of hardware adapters, but the company will not support any adapter it has not certified to run with its NOS. However, it is possible to mix adapter hardware brands and topologies. A 386 or 486 computer will work as a server (although the faster PC, the better) and you can use almost any PC as a workstation. Even the DEC VAX and many Unix machines can be used as file servers with NetWare for VMS or Portable NetWare.

NetWare is known for better-than-average performance that comes from a combination of techniques. These include: turbo FATs (indexed file allocation tables), elevator seeking, caching, and split reads (splitting read requests among two mirrored disks). NetWare also supports most recognized network standards including NETBIOS as well as gateways to TCP/IP and other standards.

Larry Manoski

BlackChrome Computer, Hoffman Estates, Illinois

Larry Manoski is a graduate in electrical engineering from Purdue. He engineered sewing machine products for Singer, but his interest in computers was sparked during his tenure as a design engineer for Bell and Howell.

While working at Bell and Howell, Larry was designing optical products using a drafting board and paper. But he and his associates discovered that other companies in the same field were using computer aided design (CAD) systems. To speed up the design process, they approached the company's management about putting together their own CAD system. The company agreed, but required they submit a proposal first. Because of his involvement in researching the proposal, Larry ended up not only designing as he did before, but also administering the new CAD network. He maintains that he had to train himself because there was no one else to do it.

As changes in the company started, Larry saw a layoff of the design people coming. Bell and Howell would eventually move to purchasing its designs from outside the firm. With his interest and experience in networks, Larry decided to start part-time in hopes of transitioning to his own full-time business when the layoffs happened. His first work was with law firms in the Chicago area doing basic PC repair and working on networks.

When the layoffs finally came, Larry said he wanted to shout for joy. He went full-time and gave his business the name "BlackChrome Computer." Why BlackChrome Computer? In the world of optics blackchrome is a plating, like chrome. It has the durability and protective quality of chrome, but without the shine. Larry says the material is tough and stable, just the image he wants to present to his customers. He wrote this statement that he gives to his customers:

In search of optimum precision technology, one's pursuit would lead them into the field of optics. Here you would find laser instrumentation and ultraprecise lenses. The mechanical components that hold these precise elements in place are made of metal alloy plated with blackchrome.

Blackchromium plating offers extreme dimensional stability united with diamond-hard surface protection. This is the shell that BlackChrome Computer is expanding around its customer base. Our clients enhance the company.

In business since 1988, Larry has several large clients. He has advertised but he gets most of his clients by referral. Even though he's not a CNE, Larry gets corporate work on Novell Networks because his clients now interview their network people, asking specific questions. "They interview other people that have CNEs, but they know with me they're getting a more competent engineer," Larry said.

If he has an especially large network job, he hires contract people part-time to help him with the wiring. Monitor repairs are another job he hires out because he can get it done at a flat rate through a technician he knows who specializes in monitors.

However, the future is certification, and Larry is already planning to get his CNE credentials. He feels the credential will open doors for him. "Sometimes companies won't even talk to you if you're not a CNE," he added.

Besides doing PC repair, Larry works on Ethernet 10BASE-T and Token Ring network topologies. He has a strong interest in WANs and connectivity. Customers want WANs to connect one office to another so everyone can have access to one central database, Larry said. His hopes are that the new asynchronous transfer mode (ATM) technology for the coming "information superhighway" will catch on. Who knows, in a couple of years I might be setting up networks with sound and video that are as fast as accessing information on your own PC, Larry remarked.

LAN troubleshooting

Network troubleshooting tools fall into three categories. These include tools to troubleshoot cabling, hardware, and software. Before you can use a tool, however, you'll need to isolate the area of the problem. This process is very much like the process we covered in chapter 5 on troubleshooting hardware.

In isolating the problem, you'll want to ask many of the same questions you ask if called in on an individual PC repair. How has it worked in the past? When did it stop working? What happened when it stopped working?

Describe to me what happens when the problem occurs. What were you doing just before it stopped working?

And, just as in troubleshooting PC hardware, you'll want to know if any changes have been made recently. Were new programs added or deleted? Was the network or a portion of it physically moved recently? Has the problem occurred before? If so, what was done? And, of course, you'll want to have any relevant documentation.

Network troubleshooting lends itself to the process of elimination methodology—what does work? For example, you'll want to know if anyone else on the network can access or "log into" the server? If so, that means the server is probably fine and so are the stations that can connect. This narrows the scope of the problem to the workstation(s) that cannot connect as well as the associated cabling and adapter cards.

Hardware and software configuration problems cause less than 20 percent of the problems in networks. The overwhelming majority of network problems, over 80 percent, are in the cabling, so we'll start there, then cover hardware and configuration problems.

While you can use other tools such as an oscilloscope or a time domain reflectometer (TDR) or a combination of both to perform cable troubleshooting, most network repair businesses we talked with have opted to use cable testers, which include the functions of both devices. These newer devices are smarter, faster, and offer more help to the occasional user.

Cable troubleshooting tools

In looking for cable problems, you'll want to do some visual inspection first. Watch for a tear or cut in the outer shield of the cabling or a crimp in the cabling. Sometimes a chair or a heavy piece of furniture resting on the cable can create a crimp that will impede the travel of electrical impulses. In this case, the damaged portion will need to be cut out and a new section of cable spliced in.

Another simple inspection is to check the cable connections. Someone might have tripped over a cable, loosening its connection, or bumped a cable connector. See to it that the cables are securely connected. If everything seems to be correctly connected, you might be faced with a problem in the cabling itself. The problem could also stem from noise in the line caused by fluorescent lighting or an electrical motor near the cabling. These problems require special equipment to find, especially if the cabling is hidden behind walls.

A number of cable testing tools will not only tell you if there is a problem in the cable, but also the location of the problem. These tools will give you the distance down the cable from the testing point to the location of the error so you can track down the problem.

Cable testers measure cable characteristics such as noise, impedance, crosstalk, near-end crossstalk (NEXT), and attenuation. *Noise* is interference from other electrical devices. *Impedance*, more important in coaxial cable than twisted-pair, is the opposition of the cable to ac current flow measured in ohms. If the shielding is damaged or a heavy piece of furniture has damaged the cable, it will show up in the impedance of the cable.

Crosstalk is the electrical interference between wires in twisted-pair cabling. NEXT is crosstalk occurring between adjacent wires at the end of the cable. Twisted-pair wiring has a tendency to pick up stray electromagnetic interference. This interference can corrupt data to the point that it is useless.

Attenuation is signal loss. All cables have a tendency to attenuation, especially over long distances and cables carrying high frequencies have the same problem. Attenuation is measured in decibels (dB) and a reading of 0 dB means no loss of data.

You'll need to know the type of cable you're dealing with in order to use the cable tester. The information about the cable type is given in the rate electricity can travel through the cable, known as *nominal velocity of propagation* (NVP). The cable tester determines the cable type by its NVP and compares the signals it receives from the cable under test to the standard readings it contains for that type of cable. If you supply the tester with the incorrect NVP for the cable you have, the unit will not give you the correct readings.

While most cable testers will come with a table of common cable NVP settings, it is recommended you calibrate the cable tester yourself. This is done by taking a piece of cable whose length you know, connecting it to the tester, and changing the NVP settings until the cable tester reports back the correct cable length. Some testers will allow you to store the new value. You'll want to do so if it is not built into the tester so you'll have it for the next visit to the client.

To test the cable, you detach both ends of the cable from the network. UTP cable requires you to attach one end of the cable to the tester, and attach a loop-back device, which usually comes with the cable tester, to the other end. The connector on STP has it's own loop-back device, so you won't need to worry about attaching one. Once the cable is connected, you simply run through the diagnostic test routines.

Cable testing devices are available from the John Fluke Manufacturing Company, Microtest, Scope Communications, and Wavetek, though there are others. Testers are available that work on a variety of cables. Catalogs are available from these companies, and contact information is in appendix C. Expect to pay between $2,000 to under $5,000 for these devices.

As we discussed earlier, protocols govern the communications between computers. A protocol facilitates the "handshaking" process the workstation needs to complete to access the network, and this involves the proper timing, the correct communication, and accurate data. A protocol analyzer is brought into play when errors begin to increase on the network.

The steps of communication are well-defined using protocols and must be taken in the following order. First, a node must gain access to the physical medium. This is usually controlled by the hardware. For example, Ethernet networks require that a request be generated for use of the network. If simultaneous requests occur, known as a collision, each node generates a random waiting time, waits that long, and tries again. Collisions are normal, but a sudden increase in the frequency of these occurrences could mean a workstation's network adapter is faulty.

After a sending node has access to the network, it needs to surround the data it is sending with routing information that directs the data to the proper receiving node. Other information might also be added, such as start and stop bits or synchronization and error-checking bits. Protocols might also specify parameters like the transmission rate. If any part of this data frame is not recognized by the receiving device, there will be no communication.

As a network grows, matching protocols becomes more difficult. Some vendors might develop protocols that vary slightly from the accepted standards. Other vendors might develop proprietary protocols, independent of all standards. Still others combine protocols from various standards to take advantage of the best features.

Even when the protocols are matched, other faults can occur that affect communications. Subtle occurrences, such as a user noticing data is randomly becoming garbled, and obvious occurrences such as an inability to log onto the network, can be caused by problems in the network protocol. Such a fault could be an error in a network interface card that might cause it to generate bad data packets or stop generating packets. A workstation incessantly generating bad or garbage data packets is called a "jabbering node," and it can tie up the network.

Protocol analyzer options   Protocol analyzers can be used for system analysis to monitor the network, but they are best used as a diagnostic tool for fault analysis. You can get detailed information about the data traveling over a network and usually locate the source of a hard-to-find network problem. Using a protocol analyzer, data can be collected in a format that can be exported to an application software package, such as a spreadsheet, where it can be easily viewed and analyzed. Most analyzers will do some simple analysis and produce reports, charts, or bar graphs showing the network use.

Many protocol analyzers can generate and monitor network traffic, which is crucial information when upgrades or changes are planned. It is typical for a network to be operating at between 20–30 percent of capacity, though failures could occur at any capacity level. You can use a protocol analyzer to simulate increased network traffic and to benchmark each piece of equipment for its capacity level. Software and hardware developers also use network protocol analyzers to be sure that the product under development conforms to the network's specifications.

When protocol analyzers first came out, they analyzed the packets sent on the network on a bit-by-bit level. The current protocol analyzers take the convoluted bit pattern in each frame and convert them into English (ASCII), or sometimes hexadecimal. Putting the information into a more usable format makes it much easier to see what is happening on the network. Many protocol analyzers have features that allow you to predict a coming problem as well.

Some network users connect protocol analyzers to the network to monitor performance on a regular basis. This method can be helpful to track the performance of the network and give you a basis for comparison. By monitoring the network, it's possible to notice changes and possibly even anticipate a failure before it happens.

Capturing network data for analysis   If you suspect a problem or just want to be aware of certain events on the network, you can set most protocol analyzers to capture databases on a set of specified characteristics using techniques known as triggering and filtering.

A trigger starts or stops the collection of data when a certain condition occurs. If you set a trigger to stop collecting data when an error condition occurs, you can back up and examine the events before the error happened. Hopefully, you'll see a pattern that occurred just before the failure. Then, in an attempt to stop the failure, you can construct a trigger to indicate the next time the same patterns occur.

A filter, like a trigger, collects specific data, but it continuously screens the data. It can be aimed at a specific part of the network, such as a part of a packet or packets going to and from a specific destination. For example, if you are interested only in one set of protocols, a filter can ignore others and only capture these. A filter can also be used to collect statistics on network use.

Hardware and software filters are available. Hardware filters are faster, but software filters are more flexible because they allow for screening of a greater variety of packets. Often, a combination of hardware and software are used. The hardware reduces the number of packets captured so the software can handle the packets. The software can then more finely filter the information, so you get just the data you're looking for.

Real-time filtering, or filtering as the events occur, is an option, but if you're not going to be there to use the data right away, there's little point in putting the extra stress on the system. You can opt to capture the packets and send the data to a hard disk drive for storage until you're available to review it. At that time, you can use the protocol analyzer software to filter through and analyze the data as needed. This method has the added benefit of maintaining an ongoing record of network performance, right through changes and upgrades.

What to look for   What are you looking for anyway? Well common network protocol errors include: CRC errors, jabber, runts, short preambles, alignment errors, and illegal interframe spacing.

Cyclical redundancy checking (CRC) is a mathematical way to "add up" the message packets. The resulting value is transmitted with the packet. The math is done again by the receiving computer, and the result is compared with the value transmitted. A CRC error means the numbers didn't match up, which indicates the packet was unsuccessfully transmitted.

Jabbers are larger-than-usual packets that disrupt the network's signal. The additional data is garbage and worthless. A "jabbering node" is a workstation that sends out garbage data incessantly, saturating the network and slowing other traffic to a standstill. The opposite problem is packets with data missing. These packets are called "short frames" or "runts."

Short preambles refer to missing portions of the coded sequence transmitted before each frame to synchronize clocks and other circuits. If the preamble is short, the synchronization needed won't occur.

Alignment errors occur when a packet is not synchronized correctly. This usually occurs when the packet is not a multiple of eight bits.

Illegal interframe spacing can cause timing problems. Timing is crucial on a network, and late events are a problem. Timing problems can also be caused by segments that are too long or the presence of too many repeaters.

Any one of these problems could indicate a problem with the transceiver, which is the combination transmitter/receiver usually located on the adapter card itself. If the transceiver is separate, the transceiver cable is suspect as well. The adapter card itself can also be at fault.

Types of protocol analyzers   Protocol analyzers come in a range of forms and prices. Some are packaged as turnkey systems in the form of a portable computer, while others are sold as a board and software that you add yourself to a portable computer for use on a network. Software-only analyzers are also available. The software can be run on any workstation on the LAN and costs less than hardware analyzers, but is usually less powerful than the hardware-based systems. You can rent the more expensive protocol analyzers as needed for work on complex networks.

Many protocol analyzers are hybrids, part protocol analyzer and part network monitor. These tools can be a cost-effective alternative to more expensive full-featured protocol analyzers. Some of these hybrids are stripped-down versions of the more expensive products, while others might cost as much as or more than older units but provide additional functions.

Many products combine the basic functions of protocol analyzers. Physical probes that tap into the cables to evaluate traffic patterns are included in these units, and software is included that filters and decodes LAN data packets. The software can translate packet protocols into graphical output, which can also be used to generate traffic reports.

The trend is away from software that performs extensive protocol decoding and toward analysis software that can monitor local and remote traffic on more than one LAN. These programs can also generate detailed reports based on programmable packet thresholds and then set off alarms when the preset conditions are detected.

Probably the best-known hardware-based protocol analyzer is Network General's Sniffer, but other competing products are available from John Fluke Manufacturing, Hewlett-Packard, Novell, and Digilog, among others. You can expect protocol analyzers to range in price from under $3,000 to under $15,000. Contact information for these companies is in appendix C.

Network analyzers

The more powerful network traffic monitors are sometimes called network analyzers, but there is a difference. Network analyzers are usually more dedicated in their function, while traffic monitors are more like instruments. Network analyzers tend to have more advanced monitoring capabilities, allow a wider range of filtering, and some even have cable-testing features. These analyzers also are able to test Ethernet transceivers and offer advanced traffic-loading ability.

You might test the network and find it is running below capacity, but a network analyzer left in place might pick up peak times when the network becomes saturated. A saturated network—meaning it is simply overloaded—can cause problems such as bad messages and subtle data errors. Network errors detectable by a network analyzer include CRC, jabber, runts, and illegal interframe spacing. Interframe problems can be caused by a faulty transceiver, jabbering controller, or malfunctioning repeater.

Network analyzers can also deliver network and station statistics to be used in determining if network traffic is too heavy and to find configuration problems, such as nodes with incorrect address configurations. One of the clues to incorrect addressing can be found in looking at the network and station statistics for nodes that transmit but never receive or nodes that receive but never transmit.

If your troubleshooting leads you to believe that there is a configuration problem, you'll need to isolate the location of the error. Configuration errors indicate the problem could be an incorrect hardware setting or the workstation or server's environment files. Since each network has its own unique configuration files and settings, you'll need to become familiar with the particular network, usually through the documentation or through vendor training, in order to locate the problem.

Configuration troubleshooting hints

Just like other cards in the PC, network cards often have dip switches or jumpers for setting up the configuration. The network adapter card usually requires interrupt settings and a direct memory access (DMA) channel. If a new device has been installed on the workstation in question, there might be an overlap.

The settings can often be made using the software drivers in the network environment files as well. You might find yourself tweaking these files, looking for better settings or incorrect settings that could cause a configuration problem.

It is also helpful to note that the environment files load additional drivers into memory that can cause memory conflicts with TSRs or other software drivers. While these drivers can be loaded into high memory, freeing up lower memory for programs running on the workstation, there might not be high memory available. The problem could be simply not enough memory on the workstation to run the particular application the user is attempting to use.

In addition, it might be difficult to add a new PC to the network if the PC already has several peripherals attached, such as a CD-ROM drive, sound card, and joystick. Sometimes the only way to get around this is to use a multiple boot configuration, creating a network setting. This might require the user to reboot the computer, or even power down, before starting the network configuration, but it will usually work.

As the saying goes, you can never be too rich or too thin. Well, we'd like to add that you can never know too much about LANs. The field is constantly changing, so while it is well-paying, it requires you to keep up. We'd like to recommend two books, the *LAN Troubleshooting Handbook* by Mark Miller for general LAN information and for NetWare, *LAN Survival: a Guerrilla Guide to NetWare* by Deni Connor and Mark Anderson. *LAN Times* magazine is another good source for up-to-date networking information, though there are several other good magazines as well. We've listed these resources and others in appendix A. As an additional resource, Novell has a forum on CompuServe you can get to by typing GO NOVELL, which you can use to look for answers to your questions and to download drivers or updates as needed.

Acquiring LAN information

The tools you need to start

Your most expensive investment will be in a cable-testing tool. A cable tester that works with a variety of media is best, especially if you plan to go from site to site working on networks. Fortunately, network vendors usually provide troubleshooting software tools with the network, and network adapter cards also come with software diagnostics. So learning to use the software provided by the vendor is going to be the most economical route.

If you're working on large networks, a protocol analyzer or, even better, a network analyzer, will be a valuable tool. This is especially true on networks with multiple protocols or gateways. By a large network, we mean one with 100 or more workstations.

Integrated tools aimed at a popular network product will become increasingly popular. Microtest's Compas (Fig. 7-2) combines the most-used functions of cable testing, protocol testing, and network diagnostics and is aimed specifically at Novell networks. The trend is also toward analyzers that are less cryptic in the way they interact toward the user and are self-configuring, as demonstrated by the Compas product. You can expect to pay more for integrated diagnostic tools such as Compas, which is retail priced at under $5,000.

7-2
The trend in network diagnostic tools is to combine the basic functions of several tools into a single product with a less cryptic interface. The Compas network diagnostic product is an example of that trend.

One of the ways to learn to use the vendor tools is from the vendor. Training for network certification will help provide you with that knowledge as well as give you additional resources you can turn to for help when sticky problems arise. We'll cover that next.

Berkeley Geddes

Network Professional Association (NPA), Provo, Utah

Berkeley Geddes is the president of the Network Professional Association, formerly known as the Novell Certified Engineer Professional Association (NCEPA). The group is a nonprofit association that is attempting to be to computer professionals what the American Bar Association is to the legal profession or the American Medical Association is to doctors.

Started in 1990 as the Novell Certified Engineer Professional Association (NCEPA), Berkeley claims the group is in its infancy in launching certification programs, even though it is the largest network association so far. He compared the NPA's current level of achievement to where the American Medical Association was in the early 1900s. Berkeley is hoping the group will be able to establish the same standards and recognition for network computing as the AMA has established for doctors.

One of the most recognized services the NPA performs are its Event Labs, a hands-on technology road show that travels to 34 annual industry events such as the Networld/Interop show held in Dallas, Texas each year. The programs have been attended by 35,000 professionals worldwide and each one requires between 20 and 50 professionals to make the labs successful.

The NPA has nearly 80 chapters, with over 10 percent of the chapters outside the United States, and plans to expand its presence outside the United States. Berkeley added that several thousand new members are expected from Germany and Australia when those governments officially recognize the association so people can join.

To be a full member of the NPA, you must be a CNE and pay $150 a year. However, the group is now actively broadening its membership requirements to include other certifications in addition to the CNE which are offered by major industry players. These are:

- Novell Certified Novell Engineer (CNE)
- Banyan Certified Banyan Specialist (CBS), Certified Banyan Engineer (CBE)
- Microsoft Certified Systems Engineer (CSE), Microsoft Certified Product Specialist
- Compaq Accredited Systems Engineer (ASE) and ASE SCO Unix
- IBM LAN Server Administrator, LAN Server Engineer, OS/2
- Lotus Notes Certified Specialist (LNCS)
- WordPerfect Certified Systems Engineer (CSE)

Financial support for the group comes from the dues of 6,500 members and from ten vendors, including Novell, Hewlett-Packard, Skytel, IBM,

Profile

Banyan, WordPerfect, Microsoft, McAfee, Grand Junction Networks, and Lotus.

Berkeley maintains that the network paradigm has placed an umbrella over the entire computer industry. "In our view, the computer industry is the network," he said. "If you learn the network environment, you have to learn a stand-alone environment. This is a fundamental change in terms of professionals. Those who have picked up the network paradigm have a vision for understanding all of it, and with that focus they want to know any new technologies that come out."

In talking about knowing the new technologies in connection with network technology, Berkeley noted that right now you can hook up a Skytel pager up to a network system so that if the main hard disk is full or another problem occurs, it will page the network administrator. As TV moves to digital, it too is moving to a networked environment. "It won't be long before you'll be able to watch a movie while you're looking over your electronic mail," he added.

One of the main goals of the NPA is to establish core certification programs, get training for those programs established in higher educational institutions, and require that individuals get certifications gained by passing those programs in order to practice. Berkeley noted that he has met with the U.S. Department of Labor Secretary and officials from the Department of Education in making initial efforts toward establishing educational programs in computing.

The NPA is beginning by placing eight fully equipped labs in university environments with the help of member vendors. Brigham Young University is the first to get a state-of-the-art technical computing laboratory with an IBM AS/400 computer, Pentium network servers from Compaq, software from WordPerfect, and other vendor-supplied equipment.

The network computing industry will only grow as fast as these professionals are able to integrate the technology and support it, Berkeley stated. "It will only happen as fast as we have this army of professionals out there who can take the technology and integrate it into a productivity solution."

(Note: The certification programs recognized by the NPA, but not related specifically to networks, are covered in chapter 8.)

It is in the interest of the vendors to have people in the field who have a working knowledge of their products. As we said in the beginning, vendors are coming to the realization that they cannot by themselves effectively support everyone out there who has purchased their products. The vendors in the more complex fields, such as networking, have known this for some time and have set up programs to create specialists who can then go out and offer support for their products. To the user, certification is a stamp of endorsement from the vendor and sets you apart from vendors who are not certified.

While we are giving you the most up-to-date information available at the time of this writing, these programs change quickly, and those changes could accelerate as the industry moves forward in the area of communication. These certification programs change without notice. We feel the information provided here will be helpful as background to help you pursue certification, but we want to caution you to check with the vendors and the testing institutes before you pursue certification to be sure you are not wasting your time and effort on materials that are out-of-date.

In addition, be forewarned that companies will not miss this chance to take a captive audience and make them memorize the advertising material. This propaganda can become rather nauseating, but it's part of the game, so expect it.

The most well-known certification program is Novell's certified network engineer (CNE), so we'll start there. In the spring of 1992, Novell added an additional certification, called the Enterprise CNE or ECNE, for those who have worked with all of Novell's networking products. The CNE certification caught on when Novell began requiring it from all its resellers. Articles have appeared in LAN publications to advise management in companies how to keep CNEs once the company pays for an employee to become a one, which will give you an idea of the kind of demand there is out there for this certification coupled with experience.

Novell's certified network engineer (CNE)

However, the supply of CNEs is increasing, so there have been some estimates that the demand for CNEs will drop, and so will the salaries. As of this writing, there were under 10,000 CNEs. The increase in the number of computers and the increasing popularity of networks might offset the increase in supply, so demand could likely continue.

Most repair professionals working on networks want to get their CNE credentials, but those who already had their CNE pooh-poohed the need for the certification. We would suggest it is better to have the certification if you plan to work on networks, even if they're not Novell-based. As you'll see in the next chapter on other types of specialization, several other vendors accept the CNE as part of their certifications.

Specifics on the CNE course requirements and testing   Part of Novell's product line is training materials for the CNE and ECNE. The CNE course is divided into four sections with two optional additions available. The basic testing includes the System Manager, the Advanced System Manager, Networking Technologies, and Service and Support categories. You might also choose the version of NetWare for which you'd like to obtain certification, including UnixWare, then take additional courses to pursue other versions or go for the ECNE. Electives include Administering NetWare for Macintosh and NetWare TCP/IP Transport. The entire basic program with hands-on training costs about $6,000 and doesn't include the exam fees.

A prerequisite exam on DOS and PC hardware or Unix operating system fundamentals is required before you can take any of the other exams. You can obtain review books from Novell as study materials for these exams.

Novell uses Drake Training and Technologies to administer the tests nationwide and internationally. You are responsible for scheduling the tests, which cost about $70 each and are given by computer. The ECNE testing is more customized and Novell schedules and administers that testing.

If you fail a test, you can take it again, but you must pay the fee again to do so. The test is good for one year. Novell suggests that you take all the tests within a year from taking the first one because the requirements are "frozen" for you for that time period. After a year, you are responsible for retaking any testing that has changed.

The tests are short, usually taking less than half an hour. The computer asks questions and, based on your answers, adjusts the difficulty of the test up or down. It is possible to pass the test by answering just a handful of questions. A certain amount of controversy surrounds the test because of this, but most testing experts agree that a few well-chosen questions can uncover your knowledge as well as a lengthy, grueling exam.

Test questions are taken straight from Novell's materials, so it is possible to pass it with no network installation or troubleshooting experience at all. You don't have to take the hands-on courses to pass the exam if you prefer to purchase the course materials and study on your own. This can significantly cut the cost of obtaining a CNE to around the $500 range. However, we strongly recommend taking the hands-on courses for the experience, unless you can get hands-on experience performing on the job or by other means.

Novell information sources   In order for you to discover the current requirements for becoming a CNE, Novell offers a fax-back service that is menu driven so you can have information faxed to you. The information you can access includes the list of Novell Authorized Education Centers (NAEC) in your area where you can order Novell training materials and receive training, overviews of course requirements, and concepts covered in the various phases of the CNE and ECNE testing. These centers can sell you any

Novell materials, even the ones they are not authorized to teach. Instructions on how to use the fax-back service are available when you call.

The NAEC centers are also where you can take hands-on training courses taught in facilities certified by Novell and by Certified NetWare Instructors (CNIs). The number for Novell's fax-back service is listed with the Novell materials in appendix B. The list of training centers available via the fax back will also give you information about what Novell certification courses each center is authorized to teach.

In addition, you can obtain the Novell Certification Assessment, a Microsoft Windows program developed by Novell and Drake that simulates the various certification tests. The program also contains the DOS and PC hardware test simulation.

You can use this program to evaluate your knowledge of NetWare, as the questions are similar to those on the actual tests. There is no limit in the program on the number of times you can repeat the tests or sections of the tests. You get an actual score, instead of a pass/fail grade, so you can evaluate your performance. The assessment program also gives you the correct answers, where those answers are found in the Novell materials, a printout of your performance, and the areas where you were the weakest. The program is available for download on CompuServe (look in the Novell forum for details), or you can obtain it from your local NAEC.

Bruce Hildebrand
CNE, Keller, Texas

Profile

Bruce Hildebrand, currently a CNE employed at a large insurance company located in the Dallas area, never finished college. He attended the University of Southern California (USC), but was forced to quit for financial reasons.

He decided to attend an electronics school. Once he completed the one-year curriculum, his first job was to troubleshoot circuit boards for a company that made programmable welders. The work was dangerous because of the high voltages involved, and Bruce started preparing himself for different work by taking a basic programming class on the side.

Through friends, he made contact and went to work for BusinessLand, a company that specialized in doing computer work for other large corporations. While employed there, he attended IBM, Compaq, and Novell training classes.

The insurance company he now works for was originally a BusinessLand client. Bruce got to know the people there while he spent his days on site working on the company's network. When a job opening came up, Bruce was offered the position.

Bruce completed his CNE training in 1992. He managed to get through most of the tests using self-study materials, but he did have to retake one of the seven tests to pass it.

While getting his certification has helped him, Bruce said the biggest benefit is being able to make lateral moves in the computer industry. "It helps to have the certification if you have to look for another job," he said.

Bruce feels the places where he's learned the most are from his experience and from tech support calls. The insurance company purchased the Novell NetWare used in their Token Ring network from IBM, known in the industry as "blue Novell." IBM then handles all the product support. "I save up my questions, and when I talk to a tech support guy, I not only ask the question I called about, but I have a few others as well. You always get better answers from the tech support guys than you do from the sales people." Bruce added.

Part of working on networks involves PC repair. Even though his company has someone contracted to do the PC maintenance, when the network goes down, there isn't time to wait three or four hours to get it fixed. So Bruce has used his PC knowledge to install memory or perform repairs to get crucial portions of the network, such as the 486-based file servers, back online.

To keep up with the technology, Bruce reads *Lan Times*, *Network Connection*, and *Communications Week*. He's also a member of the NPA and says the NPA's magazine helps him look out for his career and keep himself marketable. He also attends the NPA's seminars at trade shows, such as the Network Expo held annually in Dallas. Bruce has also joined a networking user group in the Dallas/Ft. Worth area.

As for advice to people who might want to get into the networking field, Bruce recommends learning the PC first, including the DOS commands and what's inside the machine. Then start learning about networks by reading books and attending less expensive training classes at adult education centers. "You'll want to see if you like it before you jump into the CNE training," Bruce advises. As for his future plans, Bruce is working on his ECNE. He also is planning to get more training in the area of network routers.

Banyan, makers of the popular client-server NOS VINES, offers the certified Banyan specialist (CBS) and the certified Banyan engineer (CBE) certifications for those interested in designing and supporting VINES networks. To obtain the CBS, you must pass two tests, the VINES Administration and the Advanced VINES administration tests. Banyan offers hands-on courses as training for those tests, but you can simply take those first two tests from Drake without taking the courses. After that, students must take both the course and the test for the rest of the curriculum. For the CBS certification, students have the option of choosing either the VINES Gateways course and test or Problem Solving for VINES course and test.

The CBE requires the CBS certification plus Technical Support I and Technical Support II courses and tests. The company offers hands-on training courses several times a year in the following locations: at the company headquarters in Westboro, Massachusetts; in Atlanta, Georgia; New Jersey; Irvine, California; and Toronto, Canada. Drake handles the testing, and you can register by calling the toll-free number for the Drake/Banyan testing listed in appendix B. Course overviews for the required courses are also available by calling Banyan.

Testing is around $125, and the charge for each course varies from about $900 to $1,900, depending on the course. If you took all the courses, it would cost you about $5,500 to become a CBS and under $10,000 to become a CBE.

Optional courses include Administering VINES for the Santa Cruz Operation Unix (SCO Unix); Administering Enterprise Network Services (ENS) for NetWare; and Administering ENS for Hewlett-Packard Unix (HP-UX). These courses are in the $2,000 range each. Self-study materials are available for the VINES Administration, Advanced VINES Administration, and Administering ENS for HP-UX. Banyan Authorized Channel Partners can get you the self-study materials. A call directly to Banyan can help you locate an Authorized Channel Partner near you.

Banyan VINES certified Banyan specialist (CBS)

IBM offers the LAN server engineer certification for its client-server oriented LAN Server network. The company offers training courses through its daughter company, Skill Dynamics, and the actual testing is offered by Drake.

To become a LAN server engineer, IBM requires that the candidate take six tests in one year from the date the first test was taken. The six tests are: Installing and Supporting OS/2; OS/2 LAN Server Administration, Part 1; OS/2 LAN Server Administration, Part 2; OS/2 LAN Server Installation and Planning; OS/2 LAN Server Performance; and an elective. The electives offered include a course on Integrated Networks, Integration with Novell's NetWare, Token Ring, Ethernet, TCP/IP, and LAN NetView. Those receiving the LAN Server Engineer certification will also be certified LAN server administrators.

IBM LAN server engineer certification

Like the CNE, the LAN server engineer certification courses will cost around $6,000, with testing charged extra. The six tests cost about $100 each. IBM estimates that self-study done by purchasing the student kits is about half the cost of taking the courses. Sample test questions can be obtained by calling Drake for IBM or by calling IBM's fax-back service directly. Both toll-free numbers are listed in appendix B.

IBM also offers test credit for those with Novell or OS/2 certifications. Novell's CNE certification means that for the IBM LAN server, you have to take one less test, and so you save about 15 percent of the cost of LAN server certification. OS/2 Accreditation from IBM's Independent Vendor League also reduces the testing by one test, and you get vouchers worth $80 toward LAN server testing at Drake.

If you can make it through the LAN server tests without the course work or self-study materials, then the only costs would be the $600 worth of tests. IBM also offers benefits to LAN-server-certified individuals, including easier access to support, a free version of its CD-ROM technical library, and subscriptions to technical journals. The company will also supply you with its camera-ready logo for your advertising or business literature.

Microsoft certified systems engineer (CSE)

Microsoft offers the certified systems engineer (CSE) for networking with the Windows operating system or the peer-to-peer operating system Windows for Workgroups. This certification requires you to pass four operating system exams and two elective exams. The operating system exams are: Microsoft Windows, Microsoft Windows NT, Microsoft Windows NT Advanced Server, and Networking with Microsoft Windows or Networking with Microsoft Windows for Workgroups. Of the electives, you must take either the Microsoft Structured Query Language (SQL) Server Database Administration for OS/2 or for Windows NT. Then a choice can be made of the following electives: Microsoft LAN Manager Advanced Network Administration, Microsoft Mail Enterprise, Microsoft SQL Server Database Implementation, or Microsoft LAN Manager Network Administration.

To facilitate your planning, you can ask for the Microsoft Education and Certification Roadmap. The Roadmap is a Windows program that gives you information on the various certification programs and classes offered by Microsoft. It will even provide you with a to-do list to help you in gaining certification. The program also offers a list of the topics covered in the exams and suggests reading in the form of online documentation that comes with the programs or other resources from Microsoft or Microsoft Press.

Training for these tests can be taken in hands-on courses offered by Microsoft Solution Provider Authorized Training Centers. Self-study materials are available from these sources as well as in video, software, or workbook formats. The videos are around $200 for the set covering each exam. Self-study materials range in price from about $150 to $500 per course. Call the toll-free number for Solution Providers given in appendix B to locate the one nearest you.

The *Windows for Workgroups Resource Kit* is also an inexpensive way to get the information you need, and it costs less than $40 in book form from Computer Discount Warehouse (CDW). The *Windows for Workgroups Resource Kit* also contains all the information included in the *Windows 3.11 Resource Kit*, so you can save yourself a few dollars. The toll-free number for CDW is listed in appendix B. In addition, you can download this information from Microsoft Online, the company's own Bulletin Board Service (BBS). There are no connect charges other than what the phone company charges for the call and other software drivers and information is available there as well. That number is also listed in appendix B.

Practice materials for the exams are available as well. The Microsoft Certified Professional Assessment Exam, a practice test, is available for download from Microsoft's CompuServe forum (GO MSWIN).

For CNEs certified by Novell and CBSs certified by Banyan, Microsoft will waive the requirement of taking either the Networking with Microsoft Windows or Networking with Microsoft Windows for Workgroups exams. Proof of current certification status is required.

The exams, given by Drake, are $100 each, and retakes are $50. Once you're certified you're offered a free CD-ROM from Microsoft's TechNet CD-ROM subscription service with the latest technical information. TechNet is normally $295 annually for a monthly subscription. Microsoft will also provide you with camera-ready Microsoft Certified Professional logo to place on your advertising or brochures.

Artisoft training

Artisoft's LANtastic products are the recognized leader in peer-to-peer networking, with almost 50 percent of the market. However, analysts say Windows for Workgroups is quickly gaining a strong foothold in that niche. If you work with small businesses, you can expect to see increasing numbers of both products.

While the company does not offer certification, it does offer official training classes to those interested in learning more about the company's products. A call to Artisoft will give you details as to the training classes, held in the company's Tucson headquarters, as well as other information. The company also supports users via a CompuServe forum (GO ARTISOFT). Information as to Artisoft's available support services is in appendix B.

Certified network expert (CNX)

This is a vendor-independent certification for network troubleshooting proficiency and involves multiprotocol, multivendor product knowledge. The emphasis is on the use of network analysis tools, such as those from Network General (makers of the Expert Sniffer Network Analyzer), Hewlett-

Packard (makers of the Network Advisor), or Wandel & Goltermann (who make the DA-30).

The certification can either be on Ethernet or Token Ring networks, where two years of network troubleshooting experience is recommended. Testing is computerized and offered by Drake.

The *CNX PreTest Guide* is available for purchase from Drake for about $50. It includes a detailed discussion of each test, including sample questions, self-study materials, and a technical discussion of issues that will be on the exam.

The CNX Ethernet exam covers current and IEEE specifications as pertaining to Ethernet/802.3 standards. The emphasis is on the carrier sense multiple access/collision detection (CSMD/CD) pertaining to collision avoidance on the network. The test guidelines recommend that you understand the similarities, differences, and areas of incompatibility between Ethernet implementations, Novell, and other networks. You should also understand bit patterns associated with frame corruption, including propagation delay problems, reflection problems, environmental noise, and faulty hardware. Media access technology is covered as well, with questions on topics such as preamble generation, bit jam, and jabbering.

The Token Ring exam requires that you know the 802.3 standard and ring operation, including use of control bits such as priority, monitor count, ring poll/neighbor notification, how to add and remove a station, and soft error reporting.

Each exam costs about $250. Network General is strongly behind the CNX certification and even offers training classes to help you pass the exams. Details about the CNX, self-study reading, and course offerings are available by contacting Network General or by calling the company's fax back line at the numbers listed in appendix B.

Third-party network certification training

There are other sources for materials and training to become network certified. Wave Technologies of St. Louis, Missouri is one such source. The company offers self-study kits with books and videotapes as well as hands-on courses. While its biggest product line is Novell certification education, the company also offers training for Microsoft's certifications and IBM certifications in addition to courses on ATM technology, linking LANs, telecommunication fundamentals, and internetworking with TCP/IP. You can expect to pay $500 to over $2,000 per course, depending on the subject. The company offers a free catalog with full course descriptions and pricing information. See appendix B for contact information.

Trends in networking

The trends in networking are toward smaller and smaller network adapters and toward wireless networking. Market researchers Frost & Sullivan are predicting the wireless office equipment market will expand 20 times by the year 2000 to a $1.9-billion-a-year market. The leading force in the move is the wireless LAN segment, which is already dominant and is projected to continue growth to over 90 percent of the wireless market by the year 2000. Growth in the wireless LAN market is expected in the manufacturing, distribution, higher education, health care, and hotel fields. Radio frequency wireless LANs are expected to be slightly more popular than other types, including infrared LANs.

Companies such as Motorola, Xircom, and others are already introducing both small form-factor and wireless LANs to the market. Credit-card-sized Personal Computer Memory Card International Association (PCMCIA) form-factor network cards are available for just about every topology, including Ethernet and Token Ring (see Fig. 7-3). Mobile, portable PC users want and are willing to pay for network access, so the popularity of these connections is increasing. These cards slip into a specially designed slot on portable computers. These specially designed slots can be added to desktop PCs as well.

Xircom

7-3
Credit-card-sized Personal Computer Memory Card International Association (PCMCIA) network cards are aimed at the laptop PC market. These cards are available for just about every topology, including Ethernet.

Wireless and cordless LANs are also being offered. These LANs can be infrared or radio-based. The distinction is that wireless LANs imply the user can go nearly anywhere, while cordless LANs are local extensions designed for use in a limited area, much in the same way a cordless phone is used. The PCMCIA receiver and transmission unit for the user shown in Fig. 7-4 is Xircom's cordless CreditCard Netwave Adapter and is radio-based. The adapter communicates with the desktop Netwave Access Point (Fig. 7-5), which acts as a Netwave-to-Ethernet bridge and can support multiple users.

7-4

Wireless radio-based and infrared technologies are expected to grow 20-fold by the year 2000, and LAN technology is predicted to lead the way. Shown is a radio-based wireless network adapter in the PCMCIA form factor.

7-5

The desktop unit receives radio signals from the PCMCIA wireless network adapter cards, acting as the access point to the network.

These products can be obtained for just about any NOS and are attractive to users because they eliminate cabling. The trick is getting the software drivers configured correctly on the portable PCs as well as on the LAN server to make the units work. Costs are also expected to decrease rapidly as the units grow in popularity.

Other vendors offer training but do not offer recognized certification. The vendor might offer you a credential of some kind as well as a special logo for your advertising materials. In addition, certifications exist for computer professionals outside the world of networking, although many of these require some training or certification in networks.

Other areas of specialization & certification

Networking is not the only area of specialization in PC repair. The next chapter covers other areas of specialization, as well as where official certification for that area is available. We'll also talk about areas of further specialization in the computer repair field, such as monitor repair or printer repair, which do not have certifications available.

8 Boost your income through specialization

"If a man empties his purse into his head, no man can take it away from him. An investment in knowledge always pays the best interest."
— **Benjamin Franklin, statesman, scientist, and publisher.**

People who have a general knowledge of PC repair are in demand, but if you want to boost your income further in this rewarding field, the secret is to specialize. We've already talked in chapter 7 about networks, which is one area of specialization, but there are many others.

Some repair technicians enjoy the variety of problems they encounter by being a "general practitioner," but even then you can pick an area of specialization that will make you look to your customers as though you are focused and knowledgeable. If you enjoy a variety of problems, specializing in upgrading PCs could be an option for you.

Fortunately, the number of areas of specialization are not limited in this field. You can choose to become certified as a general practitioner; you can hitch your business to the successful business of a vendor and specialize in certain brands of PCs—even getting endorsement from the vendor by way of certification.

Peripherals such as monitors and printers need repair, and specialization can be lucrative. Software is another area where you can become an expert, ranging from operating systems to specific software applications, with certification programs available in these areas as well.

In this chapter, we've decided to spend our efforts on the most lucrative areas of specialization and the ones with training and information readily available.

We're focusing on areas we believe have a future, coupled with help so you can get into those areas.

First, we'll talk about certification in general, the difference between certification and vendor authorization, and how to go about obtaining certification. We'll move from there to areas of general PC repair certification, vendor-specific hardware certification programs, and software certification programs. Leaving certification specializations, we'll focus on service areas, including upgrades, data recovery, and repair of PC peripherals. There we'll also cover the two most lucrative areas of fixing peripherals: monitor repair and printer repair. Finally, we'll mention other areas of specialization that do not have formal training available but offer opportunities.

Certification overview

Certification is much like the "Good Housekeeping Seal" to your customers. It's the stamp of approval that says you have achieved a certain level of competence. Though we were unable to find a state in which certification was required, there wasn't one technician without certification in our interviews who wasn't planning on getting a certification of some kind. The reason? They felt it would validate their skills and generate business.

Certification versus authorization

While the distinction is sometimes blurred between vendor certification and being an authorized dealer or service center for a vendor, there is a difference. Certification usually requires the investment of money as well as time on your part. Authorization doesn't usually cost you anything to get, even though it involves training. This is because authorization means vendors are looking for you to sell or otherwise promote their products. A specific vendor might also require a minimum amount of sales volume from your business in order to even consider you for authorization. In return, the vendor will refer customers to you. However, in certification or authorization, the vendor is expecting a commitment from you. Authorization means a greater commitment since vendors have a certain amount of muscle to enforce the agreement.

The future holds certification requirements

There are groups actively working to make certification of computer repair technicians a federal requirement, so this is a subject you can expect to see more and more often. The reasons are numerous. Repair technicians in the field want to protect their reputations and the monetary amounts they can command. Those outside computer repair want to have a way of gauging the competence of people they want to hire for repair work. Repair provider companies want a market advantage and feel they can get it if their technicians are certified while others are not.

As PCs become more popular and more complex, it is becoming necessary for some type of formal training to be put into place. But formal training is expensive, so higher educational institutions have been reluctant to invest in state-of-the-art equipment. Even private training schools, who openly boast that their graduates can perform, are not investing in up-to-date equipment.

Neil Wyenn of CPR Computer Repair in Granada Hills, California told us that he used to hire graduates of schools advertised on afternoon television as training centers for computer repair technicians. He stopped hiring these new graduates because he discovered that the schools provide these trainees with very, very old equipment, so most of them have never seen an up-to-date PC on the inside and have to be retrained anyway.

Obtaining certification

To obtain certification, you must pass tests. Most certifications are offered by vendors, but there are a few that are offered by groups of vendors who have formed organizations for the purpose of certifying repair technicians in general. Certification tests are available in many fields, including the computer industry, and third-party companies specialize in administering these tests for the computer industry as well as other fields such as air conditioning contractors, chefs, animal science professionals, and a myriad of others. Drake Training and Technologies is the largest testing company, and the one you'll hear about most often for testing in the computer industry.

The companies administer the tests periodically at sites all over the United States and even internationally. Drake boasts 600 testing sites in 52 countries. Usually several testing locations are available in each state, and it is your responsibility to schedule for the testing in advance and to get yourself to the site. A fee is usually involved as well. Most testing fees are in the $70 to $200 range. Should you fail a test, you can usually retake it, but you can expect to pay the fee again.

Also, as the certification is updated, you might be required to be tested again in order to keep your certification current. Some vendors go to the trouble of revoking your certification, sending you a notice in the mail, if you do not continue to meet their education and testing requirements. On the average, you'll probably be facing tests every two years to keep your certification.

Study materials and sample test questions are available for most of the exams. The study materials or training classes are usually where you'll spend the most money. You might also find books published to help you get the more popular certifications. We will talk about each certification as we cover that field of specialization, as we did in the chapter on networks, chapter 7.

As quickly as the computer industry changes, so do the certifications and the requirements to get them. The vendor materials say repeatedly that the information can be changed without notice, and the vendor cannot be held responsible for errors or omissions. If the vendors take that stance with their own tests, we cannot take a stronger one. Take our information as a general guideline, but be sure to do your own investigation.

A few general certifications exist for PC repair technicians. The test to obtain the certification is an overview of repair skills needed, and some tests go into topics such as customer relations as well as repair.

Formerly known as the "ABCD," the Computing Technology Industry Association (CompTIA or CTIA) announced a program for establishing an industrywide competency standard for service technicians. Called the A+ certification, CompTIA said over 40 computer industry vendors participated in the program, including Apple Computer, Packard Bell, Toshiba, and computer retailer CompUSA. The A+ certification is to be implemented in four phases. Service technician certification is first, with certification tests and training for sales representatives, managers, and engineers following.

Administered by Drake, the A+ certified service technician test covers microcomputers; displays; storage media; printers; basic operating systems such as DOS, Macintosh, and Windows; and basic data communications. For an outline of the exam topics, the type of questions used in the exam, and references for further study, you can get the booklet "Twenty Things You Need to Know to Prepare for the CompTIA A+ Certifications Exam" by calling Drake at the toll-free number listed in appendix B under the A+ certification. The exam costs $165 unless you happen to be employed by a CompTIA member organization, in which case the fee is $150.

IBM offers a self-study training kit that includes a 460-page workbook with 400 self-evaluation questions; a videotape on electrophotography/laser printer concepts; a videotape covering electrostatic discharge; *The Complete PC Upgrade and Maintenance Guide, 3rd Edition*; *Microsoft MS-DOS 6, Step-by-Step*; *IBM PC DOS v6.1 User Documentation*; *Outside the IBM PC and PS/2, Access to New Technology*, and the *Macintosh Bible, 4th Edition*. The kit is around $400 and is available by calling IBM's company, Skill Dynamics, toll-free. Most of the materials in the kit are available at your public library. If you need to, you can buy these books (listed in appendix A) or equivalent books at your local bookstore for a lot less than you'll pay for the kit.

The A+ certified service technician exam has received criticism from opponents who say it does not accurately measure the knowledge a service technician has to solve a problem, and it is simply too easy. CompTIA clearly states that the test does not include vendor-specific procedures or product information. The exam is based on ". . . recognized and approved job tasks for technicians who service customers' microcomputers and related equipment in a businesslike manner." With its strong support by leading computer industry companies and its widely publicized certification, the CompTIA has a good chance of coming out on top in the general practitioner certification game.

Certified electronics technician (CET)

The International Society of Certified Electronics, founded in 1965, offers the certified electronics technician (CET) professional certification, which includes a journeyman specialty in computers. The basic exam for certification is multiple-choice and covers basic electronics, math, dc and ac circuits, transistors, and troubleshooting. An additional specialty portion must be taken for permanent journeyman status. That portion can be one of nine optional tests on subjects such as consumer electronics, industrial electronics, Federal Communication Commission (FCC) rules and regulations, audio equipment, medical electronics, radar, video, communications, and computers.

The computer option covers basic arithmetic and logic operations, computer organization, input and output equipment, memory, and storage. Some very basic knowledge of software and programming is also needed, as well as the ability to explain troubleshooting procedures. Those with less than four years of experience or education may take the associate level exam, which is the electronics portion of the full-credit CET exam, without the specialty option. The associate level status is good for four years, then it must be upgraded to CET journeyman status.

Sample tests and CET study material are available from the ISCET for a nominal charge, or you might even find those materials available in your public library. In addition, the ISCET offers videotapes on a rental basis that were donated by Sony National Parts and can be purchased from Sony. One particular tape includes a 17-minute presentation on how to solder even the smallest high-density flat pack integrated circuits (ICs) using different soldering systems, and this could be helpful should you decide to pursue component-level repair. The tape is Audio Tape Deck Mechanism, CRT Setup, and Go Ahead, Solder It!.

The tests themselves are given nationally and internationally on a regular basis. The ISCET will give you on request a list of contacts in your state for testing dates and information. The fee for the CET exam is $25 and includes the associate exam and one journeyman option. Each additional journeyman option is an additional $25. Retaking the exam is half-price the first time, then goes back to the original rates. The associate exam is $25 as well. Those who pass the associate exam are certified as an associate CET for four years and are eligible to join the ISCET. Those passing the full CET exam who have four years of education or experience receive journeyman status, a permanent wall certificate, and are eligible to join the ISCET. They may also use the CET logo and purchase CET-logoed materials.

ISCET membership is $35 a year. It includes an annual yearbook, a subscription to a bimonthly electronics news magazine, a quarterly newsletter about the ISCET, and an annual membership bonus. Previous bonus items have included items such as a free book from an electronics course. The ISCET is headquartered in Fort Worth, Texas and will send you information concerning the CET and CET materials on request. Contact information is available in appendix B.

Level 2 certification was initiated by National Advancement Corporation (NAC) of Santa Ana, California. Company president Don Doerr says he considers the CET journeyman in computers "Level 1" and therefore called his company's test "Level 2." NAC specializes in training for repair of computers and computer peripherals.

NAC says 40 percent of the circuit boards sent in for repair have nothing wrong with them, and 80 percent of the hard drives replaced in the field should not have been replaced. The problem is unskilled technicians hired to do repair work they are not qualified for, according to Doerr. Since 1985 Doerr's company has offered PC repair training to corporations with in-house repair staffs. NAC said this experience qualifies the company to set up the Level 2 vendor-independent certification.

Doerr's company is currently the only company that offers training for passing the Level 2 test. However, Doerr claims the test is not one you can pass with only "book knowledge," so only about 40 percent of the people who take NAC courses pass the Level 2 exam. Of repair technicians as a whole who have taken the test, only about 20 percent pass. If someone passes the Level 2, he or she is the cream of the PC repair crop, according to NAC, who maintains a list of Level 2 certified technicians for recommendation.

No sample test questions or self-study materials are available for the Level 2. The test fee is $150, and testing is administered by Drake. The test covers: component recognition, to test a technician's knowledge of major system components and the meaning of chip markings; data recovery, especially getting data off a nonfunctioning hard drive; diagnostics and troubleshooting relating to the ability to reason through field problems often misdiagnosed; general electronics; general PC knowledge; industry knowledge such as where to get replacement parts; monitor knowledge and the ability to spot problem symptoms and understand the operation of monitors; software knowledge such as recognizing improperly setup environment files, virus recognition, and software conflicts; and terminology.

Courses offered by NAC cover PC maintenance, printer repair, Macintosh maintenance, and two courses on network installation. Course prices range from about $1,300 to $2,500 each, depending on the course. Discounts are offered for prepayment. Course attendees are given NAC's own technical reference materials with case-specific fixes included, updates for one year to the reference materials, toll-free technical support, and a free "second time through" the particular class within a year. Courses are offered in Southern California, New York, Chicago, Dallas, Atlanta, Boston, Washington, and other major cities in the United States NAC also offers videotapes for instruction in monitor and printer repair. More information is available by contacting NAC at the toll-free number listed in appendix B.

Vendor–specific computer certifications

Several of the more popular vendors have come up with repair certification programs of their own. These vendors offer proprietary hardware, usually at a premium price. For a repair technician, this can mean a higher income, as the customer is used to paying more for the equipment and expects to pay more to have it repaired.

Compaq ASE

Compaq, one of the top PC vendors, offers the accredited systems engineer (ASE) certification. This certification requires two tests and a certification from one of four other vendors. Compaq offers a training course for the ASE, called the Systems Architecture Concepts Course, and then the student can choose from one of the four platform-specific tests offered by Compaq. Courses are offered for the platform-specific portion as well, and they include: Compaq/NetWare Advanced Performance Integration, Compaq/Microsoft Windows NT Performance Integration, Compaq/Banyan VINES Advanced Performance Integration, and the Compaq/SCO Unix Advanced Performance Integration. The cost of the courses is in the $2,000 range.

Students can test out by simply taking the tests at Drake, but Compaq strongly recommends taking the classes to prepare for the courses. Testing is about $150 per test. In addition, students must show one of the following to get their ASE certification for the first year: Novell's CNE; Microsoft certified professional or Microsoft certified product specialist for Windows NT; Banyan VINES Technical Support I course completion; or SCO Unix System V/386 administration and SCO TCP/IP and SCO NFS administration and configuration. (The Microsoft product specialist is covered later in this chapter, and references are made in appendix B as to how to obtain information on the SCO Unix certifications and course information.)

After the first year, ASE candidates must show proof of completion of one of the following accreditations in order to maintain their ASE certification: the Novell ECNE, the Microsoft certified professional-Microsoft certified systems engineer, the Banyan VINES BCE, or the SCO advanced certified engineer (ACE). In addition, Compaq requires certified candidates keep up on additional information through courses, self-study, and additional testing.

Information on the ASE program is available via Compaq's PaqFax fax-back service, which you can call toll-free using the number listed in appendix B. You can also obtain a self-assessment guide from the PaqFax service, which tells in general terms what you need to know to pass the tests.

Compaq offers support via online services such as CompuServe (GO CPQFORUM) and America Online. The company also offers training videos for under $50 that provide specific information about each of its computer products. In addition, for under $100, Compaq offers video self-study on its laser printer line.

Dell has a third-party maintenance program through which it provides training and reimburses for warranty work done on its products for its customers. In order for a repair shop to work on Dell equipment under warranty, the Dell customer involved must write a letter to Dell stating that the customer prefers that his or her own repair service technician work on their Dell equipment.

As a certified third-party maintainer for a customer with Dell equipment, Dell will pay you, at the customer's option, $15 per quarter per PC under warranty or a $75 fee per repair incident for qualifying repair calls.

Obviously, this program is not particularly lucrative, as it is aimed at large Dell customers such as universities and government installations who might have their own in-house repair people or a contract already in place with a PC service provider. However, it could be a way for you to get your foot in the door at a large installation and get some training that could help you with other brands of PCs as well.

Training for certification on Dell equipment is based on "kits" that cover the technical details of various products offered by Dell. Third-party maintainers order the kit for a product on which they wish to perform service, go through the kit, then take a test offered through the company's training facility, "Dell University." In order to pass, you must score an 85 or higher on the test. The kits are less than $150 each and include a training video, a student guide that contains material to help study for the test, a service manual, and a "how-to" sheet. Testing is included in the price of the kit, and you can request the test from Dell University when you're ready to take it.

Hands-on courses are also offered at Dell's training facility in Austin, Texas. These are three-day courses and the cost is about $1,000 per course. Testing is included in the course as well.

Third-party maintainers, once certified, have access to 800-number technical support, Dell's TechFax/Bulletin Board for online technical information, and the payments we outlined earlier as part of the warranty program. A toll-free number for Dell University is listed with the other Dell information in appendix B, where you can get more information on becoming a third-party maintainer.

In taking a wholistic approach to PC repair, we can hardly overlook the role software specialization and certification plays in the repair business. Since the NPA has decided software certifications should be included in the credentials it accepts for members, and since software is such a crucial component of the overall operation of computers in general, it seemed appropriate to include the various software specialization fields in this chapter. We'll start with the operating system certification available for IBM's OS/2, then talk about various product certifications including the certified product specialist, the WordPerfect certified systems engineer (CSE), and the Lotus Notes certified specialist (LNCS).

IBM OS/2 certification

IBM offers certification for its graphical operating system OS/2. This certification requires you pass 4 tests, given by Drake. The tests include Using and Customizing OS/2, Installing and Supporting OS/2, OS/2 Advanced Support, and either OS/2 Performance and Tuning or OS/2 Problem Determination/Problem Source Identification. Student kits are available for independent study, but IBM cautions that the materials are less aimed at self-study than they are focused on reviewing what an individual already knows. Hands-on training is available from Skill Dynamics.

Sample tests with answers are available from IBM's fax service, listed in appendix B, and information about obtaining student kits is available from the Drake number listed in the appendix. A program certification catalog is available from Drake as well. The OS/2 engineer certification is acceptable for membership in the NPA and is good towards obtaining a certified LAN server engineer credential as well.

Depending on the amount and type of training, the certified OS/2 engineer could cost you between $400 for the four tests alone, to $3,100 for hands-on training courses and the testing costs.

Microsoft certified product specialist

Microsoft offers four certification programs covering its word-processing product Word for Windows, its spreadsheet Microsoft Excel, its project management software Microsoft Project, and its electronic mail application for PC networks Microsoft Mail. To be certified you must take and pass an operating system exam on either Windows or Windows NT, then an exam on the application you wish to be certified for. You may take the exams for more than one application after you take the operating system exam, so with five exams you could be certified in all four product areas.

The same Microsoft Education and Certification Roadmap program that offers information on the company's network certification also offers certified product specialist information. A Windows program, the Roadmap gives you information on the various certification programs and classes offered by Microsoft, a list of the topics covered in the exams, and suggested reading in the form of online documentation with the application programs themselves. It will also recommend books, and you can even use it's to-do list function to build yourself a plan of action for obtaining the certifications you're interested in. Most of the application products are widely supported, so third-party books and training materials are likely to be available. You might want to check with your local library for such materials.

Hands-on courses are offered by Microsoft Solution Provider Authorized Training Centers, and self-study materials are available from these sources as well. The self-study materials come in video, software, or workbook formats.

The videos are around $200 for the set covering each exam. Self-study materials range in price from about $150 to $500 per course. Call the toll-free number for Solution Providers given in appendix B to locate one near you.

WordPerfect Corporation was purchased in 1994 by Novell and has become the Novell Applications Group. Probably the most well-known certification is its certified systems engineer (CSE) credential offered for expertise with its WordPerfect word-processing software. WordPerfect has used Drake as well as other companies for its certification testing services.

WordPerfect certified systems engineer (CSE)

Novell is now handling certification related to all WordPerfect products, and changes are occurring both in WordPerfect's support and certification policies. However, as of this writing, the new policies were not formalized. Novell officials said information regarding the WordPerfect certification can be obtained when it is available by contacting Novell using the information provided in appendix B.

Notes, Lotus' well-received office automation software package is aimed at network computing. The package provides database capabilities, messaging on the network, and connection with other, outside electronic mail sources such as CompuServe and MCI Mail. Notes' strengths are flexibility, the ability to work with other applications via the vendor independent messaging (VIM) standard, and customization to a specific set of tasks using an application programming interface (API).

Lotus certified Notes consultant (LCNC)

Lotus offers training and certification for Notes, and testing is performed by Drake. There are three certifications available for Notes, but the certification of interest to a third-party repair business would be the Lotus certified Notes consultant (LCNC). Certification as an LCNC requires that you take and pass three exams: the Notes Technical User exam, the Application Development I exam, and the System Administrator I exam.

Training materials include courses, courseware in book form, and computer-based training (CBT), which are available at Lotus Authorized Education Centers (LAECs) throughout the United States. The company also has LAECs in Brazil, Canada, and Mexico. Hands-on training courses range in cost from $400 to $1,200, depending on the course. CBT training is about $1,500 a module. The CBT training allows you to work at your own pace, repeat sections of the training if needed, and keep track of your progress. Including exam testing costs of under $100 an exam, LCNC certification costs can range from about $2,400 for hands-on training to $5,000 if the CBT training route is chosen.

Lotus offers detailed course outline information via a fax-back service. More information is available from Lotus Education at the toll-free number listed in appendix B. Testing must be scheduled with Drake. The exams themselves are composed of 45 to 90 questions and take about an hour to complete.

Recertification is expected as new versions of Notes are released. Lotus provides updated materials while the new version is in the final testing stages, and if you are certified, the company will notify you of the upcoming testing requirement. An outline of the material covered on the update exam is available via the fax-back service as well.

Service specialization

Specialization isn't limited to what certifications you can acquire. There's a large market in taking a service segment of the repair business and focusing on it. For example, you can upgrade or offer maintenance services to customers. We'll talk about both of these opportunities next.

Profile

Winn Rosch
Author of the *Winn L. Rosch Hardware Bible*

Some of the best opportunities in the PC repair business are in upgrading, according to Winn Rosch, author of the PC repair book the *Winn L. Rosch Hardware Bible.* Repair businesses can do what people are afraid to do, and that is add new capability and horsepower to their PCs.

"PCs aren't breaking as fast as they ought to for the repair industry; they're pretty reliable hunks of sand, metal and plastic," Winn remarked. "But they often need upgrades to keep up with advances in the industry."

People aren't afraid to upgrade for no reason. Winn says that if you do the math on the number of accessories available on the PC, you run out of universe to encode the data for all the possible permutations. For example, if there are 1,000 expansion boards, 8 slots, any of 1,000 boards that can go into one slot, any of 1,000 boards that can go into the second slot, pretty soon you come up with a number that's impossibly large. This assumes that we disregard peripherals such as mice, as well as the number of motherboards available. Fortunately, the universe of accessories decreases rapidly when you eliminate oddball stuff and stick with the most popular accessories.

Smart upgrading is also a factor. Winn notes that a user can ". . . upgrade to a Pentium for half the price of one of those silly upgrade chips." The first step to getting into the upgrade market is to track your customers. "Any good businessperson keeps a database of his customers," Winn remarked. Special mailings to offer upgrades can then be made. The mailings could also be customized so that upgrades can be targeted to certain users based on their system configuration and purchasing history.

PCs that are two to three years old are good targets for upgrades. Winn advises that you might want to itemize a list of upgrade possibilities for a customer, then offer to do the upgrades in smaller steps, one piece at a time. You might offer to do a motherboard upgrade to the latest local bus architecture, then in the next month or so the customer could upgrade his or her video card, and then later add a larger hard disk drive. This way, upgrades can be done at a pace customers can afford, and you have a steady flow of repeat business.

You should also be offering specials for any major change. For example, you can target a mailing about a new Windows operating system upgrade and an update of any existing software the user has to work with it. If you properly target the letter, you can get as high as a 10 percent response, which is unheard of in the direct mail business.

The second part of this type of promotion is to look for low-cost suppliers for the components you purchase. Mail order sources can be good. Check your local sources as well. You can usually get a lower price if you order in some volume, so keep that in mind.

Upgrades

You might think that new PC buyers are not a market for upgrade services, but these people might be some of your best candidates for upgrades. New users often discover shortly after a PC purchase that they didn't buy enough to do what they had in mind when they purchased the machine in the first place. Also, it's easier to upgrade a PC in the first year after a purchase than later, as these recently sold units are more likely to be supported by their manufacturers and have the horsepower to make an upgrade worthwhile.

Popular upgrades include adding horsepower to a PC by adding a faster processor, turning it into a multimedia PC, or adding the capability to accept PCMCIA cards for sharing data with a laptop computer. You might also want to specialize in setting up PCs for access to the information superhighway, which would include adding a modem, software, helping the user get accounts with online services, and perhaps even training.

Upgrades can fix PC buyer remorse   A survey done by Channel Marketing showed that PC buyers were often unhappy with their purchase. Nearly seven out of ten respondents wished they'd gotten more expansion slots in the PC for adding peripherals such as an internal modem. Almost half of those surveyed regretted not choosing a better-quality monitor and wished they'd gotten more memory. Just about four out of ten respondents said they should have gotten a larger hard disk drive. Just about the same number declared that both high-density 3.5-inch and a 5.25-inch drives are what they should have chosen instead of just one or the other.

To get more expansion slots, the user would need a motherboard upgrade. A better monitor would mean upgrading the monitor and the graphics card. More memory could involve taking out the memory already in the PC to add new memory. A larger hard disk drive might also mean a BIOS upgrade to support the drive, depending on the BIOS. Adding a floppy disk drive is a relatively simple operation if the PC has a slot available in the front to house the drive.

Upgrading requires a change to the CMOS to tell the computer about the new component. Some of the newer computers are smart enough to recognize that more memory and two warm boots resets the CMOS, but other types of upgrades require that you change the CMOS.

The first thing to determine is whether or not the upgrade can be done. Memory upgrades depend on whether or not the memory slots are full and whether or not the motherboard is designed to support different-capacity SIMMS in the slots. Some motherboards require all the SIMMS be the same capacity, so if there are four slots and four 1MB SIMMS in those four slots, then the only way to upgrade the memory is to take out the 1MB SIMMS and add higher-capacity memory modules such as 4MB or 8MB SIMMS.

You'll need to know what the motherboard will support before you go swapping out SIMMS. You can get that information from the documentation that came with the unit, or if that isn't available, you can call the manufacturer, try to look it up in a technical reference such as the reference materials from Micro House, or try to see if the manufacturer has an online forum that will offer technical information.

Processor upgrades   Other types of upgrades are common as well. Upgrading the microprocessor chip on PCs is becoming a common practice, facilitated by chip makers and board designers. Boosting the speed of an Intel-based PC by adding a double-speed processor is relatively easy, though users might not know how to tell the BIOS about the change. Sometimes the change can involve a board swap, instead of a single chip, as in Fig. 8-1, where the technician is shown upgrading the DEC PC from a 486 to a Pentium processor. Often, chip upgrades involve changing the BIOS as well, but that probably won't involve a chip replacement.

New flash BIOSs make upgrading the BIOS easier, should it be necessary. Like RAM or CMOS, flash chips can have the information stored in them changed, but unlike RAM or CMOS, flash chips can retain the information without any power backup at all. This means the BIOS chip itself can be upgraded using software from a floppy disk. However, the most popular and the fastest way to get BIOS upgrades is to download them from the bulletin board of either the processor manufacturer or the BIOS maker. A call to the BIOS maker or the manufacturer of the upgrade processor will get you the information you need. In addition, Intel and other companies have forums on CompuServe (GO INTEL) and America Online to offer technical information and download information to support personnel. Contact information for chip manufacturers is in appendix B.

Storage space upgrades   The number of installed programs per computer will increase, driving the need for more computer storage space, according to market

8-1
Jeff Austin, head engineer at Dell, swaps out a 486 microprocessor card for a Pentium 60-MHz card.

Dell Computer

analysts Frost & Sullivan. Graphics-intensive, disk-hungry software and 32-bit operating systems are also contributors to the need for storage real estate.

Growth projections on the conservative end are predicting that the storage market will be five times the 1993 figure of $8.3 billion, while on the high end, analysts are saying that the need for storage could mushroom the market to 15 times that number by the end of the decade. Declining prices of both hard disk drives and removable disk drive storage are also fueling the demand.

A faster hard disk drive can also make an enormous difference in Windows performance, even on a fast PC. Smaller, faster, cheaper hard disk drives in capacities well over one gigabyte are becoming widely available.

The success of the upgrade will depend on how old the PC is, what the BIOS will support, and whether or not you can upgrade the BIOS if need be. The newer drives are smaller, faster, run cooler, and are often almost a plug-and-play proposition for you.

Usually, an IDE card will only support two drives, one as a master and one as a slave, and that's something to watch for when adding a hard drive. The master drive is the boot drive. Jumper settings on the back of the drive usually make the determination as to whether the drive is a master or slave. New drives usually come set to be the master drive. If the new drive is to be the slave, you can probably get the slave jumper settings without a great deal of trouble from the documentation, or you can ask for the jumper information from whoever sells you the drive.

The biggest problem is when the user wants the new, faster drive to be the master. This is a logical choice, but when the user wants to keep the old drive as well, it could get tougher. Since the drive already in the PC is set to be the master, it might be a challenge to get the jumper settings to make that sure-to-be-older drive the slave.

This is where a technical reference like the Micro House Technical library comes in handy. If you can't find the settings there, or you don't have a copy of the library, you can try calling the drive manufacturer. A copy of the *Pocket PCRef*, the *Computer Industry Almanac*, or similar reference book is a big help in attempting to locate the phone number of the manufacturer. Available for under $50, the *Computer Industry Almanac* also contains other useful information such as conferences and trade shows, industry awards, and average salaries for computer industry jobs in various locations of the country. You can also contact BIOS manufacturers using information available from the book. More information on the almanac is available in appendix C.

Multimedia upgrades   The market for multimedia hardware and software in the United States alone is expected to quadruple by the year 2000. Spurred by a booming desktop video market, the amount of multimedia authoring is expected to increase, as are the numbers of people who will purchase these new multimedia products. You can get in on this boom, helping customers upgrade existing computer hardware to multimedia standards.

A multimedia upgrade includes adding a CD-ROM drive and a sound card to a PC. You can purchase CD-ROM upgrade kits with instructions that will allow you to add the new devices for under $200 on the retail market. Instead of adding two cards, one for sound and one for the CD-ROM drive, most CD-ROM upgrade kits come with a single card that handles both, so only one expansion slot is needed. In addition, the CD-ROM drive can be mounted either internally or externally, depending on whether or not the user has a free space in the form of a drive slot for adding the drive internally.

One consideration here is the horsepower of the PC being upgraded. Most users are going to be unhappy adding a multimedia upgrade to even an Intel 386-based PC. Hard disk space is a consideration as well because most CD-ROM-based multimedia programs require some hard disk space to operate, and on a small drive, this could limit the number of programs the user can enjoy. In addition, the synchronization of the sound with the images from the hard disk drive is heavily dependent on the speed of the PC.

Some users are just adding CD-ROM capability to their PCs in order to take advantage of the vast amount of text-based reference material available on this media. In this case, a CD-ROM drive can be added to a PC with horsepower as low as a 286, although the faster, the better.

Add PCMCIA to a desktop PC As the popularity of laptop PCs increases, the exchange of data between the credit-card-sized PCMCIA flash storage cards or "PC cards" and desktop PCs is becoming more of an issue. Driven by the exploding demand for portable computers, the PC card market is expected to grow by more than ten times worldwide into a 5.8-billion-dollar market by the end of the decade, according to Frost & Sullivan.

While the PCs can be cabled together via the serial or parallel ports, and the data can be transferred using software such as LapLink from Traveling Software, most users find this process painful, to say the least. What they would like is a PCMCIA slot on their desktop PC and the ability to simply take the PC card from their laptop computer and place the card into the PC to be used there, as illustrated in Fig. 8-2.

8-2
Karen McIntosh, finance manager at Dell, inserts a PCMCIA card to transfer a spreadsheet from a laptop to a desktop PC.

Dell Computer

Adding PCMCIA capability is more than simply adding a drive. Software drivers for PCMCIA must be added as well so the computer can access the card when inserted into the drive slot. In addition, PCMCIA slots in laptop PCs have the capability of supporting a number of different PCMCIA cards, including network cards, modem cards, hard disk drive cards, wireless electronic mail or pager cards, as well as data storage cards in varying capacities. You might need to load drivers for all those capabilities, depending on what your user wants to be able to do. These drivers take up memory and might need to be loaded into high memory so the user still has access to the programs and functions that were available before the PCMCIA slot was added.

Information superhighway access upgrades   Adding a modem to a PC, whether you add an internal modem to a free expansion slot or an external modem to a free serial port, will give your user the first step to accessing the information superhighway. The essence of information highway access is the Internet, the worldwide network of that includes colleges, governments, universities, and individuals around the globe.

That might prove to be a big step for a new user however, so a Prodigy account might be a good way to begin. America Online is a good place to start and you can usually get the software starter kit by simply calling the AOL toll-free number and asking. AOL is graphical, requires Windows, and offers new user tutorials.

If your user wants to access the Internet, there are graphical Internet access programs available. Even CompuServe users can have graphical access through a number of access kits. More information is available by contacting CompuServe directly using the information provided in appendix B.

Upgrade testing

Any new piece of equipment you install in a PC should be tested. From a new hard disk drive to more memory, testing the new component is called a "burn-in." Usually, a 24-hour burn-in on a new component is sufficient to be sure the part will not fail in the field. The only place where you might not want to perform more than an hour of burn-in is on a floppy disk drive. After all, you don't want to wear it out before the customer even gets the machine home. But on other components, a burn-in will save you a number of headaches.

For your convenience, we've included with this book a program to test your upgrade installations, and it just happens to be called BurnIn. BurnIn will allow you to test one or all of the PC's main components. It performs video tests in text and graphics mode, disk tests, math and CPU tests, and it will even test a printer. If there's a problem, the program creates a log file to tell you what the problem was, so you can run the program unattended all night if you'd like.

While the program will test a printer, we don't recommend that you run the printer tests unattended. Someone needs to be available to shut the printer down if the paper gets jammed. Something as simple as a paper jam left unattended could cause expensive damage to an impact printer.

We've found BurnIn to be invaluable in testing new equipment, and we recommend the program to new computer users to perform a burn-in of the entire new system. In testing new PCs, we've found problems new users might not have found for weeks or months, including problem monitors, bad hard disk drives, and even some mechanical problems.

Once we discovered a floppy disk drive that wouldn't even accept a disk when we tried placing a disk into the drive in preparation for the floppy disk test. (By the way, you can format a disk from within BurnIn.) This particular PC was purchased at a warehouse-type retail outlet.

While that might not seem like a big deal, it is much easier to tote the unit back to the store and exchange it the next day than to find out after two months that you can't get the disk in the drive and need to get something done. In the first 30 days, most warehouse buying outlets will take back a bad product if the box and the purchase receipt are handy. After that, you usually have to deal with the manufacturer. In this case, we traded for another new PC for the customer, finished the burn-in, and the unit has run just fine ever since.

You might also want to carry a copy of BurnIn with you to test used computer equipment you might purchase. Some computer buyers carry a portable universal power supply and a copy of BurnIn to computer swaps to test PCs.

Data recovery

Data recovery is lucrative and requires skill. Every PC technician should know at least the basics of data recovery, since the data is the most important part of the PC to any user, and it is far more valuable than the hardware. What you have to do to recover damaged or lost data depends a good deal on what data needs to be recovered and why it can't be recovered by the user.

Mirror

In DOS version 5.0 and above, you'll find the Mirror command available. Mirror can be used to capture the FAT and root directory information as well as the DOS partition information, which can be used by the Undelete and Unformat commands to recover data. While the FAT and root directory information changes often, the partition table information does not usually change. Without the partition table, the drive won't be able to find the DOS kernel to boot, so having a copy of this crucial portion of drive information can be very handy.

The Mirror command can be executed in the AUTOEXEC.BAT to capture crucial information to the MIRROR.FIL file, stored in the root directory of the drive. You can save information about a single drive, or multiple drives, by simply listing the drives after the MIRROR command, separated by spaces like this:

```
MIRROR C: D: E:
```

Another crucial task for Mirror is to save the partition information generated in a file to a floppy disk. We recommend that this disk be a bootable floppy disk that also contains the environment files, any necessary drivers, and other crucial information. This "rescue" disk can then be stored by the client or by you for an emergency. To create the PARTNSAV.FIL file, use the following command.

```
MIRROR /PARTN
```

You'll be prompted as to which floppy disk drive you want to save the PARTNSAV.FIL information to, and you'll be informed as to whether or not the operation was successful.

Mirror can be loaded as a memory-resident utility to track information about files that are deleted. This information can then be used to recover deleted files, although files can be recovered without it. There's a trade-off here, however, as the TSR takes away from the performance of the system. The /TC switch is added to the Mirror command to track file information, including how many files you want mirror to keep information about. The command:

```
MIRROR /TC
```

tracks just the last file deleted, but you can track up to 999 files by adding the number to the TC switch with a dash. For example, to track the last five files deleted the command would be:

```
MIRROR /TC-5
```

The Mirror command can also be removed from memory after it is installed by using the /U switch like this:

```
MIRROR /U
```

As a side note, while you'll find most of the DOS commands in the online help supplied with versions of DOS 5.0 or higher, you will not find the Mirror command listed there.

Undelete

The simplest data recovery jobs are getting back files deleted by the user, especially if these files are recovered fairly soon after deletion. As you know, DOS maintains the FAT, a directory of the attributes, and locations of all files on the hard disk drive. When a file is deleted, all that is changed is the FAT, not the file itself. So, if you discover early that the deleted file is one that's needed, you can simply undelete the file. MS-DOS 5.0 or later, and Windows 3.1 or later offer Undelete utilities. Both the Windows and DOS versions of Undelete will show you what files are available for recovery in the current directory.

In order to undelete, a first character must be assigned to the file name because the original first character has been eliminated in the delete process. If you're attempting to recover a program, you can run into difficulty if you don't remember the first letter of the name of every file you undelete. If you get the first letter of one of the files wrong, and the program depends on a file by a certain name, the program might not run.

In recovering data files, it's less crucial to remember the exact file name. If you're just recovering data files, you can set a switch in the DOS UNDELETE to automatically undelete, which selects the "#" character for the first letter of the file names. Of course, if data has been written to the disk since the file was deleted, your chances of getting the file back decrease. Whether or not you can get the data back depends on how much the file has been overwritten by new data written to the drive.

Both DOS and Windows, as well as other programs like Norton Utilities, offer TSR programs that will help undelete by either keeping good records of the files or by even copying the files to another place so they can be recovered. Such activity can slow the system down and cost a lot of disk space. It is up to you and your client to decide if the price of the TSR is worth the extra protection. You can get more information in Windows about the TSRs under "File" in File Manager by selecting "Options," then "Configure Delete Protection" from the Microsoft Undelete menu. Further instructions for the DOS version are available by typing "HELP UNDELETE" at the DOS prompt.

To use the Mirror file information to undelete the files, type:

```
UNDELETE /DT
```

As we've already said, using the Mirror command to track deleted files reduces the system resources for other tasks. But it does significantly increase the probability of getting deleted files back.

Unformat

Unformatting is also possible. If a drive has been accidently formatted, the DOS UNFORMAT command, available in MS-DOS 5.0 or higher, can get the contents back, assuming the disk hasn't been overwritten with other data. To determine if the disk in question can be unformatted, type "UNFORMAT A: /TEST." The test will not actually unformat the drive, but it will let you know the results if the drive was to actually be unformatted.

Unformat can also use information generated by the Mirror command to put back the partition table on a drive where that information is damaged. The Mirror command must be used beforehand to save the partition table information. To use the Mirror PARTSAV.FIL to restore the partition, type:

```
UNFORMAT /PARTN
```

You can check to see if the Unformat will work with the information you've saved using the Mirror command. For example, to test the likelihood of a successful Unformat of the C: drive using the Mirror information, use the /J switch like this:

```
UNFORMAT C: /J
```

This check is a good idea. It could uncover surprises for you, such as the client's unexpected upgrade to a new version of DOS during your absence.

Get data off a reluctant hard disk drive

Most other data recovery services have to do more with getting the hard disk drive working because once the drive is operational, you can usually get the data off it. Getting the hard disk drive working depends on the type of drive and the type of problem. You should check the power to the drive, the drive's connection with the drive controller card, and the other steps we've already outlined.

Tricks to get the drive to spin up   If you determine that the problem is the hardware of the drive itself, then it depends on the type of drive you're working with as to what to do next. A common trick, which should be used as a last resort when you're pretty sure the drive isn't spinning up, is to take the drive out of the computer and rap it on the table. The idea here is to free stuck heads. You want to rap it just hard enough to jar the heads loose, not destroy the drive. Be sure it's connected to the necessary cables when you put power to it again, so if it spins up, you can leave it running and copy off the data.

Older drives are often sensitive to temperature changes, and once you allow them to warm up they work. This might mean you'll need to allow the drive to sit in the case with the power on for an hour or so before you reboot and try to access it again. Some of the old Seagate series 200 drives are especially sensitive to temperature changes, so loosening the screws on the bottom of the drive can sometimes help.

Some drives with stepper motors had trouble with the formatted tracks drifting so the heads can't read the tracks. One way to attempt to get the data off the drive is to physically take it out of the computer and hold it at varying angles until the heads can read the data. It's a trial-and-error process, but it can work.

Check the partition   If you see some life from the drive, but the computer won't boot, you should check to see if the partition still exists. You can do this with the DOS FDISK command. You'll need to boot from a floppy disk drive, then use FDISK from the floppy to determine if there's a problem with the partition. If FDISK says no drive exists, then recheck the hardware connections.

If FDISK loads, then you know you can access the drive. Choose the "Display Partition Information" option to see the available partitions. If software such as Disk Manager or SpeedStor was used to partition and format the drive, you might see a small DOS partition, then a larger non-DOS partition. That's not a problem, as these software products create a small (under 3MB) DOS partition, then create their own partition and load their own drivers to access the hard disk drive. (If you watch during bootup, you'll sometimes see the device driver from these software packages flash a copyright message on the screen.)

But if FDISK says it's a non-DOS partition, and the partitions don't follow the above pattern, the partition table could be damaged enough that DOS doesn't recognize it. If FDISK gives you the message "No partitions defined," that means the DOS partition has been damaged or destroyed.

The thing to do now is to exit FDISK. If you use FDISK to create a new partition, it is likely you'll lose all the data on the hard disk drive, as FDISK has a tendency to overwrite the FAT.

This is when a copy of the partition made with the Mirror command comes in handy. If you have a copy made with the Mirror command, you can use Unformat to put it back. If you're in an environment where there are other, similar PCs available, you can use the Mirror command to copy the partition to a floppy disk and use the Unformat command to restore it to the drive where the partition is needed. Be sure the DOS versions are the same, the hard disk drives are the same, and the partitions are the same on each drive. (The only way to know if the partitions are the same is to ask the user.)

If you're working with earlier versions of DOS, you can use a software product designed to copy sectors of the hard disk drive by location. To copy the MBR, you need to copy head 0, cylinder 0, track 1 of the good hard disk drive and restore the copy to the damaged hard disk drive. Software tools are available for this purpose, such as the GETSEC and PUTSEC utilities from the hTEST/hFORMAT hard disk recovery tools offered by Kolod Research. C.P.R. Data Recovery Tools from Tech Assist are also designed for this type of work, as is Rescue Data Recovery Software from AllMicro.

Should you not be fortunate enough to have another similar drive around to copy from, there are tools available to rebuild the partition. The Norton Utilities from Symantec, The Fix by Consolidated Software, Micro-Scope from Micro2000, and others will rebuild the partition, assuming portions of it are still available. Some of these products, such as Micro-Scope, will rebuild the entire MBR, including the partition. Be advised that if a virus is responsible for the damage to the partition or the MBR, these products could bring back the virus as well. However, this will give you an opportunity to get the user's data off the drive.

You'll find good troubleshooting information on hard disk drives that are not responding, including how to copy the MBR yourself using the DOS utility DEBUG in Mark Minasi's book *Maintaining, Upgrading, and Troubleshooting IBM PCs, Compatibles, and PS/2 Computers*. In *Que's Guide to Data Recovery*, Scott Mueller discusses how to rebuild the partition using software utilities that allow you to view the beginning portions of the disk directly.

Check system files   If you've successfully recovered the partition, or if the partition is fine, you might find yourself with a computer that still won't boot from the hard disk drive but you get the error message nonsystem disk or some other boot failure message. This could be due to damage to the system files. You'll need to restore the system files using a bootable floppy with the same version of the operating system and the DOS SYS command. You type at the DOS prompt:

```
SYS C:
```

to recopy the system files from the floppy to the hard disk drive. If this doesn't work, it might be due to a file that's already in the space the system files take up, in which case that file will need to be moved and the area erased. This can be done with software tools such as the Norton Utilities or Micro-Scope.

FAT check   If you can boot from a floppy and access the disk, you might want to try to run the DOS CHKDSK utility, which checks the FAT. SCANDISK, offered with DOS 6.22, is a more detailed check of the FAT and the hard disk that will even do a surface check of the media itself. The same utilities that will rebuild the partition will often take a look at the FAT as well, and even restore the data from the second copy of the FAT.

Get the data off   If things are uncertain and the disk is acting as though it might die again, you might just want to start getting the data off. The Fix comes with cables and a utility so you can transfer the data off one computer's hard disk onto another. This same function can be performed with one of the many programs that link two computers via the ports for file transfers, such as LapLink, or you might use a portable tape backup drive.

There are software tools you can use to get data from the drive reading sector by sector if need be, such as the C.P.R. Data Recovery Tools. The idea here is to make an exact copy of the drive onto another duplicate drive in order to recover the data. You need to know detailed information about the file and directory structure in order to make these kinds of recoveries. You can get that information from books, some of which have been written for programmers. *The DOS Programmer's Reference* by Terry Dettman (Que, 1991) does a good job in chapters 8 and 9 explaining the DOS file structure. Peter Norton's books on the PC are also helpful in explaining how data is stored.

Data recovery software tools

Data recovery software tools are crucial to most data recovery operations. None of these tools are perfect, so if you suspect trouble, the best thing to do is get access to the data, then move the data off the drive anyway you can. Then you can "futz around" to determine the exact cause of the problem. We've already discussed several products, including the Norton Utilities, Micro-Scope, Tech Assist's C.P.R. Data Recovery Tools, Rescue Data Recovery Software from AllMicro, and The Fix from Consolidated Software. Both C.P.R. and Rescue allow you to ignore one or more of the drive heads if need be to recover data, especially if one of the heads has crashed or is out of alignment. If a head is out of alignment, the data from the other heads is recovered first, then the drive is moved at various angles until that head will read the data, and the data is then recovered as well.

If the drive has a bad motor or you simply can't get the data off, you might contract with data recovery services to perform the job. If the drive needs to be opened up, you'll need to look for a service that has a Class One clean room environment. OnTrack, C.P.R. and others offer these types of data recovery services. Those services are listed in appendix C, along with the contact information regarding the data recovery software products we've mentioned in this chapter.

Data recovery would seem like it would be less crucial in the case of a damaged floppy disk drive, but sometimes it is even more crucial than recovering data from a hard disk. It is surprising how many users will keep crucial data on a floppy disk for portability and security reasons, and never make a copy of the disk. For that reason, we included the shareware utility Read My Disk! (RMD!) with the utilities in this book.

Get data off damaged floppy disks

The day coffee gets spilled on a crucial disk or the disk falls from a folder onto a driveway to be run over by a car, your clients might find themselves with crucial data recovery problems. Any disk that can be spun in a floppy drive can be read with Read My Disk! Disks damaged by coffee spills should be taken out of their protective case, rinsed with water, left to dry, then placed in another protective case before insertion into the floppy disk drive.

Severely damaged disks will produce a read-error, but Read My Disk! will read them anyway if the capacity of the disk is entered into the program. The product creates files in the directory from which it is run with the extension .DAT, and it contains the data from the disk in ASCII. The only portions of the disk that won't be read are portions that are missing (such as data that was stored where a screwdriver punctured the disk) or blank sectors of the disk.

If the drive is compressed using DoubleSpace, DiskSpace, or Stacker, the main drive you're accessing when you boot from a floppy is the uncompressed drive (usually the II: drive). Now you have a more delicate situation on your hands because you have an enormous "virtual" drive in the form of a single compressed file as well as the other compression utility files and the two kernel files IO.SYS and MSDOS.SYS.

Data recovery on compressed drives

You might not even be able to see any files on the drive at all without running DIR /A, which shows all hidden and system files. This is when you turn to the user and ask innocently if they have a recent backup of the system.

However, all is not lost, as Rescue and the Norton Utilities will also work on compressed drives. As the rest of the diagnostic tools catch up to the introduction of disk compression, you'll see more tools with the ability to deal with compressed drives as well.

Recovery of database data

A company is usually crucially dependent on the information in its database. If that information should become corrupted, it becomes imperative to get the problem fixed. The Xbase file format for databases, formerly known as the dBASE file format, has a special header that supplies information to the application software working with the database. This information includes the names, types, and lengths of data fields and other crucial information. Should this header become corrupted, it requires special knowledge to repair.

You'll need to know something about databases to perform this type of recovery, but there are tools and reference materials available to help you. Paul Heiser has made it his specialty to repair corrupted database files at the rate of hundreds of dollars an hour.

He has written a book to share his expertise with you called *Salvaging Damaged dBASE Files*. His software program, dSalvage Professional, available for about $200 from Comtech Publishing of Reno, Nevada, is designed to make repairs to Xbase files for you. The database world also has its own magazine, DataBased Advisor, which provides information and trends in the database field. We've included information on Heiser's book, dSalvage, and DataBased Advisor magazine in appendix A.

As you start your venture into the field of data recovery, you'll want to read the reference books available in that area, which include *The Paul Mace Guide to Data Recovery* by Paul Mace and *Que's Guide to Data Recovery* by Scott Mueller and Alan C. Elliott.

Peripheral repair

These days, a computer isn't considered much good if it doesn't have a monitor or a way to print. Both a monitor and a printer are considered essentials by PC users, and both are relatively straightforward to learn to repair. As we've already talked about, monitor repair is fertile ground for a budding repair business. Printer repair also offers strong opportunities, especially in laser printer repair.

Monitor repair

Monitors, especially color monitors in higher resolutions, are in demand and are worth repairing. The average cost for a color SVGA monitor these days is $500 to $700, depending on the quality of the monitor and the screen size. It is not unusual to pay over $1,000 for a good-quality monitor, and special-purpose monitors used for computer-aided design or desktop publishing can cost several thousand dollars.

At these prices, it is worthwhile to the consumer to fix an SVGA monitor if the repair cost is under $200, rather than replace the unit. Older-model monitors, both color and monochrome, can be repaired for significantly less because the components cost less.

Monitor repair is much like television repair but is more straightforward because you don't have to worry about the tuner, which is the part that brings in the various broadcast stations on a television. In fact, computer monitors can be used as televisions sets, if the broadcast signal is converted to a form the monitor can display. This is happening with increasing frequency, as demonstrated by the new computers that are cable-ready for television and the add-on television cards that turn PCs into TVs.

Monitors convert the low-voltage signal from the PC into tens of thousands of volts needed to pulse through the "guns," which shoot at and excite the phosphor in the CRT to produce the what we see. Color monitors have three guns to make the red, green, and blue (RGB) picture elements (pixels) that make the color combinations for the screen. Some components in the monitor are designed to hold a large portion of that electrical charge even when the monitor is off. This is where the danger lies in working on monitors, as this voltage can kill you. *The bottom line here is to use caution.* It is best to know what you're doing and avoid taking risks.

Most general PC repair shops have made contact with someone who can do monitor repair for them for a flat rate. Some repair shops who said they could do the repairs found it easier to contract the work out because they said monitor repair requires them to dust off skills they don't use in computer repair work. It's more economical for them to pay someone else who does the repair all the time than to spend the time sharpening their skills for the occasional monitor repair.

This specialty is also a business in which you can have less direct contact with consumers. This means you can deal with a smaller number of people who understand more about the business and will probably pick up and deliver the units to you as well. Some have been operating monitor repair businesses as a nationwide mail order repair operation. However, damage due to shipping problems has prompted some businesses to go local for their monitor repairs. Tony Hemmelgarn, head technician at the computer parts specialty company Midwest Computer Support of Toledo, Ohio, said the first repair work his company started doing was monitor repair because of the rework on monitors caused by shipping. The company purchased a training video, technical support, and some diagnostic hardware and is now repairing 120 monitors a month in addition to the parts business. However, since you have a smaller client base, it's important you get the word out to repair shops that you are available and offer reliable service.

Not counting the cathode-ray tube (CRT), most monitors have three major components, each of which costs around $30 each. Since the chances of all three components going bad are slim, most monitor repair shops can charge a flat rate of under $100 for repairs on even SVGA monitors and still come out ahead. At this rate, the PC repair shop can send the monitor out for repair, double the repair price, and still be well under what consumers are willing to pay. If the monitor is an expensive one, replacing the CRT at a cost of about

$200 might also be worthwhile, especially if it costs several thousand dollars to replace the monitor. Warranties on repairs are typically for 90 days.

Basic electronics knowledge is needed for monitor repair because you might need to read schematics. Monitors have a tendency to be very much alike, and some repair shops claim the schematics of one monitor can be used to repair another. However, schematics are not always needed to repair monitors, and many repair outfits are getting along without these diagrams.

In addition, you might find you need special tools to get inside certain monitors, such as those from IBM. These special tools are usually available from the vendor or from third-party sources. Jensen Tools offers the IBM PS/2 monitor repair tool set depicted in Fig. 8-3.

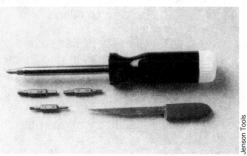

8-3
Some monitors require special tools. Shown is the IBM PS/2 monitor repair tool set.

Jenson Tools

Monitor repair training is available in the form of videotapes and courses from companies who offer computer repair training. Videotape monitor repair courses are going to cost you around $500, including books and technical support charges during your learning period. You might also opt to continue the technical support from the training facility at an additional charge, just to be sure you can get the answers you need. Courses can cost three times or more than self-study videos, including the additional cost of travel and lodging if you have to go to another city for the course. But courses offer you hands-on experience with equipment and allow you to ask questions that might not have come up otherwise.

Video self-study materials are available from Wheat Ridge, Colorado-based Peripheral Diagnostics and previously mentioned NAC. NAC also offers hands-on training. Both companies offer technical support and parts sources. Information on these companies and additional monitor parts sources are listed in appendix B.

Tony Hemmelgarn, Depot Services Manager
Midwest Computer Support, Toledo, Ohio 43624

Midwest Computer Support specializes in finding computer parts and repair services, acting as a broker in this field. They also brokered monitor repair services, but found that shipping the monitors off for repair caused them warranty rework for units that were damaged in shipment.

Tony Hemmelgarn, depot services manager for Midwest, said the company started looking into doing monitor repair services themselves. For the how-to's, the company purchased Peripheral Diagnostics Monitor Repair Training Video and the technical support and learned how to do monitor repair themselves.

"We started advertising locally, and now we're doing 120 monitors a month," Tony said. Peripheral Diagnostics' niche is video training in monitor repair without using schematics. While schematics are helpful, Tony indicated that the diagrams weren't really necessary, as the video teaches you what to look for. "You start seeing the same types of problems over and over," he said.

Midwest's standard repair rate for most monitors is $85, not including the flyback transformer or the CRT. "If those components are bad, we call the customer, let them know how much more it will be, and let them decide," Tony added.

To aid in diagnostics, Midwest purchased a monitor analyzer and a tube restorer from Sencore of Sioux Falls, South Dakota. The tube restorer helps them test for a bad CRT and allows them in some cases to repair the CRT. Replacement CRTs can be as high as $1,000, depending on the type of monitor, but most are in the $150 to $200 range. Flyback transformers range from $9 to $70, depending on the monitor.

Most of the parts needed for repairs can be obtained at an electronics parts store, and since Midwest specializes in parts, they can usually find other needed parts. Peripheral Diagnostics provided parts sources as well.

While they repair mostly VGA and SVGA monitors, they get monochrome monitors in for repair as well. Tony commented that his least favorite type of monitor for repair are monochrome monitors because he feels as though most of them aren't very well made, which makes them more difficult to repair. Also, it can be more difficult to track down parts for these monitors, especially if the company who made the monitor is out of business. The company has continued to pay for technical support from Peripheral

Diagnostics to help them in those oddball situations that arise from time to time, Tony stated.

Midwest's success rate in repair is pretty high, Tony remarked, as he's unable to repair only about 3 percent of the monitors that come in. Monitor repair has been a profitable addition as well and has become 10 to 15 percent of the company's overall business.

Printer repair

Printer repair falls into two major categories, laser printer repair and repair of impact printers. Laser printers are much like copy machines in that they use toner and a heat process to fuse an image to paper. Impact printers form images on the paper by striking the paper through inked ribbon, either with the shape of the character such as a daisy wheel printer or by making the shape of the character with repetitive dots such as a dot-matrix printer.

There are printer repair businesses that specialize in one type of printer and some that work on all printer types. While it might appear that the computing world is moving toward laser printers, impact printers are still faster, less expensive to operate, and work well for making multiple copies in a single print session. Like copiers, laser printers also keep a running copy count, which implies there is a maximum number of pages that can be printed before the laser printer simply wears out. Impact printers do not face that limitation.

Materials on the repair of daisy wheel and dot-matrix printers are available, many from the manufacturer. Materials on the repair of laser printers are less plentiful, but we feel from our research that laser printer repair can be more lucrative. For one thing, an exclusive agreement between HP and Canon has kept Canon in a low-profile position when it comes to marketing laser printers on its own. That agreement has reached its expiration date, however, so you can expect falling prices and increased demand for laser printers as Canon comes full-force into the market with its own thoroughly tested and compatible laser printer product line. The competition is expected to be especially fierce in the SOHO market, where there's a lot of pent-up demand but the price point has kept these businesses from making the investment.

Another force is the lack of established laser printer repair channels. Even though laser printers are much like copiers, copy machine repair shops often won't work on these types of printers, mostly because they're afraid of the computer end of things. This leaves the door wide open for new people with repair operations to jump into the market.

Most laser printers, including the LaserJet printers from Hewlett-Packard (HP) and the LaserWriter from Apple Computer, use a printer engine made by Canon. In fact, 80 percent of the laser printers on the market use Canon's engine. Of the printers that use the Canon engine, 80 percent are made by Hewlett-Packard. This means that if you understand the basics of repair of the Canon engine or the HP laser printer, you can repair the majority of laser printers on the market today.

Laser printers are made up of an engine and a circuit board that controls the printer. A variety of companies can have the circuit board made to go with a popular engine, such as the Canon engine, and that circuit board is where most of the variety in laser printers comes from.

A common repair on laser printers is the replacement of the fuser assembly, the part of the engine where the heat is applied to the paper. Replacement of these assemblies can cost several hundred dollars, but repair in most cases can be done for well under $100. This repair can be performed in under an hour by a trained technician, while those with more experience can do it in about 15 minutes.

NAC offers a training video that shows how to repair the various types of fuser assemblies available. The video identifies each fuser assembly, offers information about the most popular make and model number of printers the assembly is used in, and shows what to look for, including how to recognize damaged components. Additional materials list hundreds of printers by make and model with the corresponding Canon print engine used in each one. Further, the video comes with the Canon part numbers for each part in the video, right down to springs and gears, and sources for those parts. (We've listed those sources in appendix B.)

The importance of listing the Canon part numbers is HP often won't list part numbers for the component parts that make up some subassemblies. It can be difficult then to obtain the needed parts for the subassembly, forcing you to order the entire assembly rather than simply replace the damaged part. If you can get the Canon manuals for the laser printers, you'll find those manuals much more complete in their parts listings. The video is $129. NAC offers a hands-on printer repair training class as well for about $1,400 each.

Another Southern California-based company, Diversified Technigraphics, offers four comprehensive courses in laser printer repair. The courses, offered at basic, continuing, and advanced levels, are held on the weekends at the company's offices in Irvine and cost under $1,400 each.

The course work is based on the company's training manual, *Mastering Laser Printer Service*, which takes the user, in over 350 pages, through step-by-step troubleshooting techniques for all Canon-based laser printers. The manual is aimed at starting a laser printer repair business and contains impressive, detailed diagrams and photos of repair disassemblies. Normally priced at just under $400, the manual is available at a discount from PC Service Source of Carrollton, Texas (see appendix B). Technigraphics even offers a $300 toolkit with all the tools mentioned in their manual. A set of four videos to explain the basics of laser printer cleaning and troubleshooting are also available for under $150. Contact information for Technigraphics is in appendix B.

Interestingly enough, besides the regular computer repair magazines we've already mentioned in this book, there is valuable information concerning the laser printer repair industry in magazines geared toward the recycling industry. This is because laser printer toner cartridge recycling is big business. These publications include *The Recycler*, *R&R News*, and *Recharger*. A trade association, ULTRA, holds shows around the country where you can find out further information on this industry. Contact information for these publications and ULTRA is listed in appendix A.

While the videos or hands-on courses will probably be your best source for profitable laser printer repair techniques, books are available that will help you learn to perform repair on impact as well as laser printers. *Maintain & Repair Your Computer Printer and Save a Bundle* by Stephen J. Bigelow and *The Printer Bible* by Scott Foerster are two excellent reference books offering the basics of printer repair as well as troubleshooting hints.

Don't limit yourself

The topics we've covered here are by no means an exhaustive list. You might find other areas of specialization, such as becoming an expert on getting rid of viruses or specializing in the repair of floppy disk drives. Further, new fields of repair are opening all the time, such as repair of CD-ROM drives, laptop computer repair, or fixing the new generation of hand-held computers.

If you pick a very narrow area of endeavor, such as recovery of damaged databases, as Paul Heiser has done, your rates can be nearly 10 times what the normal technician makes doing general PC repair. However, you'll need to get your name known nationally, as Paul has done, in order to get enough work.

Don't let that stop you from pursuing other areas where training is skimpy, but the rewards are generous. We know of one technician who learned almost by accident that certain mainframe circuit boards tend to have a specific flaw. This person now goes from factory to factory in his tool-equipped Winnebago repairing these mainframe circuit boards at $1,000 each.

Whether you decide to specialize or not, there is information on the business aspect of the business that you need to know. Your liability for computer equipment, insurance issues, federal regulations that might affect your plans, getting paid, finding parts sources, maintenance or service contracts, and negotiating for favorable terms with suppliers are all part and parcel of this business. We'll talk about how you can tackle those issues next.

9 Common pitfalls & how to avoid them

"It is a good thing to learn caution from the misfortunes of others."

— Publilius Syrus, a Syrian-born actor who started as a slave but earned his freedom and became the leading performer of ancient Rome.

As with any business, computer repair has its own set of liabilities, trouble spots, quirks, and special requirements. Some of these issues are ones any start-up business has, but others are more unique. If you know about these issues going into the business, you'll have a much easier time and make fewer mistakes getting your business off the ground. This chapter is aimed at giving you that information.

We'll talk about when you should consider getting your business license, what requirements your state might have for operating a business, and where you can find out more about those issues. In addition, we'll discuss your liability for equipment that doesn't belong to you that you're working on, insurance issues, and resale permits. Other issues of importance are finding the parts you need, issues to discuss when negotiating with suppliers for terms that favor you, getting paid by your customers, getting paid by large businesses or government agencies, and the advantages and disadvantages of maintenance or service contracts.

Once you decide you want to start your business, you should get a business license and a business name, establish the business name, and get a resale permit for sales tax purposes. We'll talk about each one of these.

Business license, DBAs, sales tax permits

Business license You will have to check with the business offices in the county that you live in, but just to do business yourself out of your home you do not necessarily have to get a business license. Many people wait, working part-time and keeping careful track of their records, to see if this is what they want to do before they jump in and get a business license.

Doing business as (DBA) You might want to get a business license for several reasons. One is if you have a business name, you cannot protect it without filing a public "doing business as . . ." or DBA statement, and to do that you must have a business license. As part of getting a business license, your business name has to be filed with the county in which you will get your license. If someone else has the name you've chosen already, you will have to choose another name. Usually, the county business office has a book of all the business names in the area that you can look in to see if your business name is being used by someone else.

Your intention to start doing business under your chosen business name will have to be published with a certain frequency over a period of time—usually four times in a one-month period. You then have to bring the clippings along with your filled-out forms to the county office, and then you can get your business license.

If you ask the county office, you can find out if there's a service that will publish your business name for you and file your proof of publication and other paperwork with the county for you at a nominal fee. Sometimes the business even has its own newspaper it publishes your DBA in, and these services can be within just a few dollars of the cost of going to all this hassle yourself. Regular, daily newspapers offer this service as well, but if it is a large newspaper with a wide circulation, running your DBA there could cost hundreds of dollars.

Running the DBA gives other businesses the chance to object to your business name. You usually don't have to worry about this if you've checked in the county's book of business names. One tried-and-true way to make sure no other business is using your name is to name your business after yourself, such as large businesses have done. J.C. Penney, Reuters, Johnson & Johnson, and a host of other companies have done this successfully.

Of course, the name doesn't say anything about what you do, and advertising agencies will tell you that's a distinct disadvantage. Names that say what the company offers are advantageous, such as Pizza Hut, Burger King, or Bank of America. Some people go with a combination of their own name and what the business does such as B. Dalton Bookseller, Goodyear Tire, and Clark Waggoner ComputerWorks. Choose your name carefully. While you can change it, it is not easy to do so, and your customers will find it confusing.

Once you've done your DBA, you can take the paperwork you get back from the county, go to the bank, and open a checking account under your business name. While another checking account is going to cost you something, it is much easier to keep track of incoming and outgoing funds this way.

Resale license or sales tax permit

Many suppliers who will offer you good terms for parts will not do business with you if you do not have a resale number. Usually called the Franchise Tax Board, this state office will allow you to purchase items for resale without paying tax if you charge tax when you resell the item. If you collect tax, you're acting on behalf of the county, and you have to file with the county and pay in the tax you collected. Suppliers like it because they don't have to hassle with collecting tax. Depending on how much tax you collect, you might have to file annually, quarterly, or monthly. The less tax you collect, the less frequently you file.

When you go in to get a sales tax license, this is not the time to recount your dreams of getting rich. Depending on where you live, the clerk who is discussing this with you has the authority to require you to place a deposit with the county if the clerk believes you will collect a significant amount of sales tax. This clerk can also make the determination of how often you will need to file.

We've seen cases where the business was simply offering word-processing training that included only an occasional sale of a taxable item. But because the new businessperson boasted about what he planned to make a month, he left having paid a $1,200 deposit on his sales tax license and had to file monthly. Other people who said they had just a few things to sell and were just trying out this business left without paying a deposit at all and were required to file annually.

Where to find out the business requirements

We've checked with several states, but as you know, each state and even each county is different as to business requirements. The government pages in the front of your phone book will give you the phone numbers of federal, state, and county agencies in your area. SCORE, a nonprofit group of retired business executives, has offices in almost every major city and can offer valuable assistance as to how you can go about getting the information you need to launch your business. These executives specialize in looking over business ideas to help new people attain success, so sharing your ideas with a SCORE executive might give you added insights into what you need to do to launch your repair business.

The chamber of commerce in your city should also have information regarding starting a business and will probably have a helpful brochure. The phone companies in larger cities have available a "Business to Business" phone directory, and in the front, information is listed about starting a business there. While the phone company wants you to pay extra for a

"Business to Business" directory, you might find one at the public library. The reference librarian might also be able to help by directing you to books and pamphlets from your local government on the steps to starting a business in your area.

Tax liability

If you are self-employed, you are expected to pay your taxes quarterly with the federal and state government, a process called quarterly filing. You will also pay extra social security tax because you're self-employed. You might never have seen self-employment tax before because when you worked for someone else that company paid half of your social security tax and you paid the other half.

If you have a spouse working for someone else, one of the ways to get out of filing quarterly is to have the amount of tax you would normally be paying deducted automatically from your spouse's paycheck each payday. You'll need to calculate the amount you owe and divide it between the number of paydays to get the figures you need.

A tax software program, such as Turbo Tax, will go a long way in helping you prepare for your annual visit with Uncle Sam on April 15th. It is always a rude surprise to new business owners to find out they owe much more than they expected come tax time. The IRS is also famous for its penalties and interest charges.

While you can get by this way for a while, what you'll really need is an accountant. An accountant will tell you things like your automobile mileage can be deducted at a set rate if your car is being used for business purposes, what's deductible, and what isn't. The accountant's fees are also deductible.

One note on the use of your vehicle for business: while it's an attractive prospect to think you can simply deduct all the expenses associated with your vehicle, the acid test is how much your vehicle is being used for business. One way to cross-reference that is for the IRS to check with your car insurance company to see if you told them the car was used for business. Telling your insurance company you're using the car for your business will probably raise your insurance rates, so you sort of get it coming or going. It's probably cheaper starting out to simply track and deduct the business-related mileage.

If you deposit your own money in your business accounts, be sure to make that obvious. For example, write a check to yourself and deposit it. Otherwise, deposits that cannot be accounted for any other way might be counted as income if you're ever audited by the Internal Revenue Service (IRS).

If you don't want to pay an accountant, the IRS will help you. IRS people are actually very personable and willing to help you get your questions answered and avoid paying in anymore than you must. The agency often offers classes aimed at small business owners and the self-employed to help you in determining what you can safely do and how to go about it. Call your local IRS office to find out about these classes and when they are scheduled.

The biggest advantage to a home-based business is you can deduct the expenses involved in the appropriate portion of home space you use for the business from your taxes. If you use a bedroom that makes up one-eighth of your total living space, then you can deduct one-eighth of your rent or house payment and one-eighth of the utility bills. Since you're paying for the space whether you have a business or not, this deduction is a big advantage.

However, that area has to be exclusively for the use of your business. You can't use the closet in the bedroom space you deducted to store your out-of-season clothes and expect to keep the deduction if you are audited by the IRS. These rules are subject to change as well, so you should check with your accountant or IRS office before you take any deduction you're unsure about.

Deduction of home space used for business

Many people who are working from home use their home telephone number as their business phone. The phone company doesn't like it, but they can't do much about it if you answer the phone with your name or by saying "hello." It'll be easier for you and your customers if you have a business phone installed, and that way you'll also get a yellow pages listing.

Your business telephone

If you have a dedicated business line and a cellular phone or a pager, you can take an older PC with a hard disk drive, install a voice mail board, and set it to contact you in emergency situations. National Semiconductor offers a voice mail, fax, modem board for PCs, and so does The Complete PC. These companies claim you can use these boards on your main PC and still use your applications while the boards answer calls in the background. The reality of the situation is the boards use memory-resident software and can significantly degrade the performance of your PC. You'll be happier if you have a dedicated PC for this. Fortunately, your voice mail system will work just fine on an inexpensive 286-based PC.

Set up your own voice mail system

Using these boards, you can set up mailboxes that are designated by numbers. If the user leaves a message in a mailbox designated as your emergency mailbox, then the computer can be programmed to call you and deliver the message or call you and leave a code on your pager so you know there's an urgent message awaiting you. You can then call the machine back, enter your access code, and retrieve the message.

It's not a must to have an emergency mailbox to do this, as you can set the PC to call you whenever any message comes in. That way you can get back to customers quickly and avoid losing business even if you have to be out on service calls.

Do you need a fax? We recommend you have a fax. It's becoming a necessity, and you're likely to be embarrassed without one. In addition, if you want to become certified, much of the material available concerning certification is available via fax-back services. You can also fax in technical questions and get an answer within 24 hours from several companies, including Artisoft, makers of LANtastic.

As we've already pointed out, you can get a modem, fax, voice mail combination card to add to your PC. It is possible to set up a voice mail system so the user presses a key to send a fax and the fax document is then stored on your hard disk. This has the advantage of using a lot less fax paper, but the disadvantage comes in when you want to send a fax consisting of documents on paper. The only way to get them into the PC is to scan them in using an optical scanner, which is another hassle and expense.

A dedicated fax line is not a necessity, however, since you can get a switching device that will automatically switch the call to the fax machine if it detects that the incoming call is from a fax. But when you get busier, it will simply be easier to have a dedicated fax phone line that you can leave connected to your fax machine than to be hung up waiting on the fax machine every time you want to make a call.

You need a modem If you have nothing else, you should have a modem. You'll need to be able to access and download software drivers or patches to programs from the vendors. We recommend you have a CompuServe account. If you're working a lot with Microsoft, you might find a GEnie account helpful as well. CompuServe will cost you about $10 a month, depending on how much you use it. You can sign up for a plan that will give you several hours of free access plus a certain number of free mail messages. Most of the vendors on the service do not charge you extra to use their forums, but it's the services where you pay extra charges in addition to regular connect time that can make online services expensive. Fortunately, the online services will tell you when you're entering a surcharged area, so you'll know and you can get the rates before you decide to venture in. For your convenience, we've included special offers for both CompuServe and GEnie in appendix B with the information on online services.

PC repair liability issues If you are working from home and using your vehicle to transport other people's equipment to and from your home, you need to be aware of certain liability issues. Your insurance agent needs to be aware of what you're doing so he or she can help you meet your insurance needs.

Insurance issues working from home One of the most commonly misunderstood issues is the role of car insurance in terms of the items transported in a car. Your car insurance will not cover any equipment transported in your car in the case of an accident, nor will it cover you if the equipment is stolen from your vehicle. The car insurance covers the car and the occupants, not possessions in the car.

Should property you were transporting in your car become damaged, it would be your homeowner's insurance that would cover the contents of your vehicle. The problem is, if those contents were there in conjunction with a business you are operating from your home, you might not be covered by your homeowner's insurance either. You'll need to check with your insurance agent to see if your insurance coverage includes your computer equipment used for your home-based business. Chances are it does not, and you'll need to purchase additional insurance.

Another issue involves people visiting your home in the course of business. If someone visiting your home has an accident on your property, your insurance might not cover it if the person was there because of business-related activity. Some business licenses preclude your having customers in your home due to zoning laws, which could make it impossible for insurance to cover your business visitors. This won't be a problem if you deliver your services to the client.

These days, you might find it attractive to rent or lease space for your business. You might want to check into doing so, especially if you need a storefront to obtain status as an authorized service source for a vendor. It probably costs less than you think, especially in those garage-type industrial parks springing up around the country.

Insurance issues in renting or leasing office space

If you decide to rent office space or a storefront, ask the leasing agent or owner of the property what insurance coverage they have. You'll probably find that the existing insurance covers the building only, and you'll need to get additional insurance for your business equipment.

Be sure you have enough insurance to cover the equipment you take in. If you have $40,000 worth of insurance and the replacement cost of the equipment currently stored in your business location is $60,000, you are underinsured. One way to handle this is to try to keep the computers you have on site under a certain dollar value. If you can't work on a certain piece of equipment until Thursday, then you might ask the client to bring it in then instead of storing it on site.

Of course, you won't need to worry as much about equipment liability if you live in a state that excepts you from liability under the circumstances of theft, fire, vandalism, etc. if you are licensed as an electronics service dealer with the state's Consumer Affairs department. But even then, you should consider the value of the tools you have and the replacement cost of that equipment should something happen.

No one in this business accepts liability for data. No one. Read the licensing agreements of the software you purchase. Ask other vendors. Even ask shops that specialize in data recovery. Nobody will make any guarantees regarding the customer's data. There are simply too many variables and too many

Don't accept liability for data

things that are outside your control. Not to mention the fact that the cost of replacing someone's data could put you out of business. Data is too expensive for any outside person to try to replace, which is why we did all that preaching on backups earlier in the book.

If no one else will accept this liability, you shouldn't either. When you go on site to work on a customer's equipment you shouldn't scare them, but there should be some work authorization that they sign that clearly states you cannot be liable for their data. However, one of the things that will set you apart from other repair technicians is caring about the customer's data. Let that be known, and do everything you can to save the data.

Limit your liability for hardware

However, you might be required to offer an estimate of the repair in writing before you work on the equipment. The estimate should clearly state what you believe the problem is and what you expect it will cost to fix the problem. If there are problems beyond what you were lead to believe by the customer that come out when you're troubleshooting the system, then you need to let the customer know the repair is going to be more and attempt to estimate how much more.

This is just like when you take your car to the mechanic, only this time you're the mechanic. When you authorize work on your car, you sign a form that reads something like this: I hereby authorize the work outlined on this form to be done, along with necessary materials. You (the computer repair person) and your employees may operate my vehicle for the purposes of testing, inspection, or delivery at my risk. You will not be held responsible for loss or damage to the vehicle or articles left in the vehicle in case of fire, theft, accident, or any other cause.

Avoid promises you might not be able to keep

As for the equipment, you don't want to guarantee that you can fix it. You can and probably should guarantee your repair for 90 days or so after the job, but we'd advise you to avoid making promises until the system is fixed.

The best approach is to say, "I've seen (or not seen) this before, but I feel pretty confident I can fix it. Give me some time to look it over." If it's a sticky problem, and you're coming in on a referral from another customer, chances are the client has already been through one, two, or even three technicians already.

What if you break something or make a mistake?

You might be held liable for equipment you damage, if it can be established that it was your fault the equipment was damaged. If you can prove that there was no way to avoid breaking the component in order to perform the repair, you can simply charge the client for the part and the labor, just as any other service technician in any other field would do.

But there are those times when things happen. Keep in mind that no one expects you to be perfect. Something like this happened to us once. We were called in on a case where the memory-resident antivirus software reported the Cinderella virus. Upon arrival on site, we were able to verify that indeed, it was the Cinderella virus that had been reported when the virus scanned the PC's memory.

We advised the client what steps could be taken to eliminate the virus, and they chose to have everything cleared out—to start over. This was an entire day's work. They approved the expense and we went to work.

We used FDISK to repartition the hard disk drive, reformatted the drive, reloaded the operating system software from the disks, reloaded the application software from the original disks, and restored the customer's data files from tape backups.

Later, upon talking with representatives from the antivirus software company, we discovered that the software incorrectly reports the Cinderella virus in memory under certain circumstances and if certain DOS device drivers are loaded in the environment files. The problem hadn't been a virus at all, but a bug in the virus-reporting software. Had we called the antivirus software company upon discovering the report, we could have avoided the entire mess.

We had to decide what to do. Should we tell the client there hadn't been a virus after all? Should we move away? (Just kidding.) If the virus-reporting software ran into the same circumstances again, it could report the same virus again. Then how would we explain all that expense to the client?

So, we decided to tell the client about our mistake and refund the portion of the money that represented the virus work (we had installed some new software for them as well). It was painful, and we thought the client would think we were nincompoops. The client didn't say much then, but they've become one of our most loyal customers and personal friends. Our advice: if it was your fault, you do whatever it takes to make it right.

How long a warranty should you offer?

On most repairs, the standard parts and labor warranty period is 90 days. It is common practice to offer as long a warranty as the supplier offers you on the parts. If your supplier offers you a warranty on the parts that is longer than 90 days, then you can also offer a longer warranty.

Obviously, you want to avoid buying parts that aren't reliable, no matter how cheap they are. If they cost you extra time working on equipment you've already repaired once, they're no bargain. The repair technicians we talked with all said the same thing on parts. Like their customers, they'd rather pay a little more and get a reliable part then be faced with an above-average failure rate no matter how cheap the parts are. The old adage "time is money" is the rule of thumb here. Time you spend on rework that you don't get paid for is "lost opportunity" time, and it costs real dollars.

Obtaining hard-to-find parts & saving money on parts

One of the problems in the repair business is it can be difficult to find parts, or if the parts can be found, they're so expensive it's not worth the money to the customer to fix the problem. This is especially true for those who specialize. Yet the parts themselves can be relatively inexpensive to manufacture and distribute.

A bone of contention in the repair industry is the tendency for original equipment manufacturers (OEMs) to keep a tight rein on their spare parts. In any market where service is a lucrative portion of the overall picture, competition can become heated between the manufacturer and the independent service provider. In some cases, the manufacturer can actually make more off spare parts sales than it did from sales of the original product to begin with. As we said in the beginning, the parallels between the burgeoning computer industry and the automobile industry are quite strong. Auto maker Ford at one point actually made more from selling parts than it did from building and selling its cars.

There is a structure in the parts chain that will help you if you understand it. The OEM might have parts available, but most of the time that is going to be your most expensive source. A distributor for the OEM will also have parts available, and distributors always insist on a discounted price to carry and promote products. If you can get the same part from the distributor, you're likely to reap the benefits of the lower price the distributor gets and save on the part. Brokers are usually independent of both the OEM and the distributor, but they have connections and purchase parts or entire computers in quantity. If you can find a broker with the part, then you'll get the best price.

While it might take some time for you to find and build relationships with the brokers, the pursuit could mean significant monetary savings for you. If a part costs $900 from the manufacturer, but the distributor for that manufacturer sells the part for $700, and an independent broker sells the part for $200, it becomes worthwhile to spend time finding the broker. While it might sound ridiculous that there could be so much mark-up, the fact is sometimes it is even worse. Your time will be richly rewarded in two cases: when you're working with parts that are expensive, or when you're working on the same type of problem over and over. If you're doing repetitive work and can find the parts you use for less, you can charge the same and make more profit.

Even if you don't specialize, you'll find most computers use the same components, and those components are made by manufacturers who are often independent of the name that's on the outside of the computer. This means you can find a part if you simply know where to look.

Where to look for part numbers

The first thing you have to know is the part number. Depending on what you're replacing, you'll usually find the part number on top. On hard disk drives, you'll find the manufacturer, part number, and model number on a label on top of the drive. You'll need both the manufacturer and the model number. You might or might not find the other information you need on the label, such as the size, number of heads, cylinders, tracks, and landing zone. That's why you'll need a reference such as the *Pocket PCRef* or the *Micro House Technical Library*.

For circuit boards, you'll need to look at the board for a silk-screened number. You'll usually find it on the outside edge on the top side of the board near a corner. You'll want to look for a manufacturer's name on the board as well. Chips usually have the manufacturer and the chip number printed on the top of the chip. Sometimes a board manufacturer will print the company logo on top of one of the main chips on the board.

Since memory chips are something you'll probably be dealing with often, you need to know a few facts concerning these components. When adding or replacing memory chips or RAM, it is important to note the capacity of the chips as well as their speed. The speed of the chip, measured in nanoseconds (ns), is listed on the top of the chip as the end part of the part number. The speed is designated by a dash and a number, so 80 ns SIMMS will have –80 as the end portion of the part number.

Most SIMMS will be in the 70 to 80 ns range, though if you see chips with a –15, those are 150 ns chips. The faster chips take less time to do their work, so 70-ns chips are faster than 80-ns chips. The faster the processing speed, the more expensive the chips.

The rule of thumb is put SIMMS of the same capacity and speed together. Some of the newer PC motherboards will accept varying capacity SIMMS, so you can put 1MB SIMMS in with 4MB SIMMS, but only in special configurations in certain SIMM slots on the board, and they must all be the same speed. You'll have to check the vendor documentation to get the details. Memory chips at different speeds sometimes won't work together at all, even if they are all the same capacity. If they do work, you'll get the overall effect of the lowest processing speed available.

Several sources for parts are available. In particular, Torch, which stands for Total Online Reference for Computer Hardware, has put together an electronic parts database that also gives you numbers and sources for parts. The product comes on floppy disk or CD-ROM and allows you to look up parts by part number, model number, manufacturer, or type of part. If alternative parts are available for the part you're looking for, Torch will supply that information as well.

The software also gives you the OEM price, the distributor price, and the broker price. Torch gets the pricing information from the published OEM and distributor prices. The broker price is attained by taking an average from three brokers. To sweeten the deal, Torch says that if you can't find the part in

Where to look for part number information

their database, you can give them a call on their 800 line and they'll find it for you. A subscription to Torch for a single user is around $500, with updates priced at $99 each. More information is available in appendix B.

As we've already noted, several manufacturers offer bulletin boards, but some offer bulletin board services (BBS) for obtaining part numbers. Hewlett-Packard is one of the companies that has a BBS service as well as a phone service just for obtaining part numbers. A separate phone number is available for parts ordering, and the service is toll-free and automated.

Other companies have quirks of their own. For example, Compaq doesn't use part numbers, but instead uses assembly numbers. So the number you see on a Compaq piece of equipment is from the company's own internal numbering system, not a part number. This number scheme can make it more difficult to obtain needed parts.

We have listed parts sources for you in appendix B. You can also find sources for parts by checking the advertising in *Service News*, the *Service News* annual *Hardware Maintenance* issue, *Computer Hotline*, *The Guide* (published by *Computer Hotline*), *The Processor*, and other publications aimed at repair professionals.

Negotiating with vendors for terms

What we've been talking about until now is how to obtain hard-to-find parts or save money on parts for proprietary machines. However, you might find yourself dealing with two or three suppliers on a regular basis. Here are some tips for dealing with any supplier, and especially with suppliers you do business with regularly.

Look carefully at supplier policies   When you purchase parts, you'll want to note the return, exchange, and warranty policies of the companies you're buying parts from. Most part supply companies ship overnight, and that can be important to you if you have a customer with a crucial piece of equipment down. You can talk most customers into waiting until the next day, even on a repair they consider of the utmost urgency.

Negotiating credit terms   In addition, you'll want to know the credit terms, if any, offered by the supplier. As you get to know suppliers, you should begin to get more favorable credit terms. Avoid using the word "credit" with suppliers, though, because they tend to cringe when that term comes up. Try talking about terms. You might ask if you can pay the invoice in a certain number of days, or by a certain date.

If you find yourself unable to negotiate a credit arrangement with the supplier, you can get caught in a cash crunch, which is a painful position at best and can be terminal for your business at its worst. You might find yourself paying for parts before you get paid, especially if you're dealing with large companies. If you can negotiate 30-day or even 14-day terms, you'll be a lot better off. Sometimes you can negotiate to pay when you get paid, but you'll have to develop a good relationship with your supplier to make that arrangement.

Make plans to avoid the cash crunch   It was this cash crunch situation that forced Fred Chapman of Weatherford Electronics to his banker in order to stay in business when he first started. You might also need to negotiate a revolving line of credit or some arrangement where you can get ready cash to purchase supplies on an as-needed basis. Don't wait until the last minute to find this arrangement. If you wait until a crisis looms, you might not be able to spend the time to set up the arrangement, or you might lose work running around trying to get this set up.

Look for cross shipment on defective parts   On those hopefully rare occasions when you do get a defective part, you'll need fast turn around. Your customer will already have faced the inconvenience of the original repair and is now in the unhappy situation of another repair. You do not want to make the customer wait two weeks while your supplier issues a return merchandise authorization (RMA), receives your part in the mail, checks it over, then ships the replacement part. You want your supplier to cross-ship parts with just a phone call from you. This means while you're shipping back the part, he's already shipped you the new part and credits you with the returned part when it arrives.

Try to avoid restocking charges   Try to avoid restocking charges as well. If you get all the parts together for that multimedia upgrade, and the customer changes his or her mind, you'll want to be able to return those components. If you know you can sell them to someone else, great, but negotiate for return terms that don't cost you anything.

We were able to negotiate return terms on an item we didn't expect to return, out of habit mostly, and we were glad we did. We purchased a second memory upgrade board for a laser printer, but negotiated with the supplier that if the upgrade board didn't work, we could return it and get a full refund. The upgrade board worked fine in the printer and contained faster memory chips than the memory board we already had in the printer. But it wouldn't work with the existing board because of the difference in the speed of the memory chips. The new board did us little good if it didn't work with the memory we already had, so we were able to call the supplier, return the board, and get a full refund.

Remember, everything is negotiable   All parts policies are negotiable, even if the supplier says they're not. If you get turned down negotiating on a portion of your agreement with the supplier, ask what the supplier wants in order to allow you the terms you want. Usually it's a matter of time. Sometimes the supplier will want you to do a higher volume of business with them first. Once you can meet the requirement, ask for the privilege you wanted again.

If your supplier is unbending, look for another supplier. Ask around and see where other people who are buying the same parts are getting those parts. It's always a good idea to form relationships with other people in your field who are not competing directly with you, as well as people who are in fields related to yours. In this way, you can get needed information. You can also find out if a supplier is reputable or not.

Profile

Tim Sullivan
MicroServ, Colton, California

Tim Sullivan was employed at Lockheed when he first took a printer repair course at the company's expense. His interest in computers grew and he started tinkering around on the side.

Pretty soon he was working on computers at Lockheed, handling every aspect of IBM hardware, software, and setting up systems. He even started moonlighting, working with a few customers after work and on weekends.

Unexpectedly, in November of 1990, Tim found himself out of a job. Lockheed had staged massive layoffs, and Tim was a casualty. He decided to go into the computer repair business for himself partly because of his wife's promptings and partly because the economy was so bad he didn't think he could get a job. "I never thought I could get enough business to sustain me financially," Tim added.

So Tim started by reading Jay Levin's book *Guerilla Marketing*, which he said had some very good ideas and was a resource he found inspiring. To try to get business, Tim started writing letters to different companies saying what he could do for them. He didn't get one response.

The smartest thing he did, though, was to join the San Bernardino chamber of commerce. It cost him $195 a year, but after going for two months, he got his first client.

The chamber of commerce gave Tim exposure to businesspeople who needed his services. On Wednesday mornings they had coffee with about 100 people, and people were allowed to stand up and introduce themselves. Each time, Tim would stand up and introduce some offer. Once he said he had used HP laser printers for sale, once he said he was having a repair special, and once he spoke a couple of minutes on preventative maintenance.

He also openly invited people to ask him questions. After three years, Tim stopped attending the meetings. He was simply too busy with his repair business to go anymore.

Reflecting back on what worked, Tim noted, "I never got anything out of advertising. People are bombarded by it. When asked why the people at the chamber chose him over other repair businesses, Tim answered, "I guess they wanted someone they knew. They saw me every week for three years."

All his clients are referrals and some of them are cities, such as the city of Loma Linda. He has also set up networks for large, private companies. When he runs across something new, Tim simply sits down with the manual and teaches himself.

His business cards are plain and have a lot of information such as he repairs IBM and compatible microcomputers, he offers after-hour and weekend service, and his title as microsystems specialist.

One thing Tim made a strong point about for new people starting out is when you're out there and you're really having a tough time, hang in there. "What makes me a good technician is I stay with the problem until it's fixed. Never quit—never, ever, ever quit."

How to get paid

As anyone who is self-employed will tell you, getting paid is a major portion of the business effort. You can do fine, quality work, but you still need to know how to broach the subject of payment.

Try to leave with the money in hand

The best policy to have is to collect your money immediately after you finish your repairs. Most service agents prepare customers for this by saying something like, "We accept cash or checks with proper identification." Most individuals who call you expect to have to pay you as soon as the work is completed, and most of the time you'll have no trouble at all getting paid right then.

Getting paid from large companies or government clients

As you saw with negotiating with suppliers, some of your best-paying clients will expect some of those credit privileges with you as well. This is especially true if you're dealing with a state or government agency. Large companies might also expect to be billed for services.

This means you have to leave a paper trail. You have to document who called for the repair, what was done, when it was completed, how much it cost, and have someone sign off on it. This is best accomplished by getting yourself some four-part forms that have blanks you can fill in for all this information.

You can usually order these forms from an office supply store, but in the beginning you might want to use your letterhead and carbon paper to get started. You can print all the information you know beforehand on your printer, making blanks for lines you fill in on sight and lines for the authorization signatures before and after the work is completed. (After all, you don't want to tell some big company that calls to wait a week while you have forms printed.)

Getting paid by the government can be tough. There are horror stories all over about how small businesses have been hung out on payments from the government. It's not unusual for a government agency to take 60, 90, 120 days or more to pay on an account. One way to assure payment is to ask for a purchase order (PO) before you begin the work. Ask the person at the government agency requesting the service to mail or fax it to you.

This requires that you give the agency an estimate up front of the likely expenses. The accounting department of the agency then treats the PO like a check that has already been drawn against the account of the particular group you're working with, and that money is set aside to pay you. Sometimes the document is called a requisition or a request for service or materials. This is considered a legal document, and it is binding if you can prove you performed the services specified.

If the people you're dealing with at the government agency say they cannot get a PO to you, then beware. This might mean they are hoping you'll do work but are waiting for the next allocation of funds before they pay you, sort of like writing checks before payday, then racing the checks to the bank.

These government employees might complain about how terribly slow it is to get the accounting people to issue POs. However, government accounting departments take a dim view of a vendor doing work that was not authorized beforehand. Verbal authorization is not enough in their view, and your invoice can end up right at the bottom of the things to be paid.

Some government agencies have a stipulation that if there's some kind of discount for paying within a certain amount of time, they have to pay those bills first. You might pad your bill by 10 percent, then knock the extra percentage off if you're paid in a certain amount of time, say 30 days. That has worked for us a time or two.

Large companies might not be as stringent about this, but you might want to check with the accounting department before you make a commitment to do very much work. Ask the person you're working with first about getting a PO, and if they can't give you a straight answer, call the accounting department and ask them. If you're hungry, sometimes it's scary to be so forceful about getting paid, but the reality of the situation is if you spend your time and money doing the work and then don't get paid, that's worse.

Win-win service calls when you can't estimate the cost

Most clients will want to know what you're going to charge before you come out, and they will want you to give them an estimate over the phone. You might have to do this if you're in a state that requires that you give an estimate as part of your licensing agreement with the Consumer Affairs division.

This isn't as difficult as it might first appear. You'll want to ask questions over the phone to determine what parts and tools you should have with you anyway. And after a while, you'll be more familiar with common problems and know by a description of the symptoms what the most likely cause of the problem is.

If the customer doesn't know what the problem is and can't describe the symptoms over the phone to you in a way that allows you to make an educated guess, you should offer to perform a maintenance call. Have a rate handy that you charge for this call, and go through the maintenance routine outlined in chapter 8 using the 10-point checklist in appendix E. While you're there for maintenance, you can then diagnose the most likely cause of the problems and offer a much more educated estimate for the repair work.

This approach solves two problems. First, it allows you to perform a diagnosis without simply working for free. Second, the client knows up front what his minimum cost is, in addition to getting a firm and educated estimate for the repair. If it ends up you simply had to plug in the power cord, or the client decides the problem isn't worth the cost, neither of you will feel as though they were somehow shorted on the arrangement.

Always assume the best

A common mistake in any service business is to treat clients as though they're out to cheat you. We're sure you've run into service people, just as we have, who groan loud and long about how they've been cheated. You can see their eyes narrow as they talk about it. This behavior is insulting to the current client. In addition, we often find ourselves wondering what this person will say about our business encounter to the next person he or she meets.

In sales, one notably effective way to close the sale is the assumptive close. You hear it all the time. Would you like the silver model or the one with the red pinstriping? Can we deliver that Tuesday or would Wednesday be better?

Consider using the assumptive close for your service calls with methods like these to ask for payment. Would that be cash or would you like to write me a check? I can stamp your check with our company name if that would be more convenient. What type of payment should I put on this invoice for you?

If you conduct yourself in a confident, businesslike manner concerning all aspects of the job, including getting paid, you're more likely to get repeat business. Everyone has customers who are difficult to deal with. That's just part of the job.

The pros & cons of maintenance contracts

To give you the conclusion first, we recommend you set up regular service contracts with customers, paid for at the time service is rendered, rather than pursue maintenance contracts. Here's why.

Maintenance contracts sound as though you've got it made—steady pay minus the work of rounding up business. You agree to supply all the needed maintenance for a set rate, paid monthly, quarterly, or all at once. So there's money in your pocket, and the customer gets that warm feeling that all's right with the world.

Essentially, you're offering insurance—taking the risk later for money paid now. If you don't correctly calculate the risk, you can be the loser. The number one problem, as anyone who services maintenance contracts will tell you, is the customer suddenly becomes much more willing to call you. And why not? They've already paid for it. You could be making several service calls a week to simply plug a power cord because no one even bothered to check before they called.

It's easy to underbid a maintenance contract. You have to know the number of machines you're contracting for, the mean-failure rating on those machines, and the cost of parts. The failure rating part is the tough one. To give you an idea what you're looking at, an insurance company who specializes in computers won't insure a computer that is more than three years old in a repair warranty program. And the insurance cost per year is 7 percent of the replacement value of the PC.

If you have a heterogeneous environment with a number of different types of PCs, it can be difficult to correctly bid the contract. This is where a parts guide, such as the Torch product mentioned in chapter 7, could come in handy. You'll also have to be able to predict with some accuracy the number of calls you might have to make and the amount of time you or someone you hire will spend making those calls.

Large companies who make the computers or the components do the warranty service work practically at a loss. They do this because they hope to sell new equipment to the client later. And, since they make the machines, their parts costs are going to be lower than yours.

As you'll recall, Dell offered its third-party maintainers $15 a machine a quarter or $75 per repair call. While new PCs under warranty are probably not going to have a lot of problems, your overhead would have to be very low or the incidence of repairs would have to be high to make a living at those wages. To make this work, you need something profitable that goes along with being a third-party maintainer in this situation, such as being able to charge your normal rates for servicing a few hundred oddball PCs the client has on the side.

There is a guide published by the American Management Association called *How to Make Profits with Service Contracts* by Michael R. Rizzo. The book implies that one of the reasons larger companies have gone to service contracts is to enable them to keep a sufficient force steadily employed to meet customer demand when the need arises. The work force employed from the proceeds of a maintenance contract can be kept busy performing maintenance work on existing customer equipment, educating customers as to how to take care of their equipment, and then also be available for crisis situations when repair problems arise.

Try service agreements instead

For the small repair shop, however, the constant drain on resources and the risk could be too great to make the maintenance agreement a worthwhile proposition. What we would recommend instead is to set up a regular service schedule for your clients. As an incentive, offer them a discounted rate for both the service and later repairs as needed. Then charge the client for service each time after the work is performed and for repairs when they come up.

This is what Don Thompson of the laser printer repair business Diversified Technigraphics offers his clients, and he claims the approach works well for his company. This approach offers the benefit to the client of a lower fixed cost and hopefully fewer repairs because the equipment is being serviced regularly. This agreement reduces the risk to the repair shop of expenses associated with maintaining the client's equipment, but still provides the customer with a ready resource should problems arise. It also provides the repair shop with income on each call, even if that income is reduced.

Use a simple agreement

A simple, single-page agreement can be drawn up to perform service annually or twice a year. The regularity of the maintenance depends on the client's needs and the type of equipment you're servicing. We would suggest you do as Technigraphics does and offer enough of a discount on the services to make them worthwhile to the customer, say 15 to 20 percent. Outline exactly what you'll do and the benefits of maintenance in the contract. You can also add a provision that the customer can cancel the agreement at any time, so there's no specified time limit that both of you might have to endure if the agreement should turn sour for some reason.

A sample of a PC maintenance agreement, with a starting place for what to charge, is available in appendix E. You'll have to check pricing for similar services in your area and modify the pricing scale accordingly.

Profile

John Krivit
La Costa Micro, Carlsbad, California

La Costa Micro is Jonathan Krivit's part-time, home-based business. By day, he's a network technical support engineer for another company, but he puts in 15 to 20 hours a week in his own network business at nights and on the weekends.

His customers, who are mostly doctors, travel agents, and industrial plants, prefer their network maintenance, repair, and upgrades to be done at night and on weekends so their business is not interrupted. Jonathan, who boasts no formal training or certifications, says the business is cyclical. There are times when he's very busy and times when the work drops off.

Working in the complex field of networks is almost like an addiction, according to Jonathan. When a problem comes up and he doesn't know the answer, he tells himself, "I'm a smart guy. I can figure this out." He uses his contacts in the industry, his experience, and the Novell Support Encyclopedia on CD-ROM to help him through the tough spots.

He emphasizes maintenance with his customers. Most have him in every three or four months to clean the equipment and defragment their hard disk drives. He uses the Norton Utilities, especially Disk Doctor and the defragmentation routine included in the product. He charges $100 to $250 per visit for maintenance on all the PCs on the network, but service calls are between $50 and $100 an hour, depending on whether or not the customer is a regular one.

Much of his work is by referral, and he says the work is hard but rewarding. Jonathan indicated he's not interested in going with his own business full-time. The part-time hours, the extra income, and taking vacations are too attractive to give up, he maintains.

FCC Regulations

The Federal Communications Commission (FCC) has jurisdiction over radio and television communications. The FCC's involvement with computers stems from the fact that any digital device has the potential for generating radio noise that can interfere with police, ambulance, fire communications, radio and television broadcasting, and air traffic control operations. The upshot is that while computers are easy to build and the components are readily available, any computer advertised publicly for sale must be FCC Class B certified.

Some mistakenly believe the FCC requires the manufacturers to certify the components before they can be sold in the United States, but as of this writing, that simply isn't true. Some peripherals, such as modems, must be FCC verified before they can be sold, but not the basic components used to build PCs.

The certification process involves the three main components of the PC: the power supply, motherboard, and case. This is because these components are the three main potential causes of radio interference. The FCC is looking for a motherboard designed to minimize radio noise emissions, a case that is well-grounded to prevent radio noise from escaping, and a power supply that is well-filtered to keep radio noise from leaking into the electrical power lines.

There are two classes of digital devices in the FCC's way of categorizing. Class A devices are marketed exclusively for use in business, industrial, and commercial environments and can be self-verified by the maker of the device. Class B equipment is defined as for consumer use and specifically includes personal computers and portable computers.

Class B certification requires the equipment be tested by an FCC authorized third-party testing facility, which then fills out paperwork the FCC wants concerning the radio frequency emissions. To qualify, the computer should not emit radio noise that would interfere with a receiver 10 meters (or about 30 feet) away.

Class A verified equipment is tested by the vendor and has a much larger interference range than allowed for Class B equipment. Among the items that can be Class A verified are PC peripherals, mainframe and workstation computers, and peripherals for mainframe and workstation computers. External switching power supplies can also be verified.

Class categories & certification

What the FCC cares about is radio frequency interference. Even if the PC is FCC certified, if it causes radio frequency interference, the FCC has the authority to make you stop operating the equipment until the interference problem is corrected. The most likely way for the FCC to discover this interference is if neighbors, police, or fire departments complain of problems. If your PC opens the neighbor's garage door, messes up television reception, or causes radio interference, and the FCC can trace the source to your unit, then you have a problem.

Radio frequency interference is what sparks FCC action

If a PC causes these problems and is not FCC certified, the FCC will want to obtain the source of the equipment from the user. All the fines and penalties are aimed at the seller of the equipment, not the user. The agency has pretty stiff penalties for selling or leasing, or offering to sell or lease, PCs that cause interference. These penalties include one or all of the following:

- Forfeiture of all noncompliant equipment.
- A criminal penalty of $100,000 to $200,000 for the individual or organization.
- A criminal fine totalling twice the gross gain obtained from sales of the noncompliant equipment.
- An administrative fine totalling $10,000 per day per violation.

The fines are often mitigated to lower amounts, such as $7,000 a day instead of $10,000, but that is still plenty of money.

Officials at the FCC say interference problems caused by computer-related devices are very prevalent. But unless the interference is caused to a safety-of-life service, like the local volunteer fire department's radio communications, it is never investigated. When there is interference, the fire department or whoever usually doesn't know what the source is, and they just call the FCC. The agency then sends out an agent who triangulates on the interfering signal to find the source. Once the source is found, a cease and desist order is issued, and action is taken.

Purchase FCC-certified "bare bones"

You can purchase an FCC-certified case, motherboard, and power supply combination from someone else and build on those components to offer new PCs to your customers. Known as "bare-bones" units, as long as they're certified the FCC doesn't care who sells them. The FCC label on the back of the PC will have this format: FCC ID:XXX123. The first three characters belong to the company who certified the equipment, and you can look that information up on the FCC Public Access Link (PAL) BBS using the access number supplied in appendix A.

Class B certification costs/steps

Just in case you might be interested in marketing your own brand of computer to the public, here are the steps to Class B certification. The process involves three steps: an initial filing to get a grantee code number; testing of the motherboard, power supply, and case combination by an FCC contract test site either in the United States or abroad; and a final certification process that is supposed to take less than 35 days to process. The entire process costs a total of about $3,000, including filing fees and testing, and can be accomplished in about six weeks.

During the final portion of the process, the FCC can request to see the equipment. Chances are, if your equipment passed the testing phase, you'll probably get the certification without any further FCC requests.

The testing center will charge you even if your equipment doesn't pass, but the charge will probably be about half of the normal testing charge. About two-thirds of the total cost of certification is for testing. In addition, you'll need photographs of the boards, external views of the case, and the power supply—about 10 photos per PC you're testing. You'll also need a block diagram of the PC with all the crystal frequencies shown and explained.

The rules did stipulate that every combination of power supply, motherboard, and case you would want to sell needs to be tested. If you had several combinations of these components you wanted to offer, it would be cheaper to have them all tested at once, as the testing site will charge less than if you tested them individually. The FCC has proposed eliminating the need for computer builders to obtain authorization for every combination of CPU board and power supply, provided that the components are individually authorized.

The contact numbers for the FCC are in appendix A, including information on obtaining all the necessary forms, lists of testing sites, and other informative documents available concerning Class B certification. This material is free for the asking. We do suggest you call the FCC PAL BBS before acting on any of the written information because the FCC posts current changes to the criteria and the rates for testing there.

Upgrading PCs is a legal and acceptable procedure to the FCC because it is considered a service and not a resale business. If you replace a motherboard in an FCC-certified computer with another motherboard, that PC is no longer considered certified. If the new motherboard causes interference that brings the FCC down on the user, you might have an angry user on your hands, but you won't be in trouble with the FCC.

Since most PC motherboards use so many of the same components, you probably don't need to stay up at night worrying about whether the motherboards you've been using for upgrades will cause FCC problems for your users. However, it is something you should be aware of.

What about upgrades?

As an individual user, you can build as many PCs for yourself as you like without any FCC certification. You are not supposed to sell them. If your PCs produce interference, you'll need to make modifications to eliminate the problem or give up use of the computers. There was a limit of five PCs that could be built by an individual, but that restriction has been lifted.

Building PCs for yourself

So now you know the tough spots of the business: the insurance hassles, the tax wrinkles, what to negotiate for with suppliers, how to get paid, and the government regulations that govern what you can and can't build for sale. Now it's time to get into additional ways, outside of PC repair, that you can leverage your expertise and produce income. That's in the next chapter.

10 Extra income with related services

"If you have great talents, industry will improve them; if moderate abilities, industry will supply their deficiencies. Nothing is denied to well-directed labor; nothing is ever to be attained without it."

— Sir Joshua Reynolds, an artist recognized as the foremost portrait painter in London during the mid 1700s.

Historians like to say that the personal computer is the most versatile tool ever offered humanity. It doesn't seem to matter what type of work or vocation you happen to name, a computer either already is or can be involved. With that in mind, gaining extra income with a variety of services that use your knowledge of the PC isn't a difficult proposition at all.

Most of the repair people we talked with said they found themselves doing the things the customers needed. "We do anything to make an honest buck," we heard over and over again in our interviews. How did these repair people find out what the customers wanted? Most of the time, they simply asked them or listened to their customers complain. In either case, they found a problem and solved it.

While this might seem to contradict what we said in chapter 7 about specialization, it doesn't at all. It seems that the more you specialize, the more business you can get because the customer understands what you are doing. A dentist who specializes in patients who have fear problems probably has a number of clients who aren't afraid. People can make the mental leap of imagining you solving their computing problem if they can get a specific mental picture of what it is you do.

Many of those we interviewed got into a special area because someone had a need and specifically asked them for help. Tim Sullivan of MicroServ started working on networks that way, and so did Fred Chapman of Weatherford Electronics and Computer Repair. So in this chapter, we not only want to present you with ideas for additional services you can offer, but we also want to encourage you to keep an eye out for special opportunities where you are.

We'll talk about obvious extra income opportunities such as backup services, performing PC maintenance checks as an incentive to attract new customers, and repairing used PCs for resale. We'll also give you ideas such as putting together voice-mail systems, special-purpose computer-driven kiosks, cashing in on the energy-savings trend by offering to make existing PCs "green," teaming up with a programmer to build custom systems, the home automation market, special systems for the disabled, remote control systems, and even refilling toner cartridges as a way to get customers for laser printer repair. You usually charge about twice as much for these special services as you do for hourly repair work. So let's get started.

Backup services

Even if you don't plan to offer data recovery services, a portable tape backup that works from the PC's parallel port can be a money-making tool. Tape backups have large capacities, and tapes are relatively cheap. In addition, market demand for tape drives is expected to climb in the years ahead. It is simply too difficult to maintain backups on floppy disks with the larger size hard disks. Analysts are saying the most popular hard disk size for 1994 was the 500MB, and 1.5GB drives are the standard size for 1996. Pent-up market demand can make this a profitable opportunity for you.

Several companies make portable tape backup units with software that you can run from the floppy disk drive, including the Conner Tape Products Group division of Conner Peripherals based in Costa Mesa, California; the Roy, Utah-based Iomega; and the Loveland, Colorado-headquartered subsidiary of Hewlett-Packard, Colorado Memory Systems.

The advantage to a portable backup drive that's compatible with the Quarter Inch Cartridge (QIC) standard is it is compatible with the most popular tape drives on the market today. The tapes are easy to get, and hold the 340MB of compressed data. The portable Trakker 350 shown in Fig. 10-1 is also backwards compatible, meaning it will read and write the tapes in the 120MB compressed format and the 250MB compressed format.

You might need a larger parallel port drive if you're working on large file servers or networks. Digital audio tape (DAT) drives also come in portable configurations that work from the computer's parallel port, but they cost more because they back up more data. Colorado Memory Systems and the Conner Tape Products Group both offer DAT drives with capacities of 4GB compressed.

Sell a tape drive after a disaster

It's always easier to sell a customer on a tape backup drive after they've lost some data. If you're on a data recovery mission, you should always mention

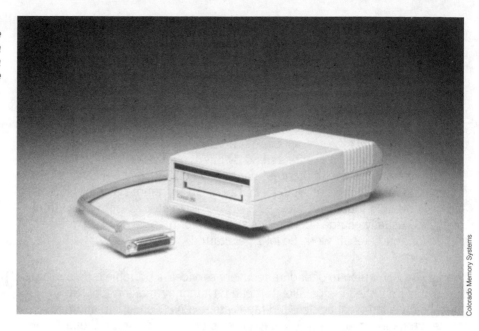

The portable Trakker tape backup drive works from a PC's parallel port and can backup 340MB per tape using compression.

Colorado Memory Systems

installing a tape backup drive. It's easy to do on most PCs because the tape drive can often run right off the floppy disk drive controller. A special cable plugs into the floppy drive controller, then the disk drive cable plugs into it. The software is easy to install as well. If the computer has a free disk drive slot, you can install an internal drive. If not, there are external drives available as well.

Set a backup schedule the easy way

Once the drive is installed, it does no good without a regular backup schedule. For the most secure backup procedure, use the "grandfather, father, son" procedure. It saves data over a period of twelve weeks and allows you to delete something from the hard disk drive, yet retrieve as much as three months later.

The procedure is outlined below.

1. You will need 10 tapes to start with.
2. Label four tapes with the days of the week from Monday through Thursday.
3. Label three tapes "Friday 1," "Friday 2," and "Friday 3."
4. Label the last three tapes with "Month 1," "Month 2," and "Month 3."
5. At the end of the day on Friday, start with the "Friday 1" tape and backup the entire drive onto that tape.
6. At the end of Monday, you do an incremental backup on the "Monday" tape, telling the software to only backup what's been changed since last Friday.
7. On Tuesday, you take the tape labeled "Tuesday" and repeat the incremental backup of step 6.

8. Repeat the procedure for the other weekday tapes until you get to Friday again, then use the "Friday 2" tape to do a full backup.
9. On Monday, use the "Monday" tape and do an incremental backup again.
10. Continue doing incremental backups each day on the appropriate day's tape until Friday, then you use the tape labeled "Friday 3."
11. Stay with the routine until the fourth Friday, then use the tape labeled "Month 1" to do that Friday's backup.
12. The next month on the fourth Friday, use the "Month 2" tape for a full backup.
13. At the end of the next month use the "Month 3" labeled tape for a full backup.
14. At the end of three months you have a complete record of twelve weeks worth of data, and you can start the tape rotation over again.

This routine has several advantages. The first is you're not dependent on the integrity of any single tape. You always have redundancy in your backups, so if a tape breaks or fails, you can recreate the data. The second is the routine can be started overnight on a weekend and the backup can be unattended. Most of the backup programs allow you to set a time for an automated backup, so you can slip in the proper tape and walk away. Third, the daily backups are short, incremental backups so they won't take a lot of time to complete.

The software will date stamp the tapes, but it's easier if the date of the last use is on the outside of the tape as well. You can write the date in small print on the label of each tape, then cross the date out and put the new date on when you use the tape next. If you need to, you can put a label over the other dates when you fill up the tape label.

One additional tip: be sure your client takes one of the tapes off-site every couple of weeks or so. Just as important documents should be copied and a copy kept off-site, so should backups. The storage location could be a safety deposit box, but there should always be a recent backup available that can't be harmed if something happens to the property where the PCs are.

Another often-overlooked issue with backups has to do with being able to recreate the run time environment used to generate the data. For example, if the end of the year comes and company statements were prepared using a certain accounting package, tax software package, and spreadsheet software product, just backing up the end-of-the-year data isn't enough. If in three years the Internal Revenue Service wants to see those records and you have to recreate them, you need to have all the software used to create the data as well as the data itself. This recreation of the run time environment should even include a copy of the operating system. Everything that was needed to create those reports should be available in case they must be recreated.

Recreate the run time environment

The reason? Software versions change, and so do operating systems. Newer versions of software products evolve, and after several years the developers drop the ability to import the old file formats from previous versions. Not only that, but it is not unusual for old versions of software products to refuse to run under new operating system versions. So if you've had some data in an archive for several years, it might be absolutely worthless if you didn't save the entire environment in which that data was created.

Your other alternative is to save the data in its native format and in a standard, vanilla format everyone uses. For example, a spreadsheet can be saved in its original format and in a tab- or comma-delimited format that can be pulled into almost any other database or spreadsheet program. Word processing files can be saved in an ASCII or text-only format. Database files can also be saved in tab- or comma-delimited formats. The disadvantage here is the vanilla formats lose all the formatting— special instructions and fonts—they were created with. But the actual data is there intact and can be pulled into another program at a later time and reformatted if necessary.

Backups with optical technology

Optical disks are like CD-ROM disks that you can write to as well as read from. You might want to offer your clients the option of optical storage because it offers greater data storage capacity on a more reliable medium than tape. This makes backups of the entire run time environment easier as well as backups of large amounts of important data. For example, insurance companies are required to keep certain records as long as ten years. However, optical technology also costs more.

The most basic writable optical medium is the write once, read many (WORM) drive. Anything written to a WORM disc is permanently stored there, so the discs cannot be reused. However, it is an excellent way to archive material, and with capacities of 600MB, you can archive quite a bit on one disc. Expect to pay $3,000 to $5,000 for one of these drives, depending on the capacity of the drive, and another $100 to $150 each for WORM discs. Sony and Toshiba both make these drives, as do other manufacturers.

Erasable CD-ROM drives are also available, but these are the most expensive optical drives available and the most versatile for storage use. These drives are in the $3,000 to $25,000 range, depending on the capacity of the drive. Iomega, Hitachi, and Hewlett-Packard are some of the companies that produce these drives.

The least expensive optical storage is magneto-optical (MO). MO drives look much like standard floppy disk drives and are rewritable storage systems that can record data an almost unlimited number of times on the same disc before wearing out. Sometimes the disks are called "floptical" to indicate the mix of optical and magnetic technology used in this storage medium.

The discs are plastic with a coating of magnetic particles, but the tracks are about ten times closer to each other so there can be about ten times the number of tracks per inch (tpi). This gives MO discs a far greater storage capacity than their magnetic counterparts.

MO discs come in 3.5-inch and 5.25-inch formats. The 3.5-inch disc can hold from 120MB to 130MB of data. The 5.25" disk can store up to 1.5GB. You can expect to pay $1,000 to $2,000 for the drives, and under $100 each for the discs. Iomega is one of the major manufacturers of this type of drive.

The New Optical Storage Technology by John A. McCormick is an excellent resource for the types of optical storage drives available, as well as manufacturer information. It even contains information on companies that specialize in mastering and producing CD-ROM titles as a service, just in case you run across a client who wants to do that.

Restore test

If you can't restore the data, you don't have a backup. Try to restore a portion of the data from your backup—data that you can verify was correctly restored. One way to tell if the data was correctly restored is to change something specific in a file after the backup, then do a restore and see if the change is gone. For example, deliberately misspell a key word in a file after the backup, then restore and see if the spelling is corrected.

Remote backup service

Most of your customers will hate making backups, so why not offer to do it for them? You can go on site with your portable tape backup and do their backup work, or you can perform backups every night remotely.

Remote backup can be particularly attractive to you and to the customer. You'll need remote access software, such as pcANYWHERE, modems installed at your site and at the remote site, access to a phone line on both sites, and the PCs you are to back up left on after business hours.

Remote backup can be a very secure process, even if the PCs are left on after everyone leaves. You can set most remote access software to answer an incoming call, then hang up and call a predetermined number back. In this way, even if someone else dials in, you can set the computer to call you back, so it becomes very difficult to gain access. In addition, you're notified if someone else attempts access.

You can also set most remote access software to disable the keyboard and blank the display on the host computer so no one else can see what you're doing. In fact, you can automate the entire process and let your computer do the backup work for you while you just come in at predetermined times and change the tapes on your own PC.

The added benefit of all this is it gives customers a backup that is off-site, which they should have anyway. Natural disasters, such as fires, floods, lightening, hurricanes, and other unpredictable events can put some companies out of business if the computer backup is destroyed in the disaster.

Your client can always buy new hardware on which to restore the backup and be in business again in a short time, if there's a reliable off-site backup.

PC maintenance

An area of specialization often overlooked by repair technicians, offering regular maintenance services, can get you in the door of companies you might not otherwise have as customers and produce other repair work for you. While maintenance could be an end in itself, it's more like the free market analysis offered by your real estate agent—a way to get yourself in the door and show a potential customer what you have to offer.

It's also a way to add value to what you do for clients. If you can point out a potentially dangerous situation or put your client on to something that will make them more comfortable, and you don't charge them extra for it, that will go a long way toward gaining your business favor with that client. Then when some other guy hits your customer up with a cheaper deal, they'll have a tough time getting the business because you're viewed as a friend and someone who cares instead of just another technician. This is how customer loyalty is built.

The maintenance work itself involves keeping the computer and peripherals clean inside and out, performing a virus check, floppy disk alignment, optimizing the hard disk drive, inventorying the components of the PC, creating a bootable "rescue" disk, and watching for ergonomic issues. This specialization requires some salesmanship, and we'll show you how that's done.

ESD check

As we've talked about before, electrostatic discharge (ESD) can present danger to the computer and peripherals. When you walk into the room where the computer is located, note the floor covering. If it's carpet, look for evidence of the buildup of static electricity. Be sure to touch something else before you touch the computer, just in case you picked up any static electricity in walking across the room.

One of the primary places to look for ESD is on the screen of the monitor. Run your hand over the surface of the monitor's screen lightly. If there's ESD buildup, that test will bring it out. You'll want to carry some antistatic spray or disposable antistatic clothes with you to wipe down the immediate surfaces of the computer to help prevent ESD.

Placement of the PC

One of the things you want to advise customers to avoid is placing the PC in a position where it could be in danger. PCs should not be near windows where direct sunlight can fall on them, they should not be under hanging plants where water might drip on the equipment, and the power cords should not be out where someone might trip and pull the monitor or the entire computer off onto the floor. In addition, the surface the PC is on should be solid, sturdy, and not easily shaken.

Check to see if the computer and peripherals are connected to an Underwriter's Laboratories (UL)-listed surge protector. Also, be sure that the UL rating applies to the actual surge-protecting capabilities of the device. Some protectors have always been approved for their electrical safety by UL. While the surge protectors that are UL-listed for surges still do not completely eliminate voltage transients, they will reduce the power surge to a level that is less likely to damage the equipment.

Look for a surge protector

Cleaning the computer involves opening up the PC and using a small vacuum or compressed air to get the dust out of the inside of the PC and out of the power supply. As we mentioned in chapter 3, dust is the enemy of all the internal components, acting like a blanket to hold heat on the internal circuits. You can demonstrate to your customer how dirty it is inside the computer without opening the case by taking a clean, white kerchief, and wiping around the opening for the power supply fan when the computer is off. The handkerchief will come up with dirt you can show to your potential client.

Check for dust buildup

Keyboards tend to get filled with all types of gunk that will eventually gum up things so badly the keyboard will need replacement. If you lay down another white handkerchief and turn the keyboard over on it, tap it, and lift it off, you'll be able to show your customer just how bad things have gotten. While keyboards aren't terribly expensive, there's no reason to be replacing them if you don't need to. You can use a small vacuum or compressed air to help clean the keyboard as well.

The monitor, just like a television screen, tends to draw dirt out of the air, which makes it difficult to see. If you use the same kerchief you used for the power supply and a clean corner of the cloth around your finger, you can quickly wipe across the monitor and show the client how much buildup is there.

We've already talked about virus checking in chapter 6, so you already know what to do here. Be sure to perform your check with a copy of the original antivirus software so you can destroy the disk if a virus is found. Protect yourself by running the virus check first, before you run any other diagnostic programs on the computer.

Virus check

You'll need a fresh floppy disk in each size and capacity to test the floppy drive alignment. You'll need a 5.25-inch 360K disk, a 5.25-inch 1.2MB disk, a 3.5-inch 720K disk, and a 3.5-inch 1.44MB disk. If the user doesn't know the drive capacities, use your Snooper program, included with this book, to determine the floppy disk drive capacity.

Floppy disk drive alignment check

Format the correct disk in the floppy disk drive and copy a data file, such as a text file, to the disk. Then take the disk to another computer in the office and try to read the disk. If the other computer can't read the disk or reads the disk with difficulty, there could be an alignment problem with the drive. Of course, since this is a free diagnostic check, you're not under any obligation to determine which drive on which computer has the problem until you have a contract.

Also note that you need to use good-quality disks for this exercise, especially if you're using 3.5-inch disks. If the disks are poor quality, they might not be centered correctly in the plastic housing. This means the tracks and sectors written during the format might not be readable once they're moved to another drive.

You can test for this by rotating the disk a quarter of the way by hand, placing it back into the drive, and attempting to read the disk again. Repeat this process until you can read the disk. If you can read the disk after a few tries, then you know you have a poor-quality disk.

Hard disk drive check

When you look at the hard disk drive, you're looking for a drive that needs space freed, fragmentation of the data on the drive, or both. First look at the disk space. The Snooper utility included with this book can tell you how much space is left on the hard disk drive. If the drive is at 70 percent or higher, it's time to start thinking about what data can be removed. As for optimization, you'll need a defragmentation program and one that will display a graphic of the fragmentation of the hard disk drive.

Fragmentation occurs because of the way DOS handles the disk space. When files are deleted and other files are written to the disk, files can become split across different parts of the hard disk. The farther apart the data is physically on the drive, the longer it takes to access that data. A severely fragmented hard drive can slow things down quite a bit.

To get a graphical display of the fragmentation, you can use DEFRAG supplied with MS-DOS 6 or higher. To tell what DOS version is on the PC, type VER. If DOS 6 is not available, you'll need to use a utility provided by Norton, PC Tools, or some other third-party vendor. Start the program, look at the graphical and fragmentation information, and write down the percentage of fragmentation displayed. DO NOT PROCEED TO DEFRAGMENT THE DRIVE. A hard disk drive should never be defragmented without a reliable backup made first, just in case. Also, you're just there to check over the drive. Defragmentation takes some time, and you want to be under contract before you proceed. Pressing the Esc key will get you out of the DOS DEFRAG program and out of most defragmentation utilities.

When you get the service contract, you'll want to optimize the hard disk drive following this procedure. Backup the drive, delete any old files or unused programs to save disk space, then defragment the drive. You'll need the user's input to delete files, however, so you might have to skip this step if the user is not available. By following these steps in this order, you can get any data back that the user suddenly decided is needed after all. You'll also get the maximum defragmentation because you did the file deletion first.

A part of PC maintenance includes attention to the health of the user of the machine. An increasing number of lawsuits are being filed by individuals who believe they have been harmed by working at computer terminals. Right now the suits are aimed at computer manufacturers such as Compaq, IBM, and Apple Computer, but you don't have to be a great legal mind to figure out that those suits will soon be aimed at employers who haven't at least taken steps to prevent computer workstation injuries to their employees. These facts should be a sales point to help you open the eyes of your client to the importance of ergonomics.

Monitor placement   Ergonomics is not a one-size-fits-all proposition. You'll need to find the person who works at the computer in question and have him or her sit down in front of the PC. The first thing to note is the placement of the monitor compared to their point of view. Is the user having to tilt his or her head down or up to see the monitor?

There is new evidence that suggests holding the head in anything but the natural straight-up position, shown in Fig. 10-2, can place strain on the neck muscles. The theory is this strain can cause the neck muscles to spasm, which pinches key nerves in the spinal column that feed down to the arm

10-2
Shown is the correct posture ergonomically for working at the computer. Note the placement of the monitor and the relationship of the chair and table to the user.

and wrist, eventually causing the symptoms associated with carpel tunnel syndrome. The way to prevent this is to make sure the monitor is placed so the user can see the screen while holding his or her head straight-up, with the eyes looking just slightly down or straightforward.

Hand and arm placement   The second thing to check is the hand and arm placement relative to the keyboard. The user should not have to lift the arms up to reach the keyboard or hold the arms at all to type. The arms should hang naturally at the sides, bending at the elbow, and the wrist should not be bent up or down to type. A wrist rest should be just in front of the keyboard to support the wrists so just the fingers can move in typing, as shown in Fig. 10-2. A rolled-up towel can work as a wrist rest, but there are commercially available rests for under $10, so there's no excuse for not having one.

Chair posture   As for chair posture, the user should not have to bend forward to reach the keyboard. The chair should be comfortable, offering lower-back support. You'll know the chair is at the right height when the user's feet are flat on the floor, yet not too low if the thighs are supported by the chair, as depicted.

Electromagnetic-field radiation emissions   The distance of the user from the monitor is a concern as well. Monitors emit electromagnetic-field (EMF) radiation, and no one really knows what effect that has on people other than to predict that it's probably bad. EMF is not deterred by standard building materials, so if you lean your head against the wall and someone's computer monitor is on the other side, that EMF radiation is coming on through the wall, just as though the wall didn't exist.

The good news is these types of fields decrease exponentially the farther away you get. So if you get about 2 feet away from a monitor, which is just under an arm's length away, the field strength decreases to just about nothing. Another thing to keep in mind is that the strongest emanations are from the back and sides of the monitor.

What all this means for monitor placement is you want people at the computer to be able to put their arms out in front of them and just barely be able to reach the monitor. You also want to watch, especially in an office, for people who are backed up against a monitor they can't see because of a physical barrier, like the wall of a cubicle or an office wall. In a home office, it's fairly common to turn a spare bedroom into an office. If you have a client with a home office, you'll want to watch to make sure the monitor isn't placed against a wall where there's someone sleeping on the other side, such as a baby's crib or child's bed.

The amount of extremely low-frequency emission in monitors is judged against the Swedish standards, which are the world's toughest. Measured in milligauss (mG), the Swedish standards recommend exposure to no more than 2.5 mG of magnetic emissions at a distance from the monitor of approximately 2 feet. If you're so inclined, you can get a TriField meter and measure the EMF from monitors, but don't be surprised to find over 100 mGs from most monitors. To put things into perspective, you might find the same emission levels from certain types of desk lamps, as well as photocopiers, fax machines, and televisions. Still, it is better to err on the side of caution and educate your customers to minimize their risk as much as possible.

The Federal Communications Commission (FCC) Office of Engineering & Technology (OET) offers a free booklet, OET Bulletin No. 56, *Questions and Answers About Biological Effects and Potential Hazards of Radio-Frequency Radiation*. The booklet explains all the types of radio-frequency radiation, including EMF radiation, and offers resources for further investigation. You can obtain this bulletin using the FCC contact information provided in appendix A.

Eye care   Eyestrain is another issue that computer users face. Facing a computer monitor all day puts you in the position of a sitting target for the onslaught of airborne particles that are bounced off the screen and into the face of the user. Some users notice an increase in skin problems on their face after using a computer for some time. Eyestrain is the worst of the problems, however, both from the particles that bounce off the screen into the face and eyes, and from looking at reflected glare or a poorly adjusted monitor.

One recommendation you can make is for a glare screen for the monitor. The good ones are made of glass and are held in place on the front of the monitor by clips and straps that attach to the air holes on the top or some sort of velcro arrangement. Using a grounding strap that reaches back to clip on the outside of the power supply, some siphon off the static electricity buildup that tends to occur with monitors. The better ones can also block EMF radiation. The most noticeable effect is to reduce the amount of reflected glare from windows or interior lighting, but the shields also prevent the individual from being bombarded in the face by particles bounced off the monitor's screen.

A poorly adjusted monitor can also cause visual difficulty. If the display is too bright, unfocused, or distorted, it can be hard on the eyes. Sonera Technologies offers DisplayMate, a software utility that allows you to make adjustments using the standard adjustment tools already on the monitor. Before it displays each test image, the software explains what image it will display on the screen, what problems to look for, and what adjustment to make in order to solve those problems.

DisplayMate can be run from a floppy disk in about 15 minutes. It can help you make adjustments that will make a big difference to the user and will make you look like a hero. If the monitor has a problem that requires repair, the product can help you pinpoint the cause and help you justify to the customer why the monitor needs fixing. It is definitely a worthwhile tool to have for PC maintenance work.

The tests cover geometry and distortion, sharpness and resolution, screen pixel resolution, color and gray scale, and there are miscellaneous tests. The program runs you through a suite of tests, but if you feel you'd like to perform further tests in a certain area, there are more tests to help pinpoint the problem or further fine-tune the display. A novice mode is available as well, which explains everything in clear and concise terms without making assumptions about what you already know.

The product comes in a Windows version, and the Professional version that supports SVGA displays in high resolution. DisplayMate for Windows is about $80, the Professional version is under $250, and the company offers both products together for under $300 if you purchase them at the same time. More information on how to contact Sonera Technologies is in appendix C.

Inventory the PC's components

As with any other complex and valuable machine, the theft of PC parts is becoming an issue. White-collar crime is on the increase, and the theft of computer parts is made easier by the modularity of the PC. An employee who wants a math coprocessor might take it out of the PC at work and install it at home. That super-duper video card might end up swapped for a mediocre one so a game-playing employee can enjoy better graphics. Even CPU chips can be easily removed, thanks to Zero Insertion Force (ZIF) sockets that have a simple release lever to free the pins of the processing chip for removal. In addition, a black market is developing for PC components, so these stolen components might be sold.

Yet these crimes can be difficult for companies to detect because the PC is rarely opened and few managers would know what to check for. In addition, knowing the components inside the PC makes it easier to make intelligent insurance claims in case of a natural disaster or theft. A company can be spending money on premium components only to be reimbursed by insurance with less than they originally paid for, simply because no inventory was done.

When doing PC maintenance, you'll want to be sure a complete inventory of all the components for each PC is on paper, and include part numbers where applicable. Snooper will tell you what's inside the PC to help you with the inventory.

Create a rescue disk

Every PC should have a "rescue disk." This disk contains all that's needed to get the PC back up and running in case of a disaster. The disk should be bootable, include all the environment files, the Windows .INI files if applicable, any device drivers, and copies of the CMOS and partition information. (You can use the DOS MIRROR command to get the partition information if the computer has DOS 6.0 or higher.) If the disk was partitioned with a third-party product, such as SpeedStor or Disk Manager, the product name and version should be noted.

This is the last step. Be sure to have a label for this disk that includes your company information, including address and phone, so you can be called should an emergency arise.

You can use these maintenance tips as things to watch for and inform your customers about problems as you see them, or you can use them as a "sample" to get in the door with new customers. We've provided a ten-point checklist in appendix E for you to use in attracting new customers using the PC maintenance tips we've already described.

The ten-point checklist

To get the maintenance business, you'll need to dress for business and carry a professional-looking bag filled with the supplies outlined above. You'll also need a sharp-looking business card, the ten-point checklist, the recommendation form, and a contract should a customer choose to retain your services. In appendix E, we provide both the forms and the list of equipment you need.

Offer to perform a free maintenance test on one computer, and let the customer show you which one he or she would like you to use. This free maintenance check is something you can advertise, or you can go from business to business offering the check.

To start the check, introduce yourself and hand the person in charge your card. Ask this person to fill out the top of the service agreement with his or her name, company name, address, and so on. You might want to carry a white lab coat in your bag to put on while the businessperson fills out the form. Get him or her to initial as authorization to perform this no-obligation service check.

Then go through the ten maintenance points on the maintenance check form. Check the yes or no boxes in the squares provided on the form. The yes box is in the center of the boxes; the no box is to the far right. The "V" for verify box is one the customer uses later in this process.

Feel free to make notes in the space out to the right of each entry. Be sure to note positive as well as negative points, where you can in the space provided on page two of the form. After all, no one wants to hear they've done everything wrong, and your honesty in recognizing the efforts of the company will be appreciated. Do not open up the PC or move the equipment.

Once you've gone through the checklist on the PC in question, use the space provided on page two to offer your recommendations as to what should be done. You'll need to ask about the inventory and the rescue disk, so you'll need to call back the person in charge, then check over the disk, if one exists, for the important information listed for you in check boxes in the recommendation portion of the form. Let the company representative hold the checklist, and have him or her check off the first box for verification as you go through each of the ten points. Be sure to tell the representative why each of these items is important.

After you've gone through the list, go through the recommendation you have prepared based on your analysis of the PC in question. You should know what you charge to correct problems for each of the ten points. Then you can offer an estimate as to how much it would cost to fix any known problems on the PC you looked over, and how much you would charge for all the PCs on site.

You can charge your hourly rate for repairs. You should charge one hour for PC maintenance, though it will probably take only half an hour per PC to perform the check once you have some experience doing it. It could take a little longer if the hard disks need to be defragmented, but that can be staggered so you can be working on one PC while the other is defragmenting. Backups should be performed before defragmentation, and that can be done by the company or you can carry a portable backup unit, performing the service at an additional charge.

Even if the client doesn't go for your offer, if treated pleasantly and with respect, you might still get that call when it's time for repair work. After all, the client has seen you in action and knows you can deliver. You might even be recommended to business associates who find themselves in need of repair work. Every favorable contact counts. You might also want to use this opportunity to sign your clients up for a service contract similar to the kind we talked about in chapter 9. We've put together a sample contract shown in appendix E, which you can modify for your own use.

Profile

Lu Howell
Computer Dust Busters, Magna, Utah

Lu Howell started out doing catering and wedding consulting. She watched her husband repair and service computers over a period of time, and she decided she could do the service work herself. "It was either learn something about computers or spend a lot of time by myself," she said.

So she decided to start Computer Dust Busters, a PC cleaning and maintenance service. The service includes cleaning the monitor, opening and cleaning the computer itself, checking the voltage on the backup battery and replacing it if needed, cleaning the keyboard, the mouse, and the printer connected to the system. She also runs a virus scan and checks the hard disk drive for fragmentation.

She has several clients, including a large steel company, and is able to show new clients how the repair bills dropped for her current clients when they started doing the maintenance work on their PCs. She has a threefold brochure about her services that includes a punch-out Rolodex card, which she indicates is popular with her clients. Lu also offers a discount to those who will put covers over their computers at night and will permanently cover their keyboards with molded plastic known as a "skin."

As part of her service, Lu also does an inventory for the customer of all the components and serial numbers on all the PCs and printers. She recommends cleaning every three months, though hard disk defragmentation usually doesn't have to be done more than once a year.

In cleaning keyboards, Lu doesn't remove the key caps on the keyboard on-site. If a customer requests what she calls a "deep cleaning" of the keyboard, Lu advises them to simply purchase a new keyboard and put a Safe Skin over it. If the customer still wants the deep cleaning, she takes the keyboard with her and cleans it at home, including taking the caps off.

As for printer maintenance, Lu works on plotters, laser printers, and dot-matrix printers. Plotters are less work to maintain than laser printers, and dot-matrix printers require the most cleaning, she remarked.

She notes that some customers don't want the plastic on their keyboards and would rather purchase new keyboards periodically. She also cautions customers to avoid covering computers while they're left on because of potential heat problems.

It's the changing keyboard industry that keeps Lu hopping. Every six months her supplier has keyboards from yet another manufacturer, and she has to get new "skins" made. But she believes keyboard covers are the way to go, and she promotes the idea to her customers.

The PC maintenance work has lead into other PC repair work for her and her husband. "Because customers know us and trust us, they ask us to do other things as well," Lu mentioned. "Your relationship with your customers is the key to success."

Repairing used equipment for resale

A lot of people would buy used computers from a reliable source if they could find them. Often, they're too worried about the investment to purchase a computer from a newspaper ad, but if they knew someone in the repair business who would warranty the system for a period of time, they'd be a lot more comfortable.

Used systems are available everywhere these days. Just some of the places you'll find used computers for sale include auctions, garage sales, government surplus sales, and computer swaps. You have to know what you're doing, but that's the beauty of being in the repair business; you do know what you're doing. You might even find clients who are getting rid of old systems that you can pick up, refurbish, and resell.

You might want to add value to the PCs you sell by doing something interesting to them such as spray-painting the outside of the case with one of those rock-look paint kits you can get at most K-Marts, Targets, or Wal-Marts. The paint makes the surface look like a type of granite or marble and can hide the fact that the monitor casing is a different shade than the CPU case and the keyboard.

Profile

Mike Burke, CNE
RST Computer Services, Hudson, New Hampshire

Mike Burke, a CNE for RST Computer Services of Hudson, New Hampshire, has been interested in computers and electronics since high school, where he took electronics, radio fundamentals, and computer circuitry. He started out of high school as a test operator for Data General.

In his fifteen years working in the computer industry, he's worked as a technician for several companies. Mike said he's had the privilege of working in some unusual locations doing repair on card readers and on-site board repair at the United Nations, the Internal Revenue Service, Airports, and even NBC.

Mike decided to start pursuing CNE certification in 1989, and he said he failed one particular test three times before he finally passed it. He purchased self-study materials that cost him $1,500 at the time. Once certified, Mike joined the NPA and has taken IBM training courses as well.

He's depended on word of mouth to get customers. Mike sets up networks, offers support, and performs service calls. However, his strongest interest is in older computers, which is why he works for RST.

RST is a reclaiming facility. Mike runs the operation, and it's his job to see that the truckloads of computer parts and peripherals the company purchases for scrap are put to the most profitable use possible. Some components are cleaned up and sold, while others are taken apart and sold for scrap metal. The most valuable machines right now are the original IBM PCs because the single-sided floppy disk drives contain gold pins.

RST gets the computers from companies going out of business and buys equipment for $1,000 to $10,000 a truckload. The company repairs are mostly on motherboards, hard disk drives, and CRTs, which are then resold at computer swaps up and down the East Coast.

At one point, Mike said he had his own computer store, but he said profit margins on hardware got too slim for him to survive. In a high-cost location, such as the New England area, Mike has found there's more money in used hardware than new hardware.

If the equipment is too old to be of much value to someone the way it is, such as an old XT computer with a 20MB hard disk drive and a 360K floppy disk drive, you can still add value to the system by selling it as a custom voice mail system. Old XT and 286 computers are plenty fast for voice mail systems, and many people have difficulty setting up such a system themselves. You can set the system up so it will call them when they get an important message, just as we suggested you do for yourself in chapter 9.

Offer voice mail systems

Small business owners are constantly looking for ways to make their business look bigger. One way to do that is to record more than one voice on the voice mail system. You can have various people record the mailbox messages for a small business owner, so there's not just one voice on the entire system.

In addition, these voice mail systems have the ability to call a list of phone numbers and deliver a message to each number. Some are even smart enough to wait for a response before they start the message. Overworked nonprofit organizations might be interested in a system that would call all their volunteers to deliver a message. For example, a church might be very interested in an inexpensive system that would call all the Sunday school teachers to remind them of a schedule change or the twice-a-year time change. Schools might want such a system to call parents to let them know their child was absent that day. Again, several companies make such boards, such as the Complete Answering Machine from The Complete PC or the TyIn 2000 board from National Semiconductor.

PC add-on manufacturers have created boards that can allow PCs to take advantage of caller ID. The service, which allows you to get the phone number of the caller before you answer the call, is growing in popularity as a business tool. New products for PCs take the phone number of the caller, look it up in a database on the PC, and display the information about the caller from the database, all before you can pick up the phone.

Caller ID systems

Even in states where caller ID is not directly available, a company with a toll-free number can often get permission to access the number of the caller. This is a growing trend and requires that the PC be equipped with a special add-on board that can intercept the caller's phone number and specialized software. AG Communication Systems offers a product called WindowPhone, which includes the add-on board and the software designed to work with Microsoft Windows. Mountain Systems offers software that will work with just a modem to perform similar caller ID functions. Such systems range in price from over $200 to under $50. Contact information is available in appendix C.

Upgrade PCs to green

Lots of energy-saving green PCs are being sold today, but there are millions of PCs sold before energy saving became something companies worried about. You can add a card to a PC to make it an energy-conscious unit that will shut down the monitor or adjust the CPU down to a low-frequency option when no actions are being performed by the user.

Micro Express offers the Green Card for making 286, 386, or 486 PCs meet the energy saving standards currently set forth in the Environmental Protection Agency's Energy Star program. The card, shown in Fig. 10-3, costs under $130 and fits into an expansion slot on the PC. It can be programmed to monitor the power consumption of any input/output device. During periods of user inactivity, the card shuts down the monitor first, which is the highest power consumption device, then shuts down the hard disk drive and the printer as well. When the user touches the keyboard, the system comes up right where the user left off.

10-3
The Green Card turns any PC into an energy-saving PC.

The disadvantage to this card is the user might have to wait for a few seconds for the monitor and the printer to warm up for use. Those working out of home offices who are conscious of the increasing costs of energy are probably the target market. However, the government is going to require its contractors as well as its offices to purchase energy efficient equipment. You can upgrade their equipment to be energy efficient so they don't have to replace it.

Home automation

Another area that we expect will be receiving more attention is home automation. There are modules available that can be controlled from an IBM-compatible computer or a Macintosh that will automatically turn on and off the lights in a home, monitor the sprinkler system, control the heating, and pretty much control anything that can be controlled. And you don't need a particularly fast Macintosh or IBM-compatible computer. (More information on the Macintosh is available in appendix F.)

Some of the simplest systems are sold by Radio Shack and are X10 compliant, a standard for automation equipment. X10 modules are available for purchase that can be controlled from a central unit. You plug the module into the wall, plug the lamp, appliance, or whatever into the module, and program the computer when you want that particular module to go on and off. Each module has alpha and numeric settings so it has a unique designation, such as A1. The control unit plugs into the computer via a serial port, and the software allows you to set which modules operate when.

For the Macintosh, Remote Measurement Systems offers a serial port connector, sensors, and software that can allow even a Mac Plus to become a home automation tool. The Macintosh can continuously evaluate external conditions via the sensors and automatically issue commands to control electrical devices such as appliances. No programming is required.

If this is an area you are thinking of pursuing, you'll want to contact the Home Automation Association (HAA). This group offers a newsletter on home automation issues including PC-based systems and a member products and services directory. Contact information is available in appendix A.

One additional area of specialization in this field is with the disabled. While their needs vary, this group is very interested in the independence offered by computer-automation of their homes. A variety of companies offer hardware and software that must be configured for the individual disabled user. Microsystems Software offers the TEAM System and popECS software that uses X10 modules and must be configured for the user. Speech synthesis, so the computer can read aloud to the user, and voice recognition, so the computer can interpret voice commands, are also popular with the disabled market. This usually requires installation of a sound card as well as software. If you're interested in pursuing the disabled market, you might check with a nearby university. The government often funds research into devices for the disabled through universities, and you'll be able to find information there.

Data acquisition systems

There are other ways to use automation systems that have business applications. One enterprising computer businessman has set up Macintosh computers with sensing equipment to monitor the temperature and soil moisture in greenhouses. He checks each system remotely from a home computer using a modem, and he inspects the systems on site on a weekly basis. This type of system is known as *data acquisition*.

Scientists and those conducting research in university environments often find themselves in need of data acquisition systems. In these situations, computers are used to simply monitor and record changes in everything from fluid levels to the amount of carbon dioxide in the air. Some equipment can be modified to send digital or analog signals that the computer can then interpret and record. A few sources for the interface needed for the computer to pick up these signals include: Digital Distributors of Santa Cruz, California; Keithley Metrabyte of Taunton, Massachusetts; National Instruments of Austin, Texas; and Omega of Stamford, Connecticut. The interface boards can either be attached to a port on a PC or installed in a slot inside the PC. Usually a simple program with the source code comes with these boards, but you might find yourself looking for outside programming help to make the systems useful to your clients. Michael F. Hordeski has two books available on this subject, *Control Technology and Personal Computers* and *Control System Interfaces, Design and Implementation Using Personal Computers*.

Team up with a programmer

You might find yourself in need of a programmer who can help you set up user-friendly systems for clients while you perform the hardware end. A client might need a specialized system that is important to business operations, and since your client knows and trusts you, he or she might ask you to manage the project. If you don't have the time or the inclination to learn to program, it's best to find someone who can do the programming for you.

Programmers aren't too difficult to find, but good programmers can be a challenge to locate. You'll want to see previous examples of their work and know something about the character of this person. Fortunately, custom programs don't have to be as sexy as retail software. It'll look sexy to the customer if it does what he or she wants.

If you and the programmer are working on a project for a client that involves a significant amount of time, effort, and expense, you'll want to divide the project into milestones. Such milestones could be the set of specifications and functionality of the program set and in writing, delivery of a test version, the setup of any specific hardware needed, and final delivery. One way to get paid is to be sure specified payment amounts are agreed to at each point in the project. When you get to that point, you get a check before you go on. That way, you minimize your loss if the client changes his or her mind or runs out of money.

Programming projects need to be specified on paper. What specific functions the program is to perform and what output the client expects should be stated in writing before any coding is done. Each screen in the program should be designed before the underlying code is written so the client knows what he or she is getting. The code should be delivered in a test format, and the client should test it, looking for needed changes or flaws. Expect problems and reassure the client when the code "falls down." This is part of the process and should be expected.

Since you brought in the programmer, you'll be the one the client looks to for answers. So you'll need to keep up with the progress on the coding of the program as well as the hardware end. Of course, instead of teaming up with a programmer on someone else's money-making idea, you could be working on your own ideas.

You might have an idea yourself or have a friend who has an idea for a special-purpose kiosk using a computer that will make you millions, as it has Matt Russell and Len Davidson of Glendale, California. These two guys started a trend in greeting cards, using a computer and custom software, that has turned into a multimillion dollar business.

Special-purpose kiosks

Working out of their garage, they built a custom system with custom software using a 386 IBM-compatible PC, a touch-screen monitor, a Hewlett-Packard 8-pen plotter, and housed the whole thing in a kiosk made from painted particleboard. They called the system CreateaCard, and its purpose is to allow people to make and personalize their own greeting cards.

The unit is entirely self-sufficient and controls everything, including placing the card stock into the plotter once the card is selected and personalized, and delivering it to the consumer after it is printed. Russell and Davidson were told in the beginning that this wouldn't work, but when they attended Comdex in 1990 in the booth of the company that makes the touch-screen monitors, Ellographics, crowds lined up to make their own cards. "Here were these technical people ooohing and ahhhing our simple project," Davidson said.

American Greetings bought Russell and Davidson's idea, and now CreateaCard kiosks are in practically every greeting card store in the United States. They're not the only ones who have taken technology that is readily available and applied it to create a product for the retail consumer market.

Styles on Video is a franchise designed for high-traffic, upscale public places such as shopping malls. The system uses a video camera, an IBM-compatible computer, and a color laser printer. A prospective customer stands in front of a video camera and allows his or her image to be captured. The operator then outlines the customer's body, subtracting the customer's hair from the image so a new hairstyle can be added.

A book of hundreds of hairstyles is available, and the customer can choose either 12 or 24 of these to "try on." The computer places the hairstyles on the image one at a time, and the entire thing can be color printed or sent by the computer to a videocassette recorder so the customer can take home a video of the experience.

The franchise costs about $15,000 to get into, can be run from a two-wheeled "mall cart" that's popular in upscale shopping centers these days, and the

Canoga Park, California-based company sells new hairstyles to existing franchises for $100 each. Customers pay between $15 and $20 for 12 styles.

What you need for a kiosk is a computer, a touch-screen monitor, software, and maybe a printer. Kiosks can be built to perform a variety of functions, from offering product information in a retail store to helping shoppers locate a store in a mall. You can even convert existing monitors into touch-screen monitors using a controller offered by Elo Touchsystems, a company that also makes touch-screen monitors. The Intellitouch Controller, depicted in Fig. 10-4, offers a single cable connection to the computer. Remote diagnostic software, the board, and the cabling are sold for about $250.

10-4
The E281-2300 controller shown can be added to any monitor to make it a touch screen.

Elo Touchsystems.

Toner refill sideline in printer repair

Refilling laser printer toner cartridges is a profitable way to keep in contact with customers who will probably need other computer services as well. This is especially true if you decide you'd like to make printer repair or laser printer repair your main specialty.

Toner refilling, despite all the bad press it has gotten from cartridge manufacturers, is a booming business. Recycled toner cartridges became so popular that even printer manufacturing giant Hewlett-Packard got into the business. It just makes sense.

Why should laser printer owners spend twice as much for new toner cartridges, at around $100 each, when they can get them competently refilled for two-thirds to one-half the price and get more copies from a refilled cartridge to boot? Even better, the process recycles cartridges that would end up wasted, lying in a city dump.

The added benefit to this work is it gives you regular contact with potential customers. If the customer has laser printers, they're sure to have computers, peripherals, and all the trappings. Marketing experts will tell you to find a way to keep yourself in the front of your customer's mind. What better way than to have regular contact with customers through cartridge refilling?

Information on cartridge refilling is available through several publications aimed at the recycling market as a whole. There are two groups that offer information and sponsor trade shows concerning laser printer recycling. One is the International Cartridge Recycling Association and the other is the United Laser Toner Recyclers Association. Publications that focus on this market include: *R&R News*, *Recharger*, and *The Recycler*. Contact information for both the trade association and the magazines are listed in appendix A.

Michael Murray

Profile

HWH Microsystems, Ponchatoula, Louisiana

Michael Murray says the "HWH" in his business name stands for "hard work helps." A high-school dropout, Michael was trying to dodge the draft during the Vietnam era, but gave up and enlisted in the army to become a helicopter pilot.

When he got out of the army, he went to college and got a business degree. Michael said he did a little bit of everything until he decided to buy a vending machine business. It was while he owned the vending machine business that he got into computers with his first taste of typesetting and desktop publishing. He used the computer to print labels for the packaged foods sold in the vending machines.

He built the vending machine business into a successful operation, sold it, and bought a Macintosh. His brother, a printer, moved to Louisiana and Michael used the Macintosh for typesetting as part of the new printing operation they both started. His enthusiasm for the capabilities of the Macintosh grew to the point that he eventually purchased the computer store that sold him the Macintosh.

Unfortunately, the store was deeply in debt and after two years, it failed. Undaunted, Michael moved the bedroom furniture out of the master bedroom of his home, turned it into an office, and looked for a problem he could solve for Macintosh users.

At that time, to connect a Macintosh to an online service, you had to purchase a modem from one person, a cable from somewhere else, and the software to make it work from yet another company. Michael got an 800 number, took out a 2-inch, one-column ad in *MacUser* and *Macworld* magazines, and offered the modem, cable, and software, along with paying the freight costs for a single low price.

"People never just call up and order a modem. They want to talk about it first," Michael said. So he used that opportunity to sell them other things, such as disks, mouse pads, and eventually even computers and printers. In this way he generated leads for customers that he still has today.

As the circulation of the magazines grew, the ads got more expensive. Michael had built a customer base, so he stopped the mail order business and focused on desktop publishing.

His company offers a suite of services to users, including computer repair, for either the Macintosh or the PC platform. HWH Microsystems has also attained the status of value-added reseller (VAR) with Apple Computer.

The term "desktop publishing" bothers Michael because he maintains, "Publishing is publishing. There is no desktop publishing because now the desktop computer is the standard for the publishing industry."

To stay in business, the most important aspect is your relationship with suppliers. "It's those individual relationships you develop, where you know you can count on your supplier to come through for you, that make the difference," Michael added.

Because he's located in a small town, Michael is looking to new technology for the future. He's done some business with state and local government and has discovered EDI. The U.S. government is planning to implement electronic data interchange (EDI) for all transactions and will force its suppliers to do so as well.

EDI allows businesses and other entities to actually engage in business transactions without paper. Orders and invoices will be transmitted electronically. Independent service organizations are to provide the needed hardware and services to facilitate these paperless transactions. Michael is investigating the possibilities of his company doing just that.

Still working from his home office after five years, Michael claims he wouldn't have it any other way. "With a home-based business you don't have employees, so you don't have to take responsibility for their actions, and you don't need to worry about absenteeism. We just do it all ourselves."

Consulting

We can't very well leave a discussion of additional services you can provide without talking about consulting. Your time and expertise with computer systems will be of value to anyone who is looking for information on solving a problem. Since you have to keep up on the technology anyway, you might as well make as much of your knowledge as possible. You can charge by the hour for this service and help your customers avoid pitfalls and mistakes.

A number of national groups are aimed just at professional consultants, including the Independent Computer Consultants Association, the Institute for Certification of Computer Professionals (ICCP), and the Association for Services Management International (AFSM). Contact information on all three of these groups is in appendix A.

The ICCP even offers certification in the following areas: business information systems; communications; data resource management; management; office information systems; procedural programming; software engineering; systems development; systems programming; systems security; and ACP programming languages, including Ada, BASIC, C, COBOL, Fortran, Pascal, RPG II, and RPG/400. Study materials are available for the certification exams from ICCP itself, on the ICCP CompuServe forum (GO ICCP), and from third-party sources listed in appendix B.

AFSM was originally focused on high-tech hardware maintenance, but has expanded to include the entire services and support industry. The group offers regional meetings, an annual trade show, educational materials, and a magazine, *The Professional Journal*.

These ideas for extra income we've outlined here are just a start, a taste, of the variety of things you can do in computer repair. There's no limit to the possibilities, many of which no one has even thought of yet. It is our hope that you, as one of the readers of this book, will find a new opportunity, either for yourself or for the entire field of computing.

Information sources, suppliers

Magazines & publications

Communications Week
600 Community Dr.
Manhasset, NY 11030
Tel: 516-562-5530
Fax: 516-562-5055

Computer Hotline
The Guide—published by *Computer Hotline*
15400 Knoll Trail Dr., Ste. 500
Dallas, TX 75248
800-999-5131
Tel: 214-233-5131
Fax: 214-233-5514

Computer Service & Repair Magazine
P.O. Box 261067
Littleton, CO 80123
Tel: 303-933-3033
Fax: 303-727-6765

Computer Shopper
One Park Ave., 11th Flr.
New York, NY 10016
Tel: 212-503-3900
Fax: 212-503-3999

Computer Sources
1038 Leigh Ave., Ste. 100
San Jose, CA 95126-4155
Tel: 408-295-4500
Fax: 408-295-0889

DataBased Advisor
4010 Morena Blvd., Ste. 200
San Diego, CA 92117
800-336-6060
Tel: 619-483-6400

InfoWorld
155 Bovet Road, Ste. 800
San Mateo, CA 94402
Tel: 415-572-7341

LAN Computing
101 Witmer Road
Horsham, PA 19044
Tel: 215-957-1500
Fax: 215-957-1050

LAN Magazine
600 Harrison St.
San Francisco, CA 94107
Tel: 415-905-2200
Fax: 415-905-2587

LAN Technology
411 Borel Ave., Ste. 100
San Mateo, CA 94402-3522
Tel: 415-358-9500
Fax: 415-364-8630

LAN Times
1900 O'Farrell St. Ste. 200
San Mateo, CA 94403
Tel: 415-513-6800
Fax: 415-513-6985

MacWeek
301 Howard St., 15th Flr.
San Francisco, CA 94105
Tel: 415-243-3500
Fax: 415-243-3651

Macworld
501 Second St.
San Francisco, CA 94107
Tel: 415-243-0505
Fax: 415-442-0766

NetWare Solutions
10711 Burnet Road, Ste. 305
Austin, TX 78758
Tel: 512-873-7761
Fax: 512-873-7782
CIS: 75730,2465

Network Computing
600 Community Dr.
Manhasset, NY 11030
Tel: 516-562-5071
Fax: 516-562-7293

PC Week
10 President's Landing
Medford, MA 02155
Tel: 617-393-3700
Fax: 617-393-3701

Processor
P.O. Box 85518
Lincoln, NE 68501-5518
800-334-7443
Tel: 402-477-8900
Fax: 402-477-9252

R&R News
4864 Market St., Ste. C
Ventura, CA 93003
Tel: 805-650-9081
Fax: 805-650-1607

Recharger
4218 W. Charleston Blvd.
Las Vegas, NV 98103
Tel: 702-438-5557

The Recycler
50 Park Rd.
N Leigh
Oxfordshire OX8 6RX
Tel: 44-0-993-883706
Fax: 44-0-993-883232

Service and Support Management
P.O. Box 399
Cedar Park, TX 78630-0399
Tel: 512-250-9023
Fax: 512-331-3900
Free subscription.

Service News
Hardware Maintenance Issue—published by Service News
P.O. Box 995
Yarmouth, ME 04096
Tel: 215-788-7112
Free subscription.

Shareware Magazine
1030 E. Duane Ave., Ste. D
Sunnyvale, CA 94086
Tel: 408-730-9291
Fax: 408-730-2107

Books

Apple Macintosh Family Hardware Reference
ISBN 0-201-19255-1
Addison-Wesley Publishing, 1988

Build Your Own 486/486SX and Save A Bundle
Aubrey Pilgrim
Windcrest/McGraw-Hill
ISBN 0-8306-4216-1

Build Your Own Macintosh and Save A Bundle
Bob Brant
Windcrest/McGraw-Hill, 1991
ISBN 0-8306-3656-0

The Complete PC Upgrade and Maintenance Guide, 3rd Edition
Mark Minasi
ISBN 0-7821-1259-5
Sybex, 1993

The Computer Industry Almanac
by Karen Petska Juliussen and Egil Juliussen
ISBN 0-942107-03-9
Published annually by Computer Industry Almanac
225 Allen Way
Incline Village, NV 89451-9608
U.S.: 800-377-6810
Tel: 702-831-2288
Fax: 702-831-8610

Control System Interfaces, Design and Implementation Using Personal Computers
Michael F. Hordeski
ISBN: 0-442-00568-7
Van Nostrand Reinhold, 1992

Control Technology and Personal Computers
Michael F. Hordeski
ISBN: 0-13-456823-0
Prentice Hall, 1992

DOS Programmer's Reference, 3rd Ed.
Terry Dettman
ISBN 0-88-022790-7
Que, 1991

Hands-on Guide to Oscilloscopes
Barry Ross
ISBN 0-07-707818-7
McGraw-Hill, 1994

How to Make Profits with Service Contracts
Michael R. Rizzo
ISBN 0-8144-5807-6
American Management Association, 1987

Inside the IBM PC and PS/2
Peter Norton
ISBN 0-13-465634-2
Brady, 1991

LAN Survival: a Guerrilla Guide to NetWare
Deni Connor and Mark Anderson
ISBN 0-12-194480-8
AP Professional, 1994

LAN Troubleshooting Handbook
Mark Miller
ISBN 1-55851-054-0
M&T Publishing, 1989

The Macintosh Bible, 3rd Ed.
Sharon Zardetto Aker, et al.
ISBN 0-940235-11-0
Goldstein & Blair, 1991

The Macintosh Bible, 5th Ed.
Darcy DiNucci
ISBN 1-566091-40-3
Peachpit Press, 1994

The Macintosh Do-It-Yourself Upgrade Book
Garry Howard
ISBN 0-782111-23-8
Sybex, 1992

Maintain & Repair Your Computer Printer and Save a Bundle
Stephen J. Bigelow
ISBN 0-8306-3507-6
Windcrest/McGraw-Hill, 1992

Maintaining, Upgrading, and Troubleshooting IBM PCs, Compatibles, and PS/2 Personal Computers
Mark Minasi
ISBN 0-87455-230-3
Compute Books, 1990

Microsoft MS-DOS 6, Step-by-Step
ISBN 1-55615-552-2
Catapult, 1993

The New Optical Storage Technology
John A. McCormick
ISBN 1-55623-907-6
Irwin Professional Publishing, 1994

Outside the IBM PC and PS/2, Access to New Technology
Peter Norton
ISBN 0-13-643586-6
Brady, 1992

PC Drives & Memory Systems
Stephen J. Bigelow
ISBN 0-8306-4551-9
Windcrest/McGraw-Hill, 1994

Peter Norton's Guide to Unix, A Book
by Peter Norton and Harley Hahn
ISBN: 0-553-35260-1
Bantam Computer Books, 1991

The Paul Mace Guide to Data Recovery
Paul Mace
ISBN 0-136544274
Brady, 1988

Pocket PCRef
Thomas J. Glover
ISBN 0-9622359-7-0
Sequoia Publishing, 1993

The Printer Bible
Scott Foerster
ISBN 0-88022-512-2
Que, 1990

Que's Guide to Data Recovery
Scott Mueller and Alan C. Elliott
ISBN 0-880225416
Que, 1991

Repairing PCs: Beyond the Basics
Michael F. Hordeski
ISBN 0-8306-3899-7
Windcrest/McGraw-Hill, 1995

Salvaging Damaged dBASE Files
Paul Heiser
ISBN 0-915391-33-3
Microtrend Books, 1989

Servicing PC-Based Equipment
Don Doerr
ISBN 0-13-808890-X
Prentice Hall, 1993

Troubleshooting and Repair Computer Printers
Steven J. Bigelow
ISBN 0-8306-3934-9
Windcrest/McGraw-Hill, 1992

Troubleshooting and Repairing Notebook, Palmtop, and Pen Computers
Stephen J. Bigelow
ISBN 0-07-005241-7
Windcrest/McGraw-Hill, 1994

Upgrading & Maintaining Your PC
Ulrich Schueller and Hans-George Veddeler
ISBN 1-55755-167-7
Abacus, 1993

Windows Resource Kit
Computer Discount Warehouse (CDW) Computer Centers
1020 Lake Cook Road
Buffalo Grove, IL 60089
U.S.: 800-800-4CDW (800-800-4239)
Tel: 708-465-6000

The Winn L. Rosch Hardware Bible, Third Edition
Winn L. Rosch
ISBN 1-56686-127-6
Brady, 1994

MediaMap Trade Show Report: MediaMap publishes the *MediaMap Trade Show Report—The Comprehensive Guide to Information Technology Trade Shows—Worldwide.* The *Trade Show Report* provides detailed listings of information technology (IT) trade shows in the U.S. and throughout the world. (Price: $495, clients; $795, nonclients).

Trade Show Report special features: 873 shows listed in the 1994 report (420 domestic (U.S.) shows, 453 international shows); show dates from 1994 through 1995 with many dates up to 1998; includes booth space costs, overview, past and projected attendance, attendee/exhibitor profiles, show management, and conference contacts. The *Trade Show Report* includes events indexed by product/market/technology and audience type, and also includes domestic and international trade and marketing resources, a comprehensive guide to other guidebooks and to government and private sector resources. The *Trade Show Report* lists the top 50 IT shows and provides information on generating media coverage. The publication also comes packaged with the "Trade Show Exhibitor Handbook," a guide to trade show marketing and exhibitor planning resources in the United States and abroad (also available separately). News and show information is updated in a monthly newsletter called Alert! (available for $495 pcr year).

MediaMap provides software and information services for information technology (IT) public relations (PR). MediaMap also offers MediaManager, software aimed at PR and marketing professionals who want to gain widespread press coverage.

Fall COMDEX

If you decide to go to COMDEX, it is important to make your travel arrangements early. During the week of the show, Las Vegas fills to overflowing during the show, and it is difficult to find lodging or transportation. If you want to play it smart, you might consider going to COMDEX near the end of the week because from Wednesday onward the crowds begin to thin and you can still get the information you need. The show requires an incredible amount of walking, so bring comfortable shoes, preferably more than one pair. Once you go to COMDEX, you can expect to begin receiving material about other computer trade shows as well.

Trade show information

Trade shows & sponsors

Spring COMDEX
Canadian COMDEX
South American COMDEX
Sponsor: The Interface Group
300 First Ave.
Needham, MA 02194-2722
Tel: 617-449-6600

Summer Consumer Electronics Show
Winter Consumer Electronics Show
Sponsor: Consumer Electronics Shows
2001 Pennsylvania Ave., NW
Washington, D.C. 20006-1813
Tel: 202-457-4900

MACWORLD Expo, Boston
MACWORLD Expo, San Francisco
Sponsor: World Expo Corporation
111 Speen St.
Framingham, MA 01701-9107
Tel: 508-879-6700

NetWare User Conference
Sponsor: NetWare Users International North America, Inc.
P.O. Box 19007
Provo, Utah 84605
Tel: 800-755-9898

NetWorld+Interop, Altanta
Sponsor: Interop Co.
303 Vintage Park Dr.
Foster City, CA 94404
Tel: 415-578-6900
Fax: 415-525-0193

PC Expo, New York
PC Expo, Chicago
Networks Expo, Dallas
Sponsor: Bruno Blenheim, Inc.
Bruno Blenheim, Inc.
One Executive Dr.
Fort Lee, NJ 07024
Tel: 800-829-3976
Fax: 201-346-1602

Service and Support World Expo
Publications and Communications, Inc. (PCI)
12416 Hymeadow
Austin, TX 78750-1896
800-727-3976

Service Tech
Sponsor: AFSM International
1342 Colonial Blvd., Ste. 25
Fort Meyers, FL 33907
Tel: 813-275-7887

ULTRA—Laser Printer Cartridge Recycling Trade Group
Sponsors trade shows
5 First St.
Dover, NH 03820
Tel: 603-749-5200
Fax: 603-749-5826

ANSI (American National Standards Institute)
11 W. 42 St.
New York, NY 10036
Tel: 212-642-4900
Fax: 212-398-0023

Organizations

Association for Services Management International (AFSM)
1342 Colonial Blvd., Ste. 25
Fort Myers, FL 33907
Administrative offices: 800-333-9786
Membership: 800-444-9786
Tel: 813-275-7887
Fax: 813-275-0794

Home Automation Association (HAA)
808 17th St. NW, Ste. 200
Washington, DC 20006
Tel: 202-333-8579
Fax: 202-223-9569

Independent Computer Consultants Association (ICCA)
933 Gardenview Office Parkway
St. Louis, MO 63141
Tel: 314-997-4633
Fax: 314-567-5133

International Cartridge Recycling Association (ICRA)
1200 19th St. NW, Ste. 300
Washington, DC 20036
Tel: 202-857-1154
Fax: 202-224-4579

International Society of Certified Electronics Technicians (ISCET)
2708 W. Berry St.
Fort Worth, TX 76109-2356
Tel: 817-921-9101
Fax: 817-921-3741

Institute for Certification of Computer Professionals (ICCP)
2200 E. Devon Ave., Ste. 268
Des Plaines, IL 60018
Tel: 708-299-4227
Fax: 708-299-4280
CompuServe: GO ICCP

Institute of Electrical and Electronics Engineers (IEEE)
345 E. 47th St.
New York, NY 10017-2394
Tel: 212-705-7555
Fax: 212-752-4929

Institute of Electrical and Electronics Engineers Computer Society (IEEE-CS)
1730 Massachusetts Ave., NW
Washington, DC 20036-1992
Tel: 202-371-0101
Fax: 202-728-9614

Service Corps of Retired Executives (SCORE)
1825 Connecticut Ave., NW
Washington, DC 20009
Tel: 202-653-6279

United Laser Toner Recyclers Association (ULTRA)
5 First St.
Dover, NH 03820
Tel: 603-749-5200
Fax: 603-749-5826

To get the necessary filing forms for Class B Certification contact:

FCC Forms Distribution Center
2803 52nd Ave.
Hyattsville, MD 20781
Tel: 202-418-3676

Ask for the Class B Digital Device Certification Pack, which includes the following list of forms. Please note that the FCC says requests by mail are processed faster than requests made by phone.

- FCC Forms 731 (2)
- FCC Form 159 Instructions (1)
- FCC Form 159 (2)
- FCC Form 159-C (1)
- Public Notice No. 34560
- Application Checksheet/Assembly Format
- Preprint of Sections 2.801, et seq. & 2.1033
- Reprint of Section 2.925 et al/Labeling Requirements
- OET Bulletin 62
- Part 15 Contract Test Firms List
- Rules Order Blank and GPO (GPO) Bookstores List
- Advance Grantee Code Assignment Pack
- Fee Filing Guide

FCC Public Access Link (PAL) BBS
BBS: 301-725-1072
300, 1200, or 2400 baud, 8 bits, no parity, 2 stop bits
(The most popular BBS setting for stop bits is 1, so you might have to adjust your telecommunications software to 2 stop bits). Information on changes to FCC rules and rate increases for certification filing, as well as other information. Note: You're only allowed 8 minutes at a time on the BBS.

Federal Communications Commission (FCC) contact information

B Third-party repair services that hire subcontractors

Third-party repair services that hire subcontractors

Bell Atlantic Services
4414 Lottsford Vista Rd.
Lanham, MD 20706
U.S.: 800-777-8800

Bell offers repair on computer equipment from PCs to minis, and mainframe computers. The company subcontracts to computer repair services who can help broaden the company's service area. The subcontracting is done through the management in branch locations. Call the 800 number and ask for the branch location nearest you, then approach the branch for possible subcontract repair work.

MCM Corporation
800 Vantage Drive, Bldg. B
San Antonio, TX 78230
U.S.: 800-274-1626
Fax: 512-377-1726

MCM offers computer repair services through a network of repair shops. To inquire about becoming a member of the MCM network, call and ask for the third-party service manager.

Certification information
Computing Technology Industry Association (CompTIA or CTIA, formerly the ABCD)

A+ Certification
Information on the A+ Program
Jean Alexander
Tel: 708-268-1818

Drake for the CompTIA
Tel: 800-77MICRO (800-776-4276)

20525 Mariani Ave.   **Apple Computer**
Cupertino, CA 95014
Tel: 408-996-1010
Fax: 408-996-0275
Customer Assistance Center: 800-776-2333
Product Support Questions: 800-776-2775

LANtastic   **Artisoft**
2202 N. Forbes Blvd.
Tucson, AZ 85745
Tel: 602-670-7100
Fax: 602-670-7101
Upgrades and Information
U.S. and Canada: 800-846-9726
Fax: 602-670-7359
International: 602-670-7100
Fax: 602-670-7101
Technical Support: 602-670-7000
Paid Support: 900-555-8324, $2.50 per minute
CompuServe: GO ARTISOFT

Certified Banyan Specialist (CBS)   **Banyan VINES**
Certified Banyan Engineer (CBE)
Technical Certification Programs
120 Flanders Rd.
Westboro, MA 01581
Tel: 508-898-1795
Fax: 508-836-0225
Course Registration & Information
800-832-4595 or 508-898-1000 ext. 1270
Applications for Certification 800-828-2404
Banyan Authorized Channel Partners: 800-2-BANYAN (800-222-6926)

Drake Testing and Technologies for Banyan
U.S.: 800-736-3926

Certified Electronics Engineer (CET) Computer Journeyman   **International**
2708 W. Berry Street   **Society of Certified**
Fort Worth, TX 76109-2356   **Electronics**
Tel: 817-921-9101   **Technicians (ISCET)**
Fax: 817-921-3741

Accredited Systems Engineer (ASE)   **Compaq**
Compaq Computer Corporation
P. O. Box 692000
Houston, TX 77269-2000
Main Phone: 713-370-0670

Support: 800-444-7575
PaqFax Automated Fax Information System: 800-345-1518
Training Registration Center: 800-732-5741
Questions regarding ASE: 714-374-2266

Drake for Compaq
800-366-EXAM (800-366-3926)

Dell Computer Corporation

2111 W. Braker Lane
Austin, TX 78758
U.S.: 800-289-3355

Dell University
Third-Party Maintainer Program
U.S.: 800-289-3355 ext. 83489
Tel: 512-728-3489

IBM

Certified IBM LAN Server Engineer
Certified OS/2 Engineer
Fax back: 800-IBM-4FAX

Skill Dynamics, an IBM Company
(A+ Certification Self-Study Kit)
U.S.: 800-IBM-TEACH (800-426-8322)

Drake Testing and Technologies for IBM
U.S.: 800-959-EXAM (800-959-3926)

National Advancement Corporation (NAC)

Level 2 Certification
Computer Repair Training Classes,
    Intel-based PCs, Macintosh, Monitors, Printer Repair
    Videos on Monitor and Laser Printer Fuser Assembly Repair.
National Advancement Corporation (NAC)
2730-J S. Harbor
Santa Ana, CA 92704
Inside California: 800-443-3384
Outside California: 800-832-4787
Outside U.S.: 714-754-7110
Fax: 714-754-7166
BBS: 714-754-7148, 8,1,n, 2400 baud
CompuServe: 70253,2400

Drake for National Advancement Corporation
U.S.: 800-340-EXAM

Lotus

Certified Notes Consultant (LCNC)
Information on certification requirements, course information, authorized
    training centers available from Fax Support.

Fax Support (fax back): 617-253-9150
More information on Lotus Notes Training,
U.S.: 800-346-6409
Tel: 617-693-4436

Drake for Lotus
U.S.: 800-74-LOTU.S. (800-745-6887)

Microsoft Certified Systems Engineer (CSE)
U.S.: 800-636-7544
Canada: 800-563-9048
CompuServe type: GO MSCESYSTEM

Microsoft Solution Provider Authorized Training Centers Referrals
U.S.: 800-636-7544
Canada: 905-568-0434

Microsoft On-line BBS
BBS: 206-637-9009, 8,n,1, 2400, 4800, 9600 and 14,400 baud with V.22bis, V.32,
    V.32bis and V.42.

TechNet CD-ROM
U.S. and Canada: 800-344-2121 ext. 589
Other: 206-936-8661

Information on Microsoft Support Network—Technical Support Services
U.S.: 800-936-3500
Offers "Fast Tips" information by fax, mail, or recording.
Microsoft GEnie Roundtable—type "m505" and <Enter> at any GEnie prompt.
Microsoft on CompuServe—type FIND MICROSOFT at any prompt to list
    more than fifty Microsoft subject forums on a wide variety of subjects,
    including: the Microsoft Knowledge Base (GO MSKB); networks (GO
    MSNETWORKS); home products (GO MSHOME); and DOS (GO MSDOS).

Drake Testing and Technologies for Microsoft
U.S.: 800-755-EXAM (800-755-3926)

Certified Network Engineer (CNE)
Enterprise CNE (ECNE)
Novell Education Information Fax Back
U.S. and Canada: 800-233-3382
Other areas: 801-429-5508
CompuServe: type "FIND NOVELL" at any prompt for a full listing of Novell
    forums or type "GO NOVELL" for the general NetWare forum.

Drake Testing and Technologies for Novell
U.S.: 800-RED-EXAM (800-733-3926)
Latin America: 612-921-4190

England: 44-71-437-6900
Germany: 49-211-500-9950
France: 33-1-4289-8749
Sydney: 61-2-444-3666
Toyko: 813-3280-7484

Certified Network Expert (CNX)

CNX Token Ring
CNX Ethernet
Network General
"Sniffer University" training for the CNX
4200 Bohannon Drive
Menlo Park, CA 94025
U.S.: 800-695-8251
Tel: 415-473-2000
Sales: 800-846-6601
Fax: 415-321-0855
Technical support: 800-395-3151
Fax back: 800-764-3329 or 415-473-2690 for testing and course scheduling
information.

Drake for the CNX
U.S.: 800-CNX EXAM (800-269-3296)

WordPerfect—the Novell Applications Group

WordPerfect Certified Systems Engineer (CSE)
Contact Novell.
BBS: 801-225-4414, 8,1,n, 2400, 9600, 14,400 baud
BBS: U.S. Robotics/HST Modem, 801-222-4325 or 801-222-4369
(CSE access via doorway, requires Telibit or Qmodem telecom software.)
WordPerfect FTP Access Via Internet: 151.155.3.17
InfoShare Fax-back Service: 800-228-9960 or 801-429-3239
SpaceWorks Third-Party BBS, offers Free on-line WP support
U.S.: 1-800-5-SPACE-5, ext. 5500 (800-577-2235, ext. 5500)

Institute for Certification of Computer Professionals (ICCP)

The following are some of the study materials available for preparing for ICCP set of examinations:

ICCP Exam Review Outlines are available for under $60 by writing:
ICCP
2200 E. Devon Ave., Ste. 268
Des Plaines, IL 60018-4503
Tel: 708-299-4227
Fax: 708-299-4280
CompuServe: GO ICCP

Review course materials on cassettes are available from:
Bird Professional Publications
   (in cooperation with the ICCP Education Foundation)
2320 Lynx Way
Boise, ID 83705
Tel: 208-384-1600

DPMA SIG-CP ICCP Certification Review Manual
Contact: Ron Carruth, CCP
Director Information Systems
The Colonial Williamsburg Foundation
P. O. Box 1776
Williamsburg, VA 23187-1776
Tel: 804-220-7298
Fax: 804-220-7717

CDP Review Manual, 5th Ed.
Lockwood L. Lyon, CCP,CDP,CSP and Kenniston W Lord, Jr., CDP,CSP
Van Nostrand Reinhold
Mail Order Service
7625 Empire Dr.
Florence, KY 41042
U.S.: 800-842-3636
Fax: 606-525-7778

Write to the following address for information on other ICCP exam
preparation materials.

M. Jean Cannon and Lockwood L. Lyon, CCP
RDE Services
P.O. Box 200
Drayton Plains, MI 48330-0233

Wave Technologies International
10845 Olive Blvd., Ste. 250
St. Louis, MO 63141,7777
U.S.: 800-828-2050
Tel: 314-995-5767
Free catalog of self-study course offerings covering network training.

Peripheral Diagnostics
11405 W. I-70 Frontage Rd. N
Wheatridge, CO 80033
U.S.: 800-845-3839
Tel: 303-940-0828
Fax: 303-940-0830
Monitor repair self-study materials, technical support.

Non-ICCP sources for self-study materials

Third-party network self-study and training

Monitor Repair Training

National Advancement Corporation (NAC)
2730-J S Harbor
Santa Ana, CA 92704
Inside California: 800-443-3384
Outside California: 800-832-4787
Outside U.S.: 714-754-7110
Fax: 714-754-7166
BBS: 714-754-7148, 8,1,n, 2400 baud
CompuServe: 70253,2400
Monitor repair training classes, videos, and technical support.

Printer Repair Certification

Epson America
20770 Madrona Ave.
P. O. Box 2842
Torrance, CA 90509-2842
U.S.: 800-289-3776
Tel: 310-782-0770
Fax: 310-782-4235
Information on becoming authorized to repair Epson printers.
U.S.: 800-338-2349

Laser Printer Repair Courses and Materials

Diversified Technigraphics
6 Morgan, Ste. 112
Irvine, CA 92718
Tel: 714-855-3838
Fax: 714-855-3959
Training courses, self-study videos and books on laser printer repair and
cartridge refilling.

National Advancement Corporation (NAC)
2730-J S. Harbor
Santa Ana, CA 92704
Inside California: 800-443-3384
Outside California: 800-832-4787
Outside U.S.: 714-754-7110
Fax: 714-754-7166
BBS: 714-754-7148, 8,1,n, 2400 baud
CompuServe: 70253,2400
Printer repair training classes, videos, and technical support.

Certification testing companies

Drake Training & Technologies
2601 W. 88th Street
Bloomington, MN 55431
Tel: 612-896-7000
Fax: 612-896-7010

America Online (AOL)
Subscription Information
U.S.: 800-827-6364
AOL has a large Macintosh user community and several vendor forums,
including an Intel forum.

CompuServe
U.S. and Canada: 800-524-3388
United Kingdom: 0800-289-458
Germany: 0130-86-46-43
Other in Europe: 44-272-255111
Other International: 614-457-0802
Major PC vendors hold forums on CompuServe. For a listing of the
information you're looking for type "FIND" and a single-word subject, such
as the vendor name or product name, at any CompuServe prompt.

GEnie
Subscription Information
U.S.: 800-638-9636
See GEnie connect offer of free sign-on plus ten free hours of connect time.
(See Fig. B-1.)

MCI Mail
201 Centennial Ave.
Piscataway, NJ 08854
U.S. Customer Service: 800-444-6245
Tel: 201-833-8484
(For vendor BBSs, see the individual vendor above.)

GEnie®
The most fun you can have with your computer on.

No other online service has more cool stuff to do, or more cool people to do it with than GEnie. Join dozens of awesome special interest RoundTables on everything from scuba diving to Microsoft to food and wine, download over 200,000 files, access daily stock quotes, talk to all those smart guys on the internet, play the most incredible multi-player games, and so much more you won't believe your eyeballs.

And GEnie has it all at a standard connect rate of just $3.00 an hour.[1] That's one of the lowest rates of all the major online services! Plus -- because you're a reader of *Start Your Own Computer Repair Business* you get an even cooler deal.[2] When you sign up we'll waive your first monthly subscription fee (an $8.95 value) and include ten additional hours of standard connect time (another $30.00 in savings). That's fourteen free hours during your first month - *a $38.95 value!*

You can take advantage of this incredible offer immediately -- just follow these simple steps:

> 1. Set your communications software for half-duplex (local echo) at 300, 1200, or 2400 baud. Recommended communications parameters 8 data bits, no parity and 1 stop bit.
> 2. Dial toll-free in the U.S. at 1-800-638-8369 (or in Canada at 1-800-387-8330). Upon connection, type **HHH** (Please note: every time you use GEnie, you need to enter the HHH upon connection)
> 3. At the U#= prompt, type **JOINGENIE** and press <Return>
> 4. At the offer code prompt enter **GCE225** to get this special offer.
> 5. Have a major credit card ready. In the U.S., you may also use your checking account number. (There is a $2.00 monthly fee for all checking accounts.) In Canada, VISA and MasterCard only.

Or, if you need more information, contact GEnie Client Services at 1-800-638-9636 from 9am to midnight, Monday through Friday, and from noon to 8pm Saturday and Sunday (all times are Eastern).

1 U.S. prices. Standard connect time is non-prime time: 6pm to 8am local time, Mon. - Fri., all day Sat. and Sun. and selected holidays.
2 Offer available in the United States and Canada only.
3 The offer for ten additional hours applies to standard hourly connect charges only and must be used by the end of the billing period for your first month. Please call 1-800-638-9636 for more information on pricing and billing policies.

B-1   *GEnie offers this book's readers free sign on, plus 10 free hours of connect time.*

Tools & sources

This appendix includes vendor contact information for tools and software products mentioned in the book. Note that FaxBack systems and bulletin board systems (BBS) are usually available 24 hours a day, 7 days a week.

Norton Antivirus.
Symantec
10201 Torre Avenue
Cupertino, CA 95014-2132
U.S.: 800-453-1150
Fax: 800-800-1438

ViruScan, Clean-Up, NetSheild, and NetScan antivirus software.
McAfee & Associates
2710 Walsh Ave., Ste. 200
Santa Clara, CA 95051-0963
Tel: 408-988-3832
Fax: 408-970-9727
Technical support: 408-988-4181

Integrity Master antivirus software.
Stiller Research
2625 Ridgeway St.
Tallahassee, Florida 32310
CompuServe: 72571,3352

Commercial software

Antivirus software vendors

Database recovery tools

dSalvage Professional.
Comtech Publishing
P. O. Box 12340
Reno, NV 89510-2340
U.S.: 800-456-7005
Tel: 702-825-9000
Fax: 702-825-1818

Diagnostic software

End-user diagnostic tools

The Norton Utilities for Windows and DOS.
Troubleshooting tools aimed at end-users and technicians.
Symantec
10201 Torre Avenue
Cupertino, CA 95014-2132
U.S.: 800-453-1150
Fax: 800-800-1438

Check-It Pro.
PC diagnostics aimed at end-user market.
TouchStone
2130 Main St., Ste. 250
Huntington Beach, CA 92648
U.S.: 800-531-0450
Tel: 714-969-7746
Fax: 714-960-1886
BBS: 714-969-0688

Disk Technician Gold.
Hard disk troubleshooting tool aimed at end-users.
Prime Solutions
1940 Garnet Avenue
San Diego, CA 92109
Tel: 619-274-5000
Fax: 619-272-4000

Skylight.
Windows troubleshooting tool aimed at end-users.
RenaSonce Group
5173 Waring Road, Ste. 115
San Diego, CA 92120
Tel: 619-287-3348
Fax: 619-287-3554

SpinRite.
Gibson Research
35 Journey
Aliso Viejo, CA 92656
U.S.: 800-736-0637
Tel: 714-362-8800

Winsleuth
Graphical PC diagnostics aimed at end-users.
Dariana Software
5241 Lincoln Avenue, Ste. B5
Cypress, CA 90630
Tel: 714-236-1380
Fax: 714-236-1390

WINProbe end-user Windows diagnostic.
PC Certify end-user diagnostics.
PC Probe PC troubleshooting software.
Landmark Research International
703 Grand Central St.
Clearwater, FL 34616
U.S.: 800-683-6696
Tel: 813-443-1331
Fax: 813-443-6603
Technical Support: 813-683-0854

Computer Consultant end-user oriented PC benchmarking and hardware
    inventory software.
Micro 2000
1100 E. Broadway, Ste. 301
Glendale, CA 91205
Tel: 818-547-0125
Fax: 818-547-0397

Professional PC Diagnostics aimed at service technicians.
Landmark SCSI Certify SCSI troubleshooting software, SCSI diagnostics and
    utilities.
AlignIt floppy disk alignment software.
Landmark Research International
703 Grand Central St.
Clearwater, FL 34616
U.S.: 800-683-6696
Tel: 813-443-1331
Fax: 813-443-6603
Technical Support: 813-683-0854

**Repair technician
diagnostic tools**

The Norton Utilities for Windows and DOS.
Troubleshooting tools aimed at end-users and technicians.
Symantec
10201 Torre Avenue
Cupertino, CA 95014-2132
U.S.: 800-441-7234
Tel: 408-252-3570
Fax: 408-255-3344

PC Tools for Windows.
PC Tools for DOS.
Troubleshooting tools aimed at both technicians and end-users.
Central Point Software (a subsidiary of Symantec)
15220 N. W. Greenbrier Pkwy., Ste. 150
Beaverton, OR 97006
U.S.: 800-925-2420
Tel: 503-690-8090
BBS: 503-690-6650, 8,n,1, 2400 baud
BBS: 503-690-4777 8,n,1, 9600 baud
TTY/TTD: 503-690-2695
Automated voice response support: 800-967-6703
FaxBack: 800-847-8766 or 503-690-2660

Floppy Tune disk alignment software with alignment disk.
PC Clinic diagnostic software for technicians available in self-booting and
    remote diagnostic versions.
Optune disk defragmentor and optimizer.
WhatCOM modem and serial COM port installation Software.
Data Depot
1710 Drew St.
Clearwater, FL 34615-6213
U.S.: 800-767-3424
Tel: 813-446-3402
Fax: 813-443-4377

QuickTech PRO-fessional diagnostic software.
UltraX
P. O. Box 730010
San Jose, CA 95173-0010
Tel: 408-988-4721
Fax: 408-988-4849

AMIDIAG diagnostic software with floppy cleaning routing and cleaning disk
    included.
American Megatrends, Incorporated (AMI)
6145-F Northbelt Pkwy.
Norcross, GA 30071
U.S.: 800-828-9264
Tel: 404-263-8181
Fax: 404-263-9381

Micro-Scope diagnostic software, comes with loop-back plugs.
Microscope Client diagnostic software for distribution.
Computer Consultant end-user oriented PC benchmarking and hardware
    inventory software.

Micro 2000
1100 E. Broadway, Ste. 301
Glendale, CA 91205
U.S.: 800-864-8008
Tel: 818-547-0125
Fax: 818-547-0397

Disk Analyst User's Guide database of hard disk drive specs,
    telephone/address of BIOS and hard drive manufacturers.
LennyLink like LapLink for data transfer between desktop PCs/laptops.
Consolidated Software Products
34650 U.S. 19 N, Ste. 206
Palm Harbor, FL 34684
U.S.: 800-737-8763
Fax: 813-789-0841

C.P.R. Data Recovery Tools.
RAMalyzer RAM diagnostics.
Amnesia CMOS recovery software.
PrinTrace printer diagnostic.
Tech Assist
5590 Ulmerton Road
Clearwater, FL 34620
U.S.: 800-274-3785
Tel: 813-571-2188
Fax: 800-226-5404

hTEST/hFORMAT Utilities for Hard Disk Repair.
Includes GETSEC and PUTSEC for absolute sector copying of MBR.
Kolod Research
P. O. Box 369
Northbrook, IL 60065
Tel: 708-291-1586
Fax: 708-291-1448

PC-Technician self-booting diagnostics, comes with loop-back plugs.
Windsor Technologies
130 Alto St.
San Rafael, CA 94901
Tel: 415-456-2200
Fax: 415-456-2244

Disk Manager
Ontrack Computer Systems
6387 Bury Dr., Stes. 15–19
Eden Prairie, MN 55346
U.S.: 800-752-1333
Tel: 612-937-1107
Fax: 612-937-5815

**Hard disk
installation
software**

DrivePro
4900 Pearl E. Circle, Ste. 101
Boulder, CO 80301
US Sales: 800-926-8299
Support: 303-443-3389
Fax: 303-443-3323
BBS: 303-443-9957

SpeedStor
Storage Dimensions
1656 McCarthy Blvd.
Milpitas, CA 95035
Tel: 408-954-0710
Fax: 408-944-1203
BBS: 408-944-1220 8,1,n, 2400 baud
BBS: 408-944-1221 8,1,n, 9600 baud

Hardware support/ information software

Micro House Technical Library on CD-ROM, includes all the following Micro House publications, each available separately: *Encyclopedia of Main Boards*, *Encyclopedia of Hard Drives*, and the *Network Interface Technical Guide*.
Micro House
4900 Pearl E. Circle, Ste. 101
Boulder, CO 80301
US Sales: 800-926-8299
Support: 303-443-3389
Fax: 303-443-3323
BBS: 303-443-9957

Hard Disk Tech Specs database of hard disk drive specs, controllers, telephone/address of BIOS, hard drive, and controller manufacturers.
Tech Assist
5590 Ulmerton Road
Clearwater, FL 34620
U.S.: 800-274-3785
Tel: 813-571-2188
Fax: 800-226-5404

Total On-Line Reference for Computer Hardware (TORCH) on CD-ROM or disk.
P. O. Box 518
N Andover, MA 01845
U.S.: 800-300-2199
Fax: 508-683-0015

Disk Analyst User's Guide database of hard disk drive specs, telephone/address of BIOS and hard drive manufacturers.

Consolidated Software Products
34650 U.S. 19 N, Ste. 206
Palm Harbor, FL 34684
U.S.: 800-737-8763
Fax: 813-789-0841

Howard Sams
4300 W 62nd St.
Indianapolis, IN 46268
U.S.: 800-428-SAMS (800-428-7267)
Reference material and schematics for IBM model PCs, Compaq, TI, NEC, Osborne, AT&T, Zenith, and the Apple II & III computers. Know the make and model you're looking for when you call.

386MAX
Qualitas, Inc.
7101 Wisconsin Ave., Ste. 1386
Bethesda, MD 20814
U.S.: 800-676-6386
Tel: 301-907-6700
Direct Sales: 800-487-1386
Fax: 301-907-0905
Technical support: 301-907-7400

Memory managers

QEMM
Quarterdeck
150 Pico Blvd.
Santa Monica, CA 90405-1018
U.S.: 800-354-3222
Tel: 310-392-9851
Fax: 310-399-3802
Technical support: 310-392-9701

MPC Wizard
Aris Entertainment
310 Washington Blvd., Ste. 100
Marina del Rey, CA 90292
800-228-2747
Tel: 310-821-0234
Fax: 310-821-6463

Multimedia troubleshooting utilities

Microsoft BBS
BBS: (206) 637-9009
Modem settings, 8,1,n supports 1200, 2400, 9600, and 14400 baud.
Includes helpful software and troubleshooting for Microsoft products in the following categories: Windows NT, Windows and MS-DOS; Word, Excel, Office and Multiplan; PowerPoint, Publisher and Project; MS Client, LAN

Operating systems
DOS, Windows, Windows NT, Windows for Workgroups

Manager, and MS Mail; Languages and Windows SDK; Works and Flight Simulator; MS FOX, MS Access, and MS Money; MS Video for Windows; and Multimedia Applications.

Microsoft FastTips Technical Library
U.S.: 800-936-4200
Fax or mail of product support information on Windows, DOS, and Windows for Workgroups.

TechNet CD-ROM
US and Canada: 800-344-2121 ext. 589
Other: 206-936-8661

Microsoft GEnie Roundtable—type "m505" and <Enter> at any GEnie prompt.
Microsoft on CompuServe—type FIND MICROSOFT at any prompt to list more than fifty Microsoft subject forums on a wide variety of subjects, including: DOS (GO MSDOS); the Microsoft Knowledge Base (GO MSKB); networks (GO MSNETWORKS); and MS Home products (GO MSHOME).

OS/2 IBM
Attn: OS/2 Service Delivery
Internal Zip 1020
1000 NW 51st St.
Boca Raton, FL 33431
U.S.: 800-992-4777
Corporate Customers U.S. Support: 800-799-7765
Fax: 800-426-6063
FaxBack technical support: 800-IBM-3395 (800-426-3395)
BBS technical support: 919-517-0001, 8,n,1
OS/2 BBS TALKLink information: 800-547-1283
Canada TALKLink information: 800-465-7999, ext. 228
CompuServe: GO OS2USER, GO OS2SUP
Prodigy: JUMP OS/2CLUB
Markham, Canada BBS: 905-316-4255, 8,1,n
Montreal, Canada BBS: 514-938-3022, 8,1,n
Toronto, Canada BBS: 416-492-1823, 8,1,n
Vancouver, Canada BBS: 604-664-6466, 8,1,n

PC-DOS IBM
1000 NW 51st St.
Boca Raton, FL 33431
FaxBack: 800-IBM-4FAX (800-426-4329)
FaxBack technical support: 800-IBM-3395 (800-426-3395)
BBS: 919-517-0001, 8,n,1
CompuServe: GO PSPAPROD (Personal Software Products Division - Products Forum)

AMIDIAG diagnostic software.
American Megatrends, Incorporated (AMI)
6145-F Northbelt Pkwy.
Norcross, GA 30071
U.S.: 800-828-9264
Tel: 404-263-8181
Fax: 404-263-9381

PC Clinic SB self-booting diagnostic software.
Data Depot
1710 Drew St.
Clearwater, FL 34615-6213
U.S.: 800-767-3424
Tel: 813-446-3402
Fax: 813-443-4377

CoSession for Windows.
CoSession for DOS.
Triton Technologies
200 Middlesex Turnpike
Iselin, NJ 08830
Tel: 908-855-9440
Fax: 908-855-9608
BBS: 908-855-9609

**Remote-control
software**

Close-Up for Windows and DOS.
Norton-Lambert Corp.
P. O. Box 4085
Santa Barbara, CA 93140
805-964-6767
Fax: 805-683-5679
Technical support: Use main no.

pcANYWHERE for Windows.
pcANYWHERE for DOS.
Symantec Corporation
10201 Torre Avenue
Cupertino, California 95014-2132
Tel: 408-253-9600
Fax: 408-253-4092

Carbon Copy for DOS.
Carbon Copy for Windows.
Microcom
500 River Ridge Dr.
Norwood, MA 02062-5028
U.S.: 800-822-8224

Tel: 617-551-1000
Fax: 617-551-1021

ReachOut.
Ocean Isle Software
1201 19th Place, 2nd Flr.
Vero Beach, FL 32960
U.S.: 800-677-6232
Tel: 407-770-4777
Fax: 407-770-4779

Windows Uninstall software

Rosenthal UnInstall
Rosenthal Engineering
P. O. Box 1650
San Luis Obispo, CA 93406
Tel: 805-541-0910

WinDelete.
Uninstaller for Windows, but has to be installed before program to be
  uninstalled is removed.
IMSI
1938 Fourth St.
San Rafael, CA 94901
U.S.: 800-833-8082
Fax: 415-454-8901

Uninstaller 2.
Microhelp
4359 Shallowford Industrial Pkwy.
Marietta, GA 30066
U.S.: 800-922-3383
Tel: 404-516-0899
Fax: 404-516-1099
Technical support: 404-516-0898

Shareware Shareware sources

Public Software Library (PsL)
P. O. Box 35705
Houston, TX 77235-5705
U.S.: 800-242-4775
Tel: 713-524-6394
Fax: 713-524-6398
CompuServe: 71355,470
Offers monthly shareware CD.
Free catalog available on request.

Association of Shareware Professionals (ASP)
14202 Carlson Avenue
Tampa, FL 33526
Tel: 813-855-1478
Distributes ASP Advantage CD-ROM of shareware titles.

CD-ROM Users Group
P. O. Box 2400
Santa Barbara, CA 93120
Tel: 805-965-0265
Fax: 805-965-5415
Distributes shareware titles and other reference materials on CD-ROM.

Snooper—Included on enclosed disk.
John Vias
Vias & Associates
P. O. Box 470805
San Francisco, CA 94147-0805
Tel: 415-921-6262
Fax: 415-922-3197

Read My Disk! (RMD!)—Included on enclosed disk.
Randy Harriman
DairySoft Custom Software
P. O. Box 2717
Bangor, ME 04402-2717
Tel: 207-945-3500

BurnIn—Included on enclosed disk.
George Campbell
OsoSoft
2122 9th St., Ste. 202
Los Osos, CA 93402-3247
Tel: 805-520-1759
BBS: 805-528-3753, 8,n,1, 300 to 2400 baud

QEdit—Included on enclosed disk.
Matthew Dial
SemWare
4343 Shallowford Road, Ste. C-3A
Marietta, GA 30062-5022
Tel: 404-641-9002
Fax: 404-640-6213
BBS: 404-641-8968

Shareware program information

Disk Drive Cleaner and Rosenthal Uninstall
Also carries cleaning disks for Disk Drive Cleaner.
Rosenthal Engineering
3737 Sequoia Dr.
San Luis Obispo, CA 93401-8313
Tel: 805-541-0910

ViruScan, Clean-Up, NetSheild, and NetScan antivirus software.
McAfee & Associates
2710 Walsh Ave., Ste. 200
Santa Clara, CA 95051-0963
Tel: 408-988-3832
Fax: 408-970-9727
Technical support: 408-988-4181

Integrity Master antivirus software.
Stiller Research
2625 Ridgeway St.
Tallahassee, Florida 32310
CompuServe: 72571, 3352

PKZip compression software.
PKWARE
9025 N Deerwood Dr.
Brown Deer, WI 53223-2437
Tel: 414-354-8699
Fax: 414-354-8559
BBS: 414-354-8670

(Note: Shareware programs included in this book are described in appendix G.)

PC hardware parts & tools
Automation, data acquisition hardware

Enviromac
Remote Measurement Systems
Tel: 206-328-2255
Fax: 206-328-1787

popECS TEAM System.
Microsystems Software
600 Worcester Road
Framingham, MA 01701

Digital Distributors
2808 Soquel Avenue
Santa Cruz, CA 95062
U.S.: 800-227-0349
Tel: 408-479-5432

Omega Engineering.
One Omega Dr.
P. O. Box 4047
Stamford, CT 06907-0047
FaxBack: 800-848-4271

Keithley Metrabyte
440 Myles Standish Blvd.
Tauton, MA 02780-1092
U.S.: 800-348-0033
Fax: 508-880-0179
Free catalog upon request.

National Instruments
U.S.: 800-433-3488
Tel: 512-794-0100
Fax: 512-794-8411
Internet: info@natinst.com
Free catalog.

Batteries

Battery Warehouse
190 E University
P. O. Box 3244
Des Moines, IA 50316
U.S.: 800-373-1310
Battery distributor and parts broker.

Fedco Electronics
P. O. Box 1403
Fond du Lac, WI 54936-1403
U.S.: 800-542-9761
Tel: 414-922-6490
Fax: 414-922-6750

Tadiran Computer Batteries
4268 Los Angeles Avenue
Simi Valley, CA 93063-3366
U.S.: 800-234-2444
Tel: 818-887-3337
Fax: 818-887-1686

Caller ID systems

WindowPhone.
AG Communication Systems
2500 W. Utopia Rd.
P.O. Box 52016
Phoenix, AZ 85072-9361
U.S.: 800-858-9236

CallAudit.
Mountain Systems
Box 830
Grundy, VA 24614
U.S.: 800-648-3108

Central processing unit (CPU) manufacturers

Intel
U.S.: 800-538-3373
Talk back: 800-321-4044
FaxBack: 800-525-3019
BBS: 503-645-6275, 8,n,1
CompuServe: GO INTEL

Cyrix
Information and FaxBack: 800-462-9749
BBS: 214-994-8610, 8,n,1, any baud rate.

Advanced Micro Devices (AMD)
Tel: 408-732-2400

Data recovery

Data recovery services

CPR&RS
7570 U.S. Highway 1, Ste. 8
Hypoluxo, FL 33462
U.S.: 800-765-9292
BBS: 407-547-5599

Data Recovery Clinic
4878 Ronson Court, Ste. A
San Diego, CA 92111
U.S.: 800-275-2823
Tel: 619-571-1700
Fax: 619-571-4898

Ontrack Data Recovery
In Minneapolis:
6321 Burry Dr.
Eden Prairie, MN 55346
U.S.: 800-872-2599
Tel: 612-937-5161
Fax: 612-937-5750

In Los Angeles:
2400 Main St.
Irvine, CA 92714
U.S.: 800-752-7557
Tel: 714-263-9245
Fax: 714-263-9246

In United Kingdom:
Surrey House, 34 Eden St.
Kingston upon Thames
Surrey KTI 1ER, UK
UK: 0800 243996
Tel: +44 0 81 974 5522
Fax: +44 0 81 974 5544

In Germany:
Tel: 0130 815 198

In France:
Tel: 05 90 72 42

The Fix diagnostic software for hard disk drive data recovery.
Consolidated Software Products
34650 U.S. 19 N, Ste. 206
Palm Harbor, FL 34684
U.S.: 800-737-8763
Fax: 813-789-0841

Data recovery software

C.P.R. Data Recovery Tools.
Tech Assist
5590 Ulmerton Road
Clearwater, FL 34620
U.S.: 800-274-3785
Tel: 813-571-2188
Fax: 800-226-5404

Rescue Data Recovery Software.
Recovery software for damaged hard drives and floppy disks.
AllMicro18820 U.S. Highway 19 N, Ste. 215
Clearwater, FL 34624
U.S.: 800-653-4933
Tel: 813-539-7283

Offers the Green Card add-on board to make standard PCs conform to Energy
  Star specifications. Also sells PCs.
Micro Express
1801 Carnegie Avenue
Santa Ana, Ca 92705
Tel: 714-852-1400
Fax: 714-852-1225

Green PC add-ons

Torch
P. O. Box 518
N Andover, MA 01845
U.S.: 800-300-2199
Fax: 508-683-0015
Electronic parts, supplier, and repair database product.

Parts & repair locators

MicroLine
35 Bonetown Rd.
Flemington, NJ 08822
Voice Tel: 800-215-0049
BBS: 908-806-2722, 8,1,n, 1200, 2400, 9600 baud
Online parts, supplier, and repair database product.
MicroLine offers two weeks free access after you first log on.

Parts brokers

Aftermarket Computer Services
U.S.: 800-578-1842
Tel: 910-725-6022
835 Reynolds Road
Winston Salem, NC 27104

Computer Commodity
1405 SW 6th Court, Ste. B
Pompano Beach, FL 33069
Tel: 305-942-6616
Fax: 305-946-7815

Computer Component Source (CCS)
P. O. Box 9022
135 Eileen Way
Syosset, NY 11791
U.S.: 800-356-1277
Fax: 800-926-2062
Canada: 800-561-9903
Canada Fax: 800-363-2141
Tel: 516-496-8780
Fax: 516-496-8984
Parts, batteries, kits for fixing common problems on PS/2s and PCs, monitor
    parts, and laser printer parts.
Free catalog available on request.

Computer Products & Services
951 Clint Moore Road, Ste. A
Boca Raton, FL 33487
Tel: 407-241-9026
Fax: 407-994-4608

Dataserv, a Bellsouth Company
19011 Lake Dr. E.
Minneapolis, MN 55317
U.S.: 800-232-4299

GE Remarketing Services
U.S.: 800-431-7716
Parts department and complete systems.

PC Service Source
1221 Champion Circle, Ste. 105
Carrollton, TX 75006
U.S.: 800-727-2787
Tel: 214-406-8583
Fax: 214-406-2787
Ask for free catalog.

KickStart 1 post card.
KickStart 2 post card.
ROM Post post card with ROMs.
Landmark Research International
703 Grand Central St.
Clearwater, FL 34616
U.S.: 800-683-6696
Tel: 813-443-1331
Fax: 813-443-6603
Technical Support: 813-683-0854

ROM POST—diagnostic ROM system, and disk alignment product.
PocketPOST post card.
PocketPOSTMCA post card for IBM's Microchannel architecture.
PC PowerCheck card to monitor and report on PC power supply performance.
Data Depot
1710 Drew St.
Clearwater, FL 34615-6213
U.S.: 800-767-3424
Tel: 813-446-3402
Fax: 813-443-4377

QuickPostPC entry-level post card.
R.A.C.E.R. II midlevel post card.
P.H.D.-16 post card with ROM included.
UltraX
P. O. Box 730010
San Jose, CA 95173-0010
Tel: 408-988-4721
Fax: 408-988-4849

PostProbe post card with included Microchannel (MCA) adapter.
Micro 2000
1100 E. Broadway, Ste. 301
Glendale, CA 91205
U.S.: 800-864-8008
Tel: 818-547-0125
Fax: 818-547-0397

Power supplies   PC Power and Cooling, Inc.
5995 Avenida Encinas
Carlsbad, CA 92008
800-722-6555
Tel: 619-931-5700
Fax: 619-931-6988
Markets high-quality power supplies.

Tape backup hardware   Largest supplier of internal and external minicartridge tape backup systems, Trakker portable parallel port tape backup.
Colorado Memory Systems (subsidiary of Hewlett-Packard)
800 S Taft Avenue
Loveland, CO 80537-9929
U.S.: 800-451-4523
Tel: 303-669-8000
Fax: 303-667-0997
QICFAX inquiry service: 800-368-9673
From Mexico: 95-800-346-9881
BBS: 303-635-0650, settings 8,1,n 1200, 2400, 9600, 14400, or 19200 baud
CompuServe Support: 71621,3022

Supplier of SuperHornet brand minicartridge tape systems and Digital Audio Tape (DAT) tape drives.
Conner Tape Products Group (a division of Conner Peripherals)
1650 Sunflower Avenue
Costa Mesa, CA 92626
Tel: 714-641-1230
Sales: 714-641-0279
Fax: 714-966-7347

Tape250 parallel port tape backup.
Iomega
1821 W 4000 S
Roy, UT 84067
U.S.: 800-777-6179
Tel: 801-778-1000
Fax: 801-778-3460
Technical support: 800-456-5522

SCSI controllers   Future Domain
2801 McGaw Avenue
Irvine, CA 92714
Tel: 714-253-0400
Fax: 714-253-0913

Jensen Tools Catalog
7815 S 46th St.
Phoenix, AZ 85044-5399
U.S.: 800-426-1194
Tel: 602-968-6231
Fax: 800-366-9662
Distributor of tools and test equipment for repairing PCs, networks, electrical
devices. Ask for free catalog.

MCM Electronics
650 Congress Park Dr.
Centerville, OH 45459-4072
U.S.: 800-543-4330
Fax: 513-434-6959
Distributor of tools and test equipment for electronics and PC repair. Ask for
free catalog.

Unicore Software
1538 Turnpike St.
N Andover, MA 01845
Tel: 800-800-BIOS

Upgrades, Etc.
2432-A Palma Dr.
Ventura, CA 93003
U.S.: 800-955-3527

DisplayMate for Windows, DisplayMate Professional.
Sonera Technologies
P. O. Box 565
Rumson, NJ 07760
U.S.: 800-932-6323
Tel: 908-747-6886
Fax: 908-747-4523

International Components Marketing
U.S.: 800-748-6232
Tel: 310-260-1444
Fax: 310-451-8727
Schematics and flybacks for monitor repair and monitor test equipment.

Computer Component Source (CCS)
135 Eileen Way
Syosset, NY 11791
U.S.: 800-356-1277
Fax: 800-926-2062
Monitor parts, laser printer parts, kits for fixing common problems on
Macintosh, PS/2's, and PCs.
Catalog available on request.

Tools distributors

ROM BIOS upgrade sources

Monitor software & hardware tools
Monitor adjustment utilities

Monitor parts

Monitor repair tools

Sencore
3200 Sencore Dr.
Sioux Falls, SD 57107
U.S.: 800-736-2673
Tel: 605-339-0100
Fax: 605-339-0317
Makes computer monitor test equipment.

International Components Marketing
U.S.: 800-748-6232
Tel: 310-260-1444
Fax: 310-451-8727
Carries computer monitor test equipment.

Touch-screen monitors

Intellitouch Controller, adds touch-screen capability to a monitor. Also markets touch-screen monitors.
Elo Touchsystems
41752 Christy St.
Fremont, CA 94538
Tel: 510-651-2340

Network tools & software

Cordless network adapters

Cordless CreditCard Netwave Adapter.
Netwave Access Point.
Xircom
26025 Mureau Road
Calabasas, CA 91302
Tel: 818-878-7600
Fax: 818-878-7630

LAN hardware vendors

Cabletron
35 Industrial Way, Box 5005
Rochester, NH 03867-0505
U.S.: 800-332-9401
Tel: 603-332-9400
Fax: 603-332-4616
Network interface cards, ethernet hubs, repeaters, transceivers.

3COM
P. O. Box 58145
5400 Bayfront Plaza
Santa Clara, CA 95052-8145
U.S.: 800-638-3266
Tel: 408-764-5000
Fax: 408-764-5001
Technical support: 800-876-3266
Network interface cards, ethernet hubs, repeaters, transceivers.

Artisoft
2202 N. Forbes Blvd.
Tucson, AZ 85745
U.S.: 800-610-0001
Tel: 602-670-4200
Fax: 602-670-7101
LAN hubs, network interface cards.

Novell
2180 Fortune Dr.
San Jose, CA 95131
U.S.: 800-453-1267
Tel: 408-434-2300
Fax: 408-435-1706
Technical support: 800-638-9273

National Semiconductor
P. O. Box 58090
2900 Semiconductor Dr.
Santa Clara, CA 95052-8090
Tel: 408-721-5000
Fax: 408-721-7662
BBS: 408-245-0671

IBM
1 Old Orchard Road
Armonk, NY 10504
U.S.: 800-426-2468
Tel: 914-765-1900
FaxBack technical support: 800-IBM-3395 (800-426-3395)
BBS: 919-517-0001, 8,n,1

Intel
5200 N E Elam Young Pkwy.
Hillsboro, OR 97124
U.S.: 800-538-3373
PC and LAN Enhancement support: 503-629-7000

SynOptics
4401 Great America Pkwy.
Santa Clara, CA 95052-8185
U.S.: 800-776-6895
Tel: 408-988-2400

Hewlett-Packard
P. O. Box 58059
MS511L-SJ
Santa Clara, CA 95051-8059
U.S.: 800-752-0900
FaxBack information on HP products: 800-333-1917
Ethertwist, PC Networks, Network printer interfaces, mass storage products.
Call for free catalog.
Part Number Information BBS: 800-635-7278, 8,n,1
Software Driver Distribution Center: 303-339-7009
Driver Software Download BBS: 208-344-1691
Software drivers available for many HP peripherals, including printers,
    plotters and scanners.

LAN software vendors

LANtastic
Artisoft
2202 N. Forbes Blvd.
Tucson, AZ 85745
U.S.: 800-846-9726
Tel: 602-670-4200
Fax: 602-670-7101

Novell NetWare.
Novell
122 E 1700 S
Provo, UT 84606-6194
U.S.: 800-453-1267
Tel: 801-429-7000
Fax: 801-429-5775
Novell Automated Support Knowledgebase (ASK)
U.S.: 800-768-9771
Tel: 801-429-2929
NSEPro CD-ROM information database sales: 800-346-7177
FaxBack technical support: 800-638-9273

LAN Server.
IBM
Old Orchard Rd.
Armonk, NY 10504
U.S.: 800-426-3333
Tel: 914-765-1900
Sales: 800-426-2968
Technical support: 800-772-2227
FaxBack technical support: 800-IBM-3395 (800-426-3395)
BBS: 919-517-0001, 8,n,1

Ergonomic
47 Werman Court
Planview, NY 11803
U.S.: 800-AKA-3COM (800-252-3266)
Tel: 516-293-5200
Fax: 516-293-5325

The National LAN Exchange
1403 W 820 N
Provo, UT 84601
U.S.: 800-243-5267
Tel: 801-377-0074
Fax: 801-377-0078

Micro House Technical Library on CD-ROM it includes:
Network Interface Technical Guide
Micro House
4900 Pearl E. Circle, Ste. 101
Boulder, CO 80301
US Sales: 800-926-8299
Support: 303-443-3389
Fax: 303-443-3323
BBS: 303-443-9957

Wavetek
9045 Balboa Avenue
San Diego, CA 92123
U.S.: 800-854-2708
Tel: 619-279-2200
Fax: 619-268-0172
Call for product information.

Network General
4200 Bohannon Dr.
Menlo Park, CA 94025
U.S.: 800-695-8251
Tel: 415-473-2000
Sales: 800-846-6601
Fax: 415-321-0855
Technical support: 800-395-3151
FaxBack: 800-764-3329 or 415-473-2690
Call or use FaxBack for product information.

Network
troubleshooting
tools vendors
(cable testers,
protocol analyzers,
network analyzers)

John Fluke Manufacturing
P. O. Box 9090
Everett, WA 98206-9090
U.S.: 800-443-5853

Tel: 206-347-6100
Fax: 206-356-5116
Call for free catalog.

International Data Sciences (IDS)
501 Jefferson Blvd.
Warwick, RI 02886-1317
800-IDS-DATA
Tel: 401-737-9900
Fax: 401-737-9911
Ask for free catalog of data communication test equipment.

Hewlett-Packard
P. O. Box 58059
MS511L-SJ
Santa Clara, CA 95051-8059
U.S.: 800-752-0900
FaxBack information on HP products: 800-333-1917
Call for free catalog.

DA-30
Wandel & Gotermann
2200 Gateway Centre Blvd., Ste. 207
Morrisville, NC 27560-9228
U.S.: 800-277-7404
Tel: 919-460-3300
Fax: 919-481-4372

Novell
2180 Fortune Dr.
San Jose, CA 95131
U.S.: 800-453-1267
Tel: 408-434-2300
Fax: 408-435-1706
Technical support: 800-638-9273

Microtest
4747 N 22nd St.
Phoenix, AZ 85016
U.S.: 800-526-9675
Tel: 602-952-6400
Fax: 602-952-6660

Optical drive suppliers

Pinnacle Micro
19 Tecnology
Irvine, CA 92718
U.S.: 800-553-7070
Tel: 714-789-3000

Fax: 714-789-3150
WORM Drives and Floptical Drives.

Hewlett-Packard
3000 Hanover St.
Palo Alto, CA 94304
U.S.: 800-752-0900
Tel: 415-857-1501
Eraseable Optical Drives.

Hitachi America
2000 Sierra Point Pkway.
Brisbane, CA 94005-1819
U.S.: 800-448-2244
Tel: 415-589-8300
Eraseable Optical Drives.

Iomega
1821 W 4000 S
Roy, Utah 84067
U.S.: 800-777-6179
Tel: 801-778-1000
Eraseable Optical Drives and Floptical Drives.

Copylite Printer Division
4061 SW 47th Avenue
Fort Lauderdale, FL 33314
U.S.: 800-989-6000
Tel: 305-581-2470
Fax: 800-327-2679
Specializing in laser printer parts.

Computer Component Source (CCS)
135 Eileen Way
Syosset, NY 11791
U.S.: 800-356-1277
Fax: 800-926-2062
Laser printer parts, monitor parts, kits for fixing common problems on
    Macintosh, PS/2's and PCs.
Free catalog available on request.

Copylite
New Town Commerce Centre
4001 SW 47th Avenue, Bldg. 201
Fort Lauderdale, FL 33314
Tel: 305-581-2470
HP series printer fuser rollers, gears and parts.

Printer repair parts sources

Eagan Technical Services
1380 Corporate Center Curve, Ste. 107
Eagan, MN 55121
Tel: 612-688-0098
Schematics for HP Laserjet printers, monitors, and PS/2 system boards.

PC Parts Express
1420 Valwood Pkwy., Ste. 204
Carrollton, TX 75006
U.S.: 800-727-2787
Tel: 214-406-8583
HP Laserjet parts, fusers, and gears.

The Printer Works
3481 Arden Road
Hayward, CA 94595
U.S.: 800-225-6116
Tel: 510-887-6116
Fax: 510-786-0589
Canon and Diablo parts, repair.

Hewlett-Packard
P.O. Box 58059
MS511L-SJ
Santa Clara, CA 95051-8059
U.S.: 800-752-0900
FaxBack: 800-333-1917
Laser and Deskjet printer as well as network printer interface products and
    information. Call for free catalog.
Part Number Information BBS: 800-635-7278, 8,n,1
Software Driver Distribution Center: 303-339-7009
Driver Software Download BBS: 208-344-1691
Software drivers available for many HP peripherals, including printers,
    plotters, and scanners.

Apple Macintosh parts & tools
Antivirus software vendors

Virex.
Datawatch
3700-B Lyckan Pkwy.
Durham, NC 27707
U.S.: 800-847-3982
Tel: 919-549-0711

Norton Antivirus.
Symantec
10201 Torre Avenue
Cupertino, CA 95014-2132
U.S.: 800-365-3186
Tel: 503-465-8420
Fax: 800-800-1438

Motorola, makes 68000 and PowerPC CPU
Texas: 512-891-2000
Illinois: 708-576-5304

Central processing
unit manufacturers

Mac OS, System 7, System 6
Apple Computer
20525 Mariani Avenue
Cupertino, CA 95014
Tel: 408-996-1010
Fax: 408-996-0275
Customer Assistance Center: 800-776-2333
Product Support Questions: 800-767-2775

Macintosh
operating system

800-WE-FIX-MACS
2306 Walsh Avenue
Santa Clara, CA 95051
U.S.: 800-933-4962
Macintosh parts broker.

Parts suppliers

Computer Component Source (CCS)
P. O. Box 9022
135 Eileen Way
Syosset, NY 11791
U.S.: 800-356-1277
Fax: 800-926-2062
Canada: 800-561-9903
Canada Fax: 800-363-2141
Tel: 516-496-8780
Fax: 516-496-8984
Kits for fixing common problems on Macintosh, PS/2 PCs, monitor parts, laser
    printer parts.
Free catalog available on request.

Intelletronics
2305 NW Kings Blvd.
Corvallis, OR 97330
U.S.: 800-935-9993
Fax: 503-752-1791
Apple authorized catalog reseller.
Free catalog available on request.

Texas Discount Computers
3812 Timms St.
Tyler, TX 75071
Tel: 903-509-2775
Fax: 903-509-2777
Specializes in resale of used and demo Macintosh hardware. Also offers resale
    of memory and parts repair.

D ASCII character set, DOS commands, Edlin

ASCII character set

ASCII characters are the numeric equivalents of the keyboard and nonkeyboard characters. To generate these characters, hold down the Alt key while typing the number on the numeric keypad, then let up the Alt key. Remember to use the numeric keypad with the Num Lock key on. The numbers above the keyboard will not work for this.

Occasionally, repair personnel will rename a DOS command so users won't be able to accidentally format the hard disk drive. For example, FORMAT.COM might be renamed to include the character (Alt-255). This makes the command nearly impossible for the novice to use, since they won't know that they have to type F-O-R-M-A-T-Alt-255 to execute the command. (See the Format command in the "DOS commands" section for more details.)

DOS commands

The problem is, if you as the repair person want to use the Format command, you probably won't be able to either, unless you know this trick. That's one of the reason's we're including the ASCII character set in the book. The other reason is because commonly used keys on the keyboard go bad first, such as the spacebar, the A and S keys, and so on. If you are in a repair situation with a problem keyboard and you need to type commands, you can use the Alt key (there's usually two, one on each side of the keyboard) and the number keys to generate a needed character in order to type a command. (See Table D-1.)

If you're going to be successful at PC repair, you need to know DOS commands. Knowing something about the editor Edlin, included in versions of DOS earlier than 5.0, can also be helpful. In order to make the DOS and Edlin commands more easily accessible to you when you're in a repair situation, we've included them on the floppy disk distributed with this book in the text

0	BLANK (NULL)	16	▶	32	BLANK (SPACE)	48	0	64	@	80	P	96	`	112	p
1	☺	17	◀	33	!	49	1	65	A	81	Q	97	a	113	q
2	☻	18	↕	34	"	50	2	66	B	82	R	98	b	114	r
3	♥	19	‼	35	#	51	3	67	C	83	S	99	c	115	s
4	♦	20	¶	36	$	52	4	68	D	84	T	100	d	116	t
5	♣	21	§	37	%	53	5	69	E	85	U	101	e	117	u
6	♠	22	▬	38	&	54	6	70	F	86	V	102	f	118	v
7	•	23	↨	39	'	55	7	71	G	87	W	103	g	119	w
8	◘	24	↑	40	(	56	8	72	H	88	X	104	h	120	x
9	○	25	↓	41	)	57	9	73	I	89	Y	105	i	121	y
10	◙	26	→	42	*	58	:	74	J	90	Z	106	j	122	z
11	♂	27	←	43	+	59	;	75	K	91	[	107	k	123	{
12	♀	28	∟	44	,	60	<	76	L	92	\	108	l	124	¦
13	♪	29	↔	45	–	61	=	77	M	93	]	109	m	125	}
14	♫	30	▲	46	.	62	>	78	N	94	^	110	n	126	~
15	☼	31	▼	47	/	63	?	79	O	95	_	111	o	127	⌂

The following eight characters are interpreted by printers to mean:

0 = NULL, 07 = BEEP, 08 = BACKSPACE, 09 = TAB, 10 = LINE FEED,
12 = FORM FEED, 13 = CARRIAGE RETURN, 27 = ESCAPE

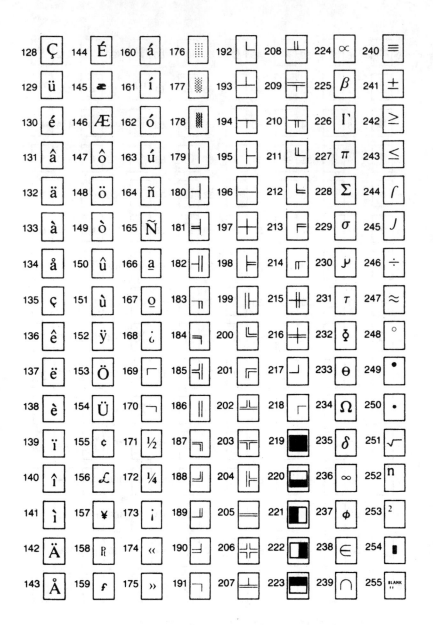

file DOS.TXT. This way, you can carry the commands with you and use them as needed. You can use QEdit, also included on the disk, to read the file or to search for a specific command. Each DOS command has an explanation of why the command is used, as well as how to use the command, and an example. There are many other useful and interesting DOS commands besides the ones we cover. We encourage you to explore the DOS manual as well as third-party reference books to broaden your technical vocabulary.

E PC maintenance forms & contracts

In chapter 10, we outlined how to go about offering a free, ten-point maintenance check as an incentive for business owners to use your services. This service is something you can advertise, or you can simply go from business to business. To perform this check, we suggest you obtain:

1. Business attire, such as a suit.
2. Sharp-looking business cards.
3. Professional bag, such as those used by doctors.
4. White lab coat.
5. Pen for filling out forms.
6. Clipboard.
7. Two clean, white cotton handkerchiefs per PC maintenance call.
8. Compressed air.
9. Antivirus software on write-protected 5.25-inch 360K disks, 5.25-inch 1.2MB disks, 3.5-inch 720 MB, and 1.44MB disks.
10. Blank disks in these formats: 5.25-inch 360K, 5.25-inch 1.2MB, 3.5-inch 720MB, and 1.44MB disks.
11. Software to check disk space—(Snooper, included on the disk with this book, can be used.)
12. Software to check disk fragmentation (MS-DOS 6.0 or higher has defragmentation utility, DEFRAG.)
13. Monitor adjustment software, such as DisplayMate from Sonera technologies.
14. Copies of the ten-point PC maintenance check (Figs. E-1A and E-1B) and the PC maintenance agreement (Fig. E-2), all with your company name printed in the appropriate places.

E-1A Ten-Point PC Maintenance Check

Performed by: Your Company, Your address, Your phone

I agree to a free, no obligation maintenance check of one PC.

Name: _____ Title: _____

Company Name: _____ Address: _____

City, State, Zip: _____ Tel: _____

Authorized by (initial here): _____

V = VERIFY, Y = YES, N = NO

V Y N
1. Electro-static Discharge (ESD)
☐☐☐   Monitor or other areas.
2. Placement of the PC
☐☐☐   Near windows.
☐☐☐   Near dangerous substances (under or near plants, liquids, etc.).
☐☐☐   On unstable surface.
3. Surge Protection
☐☐☐   PC.
☐☐☐   Monitor.
☐☐☐   Printer.
4. Dust Buildup
☐☐☐   Power supply fan clean of dust and debris?
☐☐☐   Keyboard clean of dust and debris?
☐☐☐   Monitor clean of dust and debris?
5. Virus Check
☐☐☐   Hard disk boot sector.
☐☐☐   Hard disk partition.
☐☐☐   Executable files.
☐☐☐   Memory.
6. Floppy Disk Drive Alignment
          Disks formatted on this PC can be read by other PCs.
☐☐☐   3.5-inch drive.
☐☐☐   5.25-inch drive.
7. Hard Disk Drive Space, Fragmentation
☐☐☐   Remaining hard disk drive space is adequate.
☐☐☐   Fragmentation present, _____ percent.
8. Ergonomic Check
          User name: _____.
       Monitor Placement
☐☐☐   About an arm's length away.
☐☐☐   At or slightly below eye level.
       Hand and Arm Placement
☐☐☐   Arm bent naturally at the elbow, no reaching to type
☐☐☐   Wrist support.
       Chair Adjustment
☐☐☐   Chair offers back support.
☐☐☐   Feet flat on the floor, knees bent naturally.
       Electromagnetic-field Radiation (EMF) Emissions
☐☐☐   No other individual within two feet of the monitor's sides or back.
       Eye Care
☐☐☐   Anti-glare screen present.
☐☐☐   Monitor correctly adjusted.

9. Inventory of Components
☐ ☐ ☐   Current and available for this PC?
10. Rescue Disk
☐ ☐ ☐   Current and available for this PC?

We want to compliment you on the following: _____

_____

_____

_____

_____

_____

Recommendations

Electro-static Discharge (ESD): _____

_____

Placement of the PC: _____

_____

Surge Protection: _____

_____

Dust Buildup: _____

_____

Virus Check: _____

_____

Floppy Disk Drive Alignment: _____

_____

Hard Disk Drive: ☐ Archive Data ☐ Defragment ☐ Optimize _____

_____

Ergonomic Check: ☐ Anti-Glare Screen ☐ Wrist Rest ☐ Monitor Adjustment

_____

Inventory of Components: _____

_____

Rescue Disk: ☐ Bootable ☐ CMOS ☐ Partition ☐ Environment Files ☐ Drivers
☐ Windows .INI Files _____

_____

Tape Backup Drive/Optical Disk Backup: _____

_____

Verified by (signature): _____

E-2   PC Maintenance Agreement

Your Company, Your address, Your phone

Number of PCs	Reg. Charge Each	Your Discount	Your Price Ea.	You Save
1–5	$65.00	16%	$54.60	$10.40
6–11	$65.00	31%	$44.85	$20.15
12+	$65.00	47%	$34.45	$30.55

Regular maintenance prevents expensive repairs by extending the life of PC components, promotes productivity in PC users, and offers data protection in case of unexpected failure. The above prices include the following services:

- ☐ Electro-static discharge prevention
- ☐ Removal of thermal dust/debris
- ☐ Power surge equip. check
- ☐ Power supply voltage check
- ☐ PC placement safety check
- ☐ Floppy drive alignment and cleaning
- ☐ Virus check

- ☐ Clean and reseat circuit boards
- ☐ Adequate hard disk space check
- ☐ Optimize/defragment hard disk
- ☐ Ergonomic check for user safety
- ☐ Monitor adjustment
- ☐ Full inventory of PC components
- ☐ Creation/update of "Rescue Disk"

This maintenance procedure is a proven process that offers protection against disaster and extends the life of PC components. We recommend this procedure be performed twice a year beginning _____.

With this agreement, we also offer repair services at a 15 percent discount for parts and labor on an as-needed basis beginning the date the first maintenance service is performed. This provides additional savings and security to you without binding you to a payment schedule for repair services that you don't need.

This agreement is our commitment to perform the services named above. You may cancel this agreement for scheduled PC maintenance and discounted repair service at any time by notifying us of your wish to do so.

Services will be performed on a C.O.D. basis, unless other arrangements are made in advance. This agreement is subject to renewal each year, allowing for the addition of PCs and changes of the content of the agreement.

Agreement starting date: _____ Review date: _____

Agreed to by:

Purchasing Agent: _____

Company: _____

Address: _____

City, State, Zip: _____

Telephone: _____ Fax: _____

Approved by:

Service Manager: _____

Telephone: _____ Fax: _____

F The Macintosh from Apple Computer

Of the total number of PCs sold, about 10 percent are from Apple Computer. Since the majority of the market is IBM-compatibles, we felt our focus should be there. But, we didn't want to leave the Macintosh out altogether, hence this appendix.

Apple's best-known products are the Macintosh line, including the Quadra, Performa, and the Power PC. While there are differences we'll talk about, you'll find that Apple's computers contain many of the same components, such as hard disk drives and chipsets, found in other PCs.

Macintosh basics

The Macintosh uses the 68000 line of CPU chips made by Motorola, but so do other desktop computers such as the Atari and the Commodore Amiga. The main difference is in the Apple ROMs. In fact, Atari has offered Macintosh-compatible MEGA 2 computers, which included Apple ROMs and would also run DOS applications.

The 68000 line of Motorola CPU chips served exclusively as the basis of the Macintosh and Performa computer line until the introduction of the reduced instruction set computing (RISC)-based PowerPC chip. IBM, Apple, and Motorola combined forces to trump the PC world by using a RISC chip as the main processor, a type of chip historically reserved for the more powerful and more expensive workstation computers running the Unix operating system. IBM has introduced the PowerPC chip in its workstation line, and Apple has made a big splash introducing the 60- and 80-MHz, 64-bit PowerPC Macintosh. The Macintosh also has several important built-in features. These include networking capability called AppleTalk, sound, and a SCSI interface.

PC Software compatibility

To dip into the Intel-based PC market, Apple has licensed SoftPC from Insignia Solutions to make the PowerPC run DOS and Windows programs.

This extra layer of processing slows the performance of the DOS and Windows programs, but has been a major sales point for the PowerPC. Apple went as far as to introduce the Quadra 610 DOS Compatible 68040-based Macintosh equipped with an Intel 486SX processor. The machine, which was on the market less than a year, would run DOS and Windows applications from one partition of the hard disk drive using the Intel processor, and Macintosh applications on another partition of the same hard disk drive.

The Macintosh operating system has always been a graphical one, dependent on the mouse, in which files and programs are designated by icons. The graphical, mouse-based metaphor is so strong that Apple charges extra for the keyboard, instead of charging extra for the mouse, which is done in the Intel-based PC world. Only in recent years, however, has Apple given in to user demand for color.

The Macintosh operating system

The graphical metaphor on the Mac is one of a desk with the screen as the desktop and the programs and data represented by folders you can open with a double-click of the mouse. Folders can contain more folders or icons to start programs.

The operating system is composed of two basic parts, the System and Finder. The Finder is the Macintosh file and program management system, and it is what places the graphical representation of the desktop on the screen. The Finder is version numbered independently of the System, and both are often updated independently of each other. Apple has said it will begin calling its Macintosh operating system the Mac OS instead of System or the System Tools.

The environment configuration is accomplished through the System folder, which is a folder icon with what appears to be a tiny Mac Classic depicted on it. The System folder contains the files the Mac needs to boot. The folders in the System folder include the System file, the Finder, Multifinder, and software drivers. This is one place where memory-resident software, or inits (short for initialization files) are loaded. Memory conflicts are a common cause of system lockups on the Macintosh, and inits, also known as start-up files, are a good first suspect.

Across the top of the Macintosh desktop are the pull-down menus, including one with a symbol of an apple with a bite out of it, (the apple menu) then File, Edit, View, and Special. If you use the mouse to click on the symbol of the apple, utility-type functions will appear on a pull-down menu. These functions include common tools such as a calculator and two applications used to make further adjustments to the environment, Chooser and Control Panel.

The Control Panel is where the time, date, sound volume, colors, and RAM cache settings are determined. Chooser allows you to load printer drivers and choose between them. Chooser is also where network drivers are loaded.

Other memory-resident software utilities can be activated via the Control Panel, and these are known as Control Panel devices or cdevs. Memory resident device drivers loaded in Chooser are known as Chooser devices or rdevs.

Floppy drives

While the floppy disk drives appear the same, the Macintosh drives are built to communicate directly with the Macintosh, sensing the insertion of a floppy disk into the drive. Once a disk is inserted, a folder representing the disk appears on the desktop. To eject a disk, use the mouse to drag the disk icon over to the trash can, and the operating system will activate the disk eject sequence. The Macintosh also ejects any disks in the floppy drives when correctly powered down. To correctly power down, or shut down the Mac, choose the Shut Down option from the special menu.

Formatting the floppy disk is known as initializing it. When a new, unformatted disk is inserted into the Macintosh floppy disk drive, the Macintosh will tell you the disk is unreadable and will ask you if you want to initialize it. If you do, you can choose to initialize or eject the disk at this point.

Macintosh computers come with either 400K, 800K, or a 2MB floppy disk drive. The SuperDrive, which is the latest version of the Macintosh floppy drive, can read disks formatted at all three capacities. The SuperDrive can also read disks from IBM or compatible PCs with the proper software. Software is available to read disks formatted on an IBM or compatible PC, and that functionality is also built into Apple's latest release of the Mac OS, System 7.5.

The Mac boot-up process

The Macintosh goes through a self-test routine, and if the memory and motherboard check out fine, it sounds a "bong" and displays a smiling Macintosh icon. In order for the Macintosh to complete the boot-up process, the System and Finder files must be on the boot disk. The Macintosh, like the PC, will boot either from a the hard disk drive or from the floppy drive, depending on where it finds the System files.

Like other PCs, Macintoshes have a battery that maintains the time and date settings and keeps track of changes such as printers and peripherals connected. Older Macs allow you to simply replace an AA battery by popping open a battery cover. On Mac SEs, IIs, and IIxs, Apple changed that and went to a lithium battery that is soldered to the motherboard. In the IIcx, ci and fx models, the battery is on the motherboard, but it is not soldered in and can be replaced easily. The battery provides the power for memory known as parameter RAM or PRAM.

Starting with the Mac SE, Apple introduced the Apple Desktop Bus (ADB) for serial communication with up to 15 peripheral devices, including the mouse and keyboard. Other devices that can be connected via the ADB port include a joystick, a puck, and graphics tablets.

A "programmer's switch" comes on the Mac, which is actually two switches—an interrupt switch and a reset switch. The programmer's switch is located either on the front or on the back of the Macintosh. The reset switch is the one used to restart the Macintosh without shutting off the power in case of a system lock-up or other problem.

Here are a few basic troubleshooting hints to get you started in working with the Macintosh. If there's no life at all out of the Macintosh, then it's time to check the power sources and the power supply. That has already been discussed in chapter 5. If you get life, but no video display, it's time to check the cabling and the monitor power supply.

If not, a sad Macintosh is displayed. On the Mac II, chords are also played, which are much like the beep error codes in the IBM-compatible PC world. A sad Mac could indicate a bad SIMM or a bad motherboard.

Simple troubleshooting tips

If you get the "Welcome to Macintosh" screen, but no light or whirring sound from the hard disk drive, then you'll need to be sure power is getting to the hard disk drive. If so, you might be looking at a hard disk problem. If you get a blinking question mark icon, you'll need to check to see that the System and Finder are both on the hard disk drive.

If a bomb icon appears on the desktop after a floppy disk is inserted, either the disk is bad or the desktop file used to display the icons is corrupted. The desktop file can be corrected, called rebuilding the desktop, by pressing the Command key (a key with what appears to be a four-petal flower symbol on it) and the Option key. In operating system versions before System 7, this rebuilding will also erase the names of the folders on the desktop.

Should a floppy disk need to come out of the drive when the Macintosh is powered down, there is a way to get the floppy disk out of the drive manually. You can activate the ejection mechanism with a paper clip or other device inserted into the tiny, round hole next to the floppy drive slot. This should be used only to get a disk out of the drive when the Macintosh is off or in an emergency situation when the Mac is on. A disk lodged in the drive might not come out by this means, and the Macintosh will have to be opened and the disk physically removed from the drive.

If the Macintosh crashes shortly after it starts up, the problem could be memory conflicts caused between one of the programs set to start automatically and an init or some other memory-resident driver. You can try rebuilding the desktop by pressing the Option and Command keys at the same time. Other options include reinstalling the System and Finder from the original disks, and checking for viruses with Macintosh virus software. Corrupted PRAM could be the problem as well.

To correct corrupted PRAM, there are two methods, depending on the age of the Macintosh in question. On Macs up to and including the Mac Plus, you can simply remove the battery for a quarter of an hour and when you replace it, the PRAM will go back to its original settings. On Macs higher than the Mac Plus, you must boot the Mac from a floppy that has the Control Panel desk accessory on it. Then you open the Apple menu and select Control Panel while holding down the Shift, Option, and Command keys. A box will open asking if you are sure you want to "zap the PRAM." Click on the "Yes" button.

System lockups on the Macintosh can be caused by memory conflicts. One of the easiest ways to check to see what is causing the conflict is to remove inits, cdevs, or rdevs one at a time until the problem disappears.

Apple recommends that older Macintosh hardware continue to run older versions of the Macintosh operating system. This is mostly due to memory constraints. For example, the company recommends that 512K Macs run System 3.2 with Finder 5.3. You can find out the versions of System and Finder used on a particular Mac by opening the Apple menu and selecting "About the Finder . . .," which will list both version numbers. If you run into an older version of the operating system and get just the version of Finder from the above procedure, you can open the system folder, highlight the System and Finder files, and select "Get Info" from the File Menu at the top of the desktop screen.

Inexperienced Macintosh users have a tendency to have multiple versions of System and Finder on their hard disk drives—a situation that can cause inexplicable crashes. This happens when the user gets a new program on a disk and uses the mouse to drag all the files on the floppy over to the hard disk icon on the desktop. Inadvertently, the System and Finder files are dropped on the hard disk icon as well, and they get copied to the hard disk with the rest of the programs and data. Apple has a Find File utility available through user groups or on bulletin boards, usually for less than $20. This program, or others like it, will allow you to search for the word "System" in a file, which will help you locate the additional copies of System and Finder if there are any.

Viruses are also a problem in the Macintosh world and can be identified by several antivirus programs. A virus check is always prudent, especially on a Mac that is in an educational or government environment. Virus-checking programs for the Macintosh are available from Symantec and Fifth Generation Systems, among others.

Apple to transition to the PowerPC Mac

In a statement to its stockholders, Apple has made it clear the company will transition from the 68000-based Macintosh entirely to the PowerPC Macintosh product line. This transition is expected to take some time. Software applications designed for the Macintosh will run on the PowerPC Mac, but they will run more slowly in an emulation mode. Developers on the Macintosh platform are scrambling to rewrite their applications to run "native" or directly with the PowerPC processor instead of in emulation mode.

This means you should invest your time in getting to know something about the PowerPC Macintosh, even if you have opportunities or a desire to work on Motorola 68000-based Macs. The future in the Macintosh world is in the PowerPC, and while some opportunities will remain repairing the old Macs, once Apple abandons the machines, they might not be worth repairing.

Apple offers certification programs for its computers and laser printers to those employed by its resellers. It will also train the in-house repair technicians of a large client, so working for an Apple reseller or a large user of Apple equipment might be a way for you to get training while earning income. Third-party training schools, such as National Advancement Corporation, also offer training in repairing Apple 68000-based Macintoshes and peripheral equipment.

Apple strongly discourages its customers to go outside its repair channels for service. But if an item is out of warranty anyway, then it might not make any difference to the customer if the computer is fixed by a source outside of Apple or by Apple-authorized repair services. The incentive for the customer to go outside the Apple-authorized repair channels is usually a significant savings in the repair cost.

If you are interested in servicing Apple computers, you'll find Bob Brant's *Build Your Own Macintosh and Save a Bundle* (Windcrest/McGraw-Hill, 1991) a helpful reference in understanding the components and upgrading older Macintosh computers, such as the Mac SE, II, IIx, or IIcx. Other helpful references are *The Macintosh Bible* books, one from Peachpit Press and one published by Goldstein & Blair. *The Macintosh Do-It-Yourself Upgrade Book* by Garry Howard has helpful illustrations on how to use special tools to get into the Macintosh case. Jensen Tools carries a set of tools designed for Macintosh work, which includes a "Mac-Cracker" for opening the computer's case (Fig. F-1). You might also find the Apple Computer official hardware reference books helpful. Your library might have some or all of these reference materials. (These books are listed in appendix A.) As for software utilities to help you service Macintosh equipment, in appendix C we've listed utility software and antivirus programs aimed at this platform.

One of the biggest problems with servicing Apple equipment is obtaining parts. In fact, that can be a problem in repairing any proprietary system. Since brokers like to turn over their inventory as quickly as possible, your better sources are the ones more frequently published, such as online services and weekly periodicals. Most of the Macintosh-oriented parts brokers advertise in Macintosh publications such as *MacWeek* or in online classified ads on America Online, which has a very large Macintosh user population.

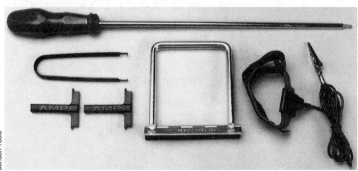

Jenson Tools

F-1 *These are tools aimed specially for working on a Macintosh, including the "Mac-Cracker" in the center for getting into the case of older Macintosh computers.*

G Included shareware titles

Shareware installation

All the shareware titles included with this book are in uncompressed format on the distribution disk. We recommend you create a directory for each program on your hard disk and copy the files from the distribution disk to the new directory. You can use the XCOPY command to recreate the programs and their subdirectories on your hard disk drive by typing the following command at the DOS prompt.

```
XCOPY A:\*.* C:\*.* /S
```

This will copy all the programs and the related directories to your PC. The programs can be run from the distribution disk, but that disk is full. If the program attempts to record information to the distribution disk, you'll get an error message.

Documentation

The documentation for each program is in its respective directory. This documentation will include instructions on how to run the program. Most of the programs have .DOC files, except BurnIn and Read My Disk (RMD). BurnIn uses the program BIDOCS.COM (for BurnIn Documents) to display its documentation. To run the program, install the software on your hard disk drive, change to the BurnIn directory, and type BIDOCS at the DOS prompt. Read My Disk uses the program MANUAL.EXE, so you'll want to follow the same procedure to read that manual.

The other programs require you to use the DOS TYPE command or an editor (such as QEdit) to view the documentation. To start QEdit after you've installed it to your hard disk, change to the QEdit directory and then type Q<Enter> to start the program. QEdit immediately begins with Quick Start Instructions you can use to become familiar with the program.

We discussed the programs in the appropriate portions of this book. To reacquaint you with the programs on the disk, we'll offer a quick synopsis of each program and its functions next.

BurnIn from OsoSoft is a PC exerciser and diagnostic tool. Its function is to give the PC and the PC's systems a workout to try to expose underlying problems or components on the edge of failure. OsoSoft recommends you run BurnIn for 72 hours on a new PC or on a PC whose warranty is getting ready to expire, before the warranty expires. In addition, BurnIn can be set to run tests on certain components of the PC, so it can be used to test new hardware added to a system before the warranty on the hardware upgrade expires. BurnIn creates a log file that records any problems so you don't have to be there to see the failure in order to know what happened.

BurnIn 4.5 PC Exerciser & Diagnostic Tool

Cleaner, from Rosenthal Engineering, is designed to safely remove debris from the delicate read/write heads of floppy disk drives. However, Rosenthal is very specific about the type of cleaning disk that should be used with cleaner.

Disk Drive Cleaner

The program offers a rigorous cleaning, and if used with inexpensive, noncloth cleaning disks, you might find yourself spending time picking pieces of the cleaning disk out of the drive. Rosenthal recommends nonabrasive cleaning disks with a cloth cleaning surface. Isopropyl alcohol is also strongly recommended. Registration of the software entitles you to a free cleaning kit, and additional cleaning kits can be purchased at a nominal fee.

A freeware program, Eject, is a simple batch file that sends a page eject command to a laser printer through the parallel (LPT1) port. The program file, EJECT.BAT, can be run under DOS or under Windows. In chapter 4, we demonstrate how to set up an icon for the file under Windows.

Eject

This .BAT file is helpful if the laser printer Form Feed light comes on, indicating the printer has something to print, but nothing is happening. This is particularly aggravating if you attempt to use the print screen key under DOS to try to print the CMOS settings. The information on the screen will be sent to the printer, but the printer might be waiting for a page eject command that it isn't going to get from the Print Screen function. This .BAT file gives it that command.

Small and fast, QEdit Advanced is a full-screen text editor distributed as shareware. A text editor is geared toward creating and maintaining program source code and other text files, as opposed to a word processor. Word processors add special characters to control the appearance of the document when it is printed or viewed on the computer screen.

Q Edit Advanced 3.0

Developed by SemWare, QEdit can be easily placed on a floppy disk and carried as part of your toolkit. It is designed to run in a minimum amount of memory and only requires one file, the Q.EXE file, in order to run. It is perfect for editing environment files, .INI files, and other text-only files.

Read My Disk! 1.3

Read My Disk! from DairySoft is an absolute disk read utility that reads every sector on any disk up to 32 megabytes. It will read the disk regardless of its condition, meaning it will read disks with missing FATs and directories, or floppy disks with holes in them. Data found on the disk is written to ASCII files, which can be edited using a word processor, and any control characters are retained.

Snooper System Information Utility

Snooper is designed to offer you comprehensive information about the system you run it on, including configuration and operating characteristics. Snooper reports back the system's components, including the processor, math coprocessor, memory, drives, hard disk space use, installed peripherals (except the printer), DOS version, BIOS version, and more. It will also print all these items, including copies of the environment files, to a log file. Developed by Vias and Associates, Snooper is fast and it is perfect for inventorying PCs.

Shareware vendor information

Each shareware vendor has included contact information with the shareware program files. We have also included this information in appendix C.

Glossary

100BASE-T   Described by the IEEE 802.3 Ethernet standard, this wiring standard for LANs operates at 100 Mbps on unshielded twisted-pair cabling.

100BASE-VG   A fast-ethernet standard for 100 Mbps transfer of data over voice-grade (VG) phone wire using all four pairs of the voice-grade twisted-pair wiring.

100BASE-X   100Base-T with CSMA/CD. Requires data-grade phone wire.

10BASE-T   An ethernet standard for a 10 Mbps data transfer rate on a network over twisted-pair wiring.

ABCD (Association for Better Computer Dealers)   See CompTIA.

ANSI (American National Standard Institute)   A group that works on voluntary national standards, especially in regard to information technology.

ASCII (American Standard Code for Information Interchange) Pronounced "ask-ee." This is a code that translates characters displayed on the screen or in print to their numeric representation for use by the computer.

ASIC (application specific integrated circuit)   A specially designed integrated circuit built to perform a specific task.

ATM (asynchronous transfer mode)   An up-and-coming telecommunication transmission technology standard offering faster data throughput.

AT   A PC based on the Intel 80286 processor.

attenuation   Signal loss over network cabling.

backbone   In the bus topology, all the workstations are wired to a single cable or "backbone."

BNC (bayonet-type network connectors)   A connector used for coaxial cable on a network.

boot sector   The area of the disk reserved for the operating system, usually located in the first few sectors of the disk.

bridge   A computer that acts as a connector between a network and a mainframe computer.

burn-in   A period of testing for electronic equipment.

bus   The pathway between hardware devices in a computer.

bus topology   A type of network topology connecting nodes on the network to a cable with terminators at each end.

byte   A basic measure of space on a computer, either on disk or in memory. One byte is composed of eight bits and is the amount of memory required to represent a single character.

cache   An area of memory reserved to improve computer performance. Pronounced "cash".

canned ring   A stand-alone network configuration connected to an MAU.

CD-ROM (compact disc read-only memory)   A laser disc format that can be used by a computer for storage of programs and data.

cheapernet   See thin ethernet.

chip set   A group of chips that work together to perform a task. Chip sets are used on motherboards for communication between the central processing unit (CPU) and the memory, in modems, and in local area network (LAN) cards.

client-server   Used on networks, this is a way of distributing the computing work to the client computers connected to the network, instead of having the main server computer do all the processing.

cluster   Disk sectors grouped together into file storage units.

CMOS (complimentary metal oxide semiconductor)   This type of circuit is known for low power consumption and with a battery backup. Stores basic information about the computer needed for operation.

CNE (certified Novell engineer)   The most widely known network certification.

coaxial cable   Like the connecting wire the cable companies use for bringing television reception into homes, this cabling can also be used to send data between nodes on a network.

collision   Two devices attempting to use the network at the same time.

collision avoidance   If two devices on the network attempt access at exactly the same time, they both back off to avoid a collision, and each wait a random amount of time before retrying.

Compression   A way to squeeze data into less disk space.

CompTIA (Computing Technology Industry Association)   Formerly called the ABCD, this is a computer industry group whose goal is to establish an industrywide competency standard for service technicians.

concentrator   Makes an Ethernet network function like a star type of network when connected to each PC network adapter.

CPU   Central processing unit. Also known as the microprocessor or processor, this chip can be thought of as the "brain" of the computer.

crosstalk   The electrical interference between wires in twisted-pair cabling.

CSMA/CD   Carrier sense multiple access/collision detection, a communications access method used on networks. It works like this. When a device wants to gain access to the network, it checks to see if the network is free. If it is not, it waits a random amount of time before retrying.

CTIA   See CompTIA.

DAT (digital audio tape)   Also used in recording, this tape is used for backup of large amounts of computer data.

QIC (quarter-inch cartridge)   The tape standard used in popular PC backup systems such as the Trakker from Colorado Memory Systems.

database   A database is a system that organizes information to serve a particular purpose.

dB   Decibels. A measure of sound used to indicate the amount of noise on a network connection.

DMA (direct memory access)   A way for peripheral devices to access the computer's memory without having to go through the central processing unit (CPU).

DOS (disk operating system)   The software that controls the hardware on the computer, such as the hard disk, and is used by all applications software to perform tasks such as writing information on the hard disk.

DRAM (dynamic random access memory)   Strictly defined, this memory is any kind of RAM used on the computer, but it has been interpreted to refer to the single RAM chips used in older computers.

drop cable   A cable connected on one end to a computer or terminal and on the other to the network cable or bus.

EBCDIC (Extended Binary Coded Decimal Interchange Code)
Pronounced "ebb-sa-dik", this table is used for the basic representation of characters on mini- and mainframe computers.

EISA (Extended Industry Standard Architecture)   A bus widely used in PCs and compatible with components designed for the ISA bus.

ethernet   A type of LAN topology defined by the IEEE 802.3 standard.

FDD   Floppy disk drive.

FDDI   Fiber-distributed data interface, a variant of the ring topology.

file allocation table (FAT)   The file directory structure used on the PC, this is the central location where all beginning data addresses for disk files are stored.

flash memory   A type of computer memory that holds data without a power source. Some ROM BIOSs are now designed with flash memory and can be upgraded from a disk instead of replacing a chip.

formatting   The addition of characters, usually outside those on the computer keyboard, to indicate special functions to the printer and to the program.

FPU   See NPU.

gigabyte   A measure of space, either on the disk or in memory. A gigabyte is 1,073,741,824 bytes, though most people just round to 1 billion bytes.

GUI (graphical user interface)   A user interface such as Microsoft Windows that uses a mouse to point and click graphical representations of commands rather than the remember-and-type approach found in the DOS command line.

HDD   Hard disk drive.

HFS   Hierarchical file system, the Macintosh system for the file directory structure.

IC   Integrated circuit.

IDE (integrated drive electronics)   A type of hard disk drive that has its intelligence built into the drive. One characteristic of IDE drives is they come already low-level formatted.

IEC (International Electrotechnical Commission)   A group that sets international electronics and electrical standards. ANSI is a member.

impedance   More important in coaxial cable than twisted-pair, it is the opposition of the cable to ac current flow measured in ohms.

init   A software application or utility loaded at start-up into memory on a Macintosh computer.

IEEE   Institute of Electrical and Electronics Engineers.

interrupt   A signal that has priority with the CPU and is usually required for I/O operations.

I/O   Input/output.

ISA (Industry Standard Architecture)   A bus widely used in PCs, sometimes called the AT-bus standard.

ISO   International Standards Organization.

KBD   Keyboard.

lattisnet   A cabling method for Ethernet.

LIFO   "Last in, first out."

math coprocessor   See NPU.

MAU   Multistation access unit, used in a networking environment.

MBR (master boot record)   A portion of the disk, usually at the beginning, where the code necessary to start the computer is stored.

MCA   Microchannel Architecture, developed by IBM.

megabyte   A measure of space, either on the disk or in memory. A megabyte is 1,048,576 bytes, though it is often rounded to 1 million bytes.

megabyte-per-second (Mbps)   The measure of how fast data moves through network cabling.

megahertz (MHz)   A measurement of speed of the CPU.

memory   Generally refers to the computer's working memory, called random access memory (RAM), though portions of the computer's hard disk can also be set aside for use as memory, known as virtual memory.

MFM (modified frequency modulation)   A hard disk magnetic encoding method generally used on floppy disks and hard disks under 40MB in size.

MCA (Microchannel Architecture)   A bus architecture developed by IBM for its brand name computers.

microprocessor   See CPU.

MULTIBUS   A bus architecture from Intel aimed at computing products developed for aerospace, industrial, and military applications.

MAU (multistation access unit or medium attachment unit)   A wiring concentrator for LANs that allows one network to be connected to another network. On Token Ring networks, MAU stands for multistation access unit. On ethernet networks, MAU stands for medium attachment unit.

near-end crosstalk (NEXT)   Crosstalk occurring between adjacent wires at the end of the cable.

network   A group of computing devices, either terminals or PCs, connected to share data and communicate.

NIC (network interface card)   This card, installed into a PC's expansion slot, connects the PC to the network via cable.

noise   On a network, noise is interference from other electrical devices.

NPU (numeric processing unit)   See math coprocessor.

NuBus   A bus by Apple Computer for its Macintosh product line.

OEM (original equipment manufacturer)   A term used to describe companies that build computer equipment and connotes a large-scale operation.

ohm   A measure of electrical resistance.

OS   Operating system.

partition   A part of the disk set aside for the operating system.

partition table   See partition.

PC (personal computer)   While the desktop computers used by individuals all qualify as personal computers, the PC, sometimes called the IBM or IBM compatible personal computer, this type of computer is characterized by using the operating system DOS. Hence it is sometimes called the DOS-based PC.

PCI (Peripheral Component Interconnect)   A bus architecture developed by Intel to handle wide data types such as video.

PCMCIA (Personal Computer Memory Card International Association)   The credit-card-sized standard for storage and peripherals used mainly in the laptop and hand-held computer market.

peer-to-peer   A type of network in which each computer enjoys the use of the resources of the other connected computers. Usually a small number of computers are networked in this manner.

ports   Physical connections used to transmit data to and from the computer.

POST   Power on self-test, performed by a PC each time it is started.

PowerPC   Developed in an alliance with Apple, IBM, and Motorola, this CPU has an RISC design, but it is marketed to compete with the Intel Pentium CPU.

processor   See CPU.

RAM (random access memory)   See memory.

repeater   Used to amplify a signal in a network cable in order to extend the cable over a greater distance.

RISC (reduced instruction set computing)   These are a type of CPU used mostly in workstation computers and known for processing speed.

RLL (run length limited)   A type of MFM, this is a hard disk drive magnetic encoding method that packs more data into the same physical disk space. RLL is also an interface for a magnetic drive. Run length limited refers to a limitation on the distance, or length, between magnetic flux reversals on the disk platter.

ROM (read-only memory)   A type of memory chip that has its contents determined when it is manufactured. Used to store control routines in computers and computing devices.

ROM BIOS (read-only memory basic input/output system)   The control routines for the PC.

router   A computer unit specifically designed to handle messages sent from one network to another.

SCSI (small computer systems interface)   A type of bus that has the advantage of allowing control of several peripheral devices through the single port.

SDK   Software developers kit.

sector   The smallest unit of storage on a disk.

Server   A data storage repository on a network.

shielded twisted pair   This is a type of twisted-pair wiring, or standard modular telephone cord, that is shielded to avoid picking up noise from other electrical devices. It looks more like lamp wire than telephone cord.

SIMM (single in-line memory modules)   A form of RAM on a small circuit board.

SOHO   Small office/home office.

SQL (Structured Query Language)   A language recognized by many databases and used to perform operations with the database (such as adding, updating, deleting, and selecting records).

SRAM (static random access memory)   Memory nearly twice as fast as standard dynamics RAM. Used to speed up particular processing activities.

STD   A bus used widely in medical and industrial equipment because it's built to take abuse and is physically small in size.

thick ethernet   The standard type of ethernet, this cabling uses a bus topology.

thin ethernet   This cabling uses a bus topology but has a maximum cable length of about 600 feet, less than half that of thick ethernet.

thin net   See thin ethernet.

TDR (time domain reflectometer)   A network testing device that works in much the same way radar does to find metallic circuit faults in cabling.

token ring   A type of network in which a token or frame is passed from workstation to workstation, and the workstation with the token may transmit.

topology   The manner in which workstations are physically connected to a LAN.

transceiver   This device transmits and receives network signals. A network adapter is an example of a transceiver.

transceiver cabling   The special cabling that comes with a transceiver to connect it to a network interface card.

TURBOchannel   A bus type developed by Digital Equipment Corporation that allows data transfer at the rate of 100 megabytes per second.

user interface   The way the computer is designed to interact with the user, particularly referring to the way program menus and screens are designed.

UTP (unshielded twisted pair)   A network cabling also commonly used as modular telephone wiring.

VESA VL-Bus   Video Electronics Standards Association standard for the VL-Bus.

VL-Bus   The Video Local Bus standard.

VME bus (VersaModule Eurocard bus)   Developed in a partnership between Motorola, Signetics, Mostek, and Thompson CSF, this bus is widely used in computers aimed at the commercial, military, and industrial markets.

WAN (wide area network)   This term implies the networking of PCs or terminals over some distance, like between New York and California.

workstation   A computer or terminal on a network.

write-back cache   Specific memory set aside to handle writing to the computer's hard disk and speed processing.

virtual memory   The practice of using a portion of the computer's hard disk drive as additional memory storage space.

XT   A computer equipped with an 8088 or 8086 Intel processor or the equivalent.s

Index

About the authors

Linda Rohrbough is the author of *Mailing List Services on Your Home-Based PC* (Windcrest/McGraw-Hill, 1994). As Dallas Bureau Chief for the Newsbytes News Network as well as other high-tech and computer industry publications, she has written more than 2,500 articles on computer-related topics for high-technology publications. Some of her work has appeared in *PC Computing, WordPerfect Magazine,* and *Texas Computing.*

Linda was honored with the Computer Press Association Best On-Line Publication Award in 1993. She has served on the board of directors of the Computer Press Association and on the board of directors of the Los Angeles Computer Society.

She lives in Plano, Texas with her husband Mark and her two children, Jessica and Margaret.

Michael F. Hordeski has a B.Sc. in Electrical Engineering from the University of Bridgeport and a M.Sc. in Electrical Engineering from the University of Southern California. He's been a registered control systems engineer since 1977.

Hordeski is the author of books, articles, and papers on microcomputer design and applications, control, and instrumentation interfaces, including: *Microprocessors in Industry,* Van Nostrand Reinhold; *The Design of Microprocessor and Control Systems,* Reston; *Microprocessor Cookbook,* TAB; *Microcomputer Design,* Reston; *CAD/CAM Techniques,* Reston; *Computer Integrated Manufacturing: Techniques and Applications,* TAB Professional and Reference Books; *Microcomputer LANs: Network Design and Implementation,* TAB Professional and Reference Books; *Transducers for Automation,* Van Nostrand Reinhold; *Communication Networks,* TAB Professional and Reference Books; *Control System Interfaces—Design and Implementation Using Personal Computers,* Prentice Hall; *Control Technology and Personal Computers,* Van Nostrand Reinhold; *Repairing IBM PCs and Compatibles—An Illustrated Guide,* Windcrest/McGraw-Hill; *Repairing PCs Beyond the Basics,* Windcrest/McGraw-Hill; *Personal Computer Interfaces,* McGraw-Hill; *Illustrated Dictionary of PCs,* 4th Edition, McGraw-Hill; coauthor of *Process Control Instrument Engineers' Handbook,* Chilton; and *Process Measurement Instrument Engineers' Handbook,* Chilton. He is also holder of Patent No. 4,011,448 on digital encoding and has been a member of the Board of Standards of Instrumentation Society of America since 1981.

About the series editors

"People are thirsty for specific how-to information that can enable them to earn a living at home," say Paul and Sarah Edwards, authors of Working from Home and Best Home-Based Businesses for the Nineties.

The McGraw-Hill Entrepreneurial PC series is designed to fill the until-now unmet need for step-by-step guidance for people wanting to make the work-home transition. The Edwards' track the trends that yield opportunities for successful home-based businesses and then find authors to provide the nitty-gritty business-specific information that can spare the home-based entrepreneur months of frustration and costly mistakes.

Paul and Sarah have been working from their home since 1974. It didn't take them long to realize they were participating in what would become a major social and economic trend—the home-based business. That spurred them to want to help others make the transition from office to home and to professionalize the image of home-based business.

Paul and Sarah are contributing editors to *Home Office Computing* magazine and write the monthly column, "Ask Paul and Sarah." They founded and manage the *Working From Home Forum* on CompuServe, an electronic network with more than 30,000 people around the world who work from home. Paul and Sarah also cohost the hour-long national weekly radio program "Home Office" on the Business Radio Network.

Other Books of Related Interest

Make Money Selling Your Shareware
—Steven Hudgik
Hudgik offers practical tips on how to write and test shareware, compose quality program documentation, supply technical support to end users, and how to get them to pay their registration fees. Other features inlcude the full results of the 1993 Shareware Industry Survey and detailed coverage of the latest shareware phenomena, rackware and CD-ROM distribution. The disk includes bulletin board and shareware vendor listings, informative articles, and sample programs.
0-07-030865-9 $29.95 Paper

Information for Sale, 2nd Edition
—John Everett/Elizabeth Powell Crowe
The book that has helped thousands start and run successful PC-based information services has been revised to include new sample searches, updated resource listings, coverage of legal issues, and the latest success stories.
0-07-019951-5 $19.95 Paper
0-07-019950-7 $29.95 Hard

Legal and Paralegal Services on Your Home-Based PC
—Rick Benzel/Kathrine Sheehy Hussey
This volume tells how to start and run a home-based legal services business with a computer. Four of the most important services are covered: court reporter, deposition digester, legal multimedia, and paralegal. Benzel and Hussey explain the growth potential of each legal service, exactly what each service entails, what skills and education are required, what computer training is needed, what legal issues are involved, and how to market the business and obtain contracts.
0-07-005109-7 $16.95 Paper

Operating a Desktop Video Service on Your Home-Based PC
—Harvey Summers
Readers are introduced to multimedia, CD-ROM, and Videodisc technologies, the components of a full-service Desktop Video shop, and techniques for planning, funding, and marketing a DTV business. Summers describes every phase of video production: script writing, directing, staging, post production, and delivery.
0-07-062545-X $17.95 Paper

Computer Consulting on Your Home-Based PC

—Herman Holtz

How to make a living developing custom software, installing hardware and software, training personnel, providing technical support, writing technical literature . . . and overcome the eight most common barriers to success.

0-8306-4449-0 $14.95 Paper
0-8306-4448-2 $24.95 Hard

Home Office Computing Handbook

—David Langendoen/Dan Costa

This book contains dozens of creative time- and money-saving tips on how to equip a home office, keep it working smoothly, and use it to your best advantage. Information is presented in bite-sized portions that are easy to read and digest.

0-8306-4577-2 $19.95 Paper

Mailing List Services on Your Home-Based PC

—Linda Rohrbough

This book shows how anyone can start, build, and run a successful mailing list business from home, with only a modest investment in hardware and software. This is a how-to book in every sense, not just in the mechanics of start-up, but also in the finer points of operation that ensure a long, profitable life for a mailing list business.

0-8306-4474-1 $14.95 Paper
0-8306-4473-3 $24.95 Hard

Health Service Businesses on Your Home-Based PC

—Rick Benzel

This book explains everything there is to know about entering the lucrative health services field. Author Rick Benzel focuses on the three most profitable health-related home businesses: billing, claims processing, and records transcription. For each he provides a solid plan of action drawn from the real-life experiences of entrpreneurs who have built successful track records in home-based health services.

0-8306-4303-6 $14.95 Paper

Bookkeeping on Your Home-Based PC

—Linda Stern

This book is a complete guide that will launch the careers of newcomers and provide valuable tips for established bookkeepers. Stern leads readers through each step in the process of starting and running a home-based bookkeeping service, with emphasis on the technology needed to make it work. The book focuses on how to equip the venture with computer, fax, modem, and telephone systems that fit the specific needs of home-based bookkeepers.

0-8306-4304-4 $14.95 Paper
0-8306-4305-2 $24.95 Hard

Upgrade or Repair Your PC
—Aubrey Pilgrim
Build-it-yourself guru Aubrey Pilgrim includes a wealth of photographs along
with step-by-step instructions to make it easy for even novices to upgrade,
enhance, or repair PCs, motherboards, ROM BIOS, floppy drives, hard disks,
monitors, printers, and more.
0-07-05011-9 $26.95 Paper

Troubleshooting & Repairing PC Drives and Memory Systems
—Stephen Bigelow
Readers learn how data storage and memory equipment operates, and the
importance of regular cleaning, maintenance, and alignment to the long,
trouble-free life of drives and memory media.
0-8306-4551-9 $22.95 Paper
0-8306-4550-0 $34.95 Hard

Troubleshooting and Repairing Personal Computers, 2nd Edition
—Art Margolis
Not limited to any specific microcomputer model or manufacturer, this all-in-
one volume presents the background theory and practical techniques
necessary to service Apple II, Macintosh, Amiga, Commodore, and IBM PC
circuitry and components.
0-8306-2186-5 $23.95 Paper
0-8306-2187-3 $34.95 Hard

Easy PC Maintenance and Repair, 2nd Edition
—Phillip Laplante
Readers will be able to prolong the life of their computer as well as save
money on repairs, lost data, and down time with the help of the book's
foolproof, step-by-step instructions.
0-07-036433-8 $17.95 Paper
0-07-036432-X $27.95 Hard

Repairing PCs
—Michael Hordeski
If you want to maximize your PC performance, minimize downtime, and save
money on repair calls, this book will help you accomplish all three. Inside,
you'll find essential information troubleshooting, repairing, and properly
maintaining a wide variety of IBM-compatible PCs, including XTs, 286, 386,
486, and Pentiums.
0-07-030523-4 $22.95 Paper
0-07-030522-6 $34.95 Hard

How to Order

Call 1-800-822-8158
24 hours a day,
7 days a week
in U.S. and Canada

Mail this coupon to:
McGraw-Hill, Inc.
P.O. Box 182067,
Columbus, OH 43218-2607

Fax your order to:
614-759-3644

EMAIL
70007.1531@COMPUSERVE.COM
COMPUSERVE: GO MH

Shipping and Handling Charges

Order Amount	Within U.S.	Outside U.S.
Less than $15	$3.50	$5.50
$15.00 - $24.99	$4.00	$6.00
$25.00 - $49.99	$5.00	$7.00
$50.00 - $74.49	$6.00	$8.00
$75.00 - and up	$7.00	$9.00

EASY ORDER FORM—
SATISFACTION GUARANTEED

Ship to:

Name _____

Address _____

City/State/Zip _____

Daytime Telephone No. _____

Thank you for your order!

ITEM NO.	QUANTITY	AMT.

Method of Payment:

☐ Check or money order enclosed (payable to McGraw-Hill)

☐ *VISA*

☐ *DISCOVER*

☐ AMERICAN EXPRESS Cards

☐ *MasterCard*

Shipping & Handling charge from chart below	
Subtotal	
Please add applicable state & local sales tax	
TOTAL	

Account No. [ ][ ][ ][ ][ ][ ][ ][ ][ ][ ][ ][ ][ ][ ][ ][ ]

Signature _____ Exp. Date _____
Order invalid without signature

**In a hurry? Call 1-800-822-8158 anytime,
day or night, or visit your local bookstore.**

Code = BC15ZZA

DISK WARRANTY

This software is protected by both United States copyright law and international copyright treaty provision. You must treat this software just like a book, except that you may copy it into a computer in order to be used and you may make archival copies of the software for the sole purpose of backing up our software and protecting your investment from loss.

By saying "just like a book," McGraw-Hill means, for example, that this software may be used by any number of people and may be freely moved from one computer location to another, so long as there is no possibility of its being used at one location or on one computer while it also is being used at another. Just as a book cannot be read by two different people in two different places at the same time, neither can the software be used by two different people in two different places at the same time (unless, of course, McGraw-Hill's copyright is being violated).

LIMITED WARRANTY

Windcrest/McGraw-Hill takes great care to provide you with top-quality software, thoroughly checked to prevent virus infections. McGraw-Hill warrants the physical diskette(s) contained herein to be free of defects in materials and workmanship for a period of sixty days from the purchase date. If McGraw-Hill receives written notification within the warranty period of defects in materials or workmanship, and such notification is determined by McGraw-Hill to be correct, McGraw-Hill will replace the defective diskette(s). Send requests to:

> McGraw-Hill, Inc.
> Customer Services
> P.O. Box 545
> Blacklick, OH 43004-0545

The entire and exclusive liability and remedy for breach of this Limited Warranty shall be limited to replacement of defective diskette(s) and shall not include or extend to any claim for or right to cover any other damages, including but not limited to, loss of profit, data, or use of the software, or special, incidental, or consequential damages or other similar claims, even if McGraw-Hill has been specifically advised of the possibility of such damages. In no event will McGraw-Hill's liability for any damages to you or any other person ever exceed the lower of suggested list price or actual price paid for the license to use the software, regardless of any form of the claim.

McGRAW-HILL, INC. SPECIFICALLY DISCLAIMS ALL OTHER WARRANTIES, EXPRESS OR IMPLIED, INCLUDING, BUT NOT LIMITED TO, ANY IMPLIED WARRANTY OF MERCHANTABILITY OR FITNESS FOR A PARTICULAR PURPOSE.

Specifically, McGraw-Hill makes no representation or warranty that the software is fit for any particular purpose and any implied warranty of merchantability is limited to the sixty-day duration of the Limited Warranty covering the physical diskette(s) only (and not the software) and is otherwise expressly and specifically disclaimed.

This limited warranty gives you specific legal rights; you may have others which may vary from state to state. Some states do not allow the exclusion of incidental or consequential damages, or the limitation on how long an implied warranty lasts, so some of the above may not apply to you.

What's on the disk

See appendix G for more information on these programs.

README.1ST
DOS.TXT
CLEANER
RMD
SNOOPER
BURNIN
QEDIT
EJECT

Important

Read the disk warranty terms on the previous page before opening the disk envelope. Opening this package constitutes acceptance of the Disk Warranty terms and renders this entire book-disk package unreturnable except for replacement in kind due to material defect.